Praise for *Until Our Lungs Give Out*

"These stimulating and wide-ranging engagements—from Noam Chomsky and Judith Butler to Robin Kelley, Mari Matsuda, and Cornel West—remind us of the range and depth of philosophical knowledge that underscores George Yancy's work as a public intellectual as well as a scholar. This collection of conversations is a must-read for those of us seeking deeper understandings of the complex interactions of race, class, gender, and justice."

—**Henry Louis Gates Jr**, the Alphonse Fletcher
University Professor, Harvard University

"Refusing to adjust to injustice, George Yancy's interlocutors speak with passion and urgency, attesting to Yancy's skill as an interviewer. Listen to what they have to say, for the insights they express speak to some of the gravest issues of our times."

—**Robert Gooding-Williams**, professor of philosophy
and African American studies, Columbia University

"Robin D. G. Kelley poignantly captures the protests for racial justice during the surge in white nationalist retaliations. He states, 'If there is such a thing as the arc of the moral universe, it does not bend on its own. We bend it one way, our enemies bend it back.' George Yancy's interviews with Kelley and many of the most important thinkers and doers of our times inspire many ways we can go forward from here. These interviews are thought-provoking, forward-thinking, and inspiring about next steps."

—**Tera W. Hunter**, author of *Bound in Wedlock: Slave and
Free Black Marriage in the Nineteenth Century*

"In this set of interviews, George Yancy invites leading intellectuals to tarry with global white supremacy, planetary anti-blackness, nocent settler-colonialism, structural misogyny, and insatiable capitalist extraction. The message and messengers are deeply political, philosophical, and pedagogical. At once an act of defiance and radical love, *Until Our Lungs Give Out* asks us to peer into a futurity its authors likely will not inhabit."

—**Zeus Leonardo**, author of *Edward Said and Education*

"*Until Our Lungs Give Out* is a timely and tremendously important book. It presents thoughtful and thought-provoking conversations between distinguished philosopher George Yancy and a dazzling array of the world's most profound, original, and generative thinkers about anti-Black racism in the U.S. and around the world."

—**George Lipsitz**, author of *The Possessive Investment in Whiteness*

"Many thanks to philosopher and public intellectual George Yancy for this bounty of engaged thought from our foremost thinkers. We need this gift now more than ever—as a source of both perception and hope."

—**Nell Irvin Painter**, author of *The History of White People*

"*Until Our Lungs Give Out* is a painfully relevant and indispensable book that brings together world-renowned scholars to collectively demonstrate what it looks like to face the horrors and deep conflicts of the world head on and to speak against them despite the dangers of doing so. As one of our nation's most searingly insightful philosophers, George Yancy has prophetically modeled speaking truth in love and has steadfastly refused to sugarcoat the truth no matter the personal cost to him."

—**Kirsten Powers**, CNN senior political analyst, New York Times bestselling author

"The title of George Yancy's new collection of interviews tells it all: he gives voice to the top critical thinkers in today's struggle against racism and sexism, thinkers who persist in their struggle to the end, until their lungs give out. I've never seen a volume which combines multiple perspectives with a united strong commitment to emancipation. *Until Our Lungs Give Out* gives hope, and hope is what we need in our dark times."

—**Slavoj Žižek**, author of *Surplus-Enjoyment: A Guide for the Non-Perplexed and Heaven in Disorder*

UNTIL OUR LUNGS
GIVE OUT

UNTIL OUR LUNGS GIVE OUT

Conversations on Race, Justice, and the Future

GEORGE YANCY

Foreword by Tim Wise

ROWMAN & LITTLEFIELD

Lanham • Boulder • New York • London

Published by Rowman & Littlefield
An imprint of The Rowman & Littlefield Publishing Group, Inc.
4501 Forbes Boulevard, Suite 200, Lanham, Maryland 20706
www.rowman.com

86-90 Paul Street, London EC2A 4NE

British Library Cataloguing in Publication Information Available

Library of Congress Cataloging-in-Publication Data

Names: Yancy, George, author.
Title: Until our lungs give out : conversations on race, justice, and the future / George Yancy.
Other titles: Conversations on race, justice, and the future
Description: Lanham : Rowman & Littlefield, [2023] | Includes index.
Identifiers: LCCN 2023005255 (print) | LCCN 2023005256 (ebook) | ISBN 9781538176429 (cloth) | ISBN 9781538176436 (ebook)
Subjects: LCSH: African Americans—Civil rights. | African Americans—Violence against. | Racism—United States. | Racial justice—United States. | Political activists—United States—Interviews. | United States—Race relations.
Classification: LCC E185.615 .Y35 2023 (print) | LCC E185.615 (ebook) | DDC 305.800973—dc23/eng/20230517
LC record available at https://lccn.loc.gov/2023005255
LC ebook record available at https://lccn.loc.gov/2023005256

This book is dedicated in memory of James G. Spady
who brilliantly showed and taught me what it
means to think with intellectual freedom

CONTENTS

Part 9: White Mob Mentality

ACKNOWLEDGMENTS

I think of the process of acknowledgment as a form of recognition of our being as fundamentally interdependent. More than a gesture of recognition, it is a process of humility. Being a philosopher continues to have traces of monasticism, which means one is working alone. There is the image of the philosopher sitting alone, hand under chin, in deep thought. Think here of Auguste Rodin's *The Thinker*. Yet philosophical voices are never alone. They are shot through with other voices, larger communities of intelligibility, and indispensable forms of intellectual labor. My voice would not be what it is without the incredible work being done at *Truthout*. By this I mean the fierce independent work, the critical discussion of ideas, and the courageous coverage that *Truthout* brings to all of us, to the world. *Truthout* provides a space where serious justice work can be articulated and amplified. I am profoundly grateful to *Truthout* for the space within which to conduct powerful interviews such as these. This would not have happened if it were not due to the editorial vision of the extraordinary editors who I continue to have the honor of working with at *Truthout*. I am deeply grateful for the continued opportunity to work with Alana Yu-Lan Price, Maya Schenwar, Anton Woronczuk, Loretta Graceffo, Britney Schultz, and Ziggy West Jeffery. As editors, they critically engage ideas, offer generative and expansive suggestions, and unhesitatingly invite critical ideas that reveal systemic forms of injustice. I am always deeply impressed with the depth and alacrity with which the editors engaged my work, especially these interviews. Their attention to detail and to fact-checking is an ethical charge that is indispensable to any news organization, especially within our contemporary moment of consciously propagated fake news and the seductive pull of echo chambers that lead to toxic forms of polarization and violence. The editors

xiii

were enthusiastic and more than encouraging when I suggested the idea of bringing the interviews together and publishing them here. Together in a single text, the interviews overlap in their persistence at dismantling various manifestations of oppressive power, systemic racism, and social injustice. I would also like to thank Rabbi Michael Lerner and Alden Cohen for their welcome response to my submissions to *Tikkun* magazine, which has stood as an important example of parrhesia, and revolutionary love of human beings, life, and the Earth itself. Permission to include within this book my interview with Peter McLaren on the critical pedagogical views of Paulo Freire is greatly appreciated. To show my appreciation to both *Truthout* and *Tikkun* is to admit that my voice isn't a solo performance act, but part of a critical collective—jazzy in its mutual exchange.

Continuing with this theme, I thank my interlocutors who gave of their time, creativity, and intellectual labor to engage in dialogue with me, to trace the threads of injustice that connect us together and that ought to force us to take responsibility for what we do or fail to do to sustain injustice. The interlocutors within this text share the understanding that there is a great deal of suffering in *our* world. It is my hope that readers of this text will feel the weight of such suffering, be able to name it, and to feel deep outrage and anger that so much suffering continues to exist. In this way, I see these dialogues as seeking to tell the truth, to unveil acts of willful ignorance, call out attempts at obfuscation, prevarication, and unbridled lying. Telling the truth, as best we can, continues to be a dangerous practice, especially within a world where so many lives are deemed nugatory and ungrievable. Fighting on behalf of the "least of these" uncovers dangerous structural forces that are in place to preserve the division between the haves and the have-nots. Refusing to be silent embodies resisting hegemonic power, vicious evil, and warmongering violence. Like my interlocutors, I refuse silence and will scream if I must.

I would also like to thank Tim Wise, a deep and sharp antiracist voice and presence in the U.S., for agreeing to write the foreword to this text. Tim, I do understand the paradox. Thank you for your self-criticality and refusal to allow the paradox to silence your voice.

Natalie Mandziuk, my editor at Rowman & Littlefield, is simply the best. Natalie continues to be an inspiration; her enthusiasm for the book ideas that at times pour out of me is greatly appreciated. She has never failed to provide rich editorial guidance, productive advice, and editorial agency. Thank you. From Rowman & Littlefield, I would also like to thank Crystal Branson for her stellar work in the production of this book.

To James G. Spady, to whom this book is dedicated, I thank you for your brilliance, patience, and generosity. I used to think that I was *the only* young burgeoning scholar whose critical capacities you dedicated your time and energy to nurturing. As I would later discover, I was not the only one. There were hundreds, perhaps more, of young scholars who you nurtured, critically engaged, and encouraged to think with audacity and freedom. You did all of this without my ever feeling as if our time was less precious, less intellectually robust and invigorating, or less affirming. As a world-class intellectual, I should have known. Your intellectual energy could not be confined to a single place, moment in history, or a single thinker; your thought processes were/are grounded in what you powerfully and beautifully call "Wayblackmemories." Thank you for the memories and for the future of what is possible.

Last but not least, I thank my children. I hope that my attempt to generate dialogue with you as children (around the dinner table, on long car rides) will provide you with the strength to cultivate your own voice, a voice that refuses to be, as Cornel West says, an echo. Don't be an echo, be a voice that is courageous, that rejects mediocrity, and that will scream if you must.

And thanks to Susan for your compassion, that sense of suffering together. Raising children isn't easy. Yet we continue to do our best even though we are not perfect. Love, however, has the power to distill those failures into more love, stronger than before. For what more can we ask?

FOREWORD

It is an honor but also daunting to have been asked to pen this foreword: an honor because of the respect I have for the work of George Yancy and daunting for two reasons.

First, because, as a white man tasked with offering introductory thoughts to a volume comprised chiefly of Black and brown wisdom, I am acutely aware of my obligations here, and I recognize all too well the privilege embodied in the ask. I have spent the past thirty-plus years as an antiracist educator, activist, organizer, writer, and lecturer whose voice was given early amplification because of the very thing much of this volume (and of Yancy's work) seeks to critique—whiteness. The contradiction, or at least the paradox, is not lost on me, nor him, I am sure.

So, too, it is daunting because I am not, unlike the others whose words are gathered in this profound set of interviews, an academic scholar. So to find myself amid those whose work has informed my understanding of race and society—but whose formal credentials I cannot match—is more than a bit intimidating. That said, Dr. Yancy believed I could share something of value to preface their words and serve as the starting pistol at the beginning of the race, so to speak, as you navigate this vital collection. So, here goes.

While white supremacy is, as several scholars in this volume point out, a global toxin, let there be no mistake that the original formula is American. Though ethnocentrism and notions of cultural supremacy are as old as organized humankind, race was a Western invention and, in its present form, an American product. Whiteness emerged from the colonial project here, and like most American inventions, we have learned well how to export it to the world along with Big Macs and Coca-Cola.

As the authors and initial mass producers of white supremacy, Americans still exert a disproportionate influence on how race is lived globally and on the distribution of resources between those who qualify for membership in the white club and those who do not. Anti-Blackness here, which has formed the indelible foundation of American racism, has parallel forms around the world, which is one of the reasons that the uprising of 2020 in the wake of the murder of George Floyd spread not only beyond Minneapolis but beyond our national borders. And it is why any solution to anti-Blackness, though it may begin here, will have to include the wisdom and energy of hundreds of millions around the globe.

These efforts will undoubtedly be fraught with risks, whether here or elsewhere. As the U.S. seeks to crawl from under the weight of Trumpism—the most recent iteration of overt white nationalism in a long lineage of the same—it is apparent that a book such as this is considered dangerous. Merely broaching the subject of racism, as these scholars do so deftly here, risks backlash from those who fear reckoning with history and its ongoing inertia. In the name of stopping critical race theory—a school of thought they couldn't define were I to hold them from a bridge, give them sixty seconds to do so accurately, or else be dropped to their deaths—reactionaries have launched an all-out war on honesty. Any narrative addressing white supremacy and its legacy must be cast into the memory hole, never to be mentioned again.

They do this in the name of presumptive colorblindness, invoking Dr. King, who, in their telling, would have been appalled at the suggestion that racism was deeply ingrained in America's national character or that it had infected whites as a collective. To persons such as this, it matters not that King said racism was as "native to our soil as pine trees, sagebrush, and buffalo grass." Likewise, they glibly skip over his insistence that the better part of white America was "poisoned to its soul" by this iniquitous force. As Simon and Garfunkel sang: A man hears what he wants to hear and disregards the rest. So, too, a nation. So, too, the world.

After George Floyd's murder, it became apparent how little some folks were prepared to hear. Although twenty million or so engaged in demonstrations in the U.S., and many millions more did the same worldwide, the backlash would prove swift and unrelenting. It was much like the aftermath of Hurricane Katrina, where Black suffering in New Orleans garnered the nation's sympathy for about forty-eight hours until the forces of reaction and white supremacy could regain their footing and turn that sympathy into a sneering judgmentalism.

Why didn't they leave before the flooding?

Because they were all on welfare and waiting for their first-of-the-month checks, came the answer.

Why didn't George Floyd comply with Officer Derek Chauvin?

Because he was a fentanyl addict whose death wasn't caused by the compression of his neck for nine minutes but rather by the drugs in his system.

By now, we know the routine. When it comes to white supremacy, rationalization is a reflex. Sadly, so too is the dominant strain of antiracism often reflexive. In this case, the reflex was to individualize the problem and the proposed solutions. Even as people spoke of "systemic racism," their default analysis too often shifted back to personal biases and shaming those who either possessed or benefited from them.

"Check your privilege," came the cries from some quarters, as if tallying up one's personal list of advantages would somehow transform the system that bestowed them.

"Stop being so delicate, Karen," came the shouts from others, whose mocking bromides about white women's tears and white fragility were passed off as structural critique.

Best of all was the insistence from corporations and even police departments that they would undertake implicit bias training to reveal subconscious prejudices, which, presumably, were to blame for Black pain. This, even though nothing about the bias animating Derek Chauvin's knee, Daniel Pantaleo's chokehold of Eric Garner, or any of the cops who shot and killed Tamir Rice, Walter Scott, John Crawford III, or so many others, had been *implicit*.

Those events were not the result of some ghostly apparition barely felt beneath the surface of those killers' psyches. Chauvin's smirk said it all. He did it because he assumed he could. And why wouldn't he? The system of law enforcement has always been predicated on the control and domination of Black bodies. That he ultimately was held accountable was a quirk of fate, made possible only because Darnella Frazier was there and had the presence of mind (and courage) to document his depravity with her cell phone.

If we are to defeat white supremacy, it will take more than guilt trips, employee workshops, and reaction-time tests administered by Harvard. It will take more than corporate diversity initiatives or freshman seminars on race, power, and privilege.

It will take more than role-playing exercises meant to demonstrate how microaggressions work. And it will surely require more than getting some teenager who posts something racist on social media fired from their fast-food job or their college offer rescinded and then pretending that either represent revolutionary activism rather than performative self-righteousness.

It will require a much more culturally transformative project than any of those quick-fix approaches would suggest. It will require the building of alternative institutions where the existing structures fail us—especially schools and public safety mechanisms other than traditional police—and an insistence that what the racist state refuses to do, nonprofits and community organizations and individuals committed to justice will do ourselves. We won't wait for elites to dispense accurate history education to our children. *We* will do that. We won't expect the law enforcement leopard to change its spots. The people will engage in violence prevention and community wellness initiatives to reduce the need for contact with such forces in the first place.

And although Black and brown folks will lead the movement out of white supremacy, such an undertaking will almost surely need a healthy dose of white antiracist solidarity, if for no other reason than to blunt the impact of the inevitable backlash on the part of the rest. Sadly, this will only likely happen if enough white folks come to see that inequality and white supremacist thinking are destructive, not only to persons of color but also to ourselves.

We saw it with COVID: millions of whites in so-called red-state America who hit the brakes on social distancing and refused to mask or get vaccines once it was known that Black folks were doing the bulk of the dying. That nonchalance then carried a price. Only 30 percent of the dead in the first two months of the pandemic were white. But by the end of 2020, over half the monthly dead were. Now, roughly 63 percent of those who have died in the U.S. from COVID have been. Because when Black lives don't matter, eventually, no one's life does.

We see it in the so-called deaths of despair that scholars keep talking about: the spike in suicide and drug and alcohol-related deaths since the late 1990s among middle-aged, noncollege-educated, working-class white Americans. Although Black folks are worse off than whites in every category of social and economic well-being, we are the ones who seem especially unable to bear up against pain and setback. Oddly, few have thought to ask why?

The answer should be obvious. Unlike Black folks who always knew the economic system was rigged and the notion of meritocracy and rugged individualism was a fairy tale, whites have had the luxury of believing in the American Santa Claus. But with globalization and the disappearance of formerly secure jobs—something Black Americans had been familiar with for decades—those who had enjoyed the privilege of obliviousness are being confronted with reality. And their skin is decidedly not thick enough, their coping skills not adequate for the reckoning. One might argue that a similar difficulty coping with change and insecurity animated Brexit and is propelling forward an emotional and psychic crisis of late-stage whiteness throughout the Western world.

White folks are like passengers on the middle and upper decks of the *Titanic*, ignoring the screams from steerage—from those who were first to know that the ship was going down. We have been ignoring them, and worse, not only to their detriment but to ours. Perhaps if we can come to see that—to truly appreciate it—we might manage to find the lifeboats needed for us all.

There is no guarantee that another volume dedicated to revealing the depths of this national and global sickness will make any difference. But one thing is for sure: if we don't keep saying it, screaming it even, nothing will change. So between these two poles—the possibility of redemption and the certainty of defeat—one should opt for hope.

Compiling these interviews was an act of hope, even as George Yancy and all the voices herein would tell you that hope can be hard to conjure. Though our perspectives on the problem and how to confront it vary, one thing unites us all: we refuse to be silent, to give up, and to relinquish our agency and voices to the forces of reaction. If we are to lose, let us go down swinging. There is no virtue in going quietly.

George Yancy's work and that of the other scholars gathered here provide us with the intellectual ammunition needed for the fight ahead. I am, once again, honored and humbled to be a small part of this effort.

Tim Wise
Nashville, TN
November 2022

INTRODUCTION

Critical Voices that Refuse to be Silenced

George Yancy

Many book titles are designed to entice, generally with the specific purpose of luring readers into making a purchase. In this sense, titles function as market devices. Perhaps there's little way around this. Yet this fact doesn't make titles any less informative or indicative of what fundamentally drives the value, integrity, and profundity of the written words and the courageous spirit within a book. The title of the book that you hold, *Until Our Lungs Give Out: Conversations on Race, Justice, and the Future*, signifies endurance, perseverance, continuance, vision, and struggle. The title also indicates a stated commitment against injustice, one with important implications regarding the critically engaging interlocutors within this text. The title speaks to their critical consciousness "to provide us," as Tim Wise powerfully argues in his foreword to this text, "with the intellectual ammunition needed for the fight ahead." There is nothing politically quiescent about the critically challenging and compellingly robust views articulated within this text. The title is about what we will do until we can't breathe; it says that we will continue to fight against racism, injustice, and search for a way toward the horizon of the *not yet*, even if for some of us the *not yet* looks horribly bleak, perhaps hopeless, perhaps even requiring the "end of the world" as we know it—an end whose grammar we cannot even fathom. In a world where so many of *us* find it hard to breathe in different ways because of systemic forms of injustice, this book is meant for you. I emphasize "us" so that I make it clear that injustice affects all of us. And I say this without any error of conflation. Injustice is suffered *differently*, and yet my suffering should not diminish my recognition of your suffering, even as you might (*will*) need to understand just how your suffering is given temporary reprieve by having me under your foot—or knee. Or, perhaps more radically and specifically,

1

how the always already imminent possibility of *my death* is a function of the stability of white structural power and even white psychic coherence and intelligibility. It was Frantz Fanon who had to remind Jean-Paul Sartre that Black bodies "suffer quite differently" from white bodies.[1] And as Ruth Wilson Gilmore powerfully reminds us, "Racism, specifically, is the state-sanctioned or extralegal production and exploitation of group-differentiated vulnerability to premature death."[2]

As a Black cis man who teaches at an R1 doctoral research university, I was born into poverty, and lived my teenage life in what are known as low-income housing projects. My mother was born *Black* and *poor* and lived as she did not because of fate, but because of a million (white) decisions *not* to see her as human. This is a case where systems must be judged and critiqued. Yet this does not mean that systems are to be reified; it is embodied people who make decisions, instantiate hatred, disgust, and, in this case, anti-Black racism. My mother told me about having to sit on the "Black side" (the "inferior," "subhuman" side) within racially segregated theaters. Think about that. I want you to imagine that being *your* mother, the one who would eventually give birth to you. When I tarry with the fact that my mother was treated in this way, I become furious, especially as I think about how white supremacist thought attempted to fix her as abject. I have witnessed with my own eyes what happens when Black people are held captive by contemporary forms of racial capitalism, where they suffer forms of racialized poverty and racialized trauma. I have seen the implosive brutality, the violent shedding of blood, the infestation of roaches, the rats, the dilapidated, shitty furniture, the heroin needles and later crack capsules in the streets, the disproportionate incarceration rates: mothers gone, fathers gone, grandparents gone. All gone missing! And then there are the mournful tears thereafter. Such a painful reality points to the *structural* vulnerability and precarity of Black lives in the U.S. James Baldwin's prophetic and courageous voice continues to be painfully relevant: "You were born where you were born and faced the future that you faced because you were black and *for no other reason*."[3] The truth of that statement is *not* born of self-victimization or a victim mentality; it is born from Baldwin's refusal to be silent. It is an indictment of the processes of structural anti-Blackness.

So, while I am aware of where I currently teach, and the benefits that come with that institutional advantage, I also know that I am racialized as Black; I know that having a PhD will not stop a police officer's bullet from piercing my chest because I'm suspected of some "crime." It will not save me from being shot in the back by a "law-and-order" police officer who perceives my Blackness as the site of "chaos," where "my crime" is being

Black. In such cases, there is nothing that I need *to do* as a prerequisite for being a criminal. Blackness is against the law. It is my being Black that is the wrongdoing. As I walk while Black, drive while Black, shop while Black, sleep within my home while Black, there is a haunting feeling of something foreboding. Within minutes, the knee of the carceral nation is on my neck, and I can't breathe, perhaps ever again. Because of so much pervasively complex suffering within our world, I have brought together a critical cadre who understands what it means to give themselves over to justice, of fighting fiercely to name, mark, trace, call out, radically critique, scream against, and undo injustice. So many of us have tried to keep outrage alive.

If you have read this far, then it is my hope that you will continue to read *Until Our Lungs Give Out: Conversations on Race, Justice, and the Future*, and that you will be moved by a powerful, generative, and encouraging form of address. I invite *you* to tarry, to remain with and to engage in the critical conversations, the dialogues, and the passionate inquiries that are contained within these pages. Notice that the mode of address is personal. I say this because you, too, are the interlocutor (*my* interlocutor, *our* interlocutor) who is being *called to* engage within this textual space of conceptual complexity, political and existential urgency, expansive inquiry, courageous listening and parrhesia (or courageous speech). The invitation that I extend to you as a reader—as an interlocutor with your own assumptions, theories, aporias, biases, foibles, fears, hurts, desperate cries in the night, political proclivities, pains, exhaustions—should be taken as an act of hospitality. What drives this invitation is the value placed upon a dialogical space of fecundity with the aim of generating greater forms of openness and critical reflections on the meaning and practice of justice. The invitation is not a demand, but an offer, the desire to create and cultivate a free space. I see this framing of hospitality, this call to engage, as a form of love. Perhaps the use of love isn't what you had expected. My sense is that we (and I leave the "we" unspecified to avoid specific finger-pointing) have failed at understanding the profound daring that is love, we have failed to honor its daring, and we have failed to act upon that daring. Perhaps some of us are afraid to engage the daring of love because we are too preoccupied with feigning the appearance of intellectual abstraction, or where "true brilliance" is defined by one's capacity for pristine rationality, or where pretentious intellectual abstruseness is rewarded. Love, after all, is an *embodied*, courageous, kenotic (emptying), and fragile phenomenon; pretense, however, runs for cover or is itself a hiding place. This does not deny that there are many among us for whom private healing spaces, sacred spaces, spaces free of relative captivity, pain, and suffering, are necessary for psychological recalibration.

Perhaps we have failed to understand, practice, and carry the weight of love within the context of a demos that is market obsessed and seduced by desires/ambitions of solidifying and acquiring more hegemonic power, moved by greed, motivated by the titillation of fame and forms of distinction that place us "above" the rest. As Cornel West reminds us, "Without Socratic questioning by the demos, elite greed at home and imperial domination abroad devour any democracy."[4] Given my own academic positionality, the personal weight of the concern that I raise here, along with its ethical implications, is not lost on me. I am also a captive (and I would say guilty of perpetuating its logics) even as I critique the insidious structures of power that come with rewards, recognitions, and neoliberal fantasies. I should clarify, though, that my use of love here is without any hint of romanticization or sentimentality. There is nothing overemotional when one is being called to allow oneself to be touched by another and to touch another through a process of profound wonder and commitment, which, in this text, is an openness to mutual critique and mutual flourishing. It is a coming together where risk is at stake. Indeed, there is nothing starry-eyed about critically examining with another the realities of life and death, to take it upon oneself to collectively bear witness to human atrocity, suffering, and pain. It is within such spaces that accountability is necessary, where one's relationship to power must be examined with honesty.

More specifically, my understanding and use of love here is the very opposite of what we generally hear in popular songs, what we see in the Hollywood production of happy endings and melodramatic portrayals of what love should look or sound like. Indeed, when I've found it difficult to articulate how I want to describe this specific form of love, I turn to the inimitable James Baldwin. He reminds me/us that love is "a state of being, or a state of grace—not in the infantile American sense of being made happy but in the tough and universal sense of quest and daring and growth."[5] For Baldwin, love involves great risk, especially the risk of the self. It is not lost on me that the "risk of the self" is complicated by differential social locations. Reemphasizing my point about market obsession, however, love implies the risk of facing the possible vacuity of one's own "happiness." We mustn't forget that there are perfunctory forms of "being made happy" that can stand in the way of forms of love that involve quest, daring, and growth. One can be "happy" by materially and symbolically fitting into the status quo. On this score, being made happy can function as a form of elision vis-à-vis one's own self-interrogation and one's interrogation of the violently stratified society within which one is made happy. Peter L. Berger writes that "by the use of various symbols (such as material objects, styles of demeanor, taste and speech, types of association and even appropriate opinions) one keeps on showing to the world just where one has arrived."[6] Love is not about grandiose arrival, but about courageously starting over, beginning anew, letting go, and daring to create an ethically capacious space (within the context of this text) for you. In this way, hospitality/love is about *making an appearance*, that you simply show up, come to the scene of the gesture. A market infused sense of arrival (and hence one's market sense of "happiness") is perfectly compatible with what Cornel West calls petty idols, illusions, seductive fetishes, "glib complacency, and pathetic cowardice."[7] In this respect, "happiness" amounts to the failure of Baldwinian quest and daring and growth that is unafraid to examine "the dark corners of one's own soul, the night alleys of one's society, and the back roads of the world in order to grasp the deep truths about one's soul, society, and world."[8] Examining the dark corners of one's own soul is consistent with Baldwin's understanding that "love takes off the masks that we fear we cannot live without and know we cannot live within."[9] Paulo Freire links love and dialogue. He writes, "Love is at the same time the foundation of dialogue and dialogue itself."[10] Furthermore, linking dialogue, love, and daring (a form of bravery), Freire notes, "As an act of bravery, love cannot be sentimental; as an act of freedom, it must not serve as a pretext for manipulation. It must generate other acts of freedom; otherwise, it is not love."[11]

When I read the conversations within this text, I understand them as dialogically generative, critical, and oppositional spaces that deeply trouble various taken-for-granted assumptions, violent ideologies, and oppressive practices. These conversations are not predicated upon manipulation or fueled by a zero-sum game. I would argue that entering such spaces (i.e., the nonmanipulative and non-zero-sum spaces) invites interlocutors to reorient their understanding of the world, themselves, and various concepts through an interplay between their own voice and the voices within this text,[12] perhaps even to the point of a fecund disorientation. Aporia is not to be feared but embraced. It allows for a productive suspension of what we think we know about ourselves, about others, and about the world. Some of my most powerful moments for which I am deeply thankful are those that reveal me to myself: "*I thought that I knew myself and I didn't.*"

I have experienced aporetic, dynamic, and ecstatic moments where, through dialogue, the self that began the conversation was not quite the self at the end of it. Something happened in the middle, as it were, that was remarkably transformative, "where," as Luce Irigaray might say, "I am no longer in the past and not yet in the future."[13] It seems to me that *critically engaging* conversations that are predicated on open inquiry have built within them, ab initio, a structural promise that one will not remain the same. I say this realizing that the movement might be subtle and not the sort of thing that leads to a dramatic collapse of one's worldview. It may not take the form of a Damascene event. *That* I converse *with you* implies (or certainly ought to) the abandonment of, or troubling of, an autarchic self, a self in complete control. Being learned or erudite isn't mutually incompatible with such a process of dispossession. (I hate to be abrupt, but I do understand, indeed, realize with pain and anger, that there are those who would rather spit in my face—and call me a "nigger"—than to genuinely engage with me, to demonstrate "vulnerability to a sudden address from elsewhere."[14]) Understanding dialogue as a gift, daring to speak the truth, taking the risk to listen with humility, and calling into question one's "innocence," is not easy. Deep and vicious backlash can result.[15]

My point here is to highlight both the importance of epistemic humility and the recognition of the alterity of the other vis-à-vis dialogue. Each of these sites imply forms of exposure, vulnerability, and openness. They signify fundamental ways in which none of us are *asocial* epistemic subjects who are beholden only to ourselves. Indeed, we are "derived, sustained by a social world that is beyond us and before us."[16] Epistemic humility refuses the poison of dogmatism, a form of intransigence whereby one becomes a prisoner of one's own insular echo chamber. Recognition of the alterity of the other refuses the reduction of the other to a rigid sameness. As Irigaray writes, "The other never suits us simply. We would in some way have reduced the other to ourselves if [they] suited us completely."[17] Critically engaged conversation (etymologically, "turning together") has the feature of "attracting me toward."[18] It is a dynamic process that "keeps me from taking and assimilating directly to myself."[19] Epistemic arrogance and atomic self-aggrandizement are centripetal, both processes of centering, forms of closure. Open (centrifugal) conversational inquiry is a site where "an *excess* resists."[20] Indeed, the other resists. And one's own interior sense of meaning, as it were, is always already postponed, deferred, which is a kind of resistance, defiance, refusal, space for the other. Moreover, dialogically, there is always something more to see, to understand, a surplus, even if one cannot or refuses to see it. The conversation continues as it must.

Within these conversations that you have available to you, and to which you are being invited to participate, the interlocutors (etymologically, those who "speak between") are painfully aware of what is at stake. These conversations are not leisurely water cooler talks, which is not to say that talk around the water cooler is to be dismissed as perfunctory or mere chatter. My point here is that the interlocutors within this text understand that the refusal to remain silent "is to be committed, and to be committed is to be in danger."[21] Being in danger involves the refusal to adjust to injustice. The interlocutors understand that, as Audre Lorde writes, "Your silence will not protect you."[22]

My invitation (to you) to this collective and critically engaging conversational text attests to my own epistemic and ontological dependence— my insufficiency. There is a fundamental *lack* at the heart of this invitation. To seek *dia*logue is to seek out the other. This brings us back to a species of humility (not humiliation), which functions as a site of generosity that "involves a dispossession of the self and is born of an affective, corporeal relation to alterity that generates rather than closes off"[23] further dialogue. As Freire writes, "How can I dialogue if I always project ignorance onto others and never perceive my own?"[24] Such a projection occludes genuine dialogue. Such a projection is structurally hierarchical and vertical. Not only is the other's voice canceled, but one's curiosity in the form of actively listening or hearing is blocked. There is no robust sense of "across" or "between" (as the prefix *dia* implies). There's simply stasis. On the one hand, the other is not heard, is left alone,[25] reduced to their own alleged ignorance. On the other hand, the one who projects the ignorance is also reduced to a monologue, which can function as a trick of "absolute mastery," an illusion of "completion," a plenum. Dialogue presupposes the vitality and fecundity of sociality, a process of being-with-the-other. My characterization of conversation/dialogue presupposes that trust both precedes and follows robust and mutually honest dialogical encounters. Indeed, there is a deepening of trust. It is certainly a form of trust, and mutual reliance, that speaks to the prolificacy of the conversations within this text. Dialoguing together, within this text, is not about control or discursive grandstanding. Rather, our coming together is undergirded by a shared desire to critique various modes of unfreedom as lived within a world of pervasive social evil and oppressive hegemonic structures. In other words, what we do within these dialogues through the lens of differing theoretical backgrounds, although with a collective and unwavering stand against injustice, is to bear witness to the ways in which people have suffered and continue to suffer, and we deploy counterhegemonic narratives, uncover ignored and rejected rich historical facts, expose gratuitous violence by the state, critique forms of political demagoguery, religious idolatry, racist hatred, and xenophobia.

In short, any specific dialogue within this text powerfully tackles deep and urgent problems of our day—problems of the twenty-first century. Combined, this text unflinchingly delineates the horrors, and the forces behind such horrors, that define the unjust social and political world that

we live in. Within this text, the unsightly social, political, and unethical entrails of the U.S. and beyond are laid bare. Twenty-eight of the twenty-nine
conversations within this text took place and were originally published at
Truthout from 2020–2022, and one was published at *Tikkun*. Hence, the
discussions reflect the different dates, and the salient events that were taking
place. In some cases, I decided to return to various discussions and to ask
the interlocutors one "final" question that didn't appear in the discussions'
original publication. In these cases, the final responses added to the already
incredibly robust discussion.

In *Until Our Lungs Give Out: Conversations on Race, Justice, and the Future*, the dialogues span the toxicity of white systemic violence; revolutionary love; the death of whiteness as a site of privilege and hegemonic nation-
building; the murder of George Floyd in 2020; the importance of critical
pedagogy; incarceration and carceral logics; poisonous class dynamics and
gender inequality; anti-Black racism in the U.S., the UK, Australia, and New
Zealand; COVID-19 and global vulnerability; the meaning of Afropessimism and Blackness as slaveness; the Black Lives Matter movement; colonialism, land, and identity; the meaning and rejection of critical race theory;
the Tulsa Race Massacre; the failures of liberal humanism; racial capitalism;
the reality of New Jim Crowism within academic institutions; the meaning
of the n-word as a weapon of white supremacy; Trump's treasonous actions,
the ugly storming of the Capitol on January 6, and the attempted undoing
of democracy; the often hidden ideology behind gun ownership vis-à-vis
anti-Black and anti-Indigenous violence; intergenerational Black faith; the
invisibility of Black women; the powerful framing of the historical Jesus as a
counter-imperial, political insurrectionist; the oppositional power of African
American and Jewish traditions within the context of fighting against white
supremacy; abolition feminism; the violence of slave ships, and "womb collector" hysterectomies, and the captivity and murder of Kevin Johnson by
the state in 2022; Black trans mobility; contemporary relevance of the Black
radical tradition; climate change; and nuclear war. This list is by no means
exhaustive, but presents a significant sample of the existentially, socially, and
politically pressing issues that are engaged within this book, issues that haunt
our world, and that could mean the end of human life as we know it.

The Doomsday Clock is currently at ninety seconds to midnight.
Once that hand hits midnight, there will be *no you* and *no me*; sociality will
be nonexistent; a nuclear (world) catastrophe will end all world-making; it
will mean the end of all human horizons. This is part of the reason why,
as a philosopher, I have come to understand that philosophy is, inter alia,
a form of suffering. How can it not be when the practice of philosophy

ought to refuse to hide from the mess that we find ourselves in, to extricate ourselves from the river of Lethe, which is the river of forgetfulness in the underworld of Hades. To critically engage the world, for me, is to suffer, especially as there is no place to stand called "innocence." It is a mode of being, a mode of feeling and cognition, that refuses to forget human suffering as it has existed, exists, and will exist. I am complicit with the world's many troubles, its violence, its failures. That is hard to admit. There are times when I want to unsuture all the structures that bind me to injustice. Just disarticulate them—*all at once!* The reality is that I am sutured, which means connected, stitched, as it were, to various ongoing *violent* processes, infrastructures, institutional, material practices, quotidian practices, habits, norms, imaginaries, libidinal economies, market processes, epistemologies of ignorance, the logics of classism, sexism, militarism, daily practices that perpetuate my carbon footprint, you name it. I feel "compelled to take stock of [my] interdependence."[26] I can't bear this alone. It's too much for any single person. None of us can, but the recognition of our being sutured (imbricated in the embodied lives of others), which has important social ontological implications for how we are complicit in perpetuating violence, should carry normative significance for us all. Judith Butler writes that "it would be incumbent on us to consider the place of violence in any such relation, for violence is, always, an exploitation of that primary tie, that primary way in which we are, as bodies, outside ourselves and for one another."[27] Therefore, these conversations/dialogues are collectively urgent and necessary. There is nothing *apolitical*, undemanding, or cowardice about how I understand dialogue within this text. Dialogues can be messy and even agonistic, but that is partly the nature of the fecundity of dialogue. There are current forces within the U.S. and within the world that are afraid of critical dialogue or are certainly aware of its dangers vis-à-vis their hold on so much inordinate power. They would rather crush dialogue, critical and radical thinking, and parrhesia beneath the force of goose-stepping conformism and mythopoetic concepts of racial "purity." Think here of any tyrannical narcissist. Trump and his "Big Lie" will do for now. Of course, he is a symptom of a larger threat of white supremacist nationalism, and the emergence of global xenophobic authoritarianism and Orwellian repression (think here of the right-wing's war on books). Frankly, and for so many reasons, I don't think that this world is safe. I am under no illusions. It is the violence experienced and enacted within this world that renders our world, at least for me, a place of deep disaffection. What happens when the world no longer feels like or has never felt like *home* to so many? That is a strange kind of uncanniness. And yet, I refuse (as best I can) to feel otherwise. To feel otherwise means (perhaps) that I have forgotten about *you*. There is something about the deep humanity that resonates with me in the words of Rabbi Abraham Joshua Heschel. There are times when his deep affect and mourning forces me to think that we were torn from the same cloth. Heschel writes, "If all agony were kept alive in memory, if all turmoil were told, who could endure tranquility,"[28] and "What have I done today to alleviate the anguish, to militate the evil, to prevent humiliation."[29]

Part One

WHITENESS AS INNOCENCE MUST DIE

1

IT'S TIME FOR "WHITENESS AS USUAL" TO END

How Do We Overcome the Death Wish of White Supremacy?

INTERVIEW WITH DAVID R. ROEDIGER

When I think about the insistence of white power and privilege—from racial inequity, the murder of George Floyd, the storming of the Capitol, and the emergence of Donald Trump, to Sen. Mitch McConnell's rejection of critical educational programs designed to bear witness to the inhuman and cruel suffering of Black people in this country—there is a sense of both disbelief and a painful recognition that this is all too familiar. Whiteness functions as one of those multi-headed creatures; it finds a way to survive. Because of its recursive existence, I thought it crucial to engage the ideological, political, economic and psychological dimensions of whiteness with prominent historian of whiteness, David R. Roediger, who is the Foundation Professor of American Studies at University of Kansas, where he teaches and writes on race and class in the United States. Educated through college at public schools in Illinois, he completed doctoral work at Northwestern University. He is the author of *Seizing Freedom: Slave Emancipation and Liberty for All*; *How Race Survived U.S. History*; *Class, Race, and Marxism*; and *The Production of Difference* (with Elizabeth D. Esch). His older writings on race, immigration and working-class history include *The Wages of Whiteness* and *Working Toward Whiteness*. His most recent book is entitled *The Sinking Middle Class: A Political History* (2020).

G. Yancy (with David Roediger), "It's Time for 'Whiteness as Usual' to End," in *Truthout*, May 23, 2021 [Editors: Alana Yu-lan Price, Britney Schultz, and Anton Woronczuk].

GEORGE YANCY: Your critically engaging work within the area of critical whiteness studies located your thinking within the panoply of critically influential Black voices that had already given critical attention to whiteness—Frederick Douglass, W. E. B. Du Bois, Harriet Jacobs, Anna Julia Cooper, James Baldwin, Toni Morrison, bell hooks, and others. Pointing out the importance of Black voices revealed the ways in which Black people had to understand whiteness and were forced to understand its subtle operations. I think that this is still an indispensable approach to understanding whiteness.

However, many white people are not invested in understanding their own whiteness. After I wrote "Dear White America"[1] in 2015, many white people decried the attempt to get them to think about their whiteness as a form of reverse racism. I also recall being told that Martin Luther King Jr. would not have approved of my use of whiteness discourse, and that I was responsible for keeping racism alive by just talking about whiteness. What is it about whiteness that makes it so hard to explain to white people the ways in which they are invested in whiteness?

DAVID R. ROEDIGER: Thanks very much for the question and for proposing the interview. It is always so great to hear your thoughts.

Let me reflect a little first on how my work critically studying whiteness took the shape that you describe. That has everything to do with my mentor, the late historian of slavery, Sterling Stuckey. When he taught me in graduate school at Northwestern, Stuckey was bent on describing "slavery from the slave's point of view," a monumental epistemological shift. Sources were of course a big part of the problem and that made Stuckey the most voraciously interdisciplinary thinker I've met—an expert on folklore, music, art and the fiction of Herman Melville, as well as on Black nationalism's intellectual history, profoundly interpreting Frederick Douglass, W. E. B. Du Bois, and Paul Robeson. At first, we read together more folktales than anything else, to try to get at their artistry and what Stuckey called an "ethos" created by the enslaved. Those, particularly the "John and Master" and Brer Rabbit tales, laid out such an ethos, much of which involved mutuality among Black people. They also involved teaching—the tales were for children—how to understand and evade, and sometimes to disarm and avenge, white terror.

The critique of whiteness thus was a part of what Stuckey called "slave culture," one that the writers to whom you allude could mine. Whiteness was a problem that the enslaved studied. My own early career in labor history, attentive to race but in fully standard ways, took me away from those inspirations. However, I began an effort in the 1980s to understand the "white worker's" contributions to the elections of Ronald Reagan—even as he helped to dismantle unions. I reread almost everything Stuckey and I read together, but as an analysis of the problem of whiteness, often of poor whiteness. The book of my own that emerged was *The Wages of Whiteness*, but my next project after that gathered Black writings in a collection called *Black on White*.

The question of why whites are so impervious to understanding their own investments in whiteness is one on which I have come to think differently over the years. Early on I argued for the idea that whiteness and white advantage were so supported from on high and so ubiquitous as norms as to be pervasive without being faced—unnamed, unseen, even invisible. That line of argument did help us reach some people, to make white people address whiteness. But increasingly I came to think that the "knapsack of privilege" is not so much invisible as it is apparent and ignored. To use Charles Mills' term, "white ignorance" is best understood as a refusal of knowledge that whites surely do have reason to possess.

For a time, I taught classes in summer schools for auto workers and steel workers. Unsure that lecturing actually worked, I took to asking those attending why anybody would want to identify as a *white* worker instead of as a worker. The classes were about 70 percent white and 30 percent not. My vague hope was that the latter would educate the former. Actually, it was the white workers who first spoke up, offering a pretty comprehensive account of the advantages of whiteness: you can more easily get a really good job in the skilled trades; you can move into any neighborhood and access good schools; cops aren't so awful to you and to your kids, and so on. Some—these were largely motivated union members—undoubtedly wished it were not so, but they lived in that world and had no idea how to leave it. This was not simply white obliviousness. It was guilty and not-so-guilty knowledge of a system working far better for white workers even if in a larger sense, given the collapses of the auto and steel industries, it scarcely worked at all.

If this knowledge was available to white people, then it was second nature within the Black tradition. If we start from that tradition's standpoint, we can hardly arrive at a conclusion that whiteness is invisible. The terror of punishments by overseers and masters was deliberately theatrical and the enslaved as a whole were made to watch. Lynchings often were likewise elaborately staged events. The much-photographed police lines in Ferguson and elsewhere, armored with the best in protective gear and aggressive weaponry, hid nothing and instead made whiteness and white power hyper-visible and seemingly unassailable. That was the strategy anyhow, though sometimes the police station got burned down and recalibration was required.

GY: I was both delighted and yet skeptical of the recent emergence of interest in reading about whiteness and the proliferation of works on whiteness. This happened within both the national and global contexts of protests regarding the killing of George Floyd and Breonna Taylor. Moreover, universities seemed ethically and politically compelled to hire scholars of color to examine white racism. Books were proliferating and academic positions were being offered. As I thought about my own work, I began to feel as if scholars, especially within philosophy, had latched on to a new fad. I thought: "Hey, I've been writing about and publishing work on whiteness for years now." I would even argue that this emergence has created a few "white gurus" within the area of critical whiteness studies. I fear this moment for various reasons. Many white people are being taught to engage whiteness as if it were an emotional issue: "Stay calm, non-defensive, and everything will be just fine." There's also this sense that administrators are rushing to do the "right thing," to hire scholars who address race and racism during this time of crisis, which feels ad hoc. My point here is that one should not hire race scholars for the purpose of creating a veneer of being "academically progressive." Hiring race scholars should be driven by radical efforts to undo the systemic pervasiveness of whiteness and the ways in which it functions both within one's academic institution and within the larger social world. Whiteness has always been there, doing violence through its normative structure. In my own field, philosophy, it feels as if philosophers are attempting to get in on the game. I recall when the subject of race was deemed philosophically nugatory, to say nothing of whiteness. For me, trying to understand whiteness is about trying to understand terror, trying not to be killed under its anti–Black imaginary. At the end of the day, this new interest in whiteness is consistent with the consumptive logics of whiteness. Whiteness will give the appearance of attacking itself by precisely finding a comfortable university home where it can do this without any real consequences. In short, whiteness can deploy itself as an object of analysis as a way of obfuscating its violence. What are some of your thoughts on the ways in which this recent engagement with whiteness is undoing the work of genuine criticality, of dismantling whiteness?

DRR: The hard questions raised in what you pose here involve some painful confrontations with what it is we have accomplished in universities and even with what it is possible to accomplish. Your observation that the small vogue in critical whiteness studies both delights and comes at a cost comports with my sense of things.

Twenty-five years ago, the great legal scholar John Powell and I consulted at a well-off private college where we tried to create a more diverse student body, faculty and curriculum. The president of the school asked what his goal ought to be. Having just helped his son pick a college, john unhesitatingly answered, "Make your student body look like your student recruitment brochures." Back then, the chilling routinization around discourses on diversity, equity and inclusion talk—the university where I teach recently added "belonging" to the list with great fanfare even as it fired its most treasured multicultural affairs staff—had not quite hardened into place. But the essential problems were already present for powell to pinpoint: the tendency to promise much and deliver little and the calculation that diversity is something to be marketed, mainly to prospective white students. Your remarks on the "new interest in whiteness [being] consistent with the consumptive logics of whiteness" capture such dynamics in their contemporary form perfectly. In a moment when we reflect on Nancy Pelosi's memorialization of George Floyd—"Thank you, George Floyd, for sacrificing your life for justice"—the placing of diversity in the service of a white nation, its evasions and its appetites for happy endings ought not surprise us.

Complicating matters, as you say, is the tendency to see emotional balance and personal development as the reason for anti-racist education training. We can't of course ignore the fact of racist aggressions, micro and macro, on campuses. However, it must be said that the confines of a listening session are much more congenial terrain for administrators, including diversity administrators, than planning to enroll far more students of color, retaining faculty of color, recruiting diverse campus workers to secure jobs that won't be contracted out, or defunding university police, talk of systemic racism notwithstanding.

From my vantage point, that of teaching the last four decades in Midwestern state universities, the larger decline of public education and academic freedom are now big parts of our inability to deliver on the promise of what you call "genuine criticality" toward dismantling whiteness. Anything grand like addressing issues of access or diversification of faculty is off the table from the start; anything controversial is seen as incompatible with winning legislators to the possibility of cutting higher education support a bit more slowly. With tiring regularity, right-wing media rediscovers the existence of critical whiteness studies and claims incredulous outrage that it is actually critical of whiteness. They seldom fail to put administrators on the defensive.

The practice in the university in ruins is to not make efforts to retain any faculty, including faculty of color. The impressive studies of the University of California system by education scholar Chris Newfield have observed that the moment when the system became a bit more democratized racially, support receded.[2] Moreover, the humanities and critical social science sites in which radically anti-racist interdisciplinary work has established itself are specifically threatened by internal university reallocations. These trends, inimical to critical ethnic studies and critical whiteness studies, emerge alongside statements by administrators lavishly supporting racial justice *off* campus. Claims of moral authority based on very meager social justice accomplishments proliferate.

Through the course of Occupy and Black Lives Matter, universities have, I think, been net importers of political energy and insurgent ideas. They have not so far deepened what has come their ways from the street and from new centers of thought on the internet. It seems to me more and more likely that what Fred Moten and Stefano Harney call the "undercommons" will not ultimately be very much university-based. That won't necessarily be a bad thing.

GY: Continuing with this theme regarding the emerging interest in whiteness, I have noticed that the terms "systemic racism" or "structural racism" have become pervasive in our national vocabulary. I'm thinking here of news anchors and politicians. Even President Joe Biden has referred to systemic racism as corrosive, destructive and costly. Indeed, he said that he ran for president because we're in a battle for the soul of this nation. Biden's use of "soul" suggests that there is something fundamentally spiritual at stake in North America, something that is tearing at the deep ethical fabric of this nation when it comes to systemic racism or structural racism. My sense is that the elimination of systemic racism or structural racism would require addressing racialized *material inequality.* Yet, to "save" the soul of this nation would require *more.* First, define how you understand systemic racism or structural racism. Second, what do you see as that "more"?

DRR: Systemic racism's proliferation in political and even corporate discourse represents a triumph for social movements. It moves us from arguing narrowly that Derek Chauvin is a "bad apple"[3] to demonstrating that his personal evil matured within patterns and practices running through law enforcement as a system.

That said, systemic racism also appeals because it remains vague and contradictory in its meanings and can require a delay in order to gather data about patterns, a pause that takes us beyond moments of particular mass anger and mobilization. At this late date, politicians propose not reparations but studies of reparations.

Vagaries as to the meaning of systemic racism are perhaps inevitable. The term "racial capitalism" helps focus discussions regarding what systems and structures prevent us from getting past white supremacy and specifically from addressing the plight of poor and working-class African Americans. Connected to the great scholar of the Black radical tradition, Cedric Robinson, racial capitalism also had significant and different origins among Marxist scholars in the South African freedom movement. The dual but overlapping origins of the term—Robinson often sought to go beyond what he saw as Eurocentric and overly mechanical aspects of Marxist accounts of race—means that systemic solutions to racial oppression can be variously inflected. The Marxist position that the structures of inequality are significantly economic remains compelling, but they are also and long-standingly political and psychological in often deeply irrational ways, carceral and educational.

Robinson and others take the argument further, arguing compellingly that capitalism emerged in a developing racial system and that race and class are typically at play together; capitalism was from the start (and remains) racial capitalism. When we think about settler colonialism as well as anti-Black racism as part of the ways in which whiteness came into the world, Robinson's approach becomes still more relevant. Structures of who owns what are vitally important, but so too is the very idea of owning, enclosing and consuming the land, and of owning the labor and the bodies of others.

So, we might inflect the racial or the capitalism when thinking about what structures are decisive in maintaining white supremacy. The liberal counterpart to an economist Marxist reductionism would hold that only those structures grounding racial difference in resources need attending to in order to move forward. Adolph Reed Jr. argues that the "professional-managerial class" serves capital by holding that if Black people share wealth equally with whites, the system is fair, no matter how wildly unequal distribution of wealth remains or becomes within Black and white populations. I think Reed inflates the extent to which such a position is held, and oversimplifies its class origins as he makes a case that universal class demands best benefit a largely working-class and often poor Black community rather than racially targeted ones. But the approach Reed describes does represent one possibility, though a less than productive one, of how to measure and attack systemic racism.

My position is that if we begin from "racial capitalism" as a naming of the systemic problem, part of the answer to the "more" in your question must be "both." That is, in addition to what you nicely call "racialized *material inequality*," the particular emergencies impacting the Black working poor deserve priority as themselves products of racial capitalism. Such a stance also implies development of vocabularies and forms, weakly present in the U.S. past and present, to imagine broad coalitions not solely based on universal demands, but ones that are able to speak to how groups sharing common oppressors are nevertheless exploited in different ways. One of our problems in this regard is that for a very long time, dramatic forward motion toward either racial justice or working-class well-being has been off the table in neoliberal electoral politics. The temptation then becomes to endlessly imagine that if we inflect racial capitalism right, all will be better. In fact, the emphasis has to fall on both words. The soul-saving might have better prospects untethered from the U.S. nation.

GY: Personally, David, I'm a pessimist. I cannot imagine the end of white privilege or white advantage, which means that I cannot imagine systemic or structural whiteness ending without a war. I think that W. E. B. Du Bois was correct where he says that "whiteness is the ownership of the earth forever and ever, Amen!" When I think about whiteness as a global phenomenon, and the possibility of its total dismantlement, I think about massive forms of resistance to its demise. The pessimist side of me says that the end of whiteness will amount to the end of the world. Here I'm referring to the tenacity of whiteness, its binary structural need for "the other," and its possessiveness of power and the world. Given my line of reasoning, I sense that many white people would prefer not to live *without* the reality of systemic or structural whiteness. In short, there is a kind of death wish associated with the end of whiteness. Perhaps this view is too psychoanalytically dismal. Any thoughts?

DRR: I am with you on the pessimist side. At the very least, it is a position we need to cultivate so that we do not lose track of its claims altogether. As activist intellectuals, we often hearken back to Antonio Gramsci's injunction holding that we need "pessimism of the intellect" alongside "optimism of the will." However, we then tend to disregard the former and act on the latter in order to keep going. That can work for a time, but such strained hope has costs, analytical and personal. Such is especially the case given the possibility that racial capitalism may well take the planet down with it in a matter of decades. As understandable as the rejoicing over the removal of Donald Trump from office surely is, the state of U.S. politics hardly allows us to see how even universal health care or defunding the police and military can succeed, let alone ending white supremacy or addressing climate disasters decisively.

We used to be able to think, as anti-colonial folk wisdom from southern Africa had it, that "time is longer than rope." That is, rulers and systems would show their malignancy over a long run, and the people would organize. The slow bending of history's arc towards justice was persuasive consolation. But because, as you put it, the evil and horror of white supremacy also includes a "death wish," time is much shorter. Such a wish seems to me tied to a failure to imagine the possibility of an egalitarian society, a society in which Black lives matter, a world system taking seriously Indigenous (including Indigenous African) respect for land, or even a pause in spiraling cycles of getting and spending. We saw the limits of racial capitalism's ability to disconnect from death in the deeply irrational responses of whites in the U.S. and elsewhere to COVID-19.

Some of the recent literature on death rates among whites, and particularly on opioid addiction and its consequences, is suggestive in these regards. I especially like Jonathan Metzl's *Dying of Whiteness*, perhaps in part because it is set significantly in Kansas where I live. We think of the Trump voter who prevents Medicaid expansion, or refuses vaccines, as "white working class," even poor, probably rural. But the death-courting, self-defeating white population reaches well into the upper middle classes and is often suburban. I try to make a case in my recent book, *The Sinking Middle Class,* for seeing, after James Baldwin, the misery and emptiness of white upper-middle class life as one key to political immobilization in the U.S. today. Of course, much older patterns of whites regarding social welfare programs as coded "Black"—even when they are universal ones like socialized health care or Aid to Families with Dependent Children, play a longstanding role here too. Whites possess whiteness, Cheryl Harris tells us, sometimes as their only possession. They are also possessed by it. The force of Baldwin on whiteness lay in large measure in insisting on airing the miseries inflicted on both sides of the color line by what he called the "lie" of whiteness. Tragically, his most redemptive passages are somehow read as hateful toward white people.

GY: Where is the U.S. headed? White nationalism is unabashedly on the rise within the U.S. and abroad. Given the historical seductions of whiteness and the ways in which elite whites worked to convince poor and working-class whites that they possessed something as vainglorious as white skin, I'm unconvinced that a critical mass of white people will see through the seductions of whiteness and establish solidarity along class lines. How do you see this? Does class mobilization have a chance, or are the public and psychological wages of whiteness, as Du Bois theorized these, still too strong to resist?

DRR: Let's take the labor one first. I do not think that the ringing traditional radical labor slogan "Black and White, Unite and Fight" offers us any solution commensurate with our crisis. Noble campaigns unfolded under that banner, but not enough of them and without sweeping enough dreams. The unity promised remained predicated on maturing trade union struggles in which largely white unions accepted and recruited workers of color in order not to see their own ability to struggle undermined. It proved too easy to suppose that workers had universal goals born of common oppression and to forget white advantage. Moreover, the feeling of inclusion, however illusory, within the U.S. state and in a relationship with management that adhered to white masculinity seeped into the practice of decreasingly militant, and now comparatively tiny, unions.

That said, working-class unity could reconstitute itself on new foundations. Increasingly, the working class in the U.S. (and in the world) is not white, and unions (or what replaces them as a vehicle of struggle) might come to reflect that. If the watchword becomes "Black and Latinx. Unite and Fight," I assume that for a time, white workers probably would not enlist wholesale, but some would join in for good reasons having to do with attraction to any renewed willingness to combat management and the state. Long ago, the brilliant theorist A. Sivanandan, writing from the U.K., argued that the very crisis of their lives might also lead to breakthroughs on race and class by white workers. "In recovering [their] sense of oppression both from alienation and a white-oriented culture," he wrote, white workers would have to "arrive at a consciousness of racial oppression."[4] The possibility of this occurring among most white workers seems small but any significant split away from the acceptance of white advantage as natural would make a significant contribution to counter-systemic movements not led by whites.

As to the future more broadly, I'd offer a sober perspective, mostly to help us think about the stakes of debates we enter. Writing while trying to understand the European-on-European carnage that was shaping up in World War I, W. E. B. Du Bois offered the view that the idea of "personal whiteness" was "a very recent thing" in human history. He put it then at about 250 years old. We could quibble about dates, but Du Bois is certainly right that owning one's own skin is a particular curse that has applied to only a little corner of a long human past. In making this point, I think he meant to provide some solace. If the past of whiteness were so anomalous and short, we could look also for its end. Your questions lead us to think about the consequences if that turns out to be an untenable assumption.

If psychoanalysis broadly describes struggles between life and death, whiteness is in a peculiar position. White supremacy seeks to make white lives and claims on the land matter above all others. But in doing so, it destroys lives of differently racialized humans and of other living things. It has not only a death wish but a deadly practice. So, Du Bois, Hubert Harrison, C. L. R. James and others in the Black radical tradition came to argue in thinking through the world wars and Nazism that such contempt for life cannot completely stop at the color line.

Let's return then to climate disaster, this time to engage in a thought exercise, à la the great Derrick Bell. Sadly, the scenario below is not of the deliberately inventive sort that he provided to help us imagine and think. It is alarmingly possible in our students' lifetimes, even likely. It is: What if global warming reaches such proportions that it makes everyday life a battle for water, shade and artificial cooling and against frequent pandemics? Suppose that for decades things worsen and finally the planet becomes largely uninhabitable?

What then would "whiteness as usual" imply about how end days unfold? Private accumulation and growth would continue to seem part of the solution even as they deepen the problem. Mars and colonization would beckon, and some might get there. Others would claim enough advantage in wealth to jockey more effectively for habitable property, presumably near the poles and away from rising oceans. Some might air-condition more dramatically and dig deeper to control underground water. The gated and perhaps in-a-bubble communities presiding over the shutting down of things would, as Dylan Rodríguez's important work tells us, include some who are "not white" in skin color but serve in the construction of a ruling "multiracial whiteness" leaving the system of racial capitalism operative. White advantage would apply, even if buying now only a few extra miserable months or years for its beneficiaries, who would almost certainly fall out among themselves.

GY: David, I would like to ask you one additional question related to the work of James Baldwin. As you know, Baldwin talks about the price of the ticket. The price was to become white. Provide a sense of how white people might return the ticket. What would that look like?

DRR: That this remains such a hard question is perhaps a good argument for the "pessimist" position that you articulated earlier, George. The price of the ticket metaphor works in two ways. One reading might see its "return" as a rejection of the ticket itself, an abjuring of whiteness itself and all badges, practices, and advantages adhering to it. The other, related but distinct, reading would envision not only returning or refusing the ticket but repaying what its issuing has cost Black and Indigenous Americans and racialized immigrant outsiders. For me, the first alone is not enough without a reparative dimension.

Years ago, in launching the magazine *Race Traitor*, the late Noel Ignatiev asked me to serve as an editor. I declined not because I thought dis-identifying with whiteness was too much to ask but because it might be too little. That is, declaring oneself not white is too easily proximate to claiming to have stepped outside the racial order and to be "colorblind." In practice, *Race Traitor* mostly did well on this matter and ultimately I worked closely with it. However, it still seems necessary to connect the dramatic disavowal of race treason with the daily practices of reparation.

Such work is hard. I have spent many years thinking, for example, about how it is that whites in the U.S. report themselves in surveys to be committed to having their kids grow up in diverse environments and still in their private consumer decisions help keep hyper-segregation in place. On the other hand, so different is wealth across the color line that if those whites did act on their diversity-seeking values new waves of gentrification would perhaps result.

Nevertheless we do get clear and repeated chances to support specific reparative demands around health care, education, defense of affirmative action, and return of land. We know too that when supporting, for example, Amazon workers organizing under Black trade union and cultural leadership in Staten Island, whites acting in solidarity, and whites working there, have a chance to return the ticket in a way that shows that in doing so they are restoring their own lost connections with humanity. White supremacy, and white pathology, are among what's being repaired.

2

TO BE BLACK IN THE U.S. IS TO HAVE A KNEE AGAINST YOUR NECK EACH DAY

INTERVIEW WITH GEORGE YANCY BY WOOJIN LIM

What drives the current rift between white and Black America, and how as individuals can we effectively contribute to the fight against the worldmaking of whiteness?

Philosopher George Yancy, a leading public intellectual in the critical study of race who received backlash for pointing out the U.S.'s yoke of whiteness,[1] argues that white supremacy breathes at the site of Black asphyxiation.

In this conversation, Yancy discusses the racialized dimensions of COVID-19 vulnerabilities, Donald Trump's displays of white nationalist aspirations, the un-sutured pain of living as a Black person in the United States, and the much-required insurrection against white ontology itself.

WOOJIN LIM: A lot has changed since you published your series of interviews at *The Stone* and penned your provocative letter, "Dear White America," in 2015.[2] How have these changes impacted your views, and which parts of your column would you revise, if at all?

GEORGE YANCY: One might think that I would revise my view within the context of the recent massive protests that are both local to the U.S. and

G. Yancy (with Woojin Lim), "George Yancy: To Be Black in the US Is to Have a Knee Against Your Neck Each Day," *Truthout*, July 18, 2020. [Editors: Alana Yu-lan Price, Britney Schultz, and Anton Woronczuk]

global. One might surmise that given the multiracial composition of the protests that I might change how I addressed white people in that letter. The protests, however, only reveal what I had in mind back in 2015: whiteness is the problem, not Blackness. Moreover, once we reach a "post–George Floyd" moment, those same whites who protested will continue to reap benefits from being white in a country that will continue to be based upon white supremacy. That is the recursive magic of white supremacy. It is able to accommodate or to consume what we throw at it. It is able to make a space for protests and even reform while precisely sustaining itself through the power of its consumptive logics. So, in retrospect, I would not change anything in terms of the argument delineated within "Dear White America."

WL: How do you understand "the more" that is necessary as the world bears witness to these protests within the U.S. and abroad?

GY: Let me first acknowledge that the protests in the U.S. and abroad have ignited an important anti-racism awakening that has been long overdue but requires far more work. There have been some meaningful outcomes, such as confederate statues toppled, the ban of chokeholds, discussions and commitments regarding the defunding of police, school districts across the U.S. committing to removing police from schools, and millions of dollars have been donated to racial justice groups. However, we need to do more. We are *not* disrupting whiteness in ways that will fundamentally make a difference in terms of how it continues to operate through various white gazes, white forms of inhabiting space, white forms of maintaining "innocence," white forms of deep structural power and normativity. What we need is an insurrection, as Judith Butler might say, at the level of white ontology itself.

I often return to James Baldwin's powerful and passionate letter to his nephew[3] where the former says that it is the innocence which constitutes the crime. Baldwin's point is that the very process of attempting to secure one's "white innocence" in the face of so much Black existential pain and suffering caused by white supremacy is a crime. The self-deception is criminal, or perhaps the effort itself is criminal. The history of white supremacy is there for all to see; North America's 400 years of anti-Black racism reveals its mythical standing as a "beacon of hope"; American exceptionalism is, for Black people, a site of un-exceptionalism when it comes to its ideals of democracy vis-à-vis its reality as a white *Herrenvolk* or "master race" polity.

Baldwin also reminds us that those who shut their eyes to reality or those who insist upon their innocence long after it is gone only create monsters. Donald J. Trump is a monster. Just consider his neofascist tendencies, his racist comments, his unabashed white nationalist aspirations, his attempts at demonizing the press, his draconian desires to silence dissent. Henry Giroux is right to call out Trump for both his "pedagogies of repression" and his "dis-imagination machine." Keep in mind that in 2017, Trump stated that there were "very fine people on both sides" in Charlottesville, Virginia. The other side to which he was referring consisted of neo-Nazis, the "alt-right" and white supremacists. This is the same man who degradingly referred to a number of African nations as "shithole countries."

Or, more recently, think of Trump's comment regarding Detroit, Baltimore and Oakland, which I take to be majority-minority cities: "These cities, it's like living in hell." Being Black in North America is like living in hell, but for reasons Trump either doesn't know, refuses to know, or knows and doesn't give a damn. Being Black in America is to be in a living hell. If you don't believe this, then resurrect those Black bodies lynched, castrated, raped and beaten during slavery and after. That hell of anti-Black racism began much earlier. Resurrect the millions of Black bodies that died during the Middle Passage,[4] bodies that could not breathe in the holds of slave ships where their bodies commingled with blood, vomit, feces, urine, disease and the stench of death. You see, not being able to breathe didn't begin with Eric Garner or George Floyd. It began in the Middle Passage. As Black people, we are still in the middle of that passage—suffocating, dying, ontologically frozen by the trauma of a white gaze that doesn't truly give a damn about Black life. It will take much more than whites protesting in the streets to grapple with that problem, especially as our failure at breathing is based upon white people's success at breathing.

I now clearly understand that Trump is the expression of a larger id of white supremacy. He is the manifestation of an unchecked domain of white racist violence, myths of white superiority, myths of white manifest destiny. But we need to keep in mind that his election wasn't the inaugural event that created what we are seeing in such blatant forms. He is a product of that. His election is the manifestation of a species of retaliation for any "Black progress." The assumption at work here is one of white zero-sum logics: Black gain is deemed white loss, which, of course, is based upon white fear and a challenge to white privilege and white ownership of power. So, I would not change anything in "Dear White America." I would remain true to its primary message, and I would do so with love: whiteness is a systemic structure and thereby to be white belies any sense of white innocence. In fact, I would argue that "Dear White America" functioned as an attempt to sting the conscience and consciousness of white people; it was a clarion call against forms of white perceived innocence.

WL: To play on words with your 2018 book, *Backlash: What Happens When We Talk Honestly about Racism in America*, what exactly happens when we talk honestly about the lived experience of racism today? What does it mean to be Black in America?

GY: In that title, the lived experience of racism had to do with the lived experience of racism that I encountered after writing "Dear White America." That experience was one of white terror, threats of physical violence, death threats, perverse projections from a deep-seated white libidinal desire in relationship to the Black body (my Black body), racist epithets, and the deployment of "nigger." That term continues to carry the weight of a punch in the face, a kick in the back; it remains assaultive. Again, pointing to Baldwin, white people really do need to ask themselves why they needed to create that term ("nigger") in the first place. By asking such a question, perhaps they will come to realize that what is necessary is that they address ways in which they have split themselves off from aspects of their own hated selves. After all, Black people did not create that term.

Thinking about the full title of that book, I would say that there is much to pay for those who refuse to tip-toe around the question of white racism, white power and white privilege. For me, that honesty and courage is not something that Black people or people of color must carry alone. White people must be prepared to talk honestly about racism in the United States, but to do so requires a certain symbolic death, where one encourages the death of the semiotics of whiteness, its oppressive material reality, where one is prepared to self-empty, to refuse the price of the ticket to "become white" and thereby anti-Black.

Another way of thinking about the lived experience of racism is to talk about the horrors of whiteness as they are experienced within the context of the mundane, the everyday. This point is so incredibly important at this moment in U.S. history. The death of George Floyd is what I would call a spectacular form of white racism on display. The emphasis is on the term "spectacular," which etymologically suggests that which is clearly seen, indicative of a show. And while we know that the brutal and slow murder of George Floyd had nothing to do with theatrics, my point is that Black people experience forms of quotidian white racism all the time, where these forms of racism are not caught on video. Let's call this the banality of whiteness.

Think about what it means to be Black at predominantly white universities and college campuses, which are the spaces within which I have taught for nearly 20 years. It means to undergo forms of deep racial alienation. Some Black students and students of color have to cope with white people, believe it or not, who have never interacted with people who are *not* white. This points to the existence of de facto racial segregation. So, out of these white spaces grow distorted racist desires and assumptions: "Can I touch your hair?" "You are very articulate." "You don't sound Black." "Tell us what it is like to witness a murder?" "What sport do you play?" "Where are you from, *really?*" "But I don't hear your accent." "You speak English so well." "You are so angry." "Stop being so sensitive." "But you've made it. Why complain?" These moments are not spectacular, but that does not mean that they are less racist or any less painful for those who feel like targets. Imagine the sense of finding it hard to breathe, hard to move within those spaces with ease or with effortless grace, imagine the impact on trying to study, imagine what it's like to take a stroll across campus after a week or even a day of such microaggressions. These interactions function as acts of micro-violence. They are nonspectacular moments of deep pain, hurt and sorrow, but still forms of racial cruelty predicated upon larger systemic necropolitical violence where state power shapes who lives or who dies, unevenly, through a racial and racist framework.

WL: So, for you, what does it mean to be Black in America?

GY: It means to be subjected to forms of white systemic violence everyday of one's life. To be Black in America is to grieve one's own death that is always already imminent or looming within a country that was founded upon a system of beliefs and practices that said that you are not human. To be Black in America means to be murdered by the white state and white proxies of the state. It means walking through a gated community minding your own business and being shot dead (Trayvon Martin), shot in the back and killed while fleeing (Walter Scott and Rayshard Brooks), shot and killed while in the "safety" of one's own home (Botham Jean, Atatiana Jefferson, Breonna Taylor), shot while out jogging (Ahmaud Arbery), arrested while innocently sitting in a Starbucks (Rashon Nelson and Donte Robinson), threatened through the weaponization of white womanhood as you ask a white woman to leash her dog (Christian Cooper). I have come to embrace a formulation, which I'm sure has its origin in Afro-pessimist theorizing, that says that the opposite of Blackness is not whiteness, but the human. In short, to be Black is to fall within the category of the "sub-person," the "subhuman" or perhaps even the "unhuman." To be Black in America is to deal constantly with white macro scenes of Black death and dying, Black disrespect, Black nullification, Black ontological truncation, Black epistemic injustice, Black degradation, Black policing, Black confinement, Black precarity, Black fatigue, Black inequality, Black poverty, Black hunger and systemic Black marginalization. In short, to be Black in America is to have a knee pressed against your neck and to die just a little each day; it is a form of gradual asphyxiation that is your birthright.

WL: As a target of white racist vitriol and death threats, what were your coping mechanisms, the guiding light that you clung to?

GY: That one is easy. I have Black children and I want them to live. The threats will come, they will continue. And while Black people cannot be the "saviors" of white people, I must attempt, with all of my strength, to protect my Black children. This is not some abstract ethical commitment but a daily and concrete loving effort that understands their reality and that recognizes their racial precarity. As a Black parent, I feel it each day when a child of mine walks out into the world, into the toxicity of anti-Black racism. You see, they don't need *to do anything* that will result in their not coming home ever again. All that is necessary is that they are Black in a white supremacist United States. What keeps me stable is that love for them. So, I must write that next essay, write that next book or edited that next book, and give that next lecture that reveals the truth about a white United States. What also grounds me, though my pessimist tendencies seem to be winning out, is the belief in an open future. After all, I don't believe that whiteness has a metaphysical monopoly on the future. Yet, there is nothing about the past or the present that says, without question, that anti-Black racism will ever completely come to an end. So, the guiding light is to save the lives of my Black children, to have them return home, not to get that call to come down to the morgue to identify the lifeless body of my Black child who has been killed because some white police officer said that they "felt threatened."

WL: What is "white America" to you?

GY: For me, "white America" is a structural lie. And by this, I mean that it was/is predicated upon abstract ideals that it never intended to apply to Black people or people of color. And even where there is "progress" for those of us whose lives don't matter, it is important to recognize that such alleged progress occurs within the framework of white interests. The critical race theorist Derrick Bell made this clear with his theory of interest convergence, which shows that racial justice for Black people only happens when white and Black interests converge. So, the implication is that Black progress is tolerated as long as it doesn't fundamentally challenge white interests. This still prioritizes whiteness.

This further speaks to the ethical vacuity of white America as a structure, as a system that consists of white people who consciously or unconsciously invest in whiteness. Returning to what I've said earlier, this means that "white America" attempts to obfuscate its practice of anti-Black violence through forms of distorted white self-narration. The lies are familiar: the majority of whites are innocent of racism; racism is an aberration enacted by a few bad whites; the U.S. doesn't see color; we are clearly a post-racial country because otherwise how could we have elected the first African American president.

This is why we need to be critically aware at this moment and nurture a critical imagination. Many whites are protesting, shouting that Black lives matter. I get it. But Malcolm X was right. If you stick a knife in my back nine inches and pull it out six inches that is not progress. He goes on to say that even if the knife is pulled out all the way, there is still no progress because progress is healing the wound that was originally made. And like Malcom, I don't see the U.S. willing to remove the knife or willing to heal the wound. It feels as if salt is being poured on that open wound every day. The protests that we are witnessing will not heal the wound. And while it is important that white people protest the killing of Black bodies and racist policing, it is also important to think about how white protestation can function as a form of virtue signaling—*you see, we are* good *whites*. I don't want white people to build monuments of white virtue on my back as I'm lying in the street dead because some white police officer could not, as Claudia Rankine says, police his or her own imagination.

WL: How would you define the project of "undoing whiteness"? How can white Americans confront the ways in which they benefit from racism?

GY: Undoing whiteness will certainly *not* happen by simply understanding that whiteness is a site of fragility. That term does some work, but it is very misleading. It often suggests that white people are these delicate creatures who would understand their racism, but only if they realize that they are operating from a defensive place of fragility. That is too consoling. White people must be prepared to accept the lie that is their whiteness. It's not about fragility. It's about white people's desire to maintain their white power, white privilege and white innocence. History has given them the blinkers, the shelters to use to protect them from facing the lie and violence of whiteness, their whiteness.

I am often asked if there is an easier way to explain to white people the meaning of their whiteness without raising the issue of their racism. I think that posing such a question presupposes white fragility. If Black people *must* face the fact that their existence doesn't matter within a white racist United States, then white people *must* face the truth that their existence is secured, protected and rendered "sacred" because Black existence isn't. That means that white people are complicit with George Floyd's death. It is not simply about Derek Chauvin. It is the fact that to be white in the United States involves, as Joel Olson would argue, never having to occupy the position of Black people, because that place is always taken.

What is needed is a form of kenosis or self-emptying. This is a process where white people die a symbolic death, a death that has deep affective, epistemological, ethical and metaphysical implications. It means ending the world of whiteness, not white people. What comes after the death of whiteness may very well produce a form of humanity that has been held captive by whiteness. Yet, this will also require removing white masks, un-veiling the systemic oppressive forms of whiteness, asking white people to be vulnerable, to tarry with forms of being un-sutured, and having their souls laid bare.

If whiteness is nothing other than oppressive and false, as David Roediger has argued, why cling to it? Back to Baldwin: "Any real change implies the breakup of the world as one has always known it, the loss of all that gave one an identity, the end of safety." That is what is necessary in order to undo whiteness, the crumbling of white worldmaking, undermining all of the fictions that reinforce white identity, and a daring act of love—not the sentimental kind—that expresses itself through the risk of looking into that disagreeable mirror called Black critique, which is predicated upon deep forms of Black pain and suffering. Unlike Odysseus, white people must be prepared to take the leap, to risk all in the name of freedom from the idolatry of whiteness.

WL: Should Black Americans be required to bear the weight of public witnessing in a world that displays "ethical cowardice and indifference," and if not, whom else? How should responsibility be apportioned to Black and white people when attempting to overcome racial gridlocks?

GY: I think that within a context of pervasive anti-Black racism, one has an ethical responsibility as a racialized Black person to bear the weight of speaking courageous speech against white racism. We can't simply as-sume that white people will do this work through moral suasion. After all, history proves that. And even if they do it, we have to be careful that they are not doing so because of white *noblesse oblige*, or because of some deeply problematic reason to be a "white hero." Those acts are perfunctory and re-center whiteness.

So, we need white people to do the work that is necessary to critically work through whiteness such that they are not reinscribing that whiteness. Unfortunately, so many white people are ethically cowardly and indifferent. The idea of losing their safety must be emphasized. In this way, they understand the magnitude of their responsibility. We can help them develop what I refer to as a form of white double consciousness, where they see themselves through the eyes of Black people. Yet, they must do the lion's share of the work when it comes to what you've called racial gridlocks. Think about what is otherwise being asked of Black people. We have to deal with white racism and then teach white people about themselves. I recall being asked by a white woman philosopher once: "What do you want from white people?" Reflecting back on that question, I'm convinced that it functioned to privilege whiteness even as it gave the appearance of something "progressive."

First, I shouldn't have to ask white people for anything. They *should* (even if they don't) see what is needed. Second, what made that white woman think that she could even provide what I needed? So, there was white arrogance. Third, structurally, her power was instantiated precisely in posing the question to me. Black people want to live, and we want to do so with our freedom and dignity intact. It is not only white people who must do the work, though. It is anti-Black racism that we are fighting against. And while whiteness is the fulcrum around which anti-Blackness moves, all non-Black people in white supremacist United States must also do the necessary work, especially if they are not Black, which, as mentioned, is a place already taken. So, there is a larger racial binary that must be interrogated, one for which whiteness is also responsible: not just Blackness and whiteness, but Blackness and non-Blackness.

I think that it's important to see how such interracial minority conflicts between—for example, Asian Americans and African Americans—are fueled by whiteness just as intra-racial conflicts are fueled by whiteness. In the former case, think about the unnecessary tension caused by the model minority myth. In the latter case think about the toxicity of colorism within Black spaces. Both are generated within the logics of whiteness.

WL: If there is one thing you would like the public to take away from your work today, what is your message?

GY: I'm not sure if there is one thing. To answer your question, though, I'll respond within the context of the gravity of our current reality. As I was thinking recently about the social and ethical challenges posed by the COVID-19 pandemic, I began to feel and to articulate what I was witnessing. What we are witnessing is the collapse of the taken-for-granted, the normative structure of everyday life. And yet, for Black people, we continue to experience more of the same, more of the same disproportionate vulnerabilities, resource depletions, food deserts and massive inequities across various indices. COVID-19 is helping to unveil these realities, but "white America" has a short memory. Black bodies are piling up. This is and has been our history. Notice the connecting themes of death and dying, and not being able to breathe without struggling to do so. Despite COVID-19, Black bodies are still close enough to stop and to harass disproportionately, to murder unarmed and to publicly lynch.

This moment reminds me of 9/11 and the horrible events that took place at Abu Ghraib prison. Regarding the latter, then-President Bush announced, "This is not the America I know." Yet, this is the America known by Black people. The xenophobic paranoia, sexual violence, sadistic brutality, we know that history. And 9/11 wasn't the first terror attack on American soil. Black people have known white terror throughout the history of this country. So, what should be taken away from my work is the importance placed on white people to face the differential horrors that Black people face, and not to turn away and claim "innocence."

For me, philosophy is a site of suffering. I ask questions about our inexplicable presence in this remarkably complex and apparently indifferent and silent universe, I bear witness to what Walter Benjamin calls "human wreckage," and I am often the target of white racist vitriol. So, for me doing philosophy, wrestling with truth, is inextricably linked to pathos. Like Theodor Adorno and Cornel West, I believe that we must let suffering speak. I also ask that white people learn how to suffer along with, and take responsibility for, the social and historical wreckage that Black people experience because of anti-Black racism that exists here in the U.S. and abroad. And for those white people who say that they do suffer in this way, then I would ask that they show me their scars, allow me to place my hand in the wound that they've endured fighting against Black degradation, and fighting against the insidious structure of whiteness—their whiteness. I want white people to know that they are not pre-social, neoliberal subjects, that we are always already entangled in the lives of others and that they are especially entangled in the lives of Black people. Because of this, there is no "white innocence."

Unlike Athena, who was born fully whole from the head of Zeus, we are born from the messiness and beauty of interlocking, collective human flesh—fragile, precarious. To echo Baldwin, I want white people to know that "everything white Americans think they believe in must now be re-examined." If not for themselves, then for the love of their white children. Indeed, returning to your question about the guiding light that I clung to, I would also add deep love for the souls of white children. If their own white parents fail them, if white society fails them, what do they have? Who will help them not to flee reality? Who will help them to remove the masks, as Baldwin would say, that they will someday come to fear they cannot live without? In fact, rethinking the second question that you posed, I would like to see white people *return the ticket* that sustains their humanity (read: white) in the U.S. This is a radical gesture as it doesn't mean simply trying to create greater instances of "diversity" vis-à-vis various traditionally white institutions or "fixing" or "reforming" the racist dimensions of the carceral system. It is not about new ways of policing. I'm asking for something far more dangerous. To return the ticket means that white people refuse to function as the social ontological normative background against which Black bodies are killed. It means refusing to bargain for something that promises the death of racialized others. To refuse the price of the ticket is to refuse to live a life of safety. It will entail a species of death, which might, as I would argue, give birth to something radically new.

3

CONFRONTING PREJUDICE ISN'T ENOUGH

We Must Eradicate the White Racial Frame

INTERVIEW WITH JOE FEAGIN

The brutal enslavement of Black people lasted for a full 60 percent of this country's colonialist history.

It is this deadly longevity of anti-Black racism that we must grasp in order to understand the currently palpable and deeply painful anti-Black racist experiences that African Americans continue to endure in the twenty-first century U.S., and the massive multiracial protests that have ensued.

U.S. anti-Black racism was founded upon the brutal enslavement of Black people. In the decades since the abolition of slavery, systemic white racism and what has been called the "white racial frame" continue to valorize white people and degrade Black people and the rich historical magnitude of Black people who have, for centuries, struggled against white supremacy.

In this crucial interview, nationally and internationally prominent sociologist and social theorist Joe Feagin explores these key concepts and historical phenomena. Feagin, who is the Ella C. McFadden Professor and Distinguished Professor in sociology at Texas A & M University, has done much internationally recognized research on U.S. racism, sexism and political economy issues. He has written over 230 scholarly articles and 79 scholarly books in his social science areas, including *Systemic Racism*, *White Party, White Government*, *The White Racial Frame*, and *How Blacks Built America*.

G. Yancy (with Joe Feagin), "Confronting Prejudice Isn't Enough. We Must Eradicate the White Racial Frame," in *Truthout*, June 30, 2020. [Editors: Alana Yu-lan Price and Britney Schultz]

GEORGE YANCY: African Americans have just celebrated Juneteenth[1] in the midst of Black-led protests that are, to my knowledge, unprecedented. Speak to the possible connection between Juneteenth and these 21st-century protests that embody long sought-after freedoms for Black people.

JOE FEAGIN: Recent Juneteenth celebrations remind all Americans that this country is founded on the human-torture system called slavery. No one should be surprised that those targeted by that system of slavery—which involved millions of African Americans—have actively protested against racial oppression and fought for human liberty and justice for centuries. From 1619 to 1865—for *60 percent* of this country's colonialist history—whites maintained a brutal enslavement system unjustly enriching whites and unjustly impoverishing African Americans.

After a brief Reconstruction period, slavery was followed by the near-slavery of Jim Crow segregation, which also unjustly enriched the white majority while unjustly impoverishing African Americans. Generation after generation, African Americans have rebelled, individually and collectively, against this white racial oppression. During the long slavery era, African Americans engaged collectively in an estimated 250 planned or implemented slave uprisings. There were also hundreds of thousands of individual protests and rebellions. During the 90-year Jim Crow era, there were also many dozens of attempted and successful collective demonstrations and uprisings, as well as many thousands of individual protests.

Today we see yet more Black-led and Black-generated demonstrations and uprisings very much in this long freedom tradition. I have rigorously argued in *How Blacks Built America*[2] that in their individual and collective protests and revolts against racial oppression African Americans have long pressed for—indeed, arguably invented—the *authentic* liberty-and-justice-for-all values that have gradually become more central to this country. The white male "founders" version of "liberty and justice" values were inauthentic, as they actually had in mind freedom for (propertied) white men, a small portion of the population, from British oppression.

GY: Since 1970, your scholarship has deepened our understanding of the dynamics of Black social protests within the United States. Speak to some of the *underlying conditions* that you see operating today that were operating within the 1960s or even the 1990s.

JF: I have researched Black antiracist movements, demonstrations and revolts since the late 1960s. With Harlan Hahn, I did the major social science book on the hundreds of violent Black revolts against systemic racism in the 1960s–1970s (*Ghetto Revolts:The Politics of American Violence*, 1973).[3] In addition, in numerous other books, such as *Racist America*,[4] I have examined, for the 1940s–1960s era, Black nonviolent civil rights demonstrations, as well as the early 1990s Black uprisings over the Rodney King beating.

Black demonstrations and uprisings today are similar in several ways to previous demonstrations and uprisings. Central to all, past and present, are what many researchers call "underlying conditions" and "precipitating events." The well-institutionalized, inhumane conditions that underlie Black demonstrations and uprisings include not only white discrimination in policing but also in employment, housing, education, health care and political rights. In survey and interview studies, most African Americans report regularly facing racial discrimination, and much research demonstrates huge racial inequalities rooted in generations of unjust Black impoverishment at the hands of unjustly enriched whites. Graphically illustrating 20 generations of white enrichment and Black impoverishment, to take just one major example, is the fact that today *the median net worth of white households is about 13 times that of Black households.*[5]

A second concept often used by researchers examining specific demonstrations and uprisings accents "precipitating events" that trigger them. A majority of such precipitating events involve discriminatory incidents where a Black person or group is publicly targeted by whites. In many cases, these involve police brutality or other malpractice incidents—especially those perpetrated by white officers.

One difference in these events today is that the general public is much more likely to see the police malpractice or other white discrimination because of phone cameras carried by many people. Unlike in the case of the 1960s and the 1990s demonstrations and uprisings, we often have a video of the triggering event that makes it much harder to deny, especially for whites. Images of the events typically become viral and appear across millions of television sets and other devices.

GY: You have articulated what you call the "white racial frame." Define what you mean by such a frame and relate it to forms of white policing of Black bodies, which often leads to horrific deaths as in the cases of Breonna Taylor, George Floyd, and, more recently, Rayshard Brooks.

JF: Today, mainstream analysis of issues involving white racism makes heavy use of concepts like prejudice, bias, and bigotry. These terms are skewed toward an individualistic, nonsystemic interpretation of racial matters. My young colleagues and I have done much research demonstrating that the concept of *systemic* racism, including the important concept of its *white racial frame*, are necessary to fully understand U.S. racial matters. For centuries, that white racial frame has provided a dominant worldview from which most whites (and many others) regularly view this society. While it includes racist prejudices, even more important are its racist narratives about society, its strong racist images, its powerful racist emotions, and its inclinations to racist actions. Especially important is that this broad white framing has a very positive orientation to whites as generally superior and virtuous (a pro-white subframe) and a negative orientation to various racial "others" substantially viewed as inferior and unvirtuous (anti-others subframes).

This frame motivates and rationalizes white racist discrimination targeting African Americans, including police brutality and violence such as that involved in the cases of African American men and women that you mention, and hundreds of others. The likely motivation for such police malpractice is more than racial bias. These events typically involve a white racial framing that not only stereotypes and interprets Black people and their actions in negative terms as unvirtuous—e.g., dangerous, criminal, violent, druggies—but also portrays whites, including police officers, as virtuous, manly, superior, and dominant. Also central in many such incidents appear to be white emotions of anger, fear, resentment or arrogance. The way in which whites view themselves in these settings is at least as important as their negative views of those they target with discrimination.

GY: Given that the white racial frame is that which is learned by whites within quotidian contexts, perhaps even at a white parent's knee, how might this form of framing be challenged and undone? I ask this because while there have been many demands for police reform, I have not heard much at all about the more fundamental problem of eradicating the white racial frame.

JF: From decades of experience researching and teaching about white racism, I have concluded it takes much long-term education and re-education for any white person, including myself, to significantly dismantle that white racial frame and replace it with an *authentic* liberty-and-justice-for-all framing that motivates meaningful anti-racist actions. This is especially true for whites who are enmeshed in family and friendship networks that vigorously enforce conformity to that frame. An example is the "blue line"—the strong police officer networks. You not only have to move white individuals into long-term deframing of their own white racial frame, but also into challenging the white racist framing of their important social groups.

Dismantling and replacing even modest amounts of that white racial frame are extraordinarily difficult because it is fundamental to the social, material, and ideological construction and operation of this country. This frame shapes what most whites believe, feel, and do in regard to racial matters. For the most part, we don't teach white youth to be deeply critical thinkers when it comes to our society's racial matters. Most home and institutional schooling encourages them to follow the lead of white economic, political, or religious leaders. Lack of critical thinking about our racist history and institutions reflects and perpetuates that dominant white racial frame.

Solid information about our racist history and institutions is a good place to start in changing that dominant racial frame. Decades of teaching thousands of college students and older Americans have led me to see that, until most whites have that accurate instruction, they do not have the essential understandings to be strongly supportive of major changes in systemic racism. Working with anti-racist organizations has revealed to me that it typically takes long hours of instruction and dialogue over many months to get whites to even begin to think critically about the racially stereotyped images, beliefs, emotions, and interpretations of the dominant white racial frame they fervently cling to.

A key problem, especially for most white Americans, is just how segregated we are from people of color—especially from regular equal-status contacts with people of color beyond the workplace. We know from social psychological studies that even getting white subjects with a strong racist framing of racial others to seriously observe or read about the latter in positive un-stereotyped settings can often begin to weaken some racist framing. This seems especially true for young children. A *substantial* breaking-down of the socially segregated spaces of whites, including with much more positive framing and information about people of color might, at least for children, begin the slow process of deframing their white racial framing.

If you examine most of contemporary schools' curricula, you will see that we are a long way from even these first steps in breaking down and replacing the worst elements of this society's still dominant white racial frame. There is no way around the hard and necessary goal of much aggressively honest education, especially for whites, about our racist history and contemporary institutions.

GY: Along with eradicating the white racial frame is eradicating white privilege, white power, white hegemony. How might white people come to understand that eliminating white racism is in their own interest?

JF: Again, aggressive re-education for whites is one essential step. For one thing, they need to be taught about the very high price many ordinary whites have paid for systemic racism at certain points in our history. For example, many whites, especially Southerners, are bamboozled by mythical notions of the slavery era and the Civil War in numerous U.S. movies, so that they do not even know that ordinary whites in the 1860s paid an extremely heavy price for what we misname as the "Civil War." This was really a treasonous uprising against an established United States led by elite white male slaveholders, a minority of Southern whites, who effectively conned ordinary whites—most not slaveholders—into supporting, often with their lives, the elite effort to preserve a slavery system that brought them great wealth. That bloody conflict took 620,000 lives on both sides. Most of those confederates were ordinary white farmers and workers who died for that elite cause.

Then as now, ordinary whites have often been conned by the ruling white elite into taking racist actions that, to varying degrees, are against their own individual or group interests. As the brilliant Black sociologist W. E. B. Du Bois underscored in his writings, in the past and present, ordinary whites have accepted the "public and psychological wage of whiteness," the sense and privileges of being racially superior, that has long been offered to them by the white male elite. Accepting this psychological wage of whiteness has made ordinary whites much less likely over the centuries to organize effectively with African American workers and farmers to improve their societal conditions. This successful elite strategy of racial divide-and-conquer has cost large numbers of ordinary white families dearly. That is, a centuries-old *lack* of united worker organizations—e.g., massive, effective and enduring unions across the color line—has meant much less desirable working and living conditions, not only for African Americans, but also for many ordinary white Americans. One can observe this negative result today in the substantial differences in the quality of the modern social welfare states (e.g., the health care systems) serving ordinary citizens in the U.S. and European countries with strong unions.

A majority of whites also pay for continuing systemic racism in elevated levels of racial fear, resentment, and ignorance. Research has shown that whites who are raised in segregated conditions and still live segregated lives are often fearful of Black people and other people of color with whom they have few or no equal-status contacts. Growing up in segregated areas, most white parents and children are unprepared to deal with the soon-to-be demographic reality of being a "white minority" in the U.S. Their fear of that significant racial change, undergirded by their racist framing of white superiority and virtuousness compared to people of color, leaves them with a limited ability to deal wisely and democratically with a racially changing country and world, in the present and future.

GY: Going forward, I tend to be pessimistic about the eradication of white supremacy and white privilege. The history of this country supports my pessimism. For those who share my view, do you see anything on the horizon for which we ought to be optimistic regarding white racism?

JF: I tend to be an optimistic pessimist. Those decades of research on our systemic white racism have made me pessimistic about the eradication of white supremacy and privilege. However, my work with effective anti-racist activist groups like the Midwestern group called Antiracism Study Dialogue Circles Metamorphosis gives me some hope for the future, as their multiracial organization has reached more than 2,000 people, many of them white, using long-term anti-racist dialogue groups.[6] Their sophisticated approach has increased the number of authentic white anti-racists. Also, the presence of millions of white Americans in recent protest demonstrations against police brutality and malpractice seems to offer a glimmer of hope that many (especially younger) whites can be educated or re-educated about our systemic racism and about anti-racist action.

Still, given the widespread white racial fears of the large-scale demographic and voter changes going on now and in the near future, I see a societal future likely to have much more sociopolitical tumult, some of which may well be violent given the growth in well-armed white supremacist groups.

GY: Indeed, despite the findings of the January 6th Committee, there is no guarantee that this will transform the white racial frame of many Trump supporters. As you and I know, though, Trump is a symptom of white supremacy. I have been thinking recently of James Baldwin's understanding of the price of the ticket. As you know, for Baldwin, the price of the ticket was to "become white." Do you have any thoughts about what it would look like for white people to *return* the ticket, i.e., return their whiteness as it were?

JF: The recent increase in overt white supremacist leaders like Donald Trump shows the white majority supports the withdrawal of the "ticket" of limited political-economic rights provided to African Americans by civil rights laws and other progressive legal and political achievements since Reconstruction. A white majority now insists on "taking back their country," referencing growing nonwhite rights and power. Yet whites' taking back the ticket of greater nonwhite rights and power is impossible short of a revolution totally destroying U.S. society. A key reason is this ticket was *never* freely extended by whites. It was forced on whites by centuries of African Americans *demanding* it by antiracist resistance and human rights organization. A century ago, the great African American scholar W. E. B. Du Bois cut through the white racist framing and its mythology: "Your country? How came it yours? Before the Pilgrims landed we were here. Here we have brought our three gifts and mingled them with yours: a gift of story and song . . . ; the gift of sweat and brawn to . . . lay the foundations of this vast economic empire . . . ; the third, a gift of the Spirit."[7] In his pathbreaking book *The Gift of Black Folk* Du Bois showed that the greatest of their gifts was Black Americans emphasizing "a vision of democracy in America such as neither [white] Americans nor Europeans conceived in the eighteenth century, and such as they have not even accepted in the twentieth century."[8]

Well into the 21st century, African Americans have emphasized this democratic vision. Reflecting on 1960s civil rights movements, in a famous *Time* article "What America Would Be Like without Blacks," Black essayist Ralph Ellison underscored this great democratic gift: "[I]t is the black American who puts pressure upon the nation to live up to its ideals. It is he who gives creative tension to our struggle for justice."[9] Most recently, African American scholar-activist Angela Davis reflected on what Barack Obama's election victory meant for an authentic democratic vision: ". . . generations of people of African descent, generations of people of all racial and ethnic backgrounds here and abroad who learned how to place justice, equality, and peace before economic profit, before ideologies of racism. . . . Let us remember the many activists in the 1930s and 1940s who paved the way for the freedom struggle of the 1950s and 1960s, those who dared to imagine a better place, a better world."[10] That is, the most important historical gift to U.S. democracy and human rights was *not* the always tentative white ticket, but the Black vision of, and insistent organization for, *real* democratic norms and values for *all* Americans.

4

WE HAVE TO LET WHITE SUPREMACY DIE IN ORDER TO TRULY LIVE

INTERVIEW WITH DAVID KYUMAN KIM

In a climate of white supremacist violence and blatant contempt for a robust democratic vision—where distrust, deception and unabashed lying run thick in the halls of power—Lindsay Graham and other Trump enablers are rubbing salt in the wound by calling on people to simply "move on."

To truly move forward, however, we will need a form of accountability that is oriented toward social transformation, rather than "reconciliation" or "unity." And those of us who are working to resist the poison of white supremacy will need to ground our actions in revolutionary love.[1]

In the interview that follows, David Kyuman Kim, Executive Director of Stanford University's Center for Comparative Studies in Race and Ethnicity, contends that in these perilous times, we must center our deepseated love of humanity—love is one of the things that separates us from the fascists.

A philosopher of religion and scholar of radical love and multiracial democracy and widely published author and editor, Kim has held appointments at Stanford University, Connecticut College, Union Theological Seminary in New York City, Harvard, Brown, the University of Pennsylvania, and the Social Science Research Council. His current book project is *The Public Life of Love.*

G. Yancy (with David Kyuman Kim), "We Have to Let White Supremacy Die in Order to Truly Live," *Truthout*, January 17, 2021. [Editors: Alana Yu-lan Price, Maya Schenwar, and Britney Schultz]

GEORGE YANCY: Let's start with the political divisiveness that we are currently experiencing in this country, though, as we know, the U.S. has always been internally divisive. How do we prevent this country from crossing the brink into a civil war, especially given the violence that took place on January 6?

DAVID KYUMAN KIM: I had previously been reticent to use the language of "civil war" to describe what is taking place in America. Regrettably, it feels irresponsible to deny how deep and extreme the divisions are in our country. The presidential election revealed that nearly half of the electorate—some 70 million Americans—voted to keep a white supremacist with deep fascist tendencies in office. And for those who are in denial that we are on the brink of civil war, the violent attack by Trump's supporters on the Capitol in D.C. and in state capitals in Washington, Kansas, and Georgia should be evidence enough that the war is upon us.

Elected officials and pundits claiming that the white supremacist mob that sieged the Capitol recently "is not America" are in a serious state of denial. The mob does not speak for all of us, but it does represent a longstanding strain of the American spirit.

The divisiveness in the country is surely a fight for the character and spirit of the nation. Are we a democracy? Are we willing and able to realize forms of democracy that have been, frankly, underdeveloped and unrealized? The civil war at hand is not simply between the left and the right, or between Trump supporters and the rest of us.

The persistence of white supremacy in the American experiment has shown that the civil war is also within us, inside of us. The storming of the Capitol was horrifying but also inevitable. White supremacy will not be contained or restrained until all of us are willing to let its hold on us die. Diversity training isn't going to save us from what George Lipsitz calls the possessive investment in whiteness.

White supremacy is as American as apple pie. The basic tenet of radical love is an unflagging commitment to the idea that we have to let basic things in us die—white supremacy included—in order to truly live. This includes the uninterrogated conceit that the police will, unfailingly, protect all of us. The footage of the Capitol Police standing aside and allowing the mob to enter the Capitol without resistance speaks to this directly.

The calls to "move on" by Lindsay Graham and other Trump enablers don't recognize that moving on and moving forward will require accountability. This is more than just punishment; it's holding ourselves to a standard of justice that says we love ourselves and our own enough to protect and preserve, to stand for the best in us rather than our basest nature.

Watching Trump give the lightest of pleas to the mob to stop and then to conclude by telling them, "We love you," is a perversion of the notion of love. Obviously, he has affection for the right-wing mob, as they do for him. But the tie that binds them is not consonant with the kind of love that insists on justice for the least amongst us—it's at odds with the love that sacrifices comfort for the sake of the good. Trump's love is a love of whiteness and power, a love of tyranny. Trump has committed all sorts of crimes over the past five years; now it seems like he is even corrupting the quality of public love.

Despite the despair, I still hold out hope. As you can probably tell, I believe that hope and love are twinned principles of our fate. Black Lives Matter, multiracial solidarity are signs of hope for our democracy in this American winter of hate. The love of (and for) people of color is a bulwark against America's commitment to white supremacy and racism. Love is an underutilized natural resource for our democracy. None of us can afford to give up on that.

GY: David, what has impressed me about your work and praxis is your emphasis on love, on its public expression. There are many who will say that love has no place in the public sphere. How do you respond to such a claim?

DKK: Folks who object that love has no place in the public sphere effectively uphold a vision of our common lives that's devoid of the very thing that makes us human. Relationships. The ties that bind. The bonds that make our lives meaningful. Even if that relationship is to oneself.

Let's extend the logic of a public sphere or public life that is devoid of love or in which love is forbidden/prohibited, as it were. This is a world and a worldview whose structure of feeling devolves from indifference and cruelty. This is how we find ourselves suffocating under a politics of cruelty rather than a politics of compassion, or what I call love-driven politics.

We are barely emerging from the bitter and exceptionally cruel Trump era—an age marked by state-sanctioned violence, the unwarranted ripping apart and separation of families, the [ongoing] caging of children, the deepening exploitation of the environment, and of course the blithe indifference to our collective and public health in the face of a global pandemic, the stoking of violent insurgence against the state. Can we really afford to back away from love in such hate-filled times?

GY: I consider literary figure James Baldwin to be a prophet of love. He links love to the process of removing the figurative masks that we are afraid to live without. In our contemporary moment, with the rise of the "alt-right" and white supremacist groups, those masks of which Baldwin spoke appear to be indelibly fixed. In fact, we seem to have little space for mutual giving, mutual sharing of generosity, and the recognition of a sense of connectedness in this country. Why is this?

DKK: I absolutely agree with you about Baldwin. He is our great secular gospel writer. The searing truth of the Gospel of Love according to Baldwin—whether we're talking about *Giovanni's Room* or *Go Tell it on the Mountain*, and of course *The Fire Next Time*—is his consistent testimony to the necessity of truth-telling to the work of realizing love. We can only survive the violence of racism, of white supremacy if we commit ourselves to loving ourselves, as Baldwin wrote over and over again. For people of color, for the severely marginalized and colonized, this commitment to loving oneself involves risk. It takes courage in the face of fear of harm. I would argue that Baldwin's interrogation was deeper than the donning of masks. Like Frantz Fanon and Audre Lorde, Baldwin was deeply concerned with the insidious ways the legacy of white supremacy has found its way into our very DNA.

And yet despite his assessment that white supremacy resides deep in our consciousness and spirits, Baldwin always held out for the possibility that love would and will prevail. This speaks to his genuine prophetic power. There was nothing Pollyannish about Baldwin's prophetic witness. He was unstinting in his capacity to reveal hard truths about himself as well as others. He insisted that the only path to realizing redemptive love is through truth-telling. For Baldwin, what I'm calling redemptive love comes into being not by forgetting the past, but rather is forged by wrestling with the harm and suffering exacted. We survive and thrive in light of a tragic past, not despite it.

Regarding your question about the paucity of mutual giving, genuine generosity and the resistance to acknowledging connection in our country, in my estimation, this has everything to do with the widespread reluctance to follow the example of love warriors like Baldwin. Redemptive love is hard. Most of us would rather avoid and evade, rather than come to terms with a devastating past. Most of us would rather condemn than attend to what we can do constructively.

GY: Personally, and I'm sure this is true for many others, there are times when optimism feels like a burden—meaningless, perhaps even Sisyphean. What can you share that might help people who continue to experience profound states of uncertainty and dread regarding the continuation of this global pandemic and the murders of George Floyd, Breonna Taylor, and others, the resulting protests last summer, global warming, etc.?

DKK: 2020 was a terrible year, for all of the reasons you mention. Uncertainty and dread are pervasive moods, as are the relentless stress and anxiety most of us have been enduring. These are not conditions for optimism. Even with Biden's election victory—and Kamala Harris's nomination as the first Asian American and African American vice president—optimism is hardly the prevailing mood of the day. Truthfully, I've never been an optimist. My orientation has always been toward hope. To put it plainly, optimism has always struck me as marked by a willful forgetting and denial of suffering and despair. Hope, in contrast, is that light that arises not in denial of a dark and difficult past and present, but rather because of it. Hope is about possibility rather than concession, about living through challenges not despite them.

Let me be clear, there have been signs of hope. Look at the protests that we witnessed in the wake of the murders of George Floyd and Breonna Taylor. These were massive expressions of multiracial solidarity. Look at the timeless work Nikole Hannah-Jones curated with *The New York Times'* 1619 Project. It's an extraordinary gift to our culture that is one part curriculum, one part living monument, all parts necessary. Look at the heroic efforts of women of color to secure our democracy from the stranglehold of Trump and the Republicans. Regarding your question about the public, all of these signs of hope are saturated with commitments of love. Each are bold statements that we have to love ourselves enough to be a part of something bigger than ourselves: untold histories; racial justice; a democracy not fully realized.

GY: The U.S. was founded upon the genocide of Indigenous people and the backs of enslaved Black people. Racism in this country didn't begin with Trump. So, it has a history, a longevity coextensive with this country's origins. Philosopher Cornel West talks about death as a form of learning or even of *kenosis* (emptying) as a form of critical reflection. How do we empty ourselves of the racist poisoning in this country?

DKK: Well, the first step is to make sure that this kenosis is a comprehensive acknowledgment that the poison is, in fact, poisonous. There's a prevailing consensus that the summer protests in response to the murders of George Floyd and Breonna Taylor (as well as the other souls murdered by police violence) are indices of a racial reckoning in America. To be honest, I'm not sure I agree with that. What do we do if white supremacists and racists not only refuse their terrorist past but double down and embrace and celebrate that legacy of evil?

A genuine racial reckoning, in my view, would involve a pervasive recognition and acknowledgment that the American experiment has been defined by an unstinting identification with white supremacy. This is hardly a novel insight. Nevertheless, it's also not a view that one would call paradigmatic for American culture.

We are not yet a nation that says that there is no justice unless there is racial justice. To your question about kenosis, while there has been progress, I'm not convinced that there is a collective will amongst white folks to let their commitment to white supremacy die in order for the nation to live. That would require them, and frankly all of us, to abide by radical love. It also would mean rethinking and re-feeling what we mean by justice.

The work that lies before us isn't so much about reconciliation or unity but rather the hard terrain of renewal and revival, of revitalization. It's a path that keeps the past, history very much in mind and structures a future in direct response to that past. It means holding all accountable for the sins of our past. It means taking the leap of faith that says we have to let that past die in us before we can live a better future.

GY: David, provide a sense of what letting the past die looks like, and say more about how love would help such a death to take place.

DKK: Letting the past die is tantamount to other forms of profound loss, which is to say, loss of a loved one, loss of a home, loss of security, loss of meaning. The death of the past—and in this instance, we are really talking about the anticipation of, the preparation for such a death—poses an existential crisis. It presses us to confront limits. Death is the ultimate limit. Whether we're talking about white people letting all expressions of white supremacy die or people of color acknowledging and addressing the racism in our communities, the changes in question mean insisting that those defining yet dehumanizing pasts that have found their way into the present will end here and now. This is hard work. It will occasion mourning, and hopefully relief.

Love is crucial for all of this. Love as forgiveness and compassion allows the past to die without fully succumbing to shame or guilt. It surfaces the possibility of transformative redemption. This expression of radical love is a bridge from the past to the present to the future. Radical love opens us up to possible futures we don't yet fully know or even understand. It's the wind that carries us in those grand leaps of faith from which all justice takes flight.

Part Two

GLOBAL ANTI-BLACKNESS

5

AFROPESSIMISM FORCES US TO RETHINK OUR MOST BASIC ASSUMPTIONS ABOUT SOCIETY

INTERVIEW WITH FRANK B. WILDERSON III

In the 21st century, what does it mean to be Black in the world? Most of us are familiar with the joyous Black aesthetic expression: "Black is beautiful." Perhaps you're also familiar with the radical, revolutionary declaration, "I'm Black and I'm proud!" Indeed, it was in 1969 that the "Godfather of Soul," James Brown, told us to "Say it Loud." And everyone around the globe knows about the momentum of the Black Lives Matter (BLM) Movement that emerged as Black people collectively took to the streets protesting systemic racism and police brutality waged against them. Like the civil rights movement, BLM is undergirded by a theme of hope and redemption, which brings back memories of Bob Marley's "Redemption Song," released in 1980.

But even as many in our communities and our movements continue to be buoyed by these joyous expressions of hope and pride, some Black philosophers are also striving to articulate the bleakest aspects of Black experience as shaped by life in a society where Blackness is unrelentingly cast as a site of the "nonhuman," and there is no redemption for Black people. In the past, I have assumed that the opposite of being racially Black is to be racially white, but Afropessimists like Frank B. Wilderson III challenge us to face the ways in which dominant white society insists that the opposite of being racially Black is actually to be human.

G. Yancy (with Frank B. Wilderson III), "Afropessimism Forces Us to Rethink Our Most Basic Assumptions About Society," *Truthout*, September 14, 2022. [Editors: Alana Yu-lan Price and Maya Schenwar]

What if the historical trajectory of Black life is, in many ways, one of social death and gratuitous violence? What if the murder of George Floyd was the result of civil society's demand for the brutalization of Black bodies? What if to be Black today is in some sense *to be* the slave? If all of this is arguably true, then Black studies/Africana studies, colonialism/ post-colonialism, queer studies, and the humanities, more generally, must be radically rethought.

To think through these incredibly important issues, I spoke with prominent theorist Frank B. Wilderson III, who argues that Blackness (being Black) constitutes a fundamental antagonism vis-à-vis civil society. It is this fundamental antagonism that the critical framework of Afropessimism interprets as a necessary feature of Black life. Wilderson, an award-winning author and a leading voice within Afropessimism, is Chancellor's Professor of African American Studies at University of California Irvine. He was one of two Americans to hold elected office in the African National Congress and was a cadre in the underground. Wilderson's most recent book, *Afropessimism*, was longlisted for the National Book Award.

GEORGE YANCY: The framework of Afropessimism challenges many disciplinary assumptions within Black Studies or Africana Studies. I'm thinking here of basic political, social and metaphysical assumptions regarding Black humanity, concepts of Black redemption, Black freedom and Black inclusivity within civil society. In fact, Afropessimism forces us to rethink what constitutes the subject matter of what we study when referring to Black life, Black humanity, Black existence. I see Afropessimism as forcing various Black disciplinary orientations to rethink their conceptual and normative frames of reference, even if they disagree with it. My contributions to Africana philosophy, critical philosophy of race, critical whiteness studies and critical phenomenology, often resonate (or so I'm told) with what I would call an Afropessimist conceptual and affective register. The Black body, as I have argued within the corpus of my own work (especially within my book *Black Bodies, White Gazes*), constitutes the site of ontological nullification, the ersatz and the opposite of the "human" (read: white). These are important and weighty claims. I conceptualize my Blackness as a site of the to-be-killed, a process of waiting to be killed by the white state. There are times when being alive feels like a temporary reprieve. The Black body, though, while waiting to be killed physically, also suffers from a form of social death vis-à-vis its dehumanization, its abject status. Yet, the Black body is both paradoxically nugatory (or inconsequential) and necessary to the functional normativity of whiteness. I have also come to see the truth that Black degradation is bottomless, and anti-Black violence is gratuitous. It seems to me that your understanding of pessimism within Afropessimism is more of a form of realism. That's where I want to begin. Talk about how Afropessimism is a form of realism. For example, how does Afropessimism understand the murder of George Floyd by the white state?

FRANK B. WILDERSON III: Thank you, George. I think what I'd like to do is first ask you what you mean by realism.

GY: Fair enough. I'm not using realism as a philosophical position within the history of Western philosophy. Hence, I'm not using it within the context of debates with idealism, where the assumption is that what constitutes ultimate reality is a mental construct as opposed to the realist claim that material objects exist independently of the mind. So, for me, realism, as I'm using it, doesn't fall within the philosophical realist and idealist binary. When I think about Afropessimism as embodying a form of realism, I mean that it doesn't avoid the nitty-gritty, everyday reality of anti-Black violence perpetrated against Black people. In this way, I think of Afropessimism as non-evasive when it comes to the constant pain, suffering and cruelty that Black people experience in an anti-Black world. Afropessimism refuses to let us (as Black people) forget just how dire our situation is, just how incredibly anti-Black the world is. That is what I mean by Afropessimism as a form of realism.

FBW III: Yes. I think that's a good point but first I'd like to give a little bit of background to readers about how this all started. Afropessimism is, in my view, more of an ear trumpet than a set of new discoveries. In other words, Afropessimism has one basic object of study, one destination, which is a diagnosis of Black suffering. Unlike Marxism, post-colonialism or feminism, etc., in Afropessimism there exists only a descriptive intervention, not a prescriptive intervention. Afropessimism doesn't answer Vladimir Lenin's question, "What is to be done?" That is because Blackness is this site of destruction of cosmological proportions—rather than, say, the economic destruction embodied in the proletariat.

In the humanities, suffering has been theorized through two urtexts: The first urtext comprises the archive of Marxism, and its theorization of a structural antagonism between the haves and have-nots. The second urtext comprises the archive of psychoanalysis, which is to say that the world is *essentially* out of joint due, not to the economic order of capitalism, but to the patriarchal order of Oedipus. These are not two diagnostic interventions that seek to reform society. They start with the premise that civil society and the state are always already unethical. The goal, ultimately, is to undo civil society and undo the state rather than to find ways to improve upon it. That's a revolutionary project.

Afropessimism shares their revolutionary (rather than reformist) sensibility that civil society and the state are, *a priori*, unethical. However, the way that psychoanalysis describes suffering, which is to say that the essential paradigm of suffering is elaborated by a patriarchal order, and the way that Marxism describes suffering, which is to say that the essential paradigm of suffering is elaborated by an economic order, are important but *inessential* paradigms of suffering for Black people.

One of the first principles of Afropessimism is that Blackness and slaveness are coterminous. Blackness is a paradigmatic position, which comes into being 1,300 years ago when the Arab world and the Chinese and the Iranians and Moroccan Jews make a kind of global consensus that the people south of the Sahara and north of Cape Town are people void of relationality; they are dishonored in their being, which means they did not perform transgressions to make them dishonored; and, that their flesh is available to the whims of others. And this comes out of, as many of your readers may know, Orlando Patterson's 1982 recalibration of what it means to be a slave.

Most scholars, prior to 1982, had described slavery as bondage, and being whipped and forced to labor without wages. But in his book, *Slavery and Social Death*, Patterson argues that those are simply examples of what it means to live *experientially* as a slave. But if we hope to understand slavery as a relational dynamic, as opposed to reportage of lived experience, then we have to understand slavery's constituent elements. What does a slave (a Black person) in 1850 chopping cotton have in common with a slave (a Black person) today in an expensive Bentley?

Patterson gives us the three constituent elements of slavery; elements which, for Afropessimism, are paradigmatically transhistorical: natal alienation (or genealogical isolation), general dishonor and openness to naked/ gratuitous violence. Natal alienation or genealogical isolation means that it doesn't matter that the slave believes he, she or they have a brother or a sister or mother or father, what matters is that the paradigm recognizes no capacity for relationality in the slave. General dishonor means that the slave cannot act in a dishonorable way because the slave is dishonored *a priori* in their flesh. This is different than [non-Black] Chicanos, Asians, the working class, women, who can transgress the rules of their oppression. Black people cannot transgress. We are always already transgressive. And, finally, there is naked or gratuitous violence: the slave is open to violence and/or accumulation for someone else's pleasure. This is comprehensive vulnerability, because the slave is not an object of violence based upon their transgression. The slave is always already, as Saidiya Hartman would say, an extension of the master's prerogative. (That is where the violence is manifest even when no injury is visible.)

Now, once we began to deepen the theorization of those constituent elements, we began to realize two things. One, every Black person in the world is an Afropessimist at some point of the day. It's just that psychically it's hard to endure the knowledge that my flesh is a compost heap of nutrients for everyone else's existence. Paradoxically, Blackness embodies the absence of capacity. This absence vouchsafes the presence that is the relational capacity for the human. That's hard to endure and contemplate every waking moment. Before 625 CE, there were no Black people. There were Maasai, Kikuyu, the Buganda, etc. They became Black through the imposition of social death, but Blackness did not have a prior plenitude of subjectivity and relationality. Blackness is elaborated simultaneously with social death. When the anti-Black world is destroyed, there will still be people like you and me, just as there were prior to 625, but they will not be Black. There will be a new epistemological order. Just like there were not working-class people all the time. A worker is a paradigmatic position that is no more than 400 years old. Workers did not exist before that. And so, the most difficult challenge for Black Studies, as you point out in your question, is also the most difficult challenge for the humanities, writ large, as well as for multiracial social movements.

The argument that Afropessimism forces everyone to address, is that in order to establish, fortify, and extend the constituent elements of human subjectivity, there must exist (in the psychic and material room) a sentient being without access to those constituent elements of human subjectivity. Someone must be socially dead. Universal humanity cannot exist. Semiotics teaches us that that would mean the word human would have no meaning if every sentient being were human. Life requires death for conceptual coherence.

Given what I've said, the murder of George Floyd should not be seen as a form of discrimination, but as a ritual, like a therapeutic act which secures the psychic health of humanity by saying, "Look, this could happen to humans, like Latinx people or non-Black women. But we would have to perceive transgression in the way they respond to their paradigms of oppression for it to happen—their deaths are not gratuitous but contingent upon their (perceived) transgressions." Blackness, however, is an embodied transgression, not a performative one. Embodied transgression cannot be reconciled with embodied contingency. Blackness lets the human say, "I am degraded, but not *a priori*, I'm still human," because Black people are not dehumanized. Blackness has no prior human status of which slavery robbed it. If Black became human, human would have no meaning.

And so, unfortunately, George Floyd was murdered by the white state, as you say, but I would say that George Floyd was also murdered by people of color who are oppressed by white supremacy and who, simultaneously, secure their status as humans (however much degraded) by anti-Blackness. The Asian cop, Tou Thao, who stood and watched the white cop, Derek Chauvin, kneel on him is undoubtedly a victim of white supremacy (perhaps even in his precinct), but he is also a beneficiary of the psychic fruits of the murder. The white cop performed a psychic form of therapy for both Asians and whites, the humanity writ large.

GY: Got it. Fascinating! In his book, *The Abolition of White Democracy*, the late political activist and theorist Joel Olson writes about how an anti-Black U.S. doesn't eliminate the reality of poor white people. In fact, it was never intended to do so. Rather, there is the assurance that white people will not find themselves, as he writes, "at the absolute bottom of the social and political barrel, because that position is already taken" by Black people. In my work, I have argued that if one eliminates class poverty with respect to Black people in the U.S., they will still be Black. And if one eliminates class poverty with respect to white people, they will still be white. In this case, white people, regardless of their class status, are still deemed and structurally situated as racially superior, while Black people, even those who are wealthy, are deemed and structurally situated as sub-persons, and inferior. In your challenging book, *Afropessimism*, you argue that being a Human being (capital "H") "can only be guaranteed to the extent to which one can say, I am not Black." Similarly, I have argued that whiteness is the normative structure that is the site of humanity. As such, Blackness or Black people fall outside the category of the human in as much as they are not white. For you, does this mean that other racialized identities/groups affirm their humanity through their distance from Blackness (or through their declaration: "I am not Black!")? You know, as many will argue, it's imperative that we don't forget about the dehumanization of Indigenous peoples.

FBW III: We have to remember that Afropessimism doesn't deny the dehumanization of Indigenous peoples, or Jews, or Palestinians (the three groups that are normally thrown up in rebuttal to Afropessimism). In fact, that *is* the point: they are being dehumanized, which exists nowhere in the paradigm of Black oppression. Many people offer what I would call a knee jerk reaction to the discussion of anti-Blackness by bringing in other op-pressed groups. What I just said, in my response to the first question, was not that Native Americans don't suffer. In fact, there's 100 pages in my second book, *Red, White & Black: Cinema and the Structure of US Antagonisms*, in the very middle that completely deals with the structure of Native American suffering, as it is articulated directly through Ward Churchill, Vine Deloria and Haunani-Kay Trask, and as it is argued indirectly through Chris Eyre's movies, and the writing of Leslie Marmon Silko. I bring all those people together to say these people are really suffering from white supremacy. And at the same time, they have, as the foundation of their existence, anti-Blackness. So those two things need to be held together. That they can't be Native American, in this day and age, prior to contact, perhaps, but they cannot be Native American, in this day and age, without anti-Blackness be-ing at the core of their being. And at the same time, they are genocided from 18 million people down to 270,000 in 1870 by the white supremacists. So, there's a way in which Afropessimism demands specificity and rigor. I mean the demands are that we separate, as we were discussing earlier, the structural elements of white supremacy and set them over here, from the structural elements of anti-Blackness and set them over there on the other side, and not try to bring those two together.

The other thing I want to say is that your intervention from Joel Olsen, who I remember quite fondly and was happy to consider him as a friend, is really, really important and that is that exploitation of the working class forms the underpinning of the world's economic structure and foundation. But once you get rid of capitalism, you will still have another bedrock under the foundation of the house and that bedrock is called anti-Blackness. And there are two ways in which you can prove this symptomatically. One is to go anywhere in the world and start trying to impose upon progressives a conversation about anti-Blackness in its singularity and watch little beads of sweat form on their foreheads or watch their shoulders jerk in what Freud would call somatic compliance, like little nervous tics. It won't be long before someone in the room accuses Afropessimism of playing Oppres-sion Olympics. Watch how uncomfortable people become when you try to say, "Okay, the working class suffers, but let's talk about Black suffering and the slave as a paradigm of suffering that bears no analogy to economic exploitation." And I have experienced this rash, symptomatic discomfort in Communist countries (in the USSR and in Cuba). For example, during six weeks that I spent in Cuba, when Black Cubans wanted to speak only to the three Black people on the delegation that I was with. And the white Cu-bans, with whom we were also touring the island were up in arms. "We're all proletariats, here, we're all people, race doesn't matter in Cuba."Yet, here were these Afro-Cubans who were saying, "Could we have one day, one day out of six weeks in which we talk to the three Black people in the group simply about the anti-Blackness of Cuba that we experience?" I, personally, had to take my passport to the hotel, Habana Libre, and hold it out in front of me as I approached the door, so that the people at the door would not think of me as a dark-skinned Cubano and, instead, would think of me as a Black American and let me in. I will tell you this. The 11 people on my tour with me who were white—and none of us were staying at the Habana Libre—would just walk in—they were kind of hippie looking people from the Bay Area, not dressed like most of the guests in the hotel—they'd walk in, no reservation, no room, go to the roof and swim in the pool. I could not do that. I've experienced this in the Soviet Union in 1973, even as the So-viets were arming *Umkhonto we Sizwe* in South Africa. I've experienced it at a party with rich white Brazilians in Rio de Janeiro. This symptomatic, and foundational, anxiety fortifies and extends civil society amongst communists as well as capitalists. It turns into a kind of hyper-anxiety where the discus-sion is overtly concerned with the elements that structure Black suffering. Few people can verbalize what they know to be true, albeit unconsciously: that at the bedrock of what organizes humanity is the realization that, "I am to the extent that I am not Black."

GY: Yes. There is that sense of being that is purchased through a form of negation. You know, there is something a bit daunting about Afro-pessimism, especially given how you think about Blackness or Black people as "hosts" in terms of which others are "parasites." Indeed, such parasites can affirm their humanity, their sense of ontological, ethical, political, and aesthetical integrity to the extent to which they are *not* Black. In your article entitled, "Afro-pessimism and the Ruse of Analogy: Violence, Freedom Struggles, and the Death of Black Desire," you write, "My parasites were Humans, all Humans—the haves as well as the have-nots." If I'm reading you correctly, civil society is made possible through anti-Blackness. The daunting part is that civil society, as we know it, along with what you see as the Human, must be undone, overthrown and deracinated if we are to gesture toward something that *isn't* based upon anti-Blackness. How does one begin to undo civil society?

FBW III: One has to understand that violence is the *sine qua non* of civil society. There cannot be civil society prior to an ocean of violence that destroys the subjectivity of one group of people in service of the elaboration of another group. When I was a student of Edward Said's, in 1989, he made this provocative statement in a seminar: "Social stability is a state of emergency for people of color." That puts the pin right on it because the media always portrays revolutionaries as violent (and criminalizes that violence), without acknowledging the soup of violence that maintains the so-called peace.

There are a lot of progressives who call themselves nonviolent. Nonsense. Everyone is violent. Everyone's condition of possibility is either sustained or destroyed through violence. You might not pick up a gun. You might not hit someone. But if you are well off, if you are psychically well off, if you are materially well off, if you are not Black, which is to be well off as a human subject, you are well off because you are fortified and extended through a structural violence that is beyond the imagination.

Afropessimism rigorously theorizes violence from an ethical (as opposed to moral) orientation. There are ways to start to get to the end of your question—How does one undo civil society?—if one understands that when the day of reckoning comes, there will be a situation in which the confrontation will be in the streets, and everyone will have to decide on a side. But what most people do, especially in the United States, is spend our lives trying not to decide. And so, one of the things that one must start to do if one is not Black—because the question how does one undo civil society is different for someone if you're Black—you have to begin to understand that your life and what has sustained you was a sacred cow, one that you should sacrifice. You can no longer afford sacred cows (i.e., a genuine desire for access to the rights and privileges of civic life). You have to attempt to undo your touchstones of cohesions, both filial (the family or other community into which one was born) and affilial (forms of association that are voluntary)—that which makes you present as a human subject in the world.

What's scary about this is no one can say, definitively, when/if one has achieved this. Anti-Blackness is a psychodynamic affair. The Black unconscious is as anti-Black as the unconscious of the human. We know this from the work of Frantz Fanon when he's not trying to be a humanist, when he's not trying to figure out how he and his white wife come together, which is a laudable question. My wife, Anita, and I confront these issues all the time. And our conversations are richer for Fanon and his work. But Fanon was anxious to reconcile, on an individual basis (one to one) what cannot be reconciled with the epistemological order in which we live and breathe. Westerners are taught that problems come with solutions. Some don't. But they must still be addressed. So, I find Fanon's elaboration of the antagonism to be instructive (say in, "The Woman of Color and the White Man" or "The Man of Color and the White Woman"). However, Fanon can go off the rails when offering humanist prescriptions to stop simply exploring the antagonism and try to reconcile it.

Antagonisms, by the very definition of the word, cannot be reconciled through the tools that you have, which are psychoanalysis or sociology or activism. One becomes fantastically hopeful and forgets that anti-Blackness is the *sine qua non* of those tools. So, you cannot actually think your way to liberation in the *episteme* in which you live. You just have to have a notion that this *episteme* didn't always exist, but it came into existence with a hell of a lot of violence over 1,300 years, and it will leave with that same kind of violence. Now, for non-Black people to fully embrace this they have to understand that that which structures them as non-Black people is the very *sine qua non* of social death for Black people. In fact, Black people were never, back to what I said about plenitude, "human" to begin with.

But I think that for Black people, the reading of Afropessimists, as well as my book, *Afropessimism*, will help in a certain way in that one comes to understand, as David Marriott writes, that when I look in the mirror, I see a threat. Not in my conscious mind because my conscious mind might be integrationist like "We're all just people." Or my conscious mind might be Afrocentrist like, "I'm Black and I'm proud and I'm Black and I'm beautiful." You might be seeing that in the mirror, but your unconscious mind is saying, "There you are. There is the imago, a threat, a threat to the world, a threat to yourself." And as David Marriott has written, your unconscious then works to fortify itself against your own image, fortify your mind against your own image, and to attack oneself constantly, to surveil oneself through the eyes of others constantly.

Now, embarking upon an analysis of that will not alleviate it, but it will help you understand that you didn't do this to yourself, that the world did this to you. And I think that that can lead to little steps, maybe baby steps, toward freeing of the Black imagination. Freeing the imagination means that I don't have to feel guilty about the kind of unvarnished hatred that seizes me in the middle of the night, and for which even the left offers me no outlet. I don't have to feel guilty about hating the police before they do anything to me. I don't have to feel guilty about hating the country or being mad at the country even though I can have a good job. I think that Afropessimism has shown how the world is sustained through the destruction of Blackness. And if you can absorb that a little bit then your preconscious mind can open, just a little, your unconscious mind indirectly and allow those very, very taboo thoughts to find expression.

GY: There is another daunting feature of Afropessimism. I've posed this question to myself. What if the collective mass of Black people in the U.S. began to understand themselves through the lens of Afropessimism? There are times when I've wondered whether traditional forms of Black protest, especially as they are often predicated upon inclusion, don't further strengthen the structures and libidinal economies of anti-Blackness. After all, Black people want recognition, equality and equity, and dignity, and to be allowed to benefit from what "white civil society" has to offer. Yet, there is a way in which our very desire for inclusion means that we desire to be a part of a system from which we are structurally barred, and which would mean our continued social death. Hence, if Black people in the U.S. collectively became Afropessimists, there would be no desire for inclusion, no desire to mimic the false category of the Human, no reason to comply with the parasitic logics of a world whose sense of its own coherence needs Blackness as the abject. I think that this would frighten the hell out of those who instantiate the category of the Human. I think that it would also frighten the hell out of Black people. What do you think?

FBW III: Yes, and I want to make it clear that I think that this is a beautiful dream that you've articulated here—all Black people becoming Afropessimists. I'm not sure what that would look like as a mass movement. . . . But your question about how Afropessimism might frighten Black people and would frighten everyone else, this whole question, takes me beyond where people like myself and Jared Sexton, Zakiyyah Jackson, Sora Han, Kihana Miraya Ross, Huey Copeland, Connie Wun, Camille Emefa Acey and Amanda Lashaw started back in Berkeley. I know I've left someone out and that not everyone agrees on everything, but those are some of the names that stick most profoundly in my mind.

We were critiquing on one side the multiracial coalition that had an unconscious symptomatic knee-jerk response to Black people in the political coalitions of the San Francisco Bay areas, as those Black people articulated the singularity of their suffering. We were critiquing that symptomatic response; and we were critiquing our graduate seminars on Marxism and psychoanalysis because we were seeing that these are really wonderful tools for understanding suffering, but they do not explain the fullness of Black suffering. And so, we were offering a critique, not a blueprint for struggle.

We are now in 2022, almost 25 years later, and Black activists, artists and intellectuals across the globe are thinking through and with Afropessimism—it's informing their political activism and their art in ways that we couldn't have imagined, in Berkeley, at the end of the 20th century. No one is more surprised by that than me. So, I'm new to the question you've posed. Afropessimism is new to the question. But I do believe that one of the reasons why the massification of Afropessimism into a movement would frighten everyone is because Afropessimism has a critique of the world writ large.

Marxism has a critique of the economic world. Psychoanalysis and feminism have a critique of the filial, oedipal, patriarchal world. All those people suffer contingent violence, all those people suffer dishonor through transgression. Afropessimism has a global critique; one which includes the whitest white supremacist and the people-of-color victims of white supremacy.

Another thing to consider is that the unconscious mind, in everyone, is a rather conservative entity. The unconscious mind desires pleasure at any cost. Anita and I were watching *Ryan's Daughter* last night. In that film you can see how unconscious desire ignores or side steps prohibitions set forth by preconscious interest. The preconscious's rules regarding marriage, worship and civic order (and here I mean the civic order of Irish Republicans, not British colonialism) collide with the unconscious mind's quest for gratification. Pleasure is to be conserved at all costs. The unconscious isn't going to just automatically put itself at risk.

Now, Black people have an unconscious also. But it is an unconscious that is garrisoned by non-Black desire; usurped; overridden by the anti-Black imperative to turn white or disappear. If we ever got to a Black unconscious informed by Afropessimism, wow! That would not mean the end of a political, economic order (capitalism) or the end of an oedipal, filial order (patriarchy). That would mean the end of the order of order. We would be on the cusp not of a crisis, but of an epistemological catastrophe. What I'm trying to say is that on the other side of anti-Blackness people could still live and breathe and have families, but no one in the world can tell you how that would look because Black people exist beyond semiotic logic.

GY: Can I get you to elaborate just a little bit on that? That Black people are beyond semiotic logic.

FBW III: Well, the way I do it with my students, because I'm a rhetorician, is to explain that the way semiotics understands conflict cannot really apply to Black people. And if people are interested in more about this, I've written on the Black Liberation Army to show why the Black Liberation Army say they are Marxist-Leninists and think that the ultimate form of oppression is economic exploitation. But if you look at the work of Assata Shakur and Dhoruba bin Wahad and Safiya Bukhari what you see are glimmers of the ways in which they suffer in *excess* to poverty. That's a colloquial way of understanding it. For a more theoretical explanation I draw a triangle on the board and at the top of the pyramid of the triangle I put a question mark. And then on the two lower corners, if I'm doing humans, is that I'd put say Native Americans on one lower corner and on the other lower corner white settlers. And the point is that they are in conflict, indeed, genocidal conflict. This triangle helps students understand why this is not an antagonism. Because at the top of the triangle, where there was a question mark, I erase the question mark and I write LAND, for example. In semiotics in order to understand conflict, whether we're talking about colonialism, patriarchy, class struggle, you have to apprehend the third term mediator. And the third-term mediator is the concept at the top of the triangle, here it's LAND, that little point at the top. That is what makes the genocide, the so-called Indian wars, *sensible*. What I mean by that is it gives it sense. So that Chief Justice Robert B. Taney in the *Dred Scott* decision can say that Dred Scott goes back to slavery, because he is not a subject of jurisprudence. He is not a subject of jurisprudence because he is not a subject of community. He is not a subject of community because Africa is a place outside of community.

Then the Chief Justice makes a point that Native Americans have fought with white people over what to do with this land, what kind of polity is apropos. He's saying, when Native people whiten-up, when they learn what settlers have been trying to teach them through 200 years of genocide, they will become full citizens. So, he's unconsciously arguing that there's a semiotic relationship between whites and Indigenous people. A third-term mediator, Land, makes genocide sensible; and also makes armed resistance sensible. With Ulrike Meinhof and Andreas Baader in the Red Army Faction in Germany, they were in struggle against the German state over temporality, which is to say the wage, economics. So, at the top of their triangle would be economics or the working day—a temporal rather than spatial third-term mediator. The unconscious, and this is true for progressives as well as Trump supporters, does not give Black flesh the capacity for spatial or temporal creation. What it says is you have no time. You have no place. Because when there's Black on one point at the bottom of the triangle and on the other point at the bottom of the triangle is white or another non-Black person, the question mark at the top of the triangle cannot be filled in with a concept, like Land or the Working Day. There's never a semiotic entity that is allowed to be coupled with Blackness. And Obama found this out when he became President. In other words, you can become president, but you cannot be presidential. You can be a professor, but you cannot be professorial. You can be a tool of everyone else's hegemony, but you cannot be a contributor to hegemony or counter-hegemony. That's what I mean.

GY: As you were talking, I was drawing your diagram and I would extrapolate that with respect to anti-Blackness there is no third term, there is no mediator.

FBW III: Yes! There's no third term mediator for anti-Blackness. And this is what makes raising kids so hard, because you try to say, "Here's how you act so you don't get shot by the police." No! It's necessary for the police to shoot you. Just like people who are suffering go to therapy. Anti-Black violence is a form of therapy for the rest of the world. You can't act in a good way because you have been dishonored *a priori*.

GY: That's an incredibly haunting way to think about anti-Black violence. And, yet the noncontingent dimensions of anti-Black violence and policing, along with their gratuity, makes sense to me. Frank, what then might we say are important ways in which Afropessimism might speak to or help junior partners (non-Blacks and non-whites) to whiteness or to humanity or hegemony to understand their positionality without taking their suffering as the standard against which all others are to understand oppression. Does that make sense?

FBW III: It makes perfect sense and it's impossible to answer. And I'm going to put it like this. It can start to happen ... sometimes between individuals. But if you think about posing your question for a group of people, they'll go crazy in their frenetic response because the question is not really asking them to understand Black suffering. The question is really asking them to understand how their stability is based upon my death. And, God damn, you have to be a really special kind of non-Black person to want to have that discussion. Perhaps, you'd have to be traumatized in some way so that your trauma opens you up to discussion. You have to have a relationship with a Black individual. (I'm spit balling, here, because I don't know the answer.) But the reason why it might not be possible on a mass scale is because people who are not Black embody a demand to reclaim something that they lost or was stolen from them. The recovery of plenitude. And now there's a black person who is part of this progressive movement and that person may not be saying this, but their embodiment is saying, "By the way, I have not lost anything, because I am not the embodiment of loss, I'm the embodiment of absence. Therefore, the actual structure of my suffering cannot be reconciled with the structure of your suffering. Do you want to talk about the structure of my suffering, because for 300 odd years I have been here to talk about the structure of your suffering. Black people are the first to jump in and help other people with their shit." I mean, Leonard Peltier talked about how the Black Panthers came to the reservations and helped the American Indian Movement (AIM) grow, organizationally, and with AIM's community service programs. But there's never been a reciprocity at the level of the coalition. There's never been a reciprocity at a mass level. No one has ever said, "hey can we spend some time just talking about your suffering and its structure, as opposed to ours?" And one of the reasons for that is because, as I said before, the unconscious is very conservative, and the demand for redress that Black flesh presents the psyche with is often unbearable. It's more than a revolutionary demand. It's a demand to want the end of everything, as opposed to access to something. And that's why everybody loves Black people in coalitions because we embody that energy, that affect that is really important to the first part of the movement, that destructive movement against the state. Then when they get their shit and they start to consolidate, they see that any consolidation of their community is going to be as threatened by a new Black presence as it was by the old white supremacy. And then they start getting all funny and siddity with us.

6

"I CAN'T BREATHE" IS A CRY WELL KNOWN TO BLACK INDIGENOUS PEOPLE IN AUSTRALIA

INTERVIEW WITH CHELSEA WATEGO

We know the "I can't breathe" cries of George Floyd and before him Eric Garner, but how many know of 26-year-old David Dungay Jr., a Black Indigenous man in Australia who cried, while in custody, "I can't breathe"[1] and died while being "restrained" by police?

The global dimensions of the struggle for Black lives were strikingly visible last year, after the killing of Breonna Taylor and George Floyd, when we all witnessed global protests from multiracial groups of people who were fed up with state-sponsored killings of Black people and anti-Black policing around the world.

In our day to day lives, however, many people in the U.S. are often unaware of the ongoing resistance occurring throughout the world. It is for this reason that I wanted to bring attention to a Black and Indigenous group in Australia, the Indigenous Blackfullas, who are often erased on the international stage of anti-Black pain and suffering.

To get at the heart of anti-Black Indigenous reality in Australia, I spoke with Chelsea Watego who is a Mununjali and South Sea Islander woman and Professor of Indigenous Health and Executive Director of the Carumba Institute, Queensland University of Technology.

G. Yancy (with Chelsea Watego), "'I Can't Breathe' Is a Cry Well Known to Black Indigenous People in Australia," in *Truthout*, March 24, 2021. [Editors: Alana Yu-lan Price, Britney Schultz, and Anton Woronczuk]

With over 20 years of experience working within Indigenous health as a health worker and researcher, Watego's work has drawn attention to the role of race in the production of health inequalities. She is working to build a new field of research committed to the survival of Indigenous peoples locally and globally, and she is a founding board member of Inala Wangarra, an Indigenous community development association. Her debut book, *Another Day in the Colony*, published by UQ Press, was released in November 2021.

GEORGE YANCY: In 2020, the world witnessed the killing of 46-year-old George Floyd as he was being held face down on the ground, and as one white police officer, Derek Chauvin, knelt with his knee on Floyd's neck. As in the case of 43-year-old Eric Garner, Floyd was heard pleading with the police officers that he could not breathe. "I can't breathe!" is a cry that has deep existential, political, social and economic implications for Black people in North America. It is cry that reflects North America's history of violent lynching of Black bodies, social and economic racist oppression of Black bodies, and the disproportionate vulnerability experienced by Black bodies and people of color regarding the impact of COVID-19. In other words, that cry isn't new. Yet, this existential motif is not specific to North America. I was excited to see Aboriginal people engaging in solidarity with the Black Lives Matter movement here. I think that solidarity must move in both directions. I find that many Americans, across racial divides, are not as aware of Aboriginal suffering under white supremacy as they ought to be. Black bodies are globally depicted as "inferior," "sub-persons," as the quintessence of "criminality." In short, Black Aboriginal people continue to find it hard to breathe within a white hegemonic settler colonial system. Discuss what you see as the structures of the anti-Black racism that haunt Aboriginal people.

CHELSEA WATEGO: I think you raise an important point about solidarity moving in both directions. As a people that are both First Nations and first-raced, we are Black and Indigenous, yet on the international stage, it is not uncommon for us to be erased from the category of Black.

Our mob[2] joked about being the "wrong kind of Black"; our creation stories don't speak of a Blackness that originates out of Africa, and nor does our emancipatory work as Indigenous peoples align neatly with the U.S. civil rights movement. As Aboriginal people, we can observe a hierarchy of Blackness in which we are placed at the bottom—that is, when we are not being excluded from it altogether. It really is something to be seen as neither human nor Black in the place where we became both.

An example was that Trevor Noah joke that surfaced prior to his Australian tour and the response to it. The joke told in 2013[3] made reference to the beauty of all women which included Black women, but then, he went on to speak of Aboriginal women specifically and separately from Black women. The punchline was something along the lines of well, maybe we aren't beautiful, but we are good at giving head, as he mimicked playing the didgeridoo (which, for the record, is a men's instrument). Noah granted an interview with me and my co-host Angelina Hurley the "Wild Black Women"[4] in which he refused to apologize for the joke, despite the interview taking place in the midst of both #MeToo and #BlackLivesMatter movements. The responses on social media from many of his Black fans were to insist that we weren't even Black because we didn't look like it.[5]

There is a betrayal of sorts when Black people read the bodies of Blackfullas to deny the legitimacy of our identity as Aboriginal people—it is, after all, a very settler thing to do. Ideas of blood quantum were fundamental to the racial violence we experienced here, yet we have resisted, and we speak instead of bloodlines: bloodlines that aren't dilutable, but that forever bind us to the country from which we became human and testify to the completeness of our Indigeneity.

Regardless of color, the bodies of Blackfullas also testify to the brutality of race in this place. David Dungay Jr. was just 26 when he uttered his last words, "I can't breathe," repeatedly.[6] The force applied, complete with a sedative injected into his body, was because he refused to stop eating biscuits in his prison cell in 2015. The coronial inquiry concluded that none of the guards should be subject to disciplinary action. Stories of Blackfullas dying at the hands of the state with investigations that deem such deaths as "inevitable" show how race continues to work all the time, everywhere, in prison cells and hospital wards as well as public streets. I would also argue, however, that Blackfullas, as genocide survivors, have something to teach the world about how to strategize survival amidst racial violence, too. After all, it is on these same streets that we chant #StillHere and #AlwaysWasAlwaysWillBe.

GY: I have had the opportunity to visit Western Australia a few times. My first public talk in Australia was in 2010. I had the opportunity to give a talk there on white privilege. I must say that the white Australians with whom I discussed that issue appeared to be shocked. I tend to be direct and candid when giving talks on race and racism. So, I'll concede that this was part of what generated their response, but during Q&A, it occurred to me that they had not done the critical work of exploring *their* whiteness. Hence, I suspect that the discussion itself was unnerving. Perhaps I was naïve to expect otherwise. From your own experience as an Indigenous scholar, as a Blackfulla, has there been any substantial movement by white Australians to come to terms not just with the ways in which their own system of white governance has been brutally detrimental to the lives of Black Indigenous people, but the ways in which their whiteness is the problem?

CW: White people are particularly out of control here in the colony, so it is not surprising to hear of these kinds of reactions. Here we are forced to speak of our supposed cultural "otherness" rather than the violence of white supremacy. Australia is very much in denial about who it is as a nation, from the founding lie of Terra Nullius (unoccupied land), to the mythologizing of itself as a place of the "fair go." It is a country that heartlessly incarcerates people indefinitely for seeking asylum. It is a country where, in one state, 100 percent of the youth prison population is Aboriginal.[7] It is a country that has suspended the Racial Discrimination Act[8] on three separate occasions and only in relation to Aboriginal and Torres Strait Islander peoples. There isn't even a place in the Australian academy to teach or study race, and if you try to, you can guarantee you'll be hard pressed finding an office to work from even if you have tenure.

It is also difficult to publish as a race scholar. Just this year, I had a peer-review publication denied by the *Australian Feminist Law Journal* on what was to be a "special issue" by Indigenous female academics on race, literature and the academy.[9] I wrote a review of a text that had routinely used animalistic descriptions in their references to Aboriginal characters. It was rejected by the editors on the basis that to imply that someone is racist, which my 150-plus footnotes appeared to do, could be seen as defamatory, even if it were true. I was allowed to write an opinion piece instead to talk to my "experience" of not being published. They also then insisted on the inclusion of a white male in this special issue of Black women's writing, to explain defamation laws. Interestingly, the alleged unpublishable article was published in my book. So yeah, there's that.

GY: In her first novel, *The Bluest Eye*, Toni Morrison has this powerful passage that reads: "Anger is better. There is a sense of being in anger. A reality and presence. An awareness of worth. It is a lovely surging." Under racist hegemonic systems, those in power would rather we suffer in silence. Or perhaps they would rather we remain hopeful. While being hopeful can keep an oppressed people alive, it can also function to keep oppressed people—and here I am thinking of Black, Indigenous and People of Color (BIPOC)—looking toward a future that may never come. In this way, I agree with Morrison. Anger operates at a different level of temporal intensity. Anger expresses our reality of presence. It says, "We are here!" It speaks to our sense of self-worth; it says that we refuse to wait, to hope, to have justice deferred. My sense is that there are forms of dehumanization that mock the privilege of hope. What are some of your thoughts on the ways in which hope itself might function as counterproductive to Black Aboriginal complete liberation?

CW: It's funny because it was your interview with bell hooks[10] when she spoke about anger and the advice from Thích Nhất Hạnh that I'll never forget. He advised hooks to "hold on to your anger and use it as compost for your garden." I felt so relieved to hear that because I had come out of a conference that had commemorated the 50th anniversary of Kwame Ture and Charles V. Hamilton's articulation of institutional racism, where all the presenters (mostly white) were talking about hope, and it made me angry![11] I am tired of being told that anger is an unhealthy emotion, particularly when it is anger that drives my work, and is the foundation of my best work.

I don't know how it is I could be human as an Aboriginal woman, and not be angry about the world that I am situated within, which Lauryn Hill captures so powerfully in "Black Rage." But just because I am angry about things does not mean I am an angry person. I have much joy in my life which I am deliberate about.

The radio show "Wild Black Women" I co-hosted for several years invoked the idea of the angry Black woman, where each week we deconstructed the events that got us wild (i.e., angry). The irony was that we laughed and snorted our way through each episode, ridiculing those who had the nerve to try and put us in our place. Our earliest complaints were from largely white listeners who were offended because we were laughing. So, we read those complaints out on air to the backdrop of violins and laughed some more. We also got our first fan mail, which I'll never forget. It was a hand-written letter from a brother in jail who spoke about how Black radio playing outside his cell got him through the glare of those fluorescent lights. To be human and to be free is to feel every damn emotion—whenever the hell we feel.

GY: I'm aware of the risks involved when Black people share their pain. It is often so easy for white people to consume it with a sense of fetishization. I recall once asking two philosophy graduate students, one Black and the other Chinese, to share with the other students, who were white, what it is like to be nonwhite in North America. That day, I learned a valuable lesson. Both students refused to share, as they didn't want their pain placed on display. I don't want to risk that here in this conversation. However, as a Black Indigenous woman living under white Australian systemic power, could you share how you cope? I ask this because there are times here when I want to scream at the top of my lungs.

CW: So, I have had to check myself on this one. I have long resisted the idea of being a victim. I just hate the idea of it. I was taught to be 10 times better as a strategy for surviving racism, so the vulnerability of victimhood was unfamiliar to me. But I've slowly realized that the requirement to be su-perhuman as a response to dehumanization is another unfair burden placed on Black bodies and souls. As a victim of racial violence, I have taken up fights through legal processes and I found myself in what I thought was the paradoxical position of victim and potential victor. I thought that to win, I had to be strong and that I couldn't let them see me as a victim. Yet, I've realized that one can occupy the dual role of victim and victor. It means a preparedness for a form of public vulnerability, but knowing who that is for and the limitations and risks of it all.

I realized I was doing a great disservice to other Blackfullas, includ-ing my children, when I pretended that the violence was not taking its toll, knowing that some days it had almost broken me. They felt it in our home, even if I didn't speak of it. What are we saying to ourselves when, having been brutalized, we don't permit ourselves to occupy the role of victim?

I know that my vulnerability will be weaponized against me by white people, but there is something just as dangerous in denying ourselves that vulnerability with each other. In rethinking victimhood, I had to rethink victory, too. I had long been obsessed with W. E. B. Du Bois's "blue sky moments," but it was an Elder Dr./Aunty Lilla Watson who sat me down one day and questioned me on my desire to win. She said to me that when we operate on their terms, we've already lost. But when we operate on our terms, we are winning. I had to think about winning not as an outcome of a court case, but instead in the turning up of things. The winning is in my being, in the exercising of my sovereignty in those moments, all the time.

GY: While I'm critical of hope, I know that Black people around the world must survive. And we may have to do so in the face of absolutely no guarantee that our lives will improve under different manifestations of white power, white nation-building, white empire fortification. What do you see as necessary for Black people in Australia in terms of their survival? And as someone who is aware of the pervasive suffering experienced by Black people in North America, what would you suggest to Black people here moving forward? I ask this because we are not, by any stretch of the imagination, beyond the white nationalist, white supremacist ethos of Donald Trump—it is there, standing back and standing by.

CW: So, I am all about retiring hope as an emancipatory strategy for Black people. Literally, a chapter in my book is called "Fuck Hope." I am interested in dealing with the reality of things, in all of its ugliness. And look, it's not like a red pill, blue pill choice as we find in *The Matrix*, though I used to think of it like that, as though we only ever have a choice between race blindness and race transcendence. Both positions are violent and exhausting for Blackfullas, and in part because both rely on the hope that race isn't real, either now or in some future time. Race isn't going anywhere, and progress is a lie white people tell to assure us of their virtue—again, in some future unknown time. I'm more interested in "nihilism" in Paul Beatty's *The Sellout* where he describes an "unmitigated Blackness."

Our people have not aspired to be like white people, seeking the same rights they have; rather, we have been insisting upon our unique rights, while knowing full well the odds are completely stacked against us because the settlers aren't going home. But Beatty writes, "sometimes it's the nihilism that makes life worth living." Unmitigated Blackness doesn't lend itself to definition, but he writes, "whatever it is, it doesn't sell . . . it's a seeming unwillingness to succeed . . . it's the serious black actor, it's a night in jail . . . simply not giving a fuck." This is the closest articulation of an embodied sovereignty that I've witnessed among Blackfullas.

I'm arguing that there is a place between white lies and Black death, and that such a place is essential to our survival—that place is an embodied Indigenous sovereignty. Such a survival is grounded in not what they grant us, but in who we are, on our terms. It means we can recognize ourselves as human, as Black, as belonging, and as worthy all the fucking time. I think sometimes Black people confuse hope with faith. Hope is in the waiting, but faith, like sovereignty, is in the knowing, in remembering who we are and where we come from. And look, if ever there was a case for "the nihilism that makes life worth living," it was the 2020 Black Lives Matter protests across the world amid a pandemic. There is so much power and possibility in a Blackness of the unmitigated kind.

GY: I was in Australian recently (2022). I have visited before. This time when I was there it became clear to me that the white Australians that I interacted with saw themselves as "progressive." I was invited to give a talk at a predominantly white church there and I was told that my talk on whiteness as anti-theological might discourage white people from having a dialogue about whiteness. The church, on this score, saw itself as finally getting some white people to talk about race in Australia, but they feared that my talk would dismantle that "achievement." What became clear to me is that there was a sense of fear to engage in courageous speech and a desire to settle for a certain kind of mediocrity. How do you understand the fear that white Australians have when it comes to talking honestly about white-settler racism? Or, is it fear at all?

CW: I've heard so much of that supposed fear over the years, fear and supposed guilt, which apparently immobilizes and/or alienates white audiences, whether they be students, policy people, colleagues or the general public. I think is yet another way in which white supremacy is sustained, in always centering white feelings about our accounts of oppression and violence at their hands. I don't buy it or buy into it. Stuart Hall's 'Teaching Race' was instructive for me when he said "Instead of thinking that the questions of race are some sort of moral duty, more intellectual academic duty which white people with good feelings do for blacks, one has to remember that the issue of race provides one of the most important ways of understanding how this society actually works and how it has arrived where it is." Much of my anti-racist work has not been about placating white resistance, but strategising for it, and the realization that the strength of resistance is in direct correlation to the extent that white supremacy feels threatened. Resistance itself therefore is a measure of the progress in the work we are doing.

7

BLACK FEMINIST "BACK TALK" ANCHORS RESISTANCE ON BOTH SIDES OF THE ATLANTIC

INTERVIEW WITH AKWUGO EMEJULU

"Britain demands that I give up my back talk and 'know my place,'" sociologist Akwugo Emejulu tells me. "I've been told to shut up, directly or indirectly, more times than you would imagine. But how could I when there's so much to be said, plainly and without artifice?"

In her work, Emejulu—a Black American feminist scholar at the University of Warwick in England—provides us with an unfiltered look at the racism and oppression faced by Black women in Britain across significant domains of unequal employment, housing and health care, especially within the context of COVID-19. She documents how Black women's suffering is exponentially increased relative to such crises as austerity in the U.K. And Emejulu also discusses the shared global dimensions of anti-Black racism vis-à-vis Black women.

As a Black male philosopher with feminist commitments, I want to do what I can to draw more attention to the importance of Black feminist "back talk": daring to disagree with hegemonic authority. I find that Black women's voices are marked by an exhaustion that is unique and specific to their social locations, and yet their voices are relentless—conceptually amplifying the hegemony of anti-Black racism through their specific modes of what bell hooks calls "back talk."

G. Yancy (with Akwugo Emejulu), "Black Feminist 'Back Talk' Anchors Resistance on Both Sides of the Atlantic," in *Truthout*, July 17, 2021. [Editors: Alana Yu-lan Price, Britney Schultz, and Anton Woronczuk]

To explore the importance of Black feminist back talk, and to highlight Black feminist similarities and differences between different political geographies, I spoke with Emejulu, the author of *Fugitive Feminism* (Silver Press, 2022) and *Minority Women and Austerity: Survival and Resistance in France and Britain* (Policy Press, 2017), and the co-editor of *To Exist is to Resist: Black Feminism in Europe* (Pluto Press, 2019). Her research interests include the political sociology of race, class and gender, and women of color's grassroots activism in Europe and the United States.

GEORGE YANCY: When I think about Black people throughout the Black diaspora, I think about a spirit of resistance, of refusal. This is one reason why I find cultural theorist bell hooks's conceptualization of "back talk" to be so powerful. The expression is indicative of having a self-empowered perspective on the world. Back talk, for hooks, functions as a site of agency. In fact, she links the process of finding and honing one's voice to processes of Black women's liberation. She calls it "the liberated voice." I take it that back talk is a key feature of Black feminist thought and practice. It is important, though, to be mindful of the social, historical and geographical specificity of Black women's suffering, political struggles and expressed agency. In this way, Black women's back talk isn't rendered monolithic. Please speak to how Black women's voices within the U.S. have impacted your own "back talk" as a Black woman in the U.K.

AKWUGO EMEJULU: I grew up in a household full of back talk. My mother and grandmother provided different kinds of role models for me about how to live a dignified life and be self-possessed. My grandmother had a steely, almost patrician air about her—she did not suffer fools and made that very plain to anyone she encountered.

My grandmother desegregated the public hospitals in Dallas, Texas, becoming the first Black nurse employed at Parkland Memorial Hospital (this is the hospital where President John F. Kennedy died after being shot by Lee Harvey Oswald in 1963). Living and thriving under Jim Crow meant that she couldn't afford to be anything but true to herself and her own wishes and desires. Her sparkling self-confidence and charisma meant that she attracted a lot of people to her, but she always warned me to choose friends wisely.

One of her favorite aphorisms was: "Love many, trust few, always paddle your own canoe." I took this to heart. I think growing up with my grandmother and coming to maturity during the civil rights movement, my mother consciously chose a different way to be a Black woman. More open and kind-hearted than my grandmother, my mother channeled her energy externally. As an English and French teacher working in one of the poorest neighborhoods in Dallas, she sought to fire up her Black students' imaginations, helping them envision other lives and other wonders for themselves through literature. In her classes, before the violence of standardized testing, she read Toni Morrison, Richard Wright, Ralph Ellison, and William Faulkner with her students and helped many of them, materially and emotionally, build different kinds of futures for themselves.

Given this upbringing, I really had no choice but to be who I am now. As a Black American living in the U.K., my back talk has constantly gotten me into trouble. I think most Americans living here are genuinely surprised by how repressed and passive aggressive most people are here. Nobody says what they really mean. Everything is coded and said indirectly. For years and years, I truly did not understand what anybody was saying to me. I'd have conversations with colleagues and later on realize that we were in a dispute—but there were no harsh voices or angry tones—just a look and a raised eyebrow. I think Sally Rooney's *Normal People* and Kazuo Ishiguro's *The Remains of the Day* are the best representations of this particularly British and Irish repression. Anyway, because Britain is a deeply hierarchical society, riddled with class anxieties (and in England in particular, racial panic), as an outsider I had to learn how to navigate these complexities. Britain demands that I give up my back talk and "know my place." I've been told to shut up, directly or indirectly, more times than you would imagine. But how could I when there's so much to be said, plainly and without artifice?

GY: I like your insistence here. This is also what I like about bell hooks. There is that courage to engage in frank speech. To further avoid the problem of erasing important differences, how would you characterize the oppressive experiences of Black women in the U.K. and, by extension, what are some of the differing ways that Black women's voices in the U.K. speak critically to their lived specificity of oppression? Of course, I'm also keeping in mind that the U.K. isn't the whole of Europe.

AE: I'll start by acknowledging the problem of a Black American woman speaking on behalf of Black British women. This remains a real source of tension between some high-profile Black American women living in the U.K.—such as myself—and various Black British activists. And this tension about who speaks, and who gets listened to and taken seriously probably best sums up the material and discursive inequalities that Black women experience here—that of erasure. Black women are more likely to be living in poverty, working in low-skilled, low-paid work and more likely to be in precarious employment, regardless of class. Black women must navigate, what we call here, both a gender and ethnic penalty in the labor market, which means that they must contend with a gender and ethnic pay gap as well as gendered and racialized labor market which reproduces segregation and discrimination. It's a double hit to earnings, wealth accumulation, career progression, and pension savings. Being trapped in low-paid work, as we know, has all kinds of knock-on effects with regards to housing and health. Indeed, a report by *Bloomberg*[1] demonstrated how Black households in London—where almost 60 percent of all Black Britons live—have been almost totally shut out of the housing market, meaning there's little possibility of living in secure housing nor building generational wealth through bricks and mortar. Further still, we see already existing health inequalities exacerbated by the COVID emergency. Because Black British women are over-concentrated in low-paid work, they have been less able to protect themselves from infection. Being a briefly honored essential worker hasn't really meant much beyond high levels of exposure to the virus and a huge number of COVID deaths. Truly, this is a catastrophe.

In my own work, which examines how women of color activists organize against austerity, my colleague Leah Bassel and I found that because Black women were already in a state of almost permanent precarity before the 2008 economic crisis, austerity measures—tax increases and cuts to public spending—have hit this group even harder. The rollback of the welfare state—from library and community center closures to benefit cuts to loss of government employment—have all had a deleterious effect on Black women's income, wealth and health. However, in Britain, we are still in the middle of a decades-long debate about how the "white working class" has been left behind and has, in response, abandoned the socialist and social democratic left for the center and far right. At no time, whether it's been public intellectuals chattering about the "left behind" nor about the racial disparities in COVID deaths, have Black women prominently featured in these public debates or policy interventions. Instead, Black economic insecurity and Black death are treated as taken-for-granted and routine. This is what erasure looks like. As both you and Charles W. Mills remind us, the racialized social order is maintained through an active state of violent ignorance and acceptance of the way things are.

GY: Thank you for bringing these realities to our attention. They confirm, for me, the often unknown or unspoken (at least from within the U.S.) ways in which Black women in the U.K. suffer from institutionalized forms of anti-Black racism and face forms of precarity and erasure. Raising a different form of erasure, as a Black male academic, I have taught within predominantly white institutions. As a Black male philosopher, however, the presence of white faces only increases. So, I know what it is like to in teach within a sea of whiteness. Black women philosophers, of course, would have a different set of experiences owing to their intersectionality in terms of being in a sea of maleness and whiteness. And while the number of Black philosophers in the U.S. is still significantly low, the U.S. has more Black academics than the U.K. Two questions: As you see it, what are some of the factors for such low numbers in the U.K.? And what is it like teaching as a Black woman, which no doubt raises all sorts of intersectional dynamics, within such white spaces, especially as you teach Black feminism? I'm tempted to say, "Black feminisms."

AE: It's no mystery as to why we see so few Black academics in British higher education.[2] For context, I am one of 25 Black women professors[3] out of more than 21,000 professors across the whole of British higher education and the first ever in the history of my university. There is one Black woman professor, the brilliant scholar, Olivette Otele, in the discipline of history, and she was only promoted to full professor a few years ago. It's a scandal. But it's a scandal that has been designed into the education system. Generally speaking, in England, Black pupils leave school with similar qualifications as their white counterparts. In Scotland, pupils of color are more likely to have better qualifications than their white peers. However, in both England and Scotland, Black pupils are less likely to be admitted to the best universities, which are collectively called "the Russell Group" here in the U.K. So, Black pupils are already at a disadvantage of being shut out of this small group of elite universities where the vast majority of our leaders are incubated.

Even those few Black pupils who do manage to gain entrance to the Russell Group, they must navigate a hostile and alienating environment in the classroom and in student halls. Time and again, we see stories of hideous racism, sexism and classism at these universities. The final blow comes in terms of degree classification. Black students are less likely to leave university with top honors[4]—what we call first-class honors, a first, or even an upper-second class honors, a "2:1." Across the Russell Group, we see the same patterns repeat: Black pupils do well enough to be admitted to these top flight universities but then something happens whilst they are at university which means that they do not graduate with the best marks.

You can see how this situation then has a knock-on effect in terms of developing the next generation of Black scholars. Without those top marks—and sadly, the imprimatur of the Russell Group—it means Black students are less likely to win prestigious studentships (scholarships) for their masters and doctoral work. This is sometimes called a "pipeline problem," and there have been some half-hearted attempts in my disciplines of political science and sociology to address this, but really, by the time students get to university, many of these dynamics that erode success are already in motion.

As for me, I love teaching—I get that from my mother. I saw firsthand how her teaching changed the lives of her students. I was also transformed by a few amazing professors during my university years, so I think I have a pretty good idea of what good teaching looks like. So, in that sense, I haven't really ever struggled in the classroom because I have self-consciously honed and developed a particular kind of teaching persona. I try to take a very informal air in lectures and seminars with lots of jokes and asides. I think this is probably in response to being on the receiving end of so much bad teaching over the years, but it's also because I think many academics think too highly of themselves and the classroom space. Yes, this is a space for learning, but it needn't be alienating nor exclusive. We can still have high-minded discussions and I can break the tension by cracking a bad joke. I don't know why this works for me. I'm sure other Black women academics wouldn't be able to get away with this informal approach.

Further, having spent the vast majority of my academic career in Scotland, one of the whitest places on the planet, I almost never had Black students in my classroom during my 15 years there. This has changed since I've moved down to England, but it is still a little disorienting to me for sure. Having taught some permutation of feminist theory or gender studies for almost 20 years, to be quite frank, the current fashion of so-called "intersectional feminism" has been a boon to me. Before this, it was a struggle to teach feminism because most students were reflexively hostile to it and it was a challenge to get them to engage meaningfully with key ideas and concepts, unlike when I taught Marxism or post-structuralism.

For the past four years, I've been teaching a new module here at the University of Warwick called Feminist Pedagogy/Feminist Activism which is about the learning and education that takes place within feminist movements. I won't lie; the first two years of teaching this module were a bit of a struggle because of some of the white students, self-proclaimed feminists, natch—were surprised and angered that Black feminism was the default, taken-for-granted position of the module, and that it was not treated as an almost forgotten add-on, as is usually the case in mainstream gender studies courses. Having to contend with an idea that gender is always classed and raced was very disconcerting for some students, and I don't think they ever really reconciled themselves to it. Which is fine by me, as that pattern is writ large across the mainstream feminist movement too.

GY: From what you've shared thus far, we must grapple with the deep political, social and affective sites of anti-Blackness in the U.K., and we must announce these to the world. Fannie Lou Hamer, who was a leading Black activist in the civil rights movement, is famously known to have said, "I am sick and tired of being sick and tired!" I think that this functions as a form of "back talk." Hamer isn't just stating a fact about being sick and tired. Rather, she is commenting on a form of exhaustion that speaks to being so exhausted. What Hamer says might be said to function as an affective tissue that describes what it means to be Black in the U.S. How would you theorize Hamer's clarion call for Black people within the U.K.? Also, please speak to how the affective gravity of Hamer's exhaustion speaks to a shared collective identity among Black women within the U.S. and the U.K.

AE: My colleague Leah Bassel and I published a paper in 2020 called "The Politics of Exhaustion," which examines the processes by which women of color activists in Europe become exhausted and how, in some cases, exhaustion can be a source for new forms of solidarity. In short, our current circumstances demand extreme physical and psychological fatigue from Black women. Whether it's the retreat of the welfare state, the normalization of the far right in mainstream politics or the ongoing deaths of refugees in the Mediterranean, the challenges are vast and allies are few.

The political situation in Europe is unstable and unrelenting. Since the start of the economic crisis (and, of course, much of this work predates 2008, but it's the intensity of the work that has changed), Black women activists have been working hard on survival, self-help, and mutual aid to stay alive. However, it is both impossible and unconscionable to allow activists to be in a state of high alert for more than a decade. But European countries have allowed this multifaceted emergency to continue, and now with COVID, there seems to be no end in sight.

These are exhausting circumstances which have sparked a mental health crisis amongst activists and is prompting many to burn out and leave the activist scene altogether. Further, for those activists still working hard at the grassroots, they must contend with comrades who cannot be fully trusted because they perpetuate and reproduce racism, sexism, ableism, homophobia, and transphobia in the ostensibly "radical" spaces of activist networks and coalitions. Those Black women activists who persist in these spaces must also contend with what we call "exhausting solidarity." They must work together with activists who perpetuate harm because the outside threat is such that they cannot afford to work by themselves. These are the untenable conditions in which many activists across Europe are having to navigate and it is heartbreaking for me.

We also found that exhaustion can sometimes operate as a kind of collective identity/identifier. That if you look around and are sick and tired of how things are, that can be an important activation to get involved to try to make things better. So, exhaustion should be understood in a nuanced way. For sure it is a byword for fatigue and emotional distress, but it can also be a resource that can sometimes be mobilized to support activist work by building the ranks and helping to identify and analyze shared grievances.

GY: Given the weight of this, where do we go from here? As I ask this question, I don't want to leave "we" uncontested. Yet, Black people of African descent have had to deal with shared painful and brutal histories of slavery and colonialism. The dehumanization is there as well as the seemingly endless mourning caused by anti-Black racism. Our Black existence is held captive by anti-Black symbolic and structural forces. And yet we continue to resist, to exist despite forces of Black social death. It isn't enough that Black unity is felt after the brutal murder of a Black body. And here I am thinking about the tragic killings of George Floyd and Breonna Taylor. How might we collectively imagine an empowered world, a more loving world, in which Black bodies matter, where finding it hard to breathe no longer exists?

AE: You have unfortunately caught me in a gloomy mood about the future, but I will do my best to think positively for this question. I return to the importance of community and connection. The activists of the Student Non-Violent Coordinating Committee called it the "beloved community." I don't think I ever believed that I would be living through bad times such as these. What makes it bearable, what allows me to breathe a bit easier, is my meaningful connection to others and our working together to make our little patch a wee bit better for everyone.

Especially in the U.K. context, we've been contending with closed opportunity structures for more than a decade and have seen living conditions worsen, especially for the most marginalized and vulnerable groups. To create possibilities for change requires diligent work locally to change political attitudes and political culture and build new forms of solidarity. This moment is so unstable; who knows what comes next, but what persists is our ability to hold each other close in pure connection.

GY: I appreciate your emphasis on community. When I think about anti-Black racism, I think about sites where Black people might find reprieve. It reminds me of the practice of marronage, where Black people attempt to free themselves from the surveillance of whiteness. At such times, perhaps many feel a sense of hope. And, yet, I know that we must return to the white world of anti-Blackness, which is where there is that sense of pessimism or perhaps nihilism. What keeps you, within the UK context, from a deep pessimist (perhaps even Afro-pessimist) or nihilist position?

AE: Pessimism is too easy and it is what is demanded from us during these catastrophic times. To sink into pessimism is to admit defeat. Pessimism is also a failure of the radical imagination—the death of Robin D. G. Kelley's "freedom dreams." It is totally understandable and unavoidable to be disheartened and disillusioned. But contained within disillusionment is a possibility to think and act otherwise—a politics of refusal. These are bad times but we can refuse to be isolated, individualized and conquered by them. Instead, we can use these bad times to find and care for each other. And in these caring relations we can dream and work towards a new world. And it's important to understand the necessity of dreams when the world is falling apart around you. The world we desire and that we collectively struggle for most likely will not be realized in any of our lifetimes. But that doesn't mean the dream—or the refusal to be defeated—is some of kind naïve indulgence. Rather, contained within that dream is an alternative way of doing and being. A way to care for the disrespected and dispossessed. A way to relate to each other outside and against of capitalist modes of comparison and competition. A way to build solidarity across the very real differences that too often divide us. It's a very tempting to fall into the abyss. However, I'm not built that way. For me, it would be a betrayal of everything my grandmother and mother worked for and desired. As long as I'm back talking and building community, I know the new world is coming.

8

ANTI-BLACK RACISM IS GLOBAL

So Must Be the Movement to End It

INTERVIEW WITH ADELE NORRIS

In her book, *Killing Rage: Ending Racism*, the late bell hooks communicates the weight of what feels like an axiomatic truth: "All black people in the United States, irrespective of their class status or politics, live with the possibility that they will be terrorized by whiteness." As we bear witness to the authoritarian violence imposed upon Ukraine by Vladimir Putin's deployment of Russia's military might, and to his perverse fantasy of a "New Russia," we must never forget that anti-Black racism in the U.S. is inextricably linked to the perverse fantasies of white supremacism and operates according to vicious, racist violence. This is one reason why, for me, *all the oppressed people of the world*—the colonized, the violated and the marginalized—must be heard, and their pain made legible on its own terms. At the end of the day, however, I know that, as Black, I am deemed by many to be the most racially abject monstrosity that there is. I continue, though, to be shocked by the global degree to which Black people experience anti-Black racism.

Adele N. Norris is senior lecturer in sociology and social policy in the faculty of Arts and Social Sciences at the University of Waikato, Hamilton, New Zealand, and coeditor of *Neo-Colonial Injustice and the Mass Imprisonment of Indigenous Women*. In my engaging discussion with Norris, which follows, she illuminates the harsh reality of the similarities of the U.S.'s anti-Black racism and that of New Zealand, which was also colonized by the British.

G. Yancy, (with Adele Norris), "Anti-Black Racism Is Global. So Must Be the Movement to End It," *Truthout*, March 14, 2022. [Editors: Maya Schenwar and Britney Schultz]

Whiteness as a normative structure pervades New Zealand. Indeed, the Indigenous Māori are disproportionately imprisoned, and Black bodies experience forms of anti-Black racist stereotyping that are found within the U.S. and places like Finland and Sweden. As a scholar who engages Black feminist methodologies to explore state-sanctioned violence against Black, Brown and Indigenous people, Norris explicates these contemporary dehumanizing forces with clarity and autobiographical insight.

GEORGE YANCY: In my own work, I have argued that the Black body is deemed *the* site of the racially deviant, the racially monstrous, the racially abhorrent and the racially abject. In the U.S., Black bodies are disproportionately stopped and placed under surveillance, incarcerated, and rendered "criminal" as a "self-evident" truth. This vicious and racist treatment of Black people is not confined to the U.S. The Western world, out of which the concept of race developed, has historically operated under myths about Black bodies and the trope of blackness as "evil," "sinister," and "ugly." Whiteness, of course, was valorized as the apex of civilization, the most intelligent and the most aesthetically beautiful. It is this last issue that I wish to discuss with you. Here in the U.S., there have been laws passed against hair discrimination vis-à-vis Black people. This cuts at the heart of Black aesthetic integrity, agency, and humanity. As you may know, Afro-Finns have started an annual celebration in the form of a "Good Hair Day"[1] to deal with complex aspects of the racialization of hair. The denigration of Black hair has also been experienced by Black people in Sweden, especially mixed-race people who have suffered from being stared at and rendered "exotic" and "strange" because of their hair. You've written about the issue of Black hair and anti-Black racism. Are you surprised that such a form of racism continues to exist in the 21st century? And what are your thoughts on the psychological toll that this sort of anti-Black racism has on Black people?

ADELE NORRIS: I remember with the election of President Barack Obama how eager people were to mark his presidency as the beginning of a post-racial era. For me, that moment is marked by the many ways his Black wife, former first lady Michelle Obama, was vilified at a national level—from her body, hair texture, to her facial expressions. A wider-white-elite society, in expressions of outrage, compared Mrs. Obama to men and monkeys. The same with Venus and Serena Williams's appearance undergoing pervasive scrutiny over their 20-year careers. What this shows is that Black women rising to the heights of global success are not exempt from the white dehumanizing gaze. The corresponding psychological burden is felt and carried within us all when we see Black women's appearance picked apart and disparaged. The night of Donald Trump's presidential election, a New Zealand colleague asked me if I thought Michelle Obama would run for president. I could tell the question was meant to virtue signal, which was confirmed after my response: "Seeing her [Mrs. Obama] compared with monkeys every day, I hope not." My colleague was visibly baffled and walked away. People are so desensitized to and comfortable with a certain amount of anti-Blackness that it hardly registers in the minds of non-Black people, including people of color.

In places where Black bodies are recent and few, there is a paucity of a language for anti-Blackness and Black racial discrimination. The language is not well developed in academic, political and social discourses. Anti-Blackness, in these contexts, is understood primarily through the ways it is expressed in the United States, especially in its most extreme forms. Last year, a 12-year-old Black girl (Zimbabwean and Samoan) from Rotorua, New Zealand, made headlines for being called the N-word and teased for her hair texture by her classmates.[2] I remember reading that she asked her principal to address her school about the harms associated with the N-word. She said the kids are learning it from somewhere and have been using it since she began school at the age of 6. Children who have never lived in the United States possessed an understanding of Black subordination. What I found most interesting about this case was the applause the young girl received for starting an anti-Black bullying and racism initiative at her school. She's only 12. Why are her adolescent years spent engaging in work that schools and parents should do? These cases are everywhere (e.g., Britain, Canada, South Africa, Sweden, the U.S.).

The psychological and emotional toll related to hair discrimination is massive for Black youth, [but] gets rarely classified as anti-Black racism. Black people's experiences of state-sanctioned violence are so severe that cases of hair discrimination are peripheral to extreme cases of police brutality against Black bodies, but they are [also] violent and disturbing. It is important to see that hair discrimination and police brutality are products of the same system.

GY: I would argue that the stigmatizing of Black hair is one mode of visual anti-Blackness. It has to do with the anti-Black dimensions of the white imaginary and the white gaze. White people have created a world within which what they see and what they imagine are what they deem to be *the only* legitimate ways to see and to imagine. As a result, Black people—and I would include people of color, as Frantz Fanon would say—suffer in their bodies, because their bodies are bombarded with racist fictions and racist stereotypes. Talk about anti-Blackness and how it operates within New Zealand (or Aotearoa, its Māori name). Do Black people find themselves facing and resisting the toxic reality of being reduced to their epidermis, where they suffer under forms of anti-Black surveillance?

AN: Experiences of anti-Blackness are often muted or subsumed by a fascination with Black culture and aesthetics. I think Black people can be deceived by non-Black people's fascination with Black entertainers and athletes and fail to understand that Black culture can be consumed by holders of anti-Black beliefs. The two are not mutually exclusive. One of the first things I noticed teaching "Introduction to Sociology" in New Zealand was how students' responses and understandings of racial stereotypes and social inequalities mirrored [those of] U.S. students. While there is a deeper understanding of the effects of colonization, which is the result of a powerful Indigenous presence, notions of Black and Indigenous people as "criminal," "deviant" and "lazy" are embedded beliefs Black people engage with daily.

Also, people may be familiar with Brown bodies, but they have rarely lived next door to a Black person or worked with one. There is an expectation for Black people to make the people around them feel comfortable, which typically involves the Black person assuming a posture of subordination. Many U.S. scholars have written extensively about this. In many ways, I think my research agenda, which heavily engages with anti-Black racism and racial inequalities, protects me. People know exactly who I am when I show up because I am not just a Black body. For example, I was approached by a white colleague to collaborate on a project for which he wanted to critique U.S. Black women's scholarship in relation to Marxism. I asked him to name five Black women authors. He stared blankly, and I walked off. While he took pride in his love for Bob Marley, he had never cited a Black woman in his 20+ years in the academy.

However, I am not surprised when I meet other Black people who are accustomed to racialized surveillance and consider racism an American invention. Some Black people from the African diaspora have spoken and written about daily experiences of racial profiling in New Zealand. With so few Black people, they are not likely supported or validated. I do think being from the U.S. links me to a tradition of resistance and a knowledge of whiteness where it does not take me long to identify covert forms of anti-Blackness and respond accordingly.

GY: The point about your white colleague is so powerful. He wanted to critique the work of Black women without being able to cite a single Black woman author. This says to me that he doesn't really give a damn about what Black women actually think. You know, I can imagine Black people and people of color from the U.S. visiting New Zealand and thinking that they will finally experience a reprieve from the daily insults of racist micro-aggressions. Given the global dimensions of anti-Black racism, however, I would not be surprised how deeply anti-Black racism runs in New Zealand. Could you say more about how you have dealt with anti-Black racism in New Zealand?

AN: Being from Mississippi, I am often asked how it feels to have left. Mississippi is one of those places recognized—and rarely contested—for its brutal history of white hostility toward Black people. People feign a look of shock when I respond that the world is like Mississippi. Mississippi just owns what it is. It is like in 2018 when Cindy Hyde-Smith, the Republican senator from Mississippi, said, "If he [a cattle rancher] invited me to a public hanging, I'd be on the front row."[3] Hyde-Smith was still elected for saying exactly how she felt. Two years later, the world held a front-row viewing of George Floyd's public lynching. For those white people seeing a large Black man rendered powerless, and his life slowly and brutally taken from him as others watched, is reminiscent of the Jim Crow era, post-slavery, where the lynching of Black people by ordinary white citizens in collaboration with law enforcement was a sanctioned practice. Floyd's public lynching represented for many people that all was right in the world and order had been restored. I work with and engage with many people like Cindy Hyde-Smith on a daily basis.

During Trump's presidential campaign, extreme-right groups around the world mobilized and expanded exponentially. Growing visibility of white supremacist groups—the True Blue Crew and United Patriots Front in Australia, and the New Zealand National Front and Right Wing Resistance in New Zealand—hardly received media and academic attention. Yet, statements such as "We are not as bad as the U.S." are commonplace. If the U.S. is your point of reference, you are doing pretty bad. Like the U.S., there is unwillingness to name and confront white supremacy here. Even after the Christchurch massacre in 2019, when Brenton Harrison Tarrant, a white supremacist, murdered 51 people at two mosques, New Zealanders were quick to point out that the gunman was Australian. A massacre of this scale should have signaled white supremacy as a national threat. Racism is seen as something that happens elsewhere.

Evasive tactics deployed to explain away systemic racism are most evident in the reluctance to use the terms "race/racism." For example, racial segregation as a result of housing discriminatory practices becomes "cultural bubbles" or "ethnic clustering," and racism becomes "unconscious bias." Racism is viewed as something people would not do knowingly. When I informed my colleagues of my first experience of many instances of racial profiling, they responded that people are just curious. Yet, two months later when I disagreed or could not undertake a task a colleague asked of me, I was called an "uppity Negro," twice. Of course, I was not outraged or surprised. Navigating white hostility and other forms of anti–Blackness (anti–African Americanness) has been a transnational burden. As a daughter of Jim Crow survivors, white hostility was always discussed in my home so that when we saw it, we could identify it and not internalize it.

GY: The structure of whiteness is to obfuscate its reality. Your insights suggest global instances of white mystification. When I think about the European imperialist violence brought to bear upon the Indigenous Māori in New Zealand, I think about the suffering, misery and death of Indigenous peoples in both North America and Australia. Collectively, I think about the themes of land dispossession, cultural ruptures in language, religious rituals and broader questions of cultural identity. European imperialism is about domination, usurpation and dehumanization. Death and dying are inextricably tied to European arrogance, xenophobia, exoticization and hatred of those deemed "less than human." Could you talk about how the Indigenous Māori continue to face contemporary forms of discrimination, inequality and oppression?

AN: Coming from the U.S. with an understanding of the racist laws and policies—such as Black codes, Pig Laws,[4] and Jim Crow that eroded the progress Black people made during Reconstruction—I saw the effects of Indigenous land dispossession, but I also saw features of Jim Crow, though it was not codified like in the U.S. Many Indigenous people were urbanized and relocated to urban hubs like many Black people, but on a much smaller scale. While segregation was not codified in New Zealand in the same way as in the U.S. via Native reservations and redlining, Māori were encouraged to migrate from rural areas where they owned land and were targeted for social housing to meet the demand of cheap labor and to further facilitate land dispossession. Like the U.S., social housing means lack of home ownership that disrupts the creation of generational wealth.

Urbanized hubs of predominantly Indigenous and Polynesian people were singled out as in need of targeted policing and social control. When I first arrived in 2015, I looked up the imprisonment rate. I thought it was a typo. While New Zealand is a small country of 5 million people, the imprisonment rate per capita for Māori is higher than the imprisonment of Native Americans. Māori women represent roughly 16 percent of the total population of women, yet Māori women represent 65 percent of women imprisoned (over four times their representation). Māori rate of imprisonment follows the trend of Indigenous people in Australia, Canada and the U.S., which is often framed through a lens of deviancy with little attention toward state-sanctioned and colonial violence. My collaboration with Indigenous colleagues strives to fill this gap in New Zealand criminal justice scholarship.

GY: Speaking about the issue of criminal justice, what impact did the killing of George Floyd by a white police officer in the U.S. have on bringing light to bear upon the disproportionate effect of policing of Māori people? I ask because I am aware of how the Black Lives Matter (BLM) movement in the U.S. galvanized protests in Australia that brought attention to the large number of deaths of Indigenous/Aboriginal peoples there while in police custody. While there are differences, there are so many shared patterns of carceral violence experienced by Indigenous peoples who are subjected to racialized and colonial oppression. This speaks to overwhelming proof that there are fundamental links between processes of otherization, race, white supremacist state power and criminalization.

AN: Issues raised by BLM protests resonated with many Indigenous, Black and Brown New Zealanders. Many Indigenous people have firsthand experiences of racialized policing, surveillance and imprisonment, and understand the implications via lived experiences. BLM became a rallying cry reinvigorating attention toward Māori mass imprisonment. However, in places like West Papua, where Black Indigenous people are experiencing genocide under Indonesia's rule, BLM was easily incorporated alongside the Free West Papua movement,[5] which has a large New Zealand base.

   While I was thrilled to see how quickly BLM traveled and spoke to specific issues in this context, I did not recognize parts of it. What happens to Black social movements when they migrate, and Blackness is not centered or understood? If we are not careful, it is like consuming Black culture. BLM was adopted in ways that did not shine light on the Black experience. Expressions of anti-Blackness in the U.S. were acknowledged, but how anti-Blackness is experienced in New Zealand was not. Black children being called the N-word by white people and [non-Black] people of color is a huge problem in a place like New Zealand, but it rarely gets attention. I only use this example to show the interesting power dynamics that influence how Blackness is articulated, if at all, when movements like BLM travel outside of the U.S.

Many people who champion BLM also regard experiences of all marginalized people as being on par, when they are not. I explain to my class that Black and Indigenous bodies are read as deviant and violent by white society and by other people of color. I remember a couple of faculty members discussing a large, irate student roaming the halls. The student was described in such a way that the two people knew who the student was except for me. I was envisioning someone at least six feet tall around 250 pounds. Finally, someone said to me that they saw me speaking with the student. The exact words were, "He accosted you in the hallway." I think I would have remembered being accosted. The student they spoke of was a young, thin Black male nowhere close to six feet tall. I found him quite timid. He always smiled when he saw me, because I always acknowledged him and inquired about his studies. Yet, it was amazing how two white faculty members held the same image of a "giant."

The implications of the perceptions of Black bodies go unexamined in New Zealand. Yet, it is a truth of Black life for which BLM shines a spotlight. In some cases, BLM became a tool people used to leverage visibility and space without a particular focus on various forms of institutional racism. Under such conditions, anti-Blackness remained at the periphery if at all acknowledged.

GY: Could you provide a sense of how you envision ways in which Black communities, though small in New Zealand, must resist anti-Black surveillance? Also, how are Indigenous communities fighting against various modes of discrimination?

AN: Aretina Hamilton advanced a concept called "white unseen" in 2020 to explicate how deeply embedded the erasure of Blackness is as it relates to Black pain, Black anxiety and Black despair. The sanctioning of this erasure is evidenced by the fact that it is so deeply normalized that it takes severe disruptions, like in the case of George Floyd, for Black rage to gain validity.

White unseen, as Hamilton describes, is an intentional thought pattern and epistemological process where the everyday actions, terrors, ruptures, and tensions faced by Black and Indigenous people are rendered invisible. As Black people, it is important for us not to fall into this thought pattern as well, such that we do not register something like hair discrimination as a form of anti-Blackness or consider it too minor of an issue to warrant action. The insidious nature of white supremacy renders something like hair discrimination as "race neutral" compared to police violence that led to the premature deaths of Breonna Taylor, Elijah McClain, Mike Brown, Atatiana Jefferson, Philando Castile, Freddie Gray, and many more. Like racial profiling, hair discrimination reveals the insidious nature of the global white gaze that demands Black subordination. Black people are expected to acquiesce under the white gaze, and everyone knows it.

We saw how Black people were treated in China when COVID-19 first emerged.[6] We see as the world watches Russia invade Ukraine how Black people are not allowed to flee Ukraine and have been forcefully removed from buses by Ukrainian police.[7] We are witnessing in real time how Black lives do not matter globally. The initial step is seeing anti-Blackness as a global phenomenon, a pandemic—not something existing solely in the United States. It is important for us to see these connections and combine our energies to make them visible.

GY: I find the concept of the "white unseen" to be a powerful one. Do you think that white people are prepared to look anti-Black pain in the face, as it were? After all, this would mean, for white people, taking more responsibility in terms of how they are imbricated in anti-Black racism. Lastly, speak to how Indigenous communities fight against various modes of discrimination.

AN: Prime Minister Jacinda Ardern, on June 20, 2022, designated the neo-fascist groups The Base and the Proud Boys as terrorist organizations. New Zealand's position came in the wake of the federal trial of the U.S. January 6th riots at the U.S. Capitol. It is important to note that Prime Minister Ardern's decision received support from the New Zealand police commissioner, Andrew Coster stating, "Those groups are respectively neo-Nazi, neo-fascist, white supremacist groups who have been responsible for some key unlawful events overseas, and so police supported the designation" (para 6, RNZ, June 30, 2022).[8] The commissioner's comments parallel rhetoric surrounding the Christchurch massacre where gunman, Brenton Harrison-Tarrant, an Australian native, was recognized as a white supremacist, but his Australian nationality was emphasized in equal measure with his actions.

The subtext is clear, white supremacy and racism are not considered an integral part of New Zealand's society, rather imports from Australia and the United States. The Christchurch massacre, fueled by racial hatred, is the largest mass shooting in modern times and should have sounded the alarm to elevate white supremacy and white supremacist ideologies as a security threat in Aotearoa New Zealand. Instead, the country rushed to distance itself from associations of white supremacy by taking a soundbite from the PM's speech. The overnight viral success of the hashtag #TheyAreUs served as a symbol or an acknowledgment of white New Zealanders' solidarity with Muslim citizens. However, Elers and Jayan (2020) situate the hashtag as an ideological tactic of whiteness that is the default norm built into the infrastructures of New Zealand's polity.[9] The authors argued that the hashtag was more a symbol of complacency with racism and daily experiences of dehumanization in New Zealand.

This example illustrates what Resmaa Menakem, in his book *My Grandmother's Hands: Racialized Trauma and the Pathway to Mending Our Hearts and Bodies*,[10] means by the institutionalized white body. The hashtag's global reception further championed the soundbite as depicting the soul of Aotearoa New Zealand rather than seeing it as a knee-jerk response subverting critical attention toward white supremacy. In this instance, whiteness was operationalized through the way it was able to quickly divert attention away from the everyday systems that breed and harbor white supremacist ideology and racism by presenting itself as the hero, a valiant force that overcame hate with love. Donna Awatere, in her 1984 groundbreaking book *Māori Sovereignty*,[11] advanced the concept of white cultural imperialism to delineate the formation of whiteness specific to Aotearoa New Zealand. Things that are celebrated as New Zealand identity, she argues, are all British imports, with one fundamental exception—white people's longstanding hostility toward Māori. She observed the tendency to downplay white racial hatred toward Indigenous people was perpetrated across all colonial systems (education, criminal justice, and housing). During the time Donna wrote, she witnessed how whiteness had mobilized to a degree that achieving justice and equality would be out of reach for Māori, even tweaks to policies would be futile. I agree with Donna. Seeing the U.S. ban on critical race theory and the treatment of anti-Blackness by this current administration illustrates that this world is quite comfortable with turning its heads in face of anti-Blackness.

Part Three

RACISM, EDUCATION,
AND PRACTICES OF FREEDOM

9

TRUMP IS ATTACKING CRITICAL RACE THEORY BECAUSE IT IS A FORCE FOR LIBERATION

INTERVIEW WITH MARI MATSUDA

Trump and his administration are on the offensive against critical race theory and diversity training. Federal workers are currently banned from participating in anti-racism trainings, and Trump used the presidential debates to further denounce such trainings as "racist."

The Executive Order on Combating Race and Sex Stereotyping that Trump issued on September 22, 2020, rejects the claim that racism "is interwoven into every fabric of America," and labels as "divisive concepts" such claims as "the United States is fundamentally racist or sexist." Indeed, the executive order rejects workplace diversity training, which it identifies as a form of "malign ideology."

Critical race theory (CRT) was developed in the 1980s within the context of a critical cadre of Black legal scholars and scholars of color who deployed, and continue to deploy, powerful narrative writing and who pulled from their personal experiences to explicate and resist the problematic entanglement of the law and legal discourse as embedded within structures of white power.

Trump's attacks on CRT are consistent with his attacks on the press, his intolerance for facts and truth, his rejection of critical consciousness itself, his rebuff of dissent, and his need to create scapegoats as a process for maintaining his predominantly white base. Yet, within a thriving democracy,

G. Yancy (with Mari Matsuda), "Trump Is Attacking Critical Race Theory Because It Is a Force for Liberation," in *Truthout*, November 18, 2020. [Editors: Alana Yu-lan Price, Maya Schenwar, and Britney Schultz]

critical thought, thoughtful dissent, and counter-hegemonic efforts and activism are crucial—the very lifeblood of an informed citizenry.

Prominent scholar Mari Matsuda is one of the founding voices of critical race theory and holds the distinction of being the first Asian American tenured woman law professor in the United States. She is a law professor at the William S. Richardson School of Law at the University of Hawaii, and has published a number of books, including *Where Is Your Body?: And Other Essays on Race, Gender, and the Law*; *Words That Wound: Critical Race Theory, Assaultive Speech, and the First Amendment*; and *We Won't Go Back: Making the Case for Affirmative Action*. In this interview, Matsuda discusses the real goal of critical race theory, the struggle against anti-Asian attacks and how to envision, and work toward, a future of healing.

GEORGE YANCY: It is such a pleasure to speak with you in this format. Yet, the occasion is dire. Trump has attacked critical race theory, white privilege training and diversity training. He supports their characterization as "divisive, un-American propaganda training sessions." I am fairly certain that Trump has no idea what critical race theory means. As one of its original creators, briefly share with us just how essential critical race theory continues to be, especially at this moment in the U.S.'s history.

MARI MATSUDA: Neither Trump nor his minions who drafted the executive order banning critical race theory have read a word of our work. Law journal articles have hundreds of footnotes. It takes work to read critical race theory, the kind of work they are not accustomed to. They have some vague sense that critical race theorists are anti-racist intellectuals. That is the basis of their attack. Their goal is to telegraph white tribalism: *We share your anxiety about replacement and only we can defend you against all enemies.* This is an old tactic that elites have used to keep power. First, invent an enemy. Then, proclaim yourself the faithful source of protection against that enemy while you pick people's pockets.

Anyone who has actually read the work knows critical race theory is not about replacing white supremacy with Black supremacy, or any kind of supremacy. The goal of critical race theory is not to make white people feel guilty, oppressed, disregarded or disrespected. Nothing in my work does that. The stated goal of critical race theory is, first, to understand the concept of race: How was race as an idea developed and deployed? Second, CRT seeks to dismantle racism as part of a project of dismantling all forms of oppression. For me, this includes a lot of utopian work: imagining a world of mutual care and mutual respect. The idea that people seeking racial justice want to put down white people is a massive projection. We want a fair and just world for everyone—white folks included, obviously, since they have been integral to progressive struggle since the founding of the republic.

GY: Speak to what motivated your conceptual and activist engagement with critical race theory. I am often motivated by a blues sensibility as I write about racism in this country. I find myself having to touch the pain and the anger caused by racism, but never allowing it to have the last word. My sense is that this blues motif and the jazz motif of improvisation motivates your work and passion.

MM: The jazz musician and theorist Vijay Iyer talks about embodied cognition, and you and I, George, talked recently about the collective experience of pain, and the transcendence of that pain, in the blues. I often ask my students, "How did reading this make you feel?" when we encounter a critical race theory text. They tell me that this is not a question they are used to. Much of standard education is about getting us to shut down that feeling of unsafety that lodges in the gut. Just forge ahead as if nothing we are discussing here is connected to the disregard of your humanity. For many people of color in the academy, listening to our bodies and writing our way out of places where we felt trapped and assaulted was the source of our intellectual work.

When I was a law student back in the '70s, I helped organize the local chapter of the National Alliance Against Racist and Political Repression, which came out of the "Free Angela Davis" movement. The National Alliance proclaimed, as one of its goals, "Outlaw the Klan." At that time, I was also volunteering for my local American Civil Liberties Union affiliate. This created a contradiction between what I knew *had to happen* to protect people I cared about, and what prevailing ideology said *could not* happen. The [Ku Klux] Klan was gunning down labor organizers in the street. The material conditions were fueling a sense of personal frustration, that I worked out, eventually, in the book, *Words That Wound: Critical Race Theory, Assaultive Speech, and the First Amendment*, written with founding critical race theorists Charles Lawrence, Richard Delgado and Kimberlé W. Crenshaw.

GY: While Asian Americans are by no means homogenous, do you see stereotypes of Asian Americans continuing to abound in this country, as you argued in your 1996 book, *Where Is Your Body?* Do you think that it has increased given Trump's unabashed xenophobia? Just think here of Trump's appellation, "China virus" to refer to COVID-19.

MM: Trump has an intuitive grasp of the fear of the foreign as a driver of right-wing populism in the U.S. He has deployed it with a snarl, and this has increased violence against Asian Americans. My family now extends to the fifth generation in the U.S. I have Chinese friends that are in their seventh generation here. These are deeper roots than many of the MAGA folks, but our kids still get "Go back where you came from" hollered at them from passing cars, or compliments for fluent use of the English language. The deployment of "foreign" in maintaining a system under which the many toil for the benefit of the few is clear if you look at Asian American history. Using the "Chinese threat" to generate violent pogroms, to keep white workers focused on the wrong target, goes back to the 19th century. I would add that this history is not taught at most elite institutions. In 2020, students are still in struggle to institute ethnic studies at Harvard.

GY: Given your status as the first tenured Asian American law professor in the U.S., how did you resist and reject images that are designed to render you static and that attempt to denude you of your complexity?

MM: Just by standing in the front of the room and talking, while everyone takes notes, an Asian woman disrupts expectations about who should speak with authority. When you are objectified, taking the subject position is a radical act. The backlash is really quite astonishing. Ask any Asian woman who has tried speaking against power. It generates a disproportionate rage, a terrorized response, when the "object" speaks. What allowed me to survive that rage is knowing that my validation has never come from the institutions where I get my paycheck. My worth is determined by my communities in struggle. If I am useful to my home communities, and if I am a useful ally to my extended family in the beautiful "another world is possible" coalition, then my work has value. Keeping clear about whom I will allow to judge me, whose criticism I need, keeps me sane. This is especially true when you tread on difficult ground: What is my responsibility, as the descendant of immigrants, to support Indigenous sovereignty struggles? What does the political goal of "no borders" mean for native Hawaiians holding allegiance to the Nation of Hawai'i, who are struggling to reinstate their stolen country? I have found that working to build solidarity leads to more complicated, nuanced and incisive analysis.

You ask about retaining our complexities: We are our most complicated selves when we are engaged political actors. The level of self-knowledge, the self-criticism, the openness to revision, the layers of understanding that work in coalition-building requires, takes us out of little, defended spaces. It brings us onto the open plain where the wind blows free and we're able to consider what we can become.

GY: This country has failed miserably in terms of effectively addressing so many existentially important issues—racism, COVID-19 and the despicable handling of immigration. I'm also thinking here of children being put in cages or breastfeeding babies being torn from their mothers by border patrol agents. Out of these catastrophes, how do you envision a future of healing?

MM: I believe, both from the empirical evidence and as a matter of political strategy, that most humans are other-regarding beings who seek joy and safety in community. Most of us feel pain watching a screaming child pulled from a parent's arms. We will make the road to a kinder world by finding every way we can to nurture our collective best impulses. We have to create experiences, now, that give people the feeling of joy that comes from working with others on something of value—whether that is a collective art practice, or a Black Lives Matter march, or a neighborhood bike repair shop, or one of those academic panels where the good ideas are flying so fast you can't write it all down.

We have to live like we want all humans to live: supporting one another and seeing what each person adds to our own experience of being sentient on a wondrous planet. I am not a dreamer about this—there is hard work to do, the work that organizers do, going door to door and talking to people very unlike themselves, people taught to fear. We will take musicians with us, and if the music is irresistible, the fear will give way to open doors.

GY: Given the resistance against CRT in the U.S., how do you conceptualize a form of critical pedagogy, one grounded in promoting freedom, that would not fear the insights of CRT? In other words, what must happen at the level of educational theory and praxis?

MM: On content, there are existing models. First, there's old-fashioned civics as was taught in the post–World War II era that I grew up in, but that my mother also learned as a plantation kid in the 1930s. The importance of democracy, every person counts, the concept of rights: free speech, freedom of religion, voting. I remember that my fourth-grade teacher sent a classmate on an errand, then explained to us that this classmate was not going to stand during the pledge of allegiance, because she was a Jehovah's Witness, which is a religion that did believe in standing for the flag or pledging to anyone except God. Since this is America, the teacher explained, we respect everyone's right to practice their religion. She added, sternly, that no one was to make this student feel uncomfortable for having a different religion—that's what Nazis did. It was an indelible message. Of course, there were reactionary elements to old-fashioned civics during the cold war, as we all know. Let's take out the hyper-nationalism and red-baiting that went against the beautiful notions of pluralism, personhood, and self-governance that were the heart of the pro-democracy message.

Second, I would add what we called in the 1970s' Third World Studies, and Marcus Rediker's history from below. We should teach the full breadth of history, showing the experiences of poor and working people, and how they resisted the structures that were trying to keep them out of the democratic process. Social movement history is a good antidote to the separatism and cynicism that is poisoning contemporary politics. There were always more people on the outside of power structures, exploited and treated cruelly, people of all races. They reacted heroically throughout history to make the promise of democracy real. This is the most patriotic story there is, the story of ordinary Americans fighting to make sure everyone has a place of respect in the polity.

Finally, I would teach critical race theory. What is race and how is it used to divide people? Why do critical race theorists believe race, and racial hierarchy, is a powerful social construction, an engine of wealth inequality, the wrecking crew making democracy impossible? What is the difference between formal and substantive equality, and what does intersectionality do to equality analysis? These ideas are essential for anyone who wants to tackle any social problem in the United States. We won't save ourselves from climate catastrophe without understanding these concepts. The concepts are hard, but teachable. I talked to high school students in Arizona who were reading critical race theory and grappling with these complex ideas, exercising their brains in that "dive into the contradictions" way.

On pedagogy, the best method I know is getting students outside the building and into the world. Studying social movement history while participating in social movements is the critical formula. Those high school students in Arizona ran a marathon from Tuscon to Pheonix to protest the ban on ethnic studies. They chained themselves to chairs at the school board meeting using their clear moral authority: "We are students, let us read books!" They felt the power that knowledge combined with action brings.

I taught Organizing in law schools. Students were required to pick a specific, attainable goal—something they could work with others to change in one semester. They learned how to develop strategy and tactics to get it done. We did this alongside reading feminist theory, critical race theory, and movement history. Many students tell me this way of learning changed their idea of how they can live, as citizens of this world. As teachers in a time of crisis, we don't have all the answers. Using the organizing model, which starts with listening, students bring their experiences to the table, and we all become teachers of one another. This was something I came to after years of work to earn respect in the role of expert in the front of the classroom. As one of the first women of color in law teaching, I thought it was important for students to see me claim that space with virtuosity. In the end, my best teaching was when I was a learner among learners. Collaborative pedagogy models how we are going to save ourselves from unknowable, precarious futures. We have to take one another in hand and heart and figure it out together.

10

EDUCATION WILL BE CRITICAL IN THE FIGHT FOR DEMOCRACY AND ANTIRACISM

INTERVIEW WITH PEDRO A. NOGUERA

What is the role of education in creating a critically-minded public that is unafraid to resist lies and deceptions perpetuated by anti-democratic forces? How do we best address the assumption that economically oppressed children can't learn? In what way does internalized racism impact students of color and how must this be addressed? In what ways should we rethink the aims of education beyond careerism?

To address these and other important questions, I spoke with Pedro A. Noguera, who is the Emery Stoops and Joyce King Stoops Dean of the Rossier School of Education and a Distinguished Professor of Education at the University of Southern California (USC). Prior to joining USC, Noguera served as a tenured professor and holder of endowed chairs at the University of California, Los Angeles; New York University; Harvard University; and the University of California, Berkeley. He is the author, co-author and editor of 15 books. His most recent books are *Common Schooling: Conversations About the Tough Questions and Complex Issues Confronting K-12 Education in the United States Today* (Teachers College Press) with Rick Hess and *City Schools and the American Dream: Still Pursuing the Dream* (Teachers College Press) with Esa Syeed.

G. Yancy (with Pedro A. Noguera), "Education Will Be Critical in the Fight for Democracy and Anti-Racism," in *Truthout*, February 5, 2021. [Editors: Britney Schultz and Anton Woronczuk]

GEORGE YANCY: As someone who has done so much to rethink what is possible within the context of classrooms—in terms of issues related to educational equality, the education gap, race and education, policy issues that do or do not promote educational success—I want to begin by asking a question about how you understand education within the context of democracy. Educational reformer John Dewey was clear about how important critical intelligence is to a thriving democratic citizenry. Define how you understand education and its role against anti-democratic forces. I'm thinking here how bell hooks argues that education should be a practice of freedom.

PEDRO A. NOGUERA: George, I've been thinking a lot about the role of education in promoting and safeguarding democracy during the Trump years. The four years of his presidency have been characterized by a full-blown assault on facts and information, as well as science, and reasoned debate. We are living in a period of hyper-partisanship and rampant misinformation. We've also seen a rise in right-wing violence and extremism. Fortunately, Trump was denied a second term, but his election exposed how vulnerable we are to right-wing authoritarianism in this country.

Numerous scholars have described education as the foundation of democracy and we now understand clearly why that is the case. Without a grounding in history, civics and an ability to think critically, people can be easily manipulated, especially by social media, and authoritarian leaders can use that to their advantage. We must keep in mind that Trump was barely defeated in the national election, which means almost half the [voting] population was ready to sign up for four more years. With the likelihood that he will run again in 2024, we must figure out how to address the fear, misinformation and conspiracy theories that he will run on, and that were used to frighten people into seeing the COVID-19 vaccine as a tool of mass extermination. It's quite scary.

As I think about how to address this problem, I agree with bell hooks that education must be a practice in freedom. However, it's not enough to assume that if we put information out for people to consume they will take it in. Too many people don't read and are easily fooled by what they find on social media. To prepare kids to participate in democracy, they must learn to think critically about their role in society. For this to happen, schools must engage their students in democratic practice in the classroom and beyond. Students must learn through experience what democracy is and what it can do to advance justice and freedom. As a former social studies teacher myself, I used debate and simulations as a way to create powerful learning experiences to reinforce a student's understanding of history and politics. For example, I once invited a friend from college to come to my class dressed as Thomas Jefferson. Prior to the visit, I had my students learn about Jefferson's life, his presidency and his personal contradictions. When my friend showed up in his Jefferson disguise, he was pummeled with questions about slavery, his relationship with Sally Hemmings (and how old she was when it began), and the true meaning of the Declaration of Independence in a society founded on slavery.

I believe that by creating powerful learning experiences students can be prepared to participate in democracy. When students understand their rights, when they can comprehend the contradictions and atrocities that have occurred throughout this country's history, and when they know how to defend their beliefs with facts and evidence, they will be better prepared to confront the injustices that are pervasive today. My hope is that such learning experiences will make it possible for young people to see that democracy requires more than just voting. They must be actively involved in addressing problems like environmental racism, racial inequality, police violence, etc. Fatalism is our enemy and education can counter it if educational experiences are visceral and illuminating.

GY: Many scholars who critique neoliberalism vis-à-vis education have argued that education is in the grips of an economic-philosophical orientation that is wedded to marketization, commodification and the production of economic value, where investment is made in the capacities of students to generate economic value for themselves, the companies for which they work and the state. Such assumptions and pedagogical practices seem inconsistent with a robust sense of education as a site that generates what philosopher Cornel West calls non-market values. What might educators do to counter this way of imprisoning the meaning and practice of education within the context of such a narrow economic ethos?

PAN: The logic of neoliberalism has been embraced by U.S. policy makers for several years. We also see it embraced by some foundations and think tanks. These groups have embraced the notion that reforming education must come at the expense of unionized teachers and employees. In some ways, this is hardly surprising. After all, that logic has found its way into almost every aspect of public life in recent years, most notably health care. Human needs and the social purposes of education not only receive less attention; in many cases, they aren't being considered at all. It's important to recognize that both Democrats and Republicans have embraced neoliberal logic when they advocate for reform.

The good news is that their prescriptions for change—high-stakes standardized testing, school "choice" through the proliferation of charter schools and vouchers, and closing schools deemed to be "failing"—hasn't worked. They've had over 20 years since the enactment of No Child Left Behind to try implement their ideas and they haven't delivered the kind of improvement they promised. Even in cities like New Orleans and Washington, D.C., and states like Florida and Arizona, where choice has been used as the policy driver, there is scant evidence that it has resulted in better schools for the poorest children.

However, I think it's not good enough to criticize these ideas. Progressives must offer an alternative vision that addresses the challenge of delivering a high-quality education to all people, but especially to communities mired in poverty. The crux of the problem that the neo-liberals have taken on and that we can't ignore is: What should be done to educate poor children of color who too often attend schools that are struggling? It's not good enough to simply say that we must focus on ending poverty, given that we know that won't happen any time soon. We certainly can't simply tell parents to wait until we reform capitalism. Parents want answers for their kids now, and as a parent, I understand their urgency and I agree with them. Additionally, it's important to recognize that as debilitating as the effects of poverty may be, it doesn't mean that kids who are poor can't learn. The question we must ask is: Until there is major social and economic change, how do we mitigate the effects of poverty, address the unequal allocation of resources to schools, and provide educators with the support required to meet the needs of their students? I believe that if we can focus the policy discussions in this way, we can make more progress than we have.

GY: The problem of race and schooling is a huge, continuous and difficult problem. To address failing schools, as these failures are tracked along the axis of race and racism, requires a broad, coalitional form of agency and a mode of analysis that is multipronged. It seems to me that we can't isolate the question of the educational performance of a Black student from the failure of teachers to believe that such a student is a living possibility, or from the ways that learning is impacted by the prison-like structures of schools. Speak to this issue of organicity.

PAN: Race as we know is central to America's educational dilemma. Structural racism is real and it is embedded in our society's policies, institutions and beliefs. There are schools that have shown that when Black,

Latino and Native American children are educated under conditions where their culture and personhood are valued and affirmed, where expectations and academic standards are high, and parents are engaged as respected partners, excellent results are possible. In several publications I have identified such schools because they serve as proof that there is nothing inherently "wrong" with the children. This might seem obvious to those who don't work in education, but I would argue that there are still many in this country who continue to subscribe to racist beliefs about genetics and intellectual ability.

I also know that it's easy to be distracted by what we might call "silver bullets": the notion that all we have to do is hire more teachers of color, or implement an anti-racist or ethnic studies curriculum, and the problems will fade away. Educational issues are more complicated than that, and on matters related to race, the complexity is important.

Schools that counter the effects of racism and capitalism do so by enacting several strategies simultaneously. They empower teachers with a clear understanding of how to meet the academic and social needs of their students. They build partnerships rooted in trust and respect for parents. They have strong, visionary leaders who work with their community to create a culture characterized by caring, collaboration and accountability. They cultivate the curiosity in children, teach them to utilize their higher-order thinking skills, and provide opportunities for them to develop their voice and to use their education to address the problems facing their school, community, society and the world.

I believe racial integration is a goal worth pursuing because we live in an interracial society and children must be prepared to live with others from different backgrounds. However, I don't think we have to wait for our schools to be integrated to deliver a better education to them. In fact, I have found that it is often easier to create the kinds of conditions I have described in schools that are racially homogenous or where no white children are present, if we have the will, resources and support needed to do so. I don't want to make this sound easy, but I do believe it can be done.

GY: After Barack Obama became president, I recall many (across racial lines) who argued that racism no longer existed, which meant that if Black children and children of color fail in school, they do so because of their own lack of effort. This view, sadly, overlooked systemic forms of racism, its history and its current manifestations. How does systemic racism continue to negatively impact Black and Brown children in North America when it comes to educational equity?

PAN: George, I believe I addressed this in my response to the previous question. The only thing I should add is that in addition to addressing structural, ideological and interpersonal racism, education must also address internalized racism.

GY: Yes! Excellent.

PAN: This is in many ways the most insidious effect of living in a racist society. As Black people, we are not only likely to internalize racist beliefs about ourselves, we are also likely to hold them toward other people of color. Frantz Fanon, Albert Memmi, Paulo Freire and many others have written about why addressing internalized oppression is so important to human liberation. The only way we can demonstrate agency in acting on our collective interests is by rejecting the dehumanizing beliefs that serve as the basis of our subjugation.

My own understanding of this process—which we might describe as an awakening to self-love, and a collective consciousness that rejects white supremacy—has been helped from learning about how the Māori have approached decolonization in New Zealand. Increasingly, they have come to understand that they can only reject white supremacy and the legacy of English colonialism by critically asserting what it means to be Māori today. This means not romanticizing the past but drawing from the best and most useful elements of their language, history and culture, to begin constructing a new collective sense of self.

Schools can play a role in facilitating this awakening by providing children with an education that affirms their identity without reinforcing narrow parochialism. This is not merely a matter of being exposed to the right content. Children must have powerful learning experiences that teach them the utility of core values (e.g., respect, character, etc.) and cultural concepts (e.g., unity, social responsibility, etc.) so that they will be prepared for life as adults. Such an education is the only effective way to counter the sense of inferiority that is cultivated among people of color, especially Black people, in America.

GY: As a Black man who engages important questions that deal with race and education, how do your experiences shape your approach regarding how young Black males can be affirmed in K-12 educational spaces? I say this with the understanding that there are proportionally more white female teachers than teachers of color.

PAN: I have argued on several occasions and in writing that what young men of color, especially Black men, need is the chance to grow and develop without being limited by what we now call toxic masculinity. Like race, the social construction of gender is deeply embedded in the fabric of society and is reinforced through hegemonic structures that cause gender roles to appear "natural." Males of color do best academically and socially when they are in environments where they are challenged, supported, encouraged to dream, exposed to new opportunities and allowed to be themselves without being limited by the stereotypes related to race and gender that are prevalent in society. Without a concerted effort to create conditions like these, the stereotypes more often than not will determine how young men see themselves and are seen by others. As a Black man, I know from experience how hard it is to do this. However, I know enough Black men who have managed to overcome these obstacles to know that it can be done.

GY: How do you envision education as a possible force and source of creating a world in which we as human beings collectively flourish or are able to heal from so many forces that divide us?

PAN: Education must do more than prepare children for college or jobs. It must empower them to think creatively about the future. It must equip them with the mindset needed to address the many challenges facing this country and the world. Right now, we're coping with the pandemic, a severe economic crisis and the growing reality that climate change will totally alter the future in ways we can barely imagine. Educational issues are rarely seen as a priority in national politics. That may be a good thing since most politicians know very little about the complex issues facing our schools. However, anyone who is at all worried about the future has to see that education is our best, and perhaps our only, resource for tackling the problems we will face.

Our schools reflect the best, and sometimes the worst, of our society. I believe that if we're going to make progress in addressing the issues that divide and undermine the progress of this nation—poverty, racism, inequality, etc.—education will have to play a central role. However, this is asking a lot of our schools and the educators who work in them. This occurred during the summer when many kids were not in school. Imagine what would have happened if kids had been in school at the time of George Floyd's murder, a murder captured on video and seen by millions of people, including children. Would teachers have known how to respond? As protests erupted, and looting ensued in some cities, would educators have been able to turn this into a "teachable moment," and if so, what would they have taught?

Education is the best tool we have for creating a more just and equitable society, but our schools have significant limitations. We hire ordinary people to become teachers and principals but expect them to do extraordinary things. Among other things, we expect them to stimulate and challenge kids, to encourage and ensure evidence of learning from those who are unmotivated, to support those with significant social and emotional needs, and to keep all kids safe while they are in school. During the pandemic we expected schools to deliver meaningful instruction to kids virtually when they had almost no time to prepare for the moment.

It's hardly surprising that so many schools fail given how much they've been asked to do. Throughout my career I have described myself as a critical supporter of public schools because no other institution is charged with meeting such a broad array of challenges. I know that many schools are set up to fail because they lack the resources to address the complex issues they face.

Despite their flaws and limitations, we have to support public schools, even as we also demand more from them. As we've seen during the pandemic, they are a vital part of the social safety net where kids can receive social support. But they must do more. They must prepare kids to engage the world around them, and not merely accept things as they are. Education must show kids how to apply what they learn to confront the problems facing the world. It must cultivate their agency and ability to think critically so that they will refuse to accept or adapt to injustice, and refuse to see racism as simply an unfortunate aspect of life. Education must empower students and provide them with the capacity to approach our collective problems with courage, resourcefulness and creativity.

George, I believe in the power of education, and this is why I have made it my vocation and avocation for over 30 years.

GY: Now that we have moved beyond what many view as Trump's harmful educational policies, speak more concretely to the importance of providing schools with the resources (including financial) that are needed to make the ideas that you cover a realized truth. Do you see the Biden administration helping in this regard?

PAN: During his first year in office, the Biden administration provided cash supplements for poor families with children. This is already done in several Western countries and it temporarily brought about a significant reduction in the child poverty rate in the U.S. We must recognize that poverty is an educational issue. In states such as California, 25 percent of all children come from families at or below the poverty level. Children in poverty suffer from a variety of hardships, from food insecurity, to housing instability, and a variety of unmet health needs. When schools can focus exclusively on teaching and learning, outcomes for children are more likely to improve. I'm hopeful that this will happen and we will begin to move in a new and better direction.

GY: I want to ask one additional question about hope. As you know, white supremacy is like a hydra. It has a way of returning. What do you say to young Black people or BIPOC that is able to sustain hope. I say this because hope is so fragile. Moreover, when we look at the bold actions of what is the raise of white nationalism (think here of the January 6th assault on the Capitol), I find it hard to sustain hope or to communicate such hope to young people of color.

PAN: George, I am currently inspired by the example of the young women in Iran who are standing up to the Mullahs and asserting their rights. I am inspired by the young people around the world who are demanding that political leaders take action now to address climate change. I want young people in this country to get off of social media and get involved in demanding change now. Their future will be determined by what we do now. I am prepared to work with them, but the youth must lead. This is where my hope lies.

11

PAULO FREIRE

Critical Education in a World in Need of Repair

INTERVIEW WITH PETER McLAREN

This year, 2021, is the 100th anniversary of Paulo Freire's birth. My introduction to Freire's radical and revolutionary work began when I was introduced to his seminal book, *Pedagogy of the Oppressed*. That text alone forced a new vision for how I came to think of education as a site of profound nurturing and reciprocity between students and teachers. In fact, for me, the very idea of the teacher and student relationship had to be rethought outside of a neoliberal framework that stressed marketization, privatization, commodification, consumerism, and a social reality believed to consist of atomic individuals whose sole raison d'être is entrepreneurial, where the aim is to maximize one's power on the basis of zero-sum logics. Such a form of "education" is ripe to support the status quo through the manufacturing of a false messianism, where those in power attempt, as Freire says, "to save themselves." Education, on this score, is not designed to trouble the social order, to disrupt complacency, and disturb milquetoast mentalities, but to produce more cogs within a hegemonic cookie-cutter society where *homo economicus* rules, that is, where human beings ruthlessly and narrowly battle to promote their own self-interests. Such a society is predicated upon those who are deemed "losers" and are left out, discarded. The "winners" take all. There is also the reigning ethos of indifference vis-à-vis the least of these, a society that willfully refuses to see those who suf-

G. Yancy (with Peter McLaren), "Paulo Freire: Critical Education in a World in Need of Repair," *Tikkun*, September 27, 2021. [Editor: Rabbi Michael Lerner]

fer, those at the bottom, the subaltern, the stranger, the denied immigrant, the pain and injustice experienced by Black, Indigenous, People of Color, those within the LGBTQI community, and those deemed "monstrous" because of visible impairments. This politically reinforced social reality that encourages violence and xenophobia is consistent with the right-wing nationalistic fervor that we see in Brazil, Germany, Hungary, Italy, Slovenia, and in the U.S. under the neofascist (white nationalist) tendencies of Donald Trump and his political minions who continue to propagate the lie that the 2020 election was rigged and stolen. How does radical education, which is designed to cultivate radical imaginations and critically informed dissent, become sustained and nurtured in the face of dogmatism, misinformation, and the "dis-imagination machine," as Henry Giroux says? This is where the indispensability of Freire's thought and action come into play.

Freire understood, through his revolutionary educational work with oppressed peasants and workers in Brazil, that hegemonic and massive in-equity creates a "culture of silence." Rabbi Abraham Joshua Heschel writes that "The prophet's word is a scream in the night." It is Freire's scream that continues to speak to us about how our "ontological vocation is to be more fully human." For Freire, it is what he calls the banking system of education, one consistent with dis-imagination, that installs fear, cowardice, aversion to resistance, and that suppresses a critically engaged demos. The banking system of education is designed hierarchically to produce passive students, and functionary teachers. It is a system where students are not taught to be active subjects of the learning process, but empty containers, which, for Freire, is "an oppressor tactic" as it creates dependence. As we here in the U.S. find ourselves on the precipice of undoing our fragile experimental democracy and falling into a draconian dystopic world of indifferent power elites, it is important that we celebrate the work of Freire. Like Howard Zinn, Freire understood that "Education can, and should be dangerous." It is dangerous, though, to those who would prefer we sleep, who would prefer we not ask questions about climate change, anti-Black racism, misogyny, homophobia and transphobia, anti-immigration, the erasure of multiculturalism, and the banning of critical race theory. Heeding Freire's voice could mean the difference between life and death, between radical love and radical global extinction. Freire is clear, "The dialogical theory of action does not involve a Subject, who dominates by virtue of conquest, and a dominated object. Instead, there are Subjects who meet to name the world in order to transform it." Let us, then, transform our world.

With this, it is with great appreciation that I have been given the honor of conducting this broad and engaging interview with the prominent scholar, activist, and public intellectual Peter McLaren. Peter discusses with deep insight not only the work of Paulo Freire, but provides us with a genealogy of his own critical thinking and emancipatory praxis. This critically engaged space speaks to the importance of critical reflection and courageous speech, especially as we continue to live within the context of an American ideology of obscurantism, one that rejects critical thinking, one that avoids processes of nurturing challenging questions, one that fears ethical daring, and one that refuses to engage in deep political and epistemological self-interrogation. Yet, a critical pedagogy—one infused with deep probing of and outrage against systemic forms of violence, hatred, and oppression—is what is necessary if we are to create sites of deep reflective praxes that resist global forms of suffering, which includes the earth itself. What is also necessary, which I see as inextricably linked to critical pedagogy, is a radical form of love, a form of love that can see beyond the barriers that have rendered us strangers to one another. It is a form of love that is fueled by a vision of mutual healing, global solidarity, and collective liberation. Peter embodies this call for radical love and takes us through an engaging process that imbricates autobiography, intellectual history, and the spirited and revolutionary work of Paulo Freire. For those of us who attempt to speak out against various manifestations of evil, to name them, and to call them out, Peter's voice moves us and encourages us to keep alive a radical spirit of loving transformation.

Peter McLaren is Distinguished Professor in Critical Studies at the Donna Ford Attallah College of Educational Studies, Chapman University. He is also Emeritus Professor of Urban Education at UCLA School of Education & Information Studies. From 2015–2020, McLaren taught as Chair Professor at the Northeast Normal University, Changchun, China. He is the Co-Director of the Paulo Freire Democratic Project where he serves as International Ambassador for Global Ethics and Social Justice. Professor McLaren is co-founder of Instituto McLaren de Pedagogía Crítica in Ensenada, Mexico. He is the author and editor of over 45 books. His writings have been translated in 25 languages.

GEORGE YANCY: Peter, as someone who knew Paulo Freire, and who has grappled with his work for a significant period of your life, I would like to ask you a series of questions related to his work that I think that you are uniquely qualified to address. Indeed, in our contemporary moment of systemic oppression of various sorts, vast forms of dehumanization, marginalization, and violence, I think that Freire's voice is indispensable and vital as we rethink a robust and loving conception of humanity.

My teaching is deeply informed by critical pedagogy, especially as articulated by Paulo Freire. As I introduce my students to philosophy, I make important connections between philosophy as a critically engaged project that disturbs the status quo and Freire's critique of the banking system of education, which is designed to keep people complacent, passive, and ignorant of their oppression. For me, philosophy is *not* simply an abstract love of wisdom and conceptual analysis, but a form of love and wisdom that extends beyond the halls of academia and touches the lives of embodied people who too often live within contexts of deep pain and suffering. In one of your important books, *Life in Schools*, you write, "Critical pedagogy resonates with the sensibility of the Hebrew phrase of *tikkun olam*, which means 'to heal, repair, and transform the world.' It provides historical, cultural, political, and ethical direction for those in education who still dare to hope." Given the venue of our interview, say more about how you understand critical pedagogy as an approach to education that heals the world.

PETER McLAREN: I very much agree with you George—unequivocally in fact—that Freire's work is indispensable today. Given the rise of identitarian ideology, ethno-nationalism grounded in ideas of racial purity and support for the racial state (but where the term race is now hidden under the cloak of "cultural differences"), and the instantiations of White supremacy and anti-Semitism that are furiously populating the ideology of Trump's base in the current U.S. context, we need Freire more than ever. Support for democracy is now evanescent among the current Republican party. In fact, White victimhood, misology, and hatred by Whites of non-White immigrants and people of color in general, has gone analogue. Professors drawn to Freire's work, foot-weary from battling truth-obliterating anti-rationalism, are being pressured to tone down their anti-fascist efficacy because it might create divisiveness on college campuses.

Right-wing extremism—claiming Black Lives Matter to be a terrorist organization or characterizing Critical Race Theory as a communist conspiracy designed to take over the United States, for instance—has become so rampant that more authoritarian populists, worse than Trump, are poised to emerge from the sidelines and make emotional connections with the aggrieved low-wage and middle-class base and deliberately call for bloodshed. The calumny against professors inspired by Freire, who challenge right-wing extremist hate on campus, is outrageous as university administrators push for progressive and left professors to tone down, as I just said, their anti-fascist efficacy because of fear of exacerbating divisiveness on campus. However, these perpetrators of hate need to be challenged by a pedagogy of everyday life that is Freire's. Dialogue is one way to do this. And we must find more creative ways of engaging in the culture wars on campuses. Every pedagogy needs to be self-critical, otherwise, in time it will degenerate into a self-righteous hypocrisy, and I am sure Freire would agree that we need to find more creative ways to fight the hate.

GY: And I'm sure that Freire would have been against a kind of self-apotheosis and where his work would be deemed beyond critical discussion.

PM: Yes, Freirean pedagogy should not be treated as a religious text and certainly not worshipped but it needs to inform the basis of our praxis as educators. Freire came to understand that oppressed learners had internalized profoundly negative images of themselves (images that Freire identified as created and imposed by the oppressor) and felt powerless to make changes in their lives and become active agents in history. Freire created the conditions for learners to examine the limits and possibilities of the existential situations that emerged from the experiences of the learners—experiences that were often traumatic and life-denying. Critical consciousness demanded a rejection of passivity and encouraged the practice of dialogue wherein learners were able to identify contradictions in their lived experiences and were able to reach new levels of awareness of being an "object" in a world where only "subjects" have the means to determine the direction of their lives; where you made a choice to create history rather than being a casualty of history. And yes, Freire's critique of "banking education" (depositing funds of knowledge into the brainpans of students) is one of his central contributions. North American students come to appreciate this critique more quickly than in other countries in which I have taught classes. For instance, this was an extremely difficult concept for graduate students who I have been teaching in China over recent years to appreciate. Students initially asked me why I was wasting class time inviting students to share their life experiences, claiming that I was the expert and they wanted to put to memory my ideas which I was encouraged to list on a PowerPoint presentation. Fortunately, they began to appreciate Freire's critique once sufficient trust prevailed among us. And eventually they started reading *Pedagogy of the Oppressed* in Mandarin (that I had written the introduction to the Chinese version to this text also helped win me some credibility).

Freirean education is not about discovering the truth of the world through theoretical study and then engaging in a step-by-step application of our knowledge to the world, but rather engaging the material world critically in ways that enable an understanding of the world that seizes the will of the learner. Those whom Freire referred to as the oppressed see a world that they believe has already been written and view themselves as having been written out of this world. Freirean critical consciousness is a type of protagonistic knowing that occurs by "re-cognizing" the world as an arena of struggle and seeking the means to overcome the privileging hierarchies that constitute it—effectively re-writing that world by being in and with the world, that is, moving outside the fatalism that pervades the technocratic logic of capitalist modernity which traps so many of the oppressed as victims of history. For Freire, becoming critically conscious is the path to humanization, to our ontological vocation of becoming more fully human, it is a path that creates the conditions of possibility of becoming agents capable of making history rather than remaining bearers of history's inevitability. This is what forms the basis of a Freirean reading of the word and the world—a reading that is co-intentional (the student as educator and the educator as student), protagonistic, and dialogical. Freire understands that protagonistic or revolutionary agents are not born, they are dialectically produced by circumstances. To revolutionize society, it is necessary to revolutionize thinking. Yet at the same time to revolutionize thinking, it is necessary to revolutionize society. All human development (including thought and speech), for Freire, is social activity and this has its roots in collective labor. It is important to understand that for Freire, process and the outcome become one—which Freire refers to as critical consciousness.

Freire provides us with a way of challenging learners with words and concepts that emerge from their own lived histories. Freire's ideas have been adapted in the United States among practitioners of what is known as critical pedagogy. Critical pedagogy has made some inroads in graduate schools of education to the extent, at least, that students will graduate with some rudimentary understanding of Freire's work. However, high school teachers who use Freire can be more closely monitored by parents and administrators where discussion of race, class, gender and LBGTQ issues have become increasingly anathema to certain pro-Trump, QAnon, and cult-driven constituencies. Too often it's the case that colleges of education offer very few courses or programs designed around Freire's work or critical pedagogy. Here, concepts from the social sciences—feminist theory, critical theory, critical race theory, Marxist economics, African American Studies, liberation theology, and so on—potentially serve as dialectical relays through which students can "read the world" against the act of "reading the word." What I mean here is the process of reading one's lived experiences, as those experiences are reflected in or refracted through various critical theories that offer explanatory frameworks that can help students make sense of their own experiences. The idea is to create conditions of critical consciousness or critical self-reflexivity among students. You can't teach anyone anything by injecting your ideas into the veins of their consciousness, you can only create the conditions for people to learn. The idea is to provide resources, including opportunities for dialectical reasoning, to help students understand how various ideologies drive social life, to help students discern how systems of intelligibility or systems of mediation within the wider society (nature, the economic system, the state, the social system, cultural system, jurisprudence, schools, religion, etc.) are mutually constitutive with the formation of the self.

GY: So, for Freire, we are not talking about a unidirectional transformation or an enclosed Cartesian process of epistemological reflection, which, I must say, bespeaks an atomistic, neo-liberal conceptualization of the self.

PM: That's right. When we talk about liberation, we are referring to self-and-social transformation and not just self-transformation; that is, we are referring to a dialectical relationship. We need not refer to the self and social relations as though they were mutually exclusive categories, antiseptically distant from each other. They are not steel cast terms but rather bleed into each other. Again, it's a dialectical relationship. It is at this point that we arrive at the notion of praxis, the bringing together of theory and practice. Of course, we demonstrate that praxis begins with personal agency in and on the world. We begin, in other words, with practice and then enter into dialogue with others reflecting on our practice. This reflection on our practice, then informs subsequent practice—and we call this process or mode of experiential learning revolutionary praxis, or self-reflective purposeful behavior, that is, exploring with others the relevance of philosophical ideas to the fault lines of everyday life and the necessity to transcend them when they foster oppressive forms of domination. So yes, I felt that the term "tikkun olam" captured the spirit of Freire's work. I know very little about the mystical writings of the Lurianic kabbalah, but I have read that historically it has referred to a specific cosmological account where Adam was exercised to restore God's divine light that had been shattered and disbursed during the act of creation. Acts of repair were meant to imply religious acts, but I am using the concept in a more contemporary sense, and in my use it can be seen as synonymous with the popular concept of social justice and God as the idea of unconditional justice. By repair I am referring to creating conditions of possibility for producing social relations of solace and hope to restive and aggrieved populations who are suffering under the forces and relations of domination and oppression—one of the lodestones of Freire's work. The term also resonates with Freire's profound contributions to liberation theology.

GY: I would like to explicitly return to Freire's work in relationship to liberation theology, but I want to ask a question about his status as a public intellectual. I see the public intellectual as one who speaks with courageous speech, who attempts to identify with those who are treated as *the least of these*, where the subaltern and the oppressed are not treated as "objects" but as subjects. In this sense, the public intellectual attempts to create a space of shared relationality of mutual concern and a collective sense of fighting against those forces that are dehumanizing. The public intellectual, in short, relates to the "funk of life," as Cornel West would say. How do you understand the role of the public intellectual, especially within a context where many in America seem to be comfortable not knowing the existential magnitude of human pain and suffering or the suffering of the earth for that matter?

PM: Cornel West wrote the Preface to my first book about Freire and I was equally grateful that bell hooks and Henry Giroux—already considered public intellectuals—agreed to contribute. You can't ask for stronger, more committed public intellectuals than these three luminaries. And Freire's work has made him the consummate public intellectual for reasons you describe. Giroux has written mightily on the concept of teachers as public intellectuals and one of his first explorations into this was his book, *Teachers as Intellectuals* where he made a distinction between "hegemonic intellectuals" and "critical intellectuals," which was inspired by Antonio Gramsci's storied work on "organic intellectuals." Do we want our teaching to be reproductive of the status quo in which so many suffer? Or do we want to challenge dominative forms of oppression? This choice posed by public intellectuals such as West, hooks, Giroux, and Freire provided for many of us a powerful rationale for doing liberatory work in the public sphere. Now the criticism was that public intellectuals were undermining tradition and historical memory and the narrative and symbolic glue that supposedly held the country together and made us proud in being Americans and defenders of the American Dream. There was also the charge that we were being anti-patriotic and hateful of American institutions—well, you can imagine the criticisms. Many public intellectuals were denounced for being "critical theorists" in the tradition of the Frankfurt School (who were all Jewish intellectuals and perceived as communists and subversive of democracy) and were followers of Herbert Marcuse who was Angela Davis's mentor during her graduate studies—mentor to a Black Panther, what could be worse during those days? But clearly it is important that we relate our work as public intellectuals to contemporary crises of humanity and make concerted attempts to address the public on such issues in terms that would be more accessible than those used in the academy without diluting the main ideas.

Becoming a media personality is not a litmus test for being a public intellectual by any means. Freire's role as a public intellectual was carved from his brilliant writings, from his activism, from his willingness to travel the world and engage with other thinkers in deliberative, critical dialogue. It wasn't easy to find the means for public intellectuals to get their ideas across to wide audiences in those days except through publishing a popular book. And you risked offending your institution—in today's terms, being "cancelled"—even if you maintained that your ideas did not represent your institution. The term "radical professor" became part of the mainstream media lexicon and public intellectuals were often censured. Sound bite media formats meant that the ideas of public intellectuals could not be sufficiently adumbrated in a manner accessible to the public and occasionally public intellectuals were deceptively framed to appear like idiots. I was certainly not recognized as a public intellectual, but I did agree to speak out in the media on the few occasions I was invited to do so. I appeared on a talk show once where during the break the producer encouraged me to turn over a coffee table in anger. I refused and my appearance was cut out of the show, and it was never aired because I refused to accept the way I was being characterized in the "teaser" to the show. It was more than "awkward." During my doctoral studies I was fortunate to enroll in a class taught by Michel Foucault who was visiting the University of Toronto at the time and who, during a trip to bookstores across the city, spoke to me about the idea of dangerous knowledge and from his lectures I came to realize much more deeply that certain intellectuals going public were too threatening to the establishment media. Think of the case of Noam Chomsky, a public intellectual I greatly admire. You don't often see him interviewed in the mainstream press even today, although for decades he has been acknowledged as one of the world's greatest intellectuals, someone who can put complex issues into accessible terminology and someone who wants to do more than understand political history, but to act upon history, to impact the world in a way that promotes human freedom. Again, what he offers is dangerous knowledge, knowledge dangerous to the public. There is less trust in academic institutions today and in the public square. Distrust—in science for example—is one reason why so many people see an argument as equivalent to having an opinion, so you can find the most outrageous ideas expressed in today's media by those who retreat into their own platforms on social media where people dance to the same opinionated beat with no desire to do otherwise. For the last few years, I have heard from many right-wing students, and some on the left, usually undergraduates: "Ok professor that's your opinion on Freire's work, and I have a different opinion." But they present no cogent evidence for holding onto their opinions. People have lost the ability to adjudicate arguments and we unceremoniously reject them in favor of opinions to the extent that people cling to their viewpoints even in the face of objective evidence to the contrary. To them, truth is all about emotional appeal and having their ideas affirmed, which are most comfortable to them. Freirean dialogue could break this impasse precisely because, as you so clearly affirm, of the ability of his pedagogy to create a "shared relationality of mutual concern and a collective sense of fighting against those forces that are dehumanizing." That's precisely why Freire, Chomsky, hooks, Giroux, and others are considered authentic public intellectuals and it distinguishes them from today's so-called thought leaders, which is one reason Freire and authentic public intellectuals are needed more than ever at a time when the country is divided in more and deeper ways than it has been for generations.

GY: I am envious in the best possible way that you not only took a course with Foucault, but that you met and knew Paulo Freire personally. Share with us what it was like when you first met him. What was it about this man that emboldened your own sense of political praxis and intellectual courage? And how did his influence broaden your philosophical, political, and pedagogical vision?

PM: I first heard Freire's name spoken in the halls of the Department of Adult Education at the Ontario Institute for Studies in Education, part of the University of Toronto in 1979, the year I began my doctoral studies. Apparently, he visited the Institute during my time there as a doctoral student and I missed him. But I first met him in person at a conference in 1985 in Chicago where he was the featured speaker, with attendees spilling over into the aisles of the auditorium eager to hear him. Henry Giroux and one of Freire's closest North American colleagues, who had immigrated from Cabo or Cape Verde, Africa, Donaldo Macedo, introduced me to Freire at the conference. Macedo, a linguistics professor, was one of the world's leading exponents of Freire's works. What shocked me was that during my conversation with Freire, he knew some of my work. This certainly bolstered my confidence in my research. Paulo would eventually write prefaces for two of my books. When in his preface to my first major work, *Critical Pedagogy and Predatory Culture*, he talked about me as his "intellectual cousin," I understood why so many referred to Freire's humility and generosity of spirit. When Paulo, Donaldo, and I came together, they would both tease me with delightful impertinence. Once during a meal at a Portuguese restaurant in Boston, which had a live band, Donaldo and Paulo asked the band to announce that it was my birthday and play "happy birthday" for me—about five or six times during our meal. Of course, it wasn't my birthday. Freire had a wonderful sense of humor and was often playful.

There was competition among North American educators around their relationship to Freire and I realized some academics were downplaying my work privately to Freire, trying to undermine our relationship but it had no effect on him. Freire had a sense of integrity to him that was consistent and profound. Freire was careful during talks to recognize publicly those in the audience whom he knew and was often worried about hurting someone's feelings for overlooking them in the audience. Freire invited me to his home in São Paulo and attended my lecture at the university and helped to translate some of my concepts into Portuguese—even though his English was not very strong. Paulo participated in a conference which became a book, *Mentoring the Mentor*, with bell hooks, Antonia Darder, and Giroux in attendance, and many other well-respected scholars. And with great humility, he invited all those in attendance to challenge or clarify concepts he had developed in his work. Some of the best Freirean scholars—such as University of Malta's Peter Mayo—did not have the opportunity to meet Freire in person, so I consider myself fortunate to have been able to spend time with him.

Freire has been a powerful inspiration throughout my life and my scholarship on him led to numerous invitations to Brazil where I was especially interested in Afro-Brazilian religion, Umbanda in particular. Afro-Brazilian members of the Workers' Party made it possible for me to witness Umbanda rituals that normally excluded outsiders. The Freirean community is now vast. Freire's work is the dialogical glue that enjoins so many of us to venture on the path to freedom. Given the contextual specificity that gave rise to Freire's work in the countryside and in urban barrios and favelas, his work was not easily generalized across and applicable to many educational settings without falling prey to misunderstanding and running afoul of political authorities. His work was always vulnerable to political domestication, as when liberal teachers in the U.S. would often reduce his work to the teacher sitting in a circle in a classroom and having conversations with students over current events or what they did over the weekend.

Not that there is anything intrinsically wrong with that, but critical pedagogy doesn't stop there. Freire was reluctant to have his ideas "exported"
across international borders where they would lose both their nuance and
specificity; hence he always encouraged educators to "reinvent" his work
rather than simply "transplant" it in geographical and geopolitical contexts
outside of Brazil. His work would therefore need to find trusted educators
who could "translate" and adapt his ideas to various national, regional, and
local contexts both inside and outside of his native country. One example of
this was during the Nicaragua's National Literacy Crusade where elements
of his pedagogical and methodological approach adapted to the specific
circumstances in Nicaragua. Reacting to criticism of the campaign as being
too partisan politically, Freire was known to respond that such a campaign
was "not a pedagogical program with political implications, but rather, it is
a political project with pedagogical implications."

For Freire, learning involves a dialectical reading of the word and the
world, of learning to recognize opportunities for changing the world that
he referred to as "untested feasibilities." The act of knowing, for Freire, does
not move in discreet methodological steps—from an epistemological shift
in consciousness brought about by a teacher skilled in the Socratic method,
followed by an ontological shift in behavior by the student signaling a
different way of being in the world and relating to others—since for him
this leads to a type of bifurcated Cartesian knowledge. It simply repeats
the anti-humanism of Western enlightenment learning that is grounded
in a Cartesian dualism separating mind and body, while also ignoring the
contextual specificity surrounding the act of knowing and its concrete
materiality. This concrete materiality of our lives that so fascinated Freire
refers to the lived experiences of the learner, experiences that are bodied
forth, that are enfleshed, where learning occurs not solely in the "mind"
but in the bone and sinew of everyday joy and hardship, in everyday spaces
of strife and struggle in the home, the school, and the streets of the favelas,
in the transformative praxis of everyday life. Here, achieving critical consciousness is not a necessary precondition for self and social transformation (i.e., you need not read the great philosophers before you are ready
to undertake political action) but rather an outcome of acting in and on
the world critically, with an important prerequisite to this praxis being a
love for the world and humanity (in this sense ethics, for Freire, precedes
epistemology). Freire helped me to understand the importance of acting in
and on the world out of a love for the world and reflecting on our actions
in an attempt to produce a deeper, more critical change in our society. His
approach has recently been compared to the "non-methodical method"

of the French pedagogue Joseph Jacotot (1770–1840), creator of universal teaching or panecastic philosophy, made famous by Jacques Rancière and his important stress on aesthetics. However, some critics of Freire view his concept of praxis as too reliant on an assumption of society as dehumanized and people dichotomized as oppressor and oppressed, but I don't agree with this assessment of his work.

GY: I would like to return to liberation theology. When I think about Paulo Freire's liberationist sensibilities, I think of liberation theology. What would you say are some of the shared conceptual and praxis-oriented similarities between his work and the emphasis upon Christology as a process of kenosis (or emptying) and radical forms of metanoia (or a transformative change of mind/heart)?

PM: A high regard for self-correction and kenosis in Freire's pedagogy appear to be implicit in his work but Freire did not detail his theological conceptions of Christ. His impact on liberation theology went in different directions which were more in keeping with social science. This made Freire's *Pedagogy of the Oppressed* the third most cited work in the world in the field of social sciences and the first in the world in education, prompting Freire to become both a target and a prophet in his own country. Freire was clearly anticlerical—who wouldn't be growing up in the face of the dogmatism and frequent hypocrisy practiced by the Church—and was opposed to the formalism and imposed neutrality of the Church, which allowed the Church to appear to be serving the oppressed while actually supporting the power elite. Accepting Church dogma uncritically was not unlike a banking approach to educating one's faith—but when you emphasize proper doctrine over praxis, you are, in effect, emptying conscientization of its dialectical content and affirming what is essentially a static, necrophilic (death-loving) consciousness, rather than creating a biophilic (life-loving) consciousness. It is the former which de facto constitutes "an uncritical adherence to the ruling class."

Freire is known for famously calling for a type of class suicide in which the bourgeoisie willingly take on a new apprenticeship of dying to their own class interests. He likened this to experiencing one's own Easter moment through a willing transcendence of the heart and mind. But this was not an endorsement of mysticism or other-worldliness—it was political to the core. Freire was uncompromising in his view that dominant class interests must be replaced by the interests of the suffering poor if Christians are to experience their "death" as an oppressed class and to be born again to liberation. Otherwise, Catholics will be ensepulchered within a Church "which forbids itself the Easter which it preaches." This sentiment is reflected in Freire's famous words:

> "I cannot permit myself to be a mere spectator. On the contrary, I must demand my place in the process of change. So, the dramatic tension between the past and the future, death and life, being and non-being, is no longer a kind of dead-end for me; I can see it for what it really is: a permanent challenge to which I must respond. And my response can be none other than my historical praxis—in other words, revolutionary praxis."

Peruvian priest, Gustavo Gutierrez, considered one of the founders of liberation theology, invited Freire to work on some components related to liberation theology and Freire began to analyze the distinct differences among what he called the traditional church, the modern church, and the prophetic church and strongly advocated the creation of a prophetic church—no wonder Cornel West was such an admirer of Freire! As a proponent of the prophetic church, Freire made considerable contributions to liberation theology, a movement that continues to this day and whose proponents risk their lives for the sake of the well-being of the poor, the exploited, and those who are the targets of brutal military regimes and government repression. True to his principles, Freire refused to exhort others to follow a path of political activism that he, himself, was unwilling to follow. Freire understood only too well that the Catholic Church was neither working for the social and spiritual liberation of oppressed peoples nor was it taking a critical stance toward existing socio-political structures or engaging in an ongoing process of challenging the structures of oppression on behalf of the poor and oppressed. Right-wing Catholics led the Church to be as corrupt as the governments they were purportedly trying to legitimize—and sometimes worse. Nita Freire captures the essence of the prophetic church that Freire envisioned when she describes it as the "one that 'feels' with you; one that is in solidarity with you, with all the oppressed in the world, the exploited ones, and ones that are victimized by a capitalist society."

It was in the prophetic church inspired by liberation theology where one could truly bear witness to faith, solidarity and hope being conjugated with the struggle and risk-taking that is necessary for creating a better world. Personally, George, I have found God on the picket line more times than I have visiting cathedrals. Nita sent me a few years ago a photo of her private audience with Pope Francis whom I understood read *Pedagogy of the Op-*

pressed during a time of banishment when some of his fellow Jesuits accused him of not doing enough to challenge the brutality of the Argentine state during the dirty war. While I would not consider Francis to embrace whole cloth the path proposed by liberation theology, he is certainly sympathetic to it and is an admirer of Freire. Just look at how he has incurred the wrath of many conservative Catholics. In the final analysis, the prophetic church is any place where people gather to believe in God, struggle to emancipate the poor, and strive for social change—so it doesn't have to be Christian specifically. Liberation theology is ecumenical and works throughout and across many faith-based religious traditions. That in itself is profoundly Freirean.

GY: The connections that you make here, Peter, are deeply insightful. Speaking of uncritical conservatism, in our contemporary moment, critical race theory is under attack by mostly conservative white people, especially various politicians. There is the deeply problematic assumption that critical race theory is *against* white people, which, as we know, it isn't. Critical race theory is aimed at generating critical analyses that critique and attempt to dismantle white supremacy. Critical race theory calls attention to the ways in which white racism has been and continues to be embedded within American institutional life and within the habits (conscious and unconscious) of those who support anti-Black racism. My sense is that attacks against critical race theory are fueled, in part, by those who are invested in the status quo, which entails the maintenance of a revisionist understanding of America's investment in white supremacy and what that investment meant and continues to mean for Black, Indigenous, and People of Color (BIPOC). Were Paulo Freire alive today, what form would his response take in response to the attempt to silence the critical insights of critical race theory?

PM: Decades ago, as a much more orthodox Marxist than I am today, I recall both my admiration for critical race theory but also my criticism of it on some theoretical grounds—mostly for not paying sufficient attention to the strategic centrality of class in our revolutionary struggle. However, Freirean dialogues with Marxist humanists over the years have convinced me that I was misguided in that assessment, especially as I have come to appreciate the magisterial work of Frantz Fanon.

Critical scholars both in today's fascist United States and Brazil—I don't believe the term "fascist" is too strong—have vociferously denounced the legacies of settler colonial societies that from their inception to the present day have been stained by acts of genocidal slavery, democide, ecocide and epistemicide, the historical memories of which too often remain buried in the crevices of history. Freire's work has been at the forefront in bringing many of these acts to light and I am confident that Freire would support critical race theory, even though his work did not sufficiently address the concept of race, gender, or sexuality. There are, to be sure, George, clear similarities between contemporary attacks on Freire in Brazil, the virulent backlash against critical race theory, and the attacks against Nikole Hannah-Jones's *New York Times* 1619 Project, which is a major critique of the centrality of racism and slavery in U.S. history. As a result, state legislators across the country are working hard to pass laws which would gravely circumscribe the ways in which slavery and racism are taught in the United States, effectively prohibiting insights gleaned from critical race theory.

Both Trump and Jair Bolsonaro (Brazil's current president) continue to wage a war on truth, using a cruel, calculated, artificial logic that has ushered in an era of post-truth politics under the slogan of "fake news." Freire reveals to us that what is true is not so much syntactical as it is pedagogical because education is about forming minds and cultivating counterhegemonic actions and for that you don't need blueprints but at the very least you require premises that are warranted. What Freire offers us is both an educated reason, and a general theory of education, a reason tempered by the realities and struggles of his own life: his imprisonment, his work in Guinea Bissau, his work in support of Latin American guerrilla movements, and his work with teachers throughout Latin America and the United States with whom he developed a deep solidarity. What the murder of George Floyd, the rise of the Black Lives Matter movement and the global pandemic has brought to the fore in the public arena is a recognition of the obscene disparities between the rich and poor, between White folks and Black, Indigenous, and People of Color, between immigrants and the so-called "real" Americans—and the pain and suffering that has ensued over the centuries among these groups. Such issues are, at most, tepidly acknowledged during times of national crisis yet tend to recede back into that dark ether of willful forgetfulness, of historical amnesia, once a crisis has seemingly passed. What critical race theory teaches us is that the legacy of racism and slavery must be examined and reexamined by each generation if democracy and the struggle for freedom is to survive, in order to avoid those "circumstances and relationships that made it possible for a grotesque mediocrity to play a hero's part" (if I may borrow some words from Marx used to describe the class struggle in France). While we would be hard pressed to expect a full-throated denunciation of the violence that the United States has unleashed into history through the unholy exercise of its sacred claim to be the defender of liberty and the protector of freedom by those ardent proponents of American exceptionalism, we should in no way stand silent while the Trumpists are destroying what remains of American democracy in their campaign against evidence-based truth and in their attempts to sacralize the Big Lie that the 2020 election was stolen from Trump, and to erase the history of slavery by using the law to prevent dialogue around these issues in classrooms. The American academy has been successful in working out ways to quarantine Freire's work away from social revolution grounded in a philosophy of praxis but that is what we need—a social revolution in our pedagogy that will bring us closer to creating true freedom and justice.

Just when we need Freire the most, attempts are being made now to rebury him along with critical race theory, to shut down all attempts to produce a critical citizenry, to make it a crime to teach the history of slavery or to provide a language of analysis designed to uncover historical events unflattering to the so-called American patriot movement. These are veiled attempts at denigrating pluralism, at promoting white supremacy and fear of immigrants, and advocating for the creation of a white Christian ethnostate. My early visits to Brazil, to São Paulo, Bahia, Porto Alegre, Santa Maria, Rio de Janeiro, Santos, Uberlandia, Santa Cruz do Sul, Cachoeira, and other places, provided me with the opportunity to glimpse a profound intersection of politics, culture and consciousness-raising among people who were struggling for social justice in ways that Freire clearly understood. I learned from Afro-Brazilian members of the Workers Party—great admirers of Freire's work—about the horrors experienced by the four million slaves forcibly taken from West Africa to Brazil by Portuguese colonizers, beginning in 1538 and continuing until its abolition in 1888. It was necessary to come to the realization that the scourge of racism was not an unintended or unanticipated outgrowth of capitalism, but that capitalism was racialized from the very beginning by virtue of already established systems of racial classification. In many ways we need to think of capitalism as "racial capitalism" in the sense that racism didn't emerge from capitalism in some linear progression but was co-constitutive with the development of capitalism. Racism is not a by-product of capitalism; it should not be considered epiphenomenal to capitalism. Admittedly, Freire understood the workings of capitalism far better than the practice of racism. Today he would have appreciated competing conceptions of the history of racism and used those to deepen his understanding. Furthermore, I was privileged to discuss the plague of racism and capitalism and many related issues with Freire at his home in São Paulo. Ultimately, Freire recognized that history does not make history, people make history. Freire's humanism is exceptionally relevant to the future that we face. The Trumpists are calling for patriotic education in the spirit of American exceptionalism, as if the country emerged onto the world stage as some ahistorical grand narrative, when, in fact, United States militarism has in too many instances left a saber slash across the cheekbones of history.

The attacks on critical race theory invites an aerosol patriotism born from a studied forgetfulness, a motivated amnesia surrounding the history and origins of the country. It is the type of poltroonish patriotism that could easily be imagined emerging from a Fox News coffee klatch. It's an aletho-phobia tinctured by white supremacy and a refusal to reckon with the coun-try's past crimes against African slaves, indigenous peoples, and non-white immigrants. The mandates surrounding this type of patriotic education enshrines its teaching in a frozen orthodoxy, a dark alchemy, where learn-ers are ensepulchered in an intellectual mausolacracy ruled by dead white men and filled with scripted memories of things long past, such as truth, democracy, courage, commitment, and justice. Furthermore, it's primed and fitted with an uncanny obligation to pay fealty to political expediency, shopworn dogma, and Trump's low rent casuistry. It's a throwback to those cherished "great again" days of Jesse Helms and George Wallace and Jerry Falwell Sr. It brings back for me images of Lee Atwater playing his blues harp while planning more Southern Strategy political maneuvers, and Karl "MC" Rove dancing to a rap song. Speaking of Falwell, it's hard to forget his fulminations against integration and the Civil Rights Movement from the refurbished bottling plant in Lynchburg, Virginia, that became the infa-mous Thomas Road Baptist Church where Falwell distributed propaganda pamphlets created by the FBI to discredit Martin Luther King. Is this the America to which we wish to return? What does Liberty University think about that?

While Freire worked as the municipal secretary of education in São Paulo at the end of the 1980s, his work was never officially integrated into Brazil's educational system. But because Freire's work is considered by his critics to be synonymous with the Workers Party, his writings have come under the same kinds of ideological attacks in Brazil as those marshalled against critical race theorists in the United States—vigorous and ugly con-demnations. That Freire was designated the official patron of Brazilian edu-cation in 2012, during the reign of the center-left Workers Party, has been a bone of contention with the right-wing in Brazil, including conservative members of the Catholic Church. Members of Bolsonaro's party, Partido Social Liberal, lump Freire into the same "social constructivist" category as Jean Piaget and Lev Vygotsky whose works they claim have socially engineered a "cultural Marxist" takeover of Brazilian education. Conservative Catholics in Brazil continue to decry Freire's pedagogy for undermining the traditional authority of the teacher in Catholic education. Of course, criticism of Freire is also part of the trend (all too familiar to American teachers, especially during the tenure of Betsy de Vos as Secretary of Education) of reducing the role of the state in education and replacing public education with private or religious schools. Brazil's authoritarian leader, Jair Bolsonaro, who has famously discriminated against women, Black people, LGBT people, Native people and quilombolas (an ancient community of escaped slaves) and immigrants and who has persecuted leftist unions and social movements, proposed that Saint Joseph of Anchieta, a Spanish-born missionary of the 16th century, replace Paulo Freire as Brazil's official patron of education. He has described Freire's work as "Marxist rubbish," and proposed to "enter the Education Ministry with a flamethrower to remove Paulo Freire."

Freire's humanist philosophy was, for Bolsonaro, one that must be driven back. However, the Jesuit rector and vice rector of the National Sanctuary of Saint Joseph of Anchieta in Brazil's southeastern state of Espirito Santo opposed this idea on the grounds that Joseph of Anchieta was being politically manipulated by the Partido Social Liberal and they made clear that they supported both Freire and Joseph of Anchieta who chose to fight on the side of marginalized and oppressed peoples. I admire the courage and integrity of these two Jesuits for clearly incurring the wrath of Brazil's president. We need people to stand up and defend critical race theory with similar verve and courage here in the United States.

GY: Paulo Freire stressed the absolute importance of dialogue. He writes, "Dialogue cannot exist, however, in the absence of a profound love for the world and for the people. The naming of the world, which is an act of creation and re-creation, is not possible if it is not infused with love." For Freire, dialogue is integral to who we are existentially, what it means for us to be alive, and to exist as human beings. In fact, domination, for him, is what he sees as pathological and anti-dialogical. We are amidst a climate catastrophe. The earth is suffering. We have proven to be unethical and derelict in our global stewardship vis-à-vis the earth. Ours has been a teleology of absolute domination over the earth regardless of its impact on conditions that must be in place for us to flourish as a species as well as other species. In short, the earth has not been treated as a dialogic partner; we assume that the earth is an "object" to be infinitely drained of its resources, and it is being done so through capitalist greed. Were Freire alive today, what would he say about our violence against the earth, and what might he suggest as a way of moving forward?

PM: I believe Freire was deeply concerned about our violence against the earth, as you so eloquently put it, the "teleology of absolute domination over the earth." He literally wandered around the globe, describing himself in his signature humility as follows, "I am a vagabond of the obvious, because I walk around the world saying obvious things, such as education is not neutral." Freire, who traveled through numerous countries on his fifteen year exile from Brazil, was a wanderer, but he also walked the world "asking questions" rather than "giving solutions." He reminds me of the famous Zapatista saying, "*andar preguntandos*" (walking we ask questions—a horizontal or participatory position that invites dialogue) as opposed to "*andar predicando*" (walking we go preaching—a "follow me"–oriented position). In other words, Freire rejected being part of a vanguard or high priesthood that possessed the answers to revolutionary change. Wandering into hinterlands unexplored—both intellectual and physical—not only provides opportunities to err, but locates making mistakes in a realm of the pedagogical encounter that provides for the possibility of growth—for recognizing human finitude and our unfinishedness, for transcendence and emancipation.

As my friend Richard Kahn notes, the struggle for eco-justice is multifaceted and some figures in the field of ecopedagogy influenced by Freire's work have noted that this did not mean that all of Freire's positions on this issue were unproblematic or insufficiently developed. That is clearly the case. But just as clearly, Freire's commitment to the global poor would have, I believe, seen him addressing the issue of climate change, ecocide, and settler colonial epistemicide in a more sophisticated way—a dialogue between social justice and eco-justice would certainly have emerged in Freire's work. Freire wandered the world and witnessed with great anguish and empathy people starving and suffering disproportionately according to geopolitical alliances involving the so-called First and Third Worlds; he witnessed the human tragedy brought about by resource degradation, capitalist expansion, hyper-industrialization, fossil fuel extraction, global warming, and global ecocide. Freire recoiled from the policy issues put out by countries such as the United States regarding geoeconomics and more importantly still, he identified and resisted the logic of domination that led to advanced capitalist countries exploiting the lands and peoples of the Third World. Most certainly he would have engaged these issues had he lived longer.

The Freirean legacy of critical pedagogy and its affinity to the more recent development of ecopedagogy would have been important to Freire given his willingness to walk with those who toil and suffer and to understand why such suffering takes the forms that it does. Certainly, there were valid shortcomings to Freire's work which were considered by some critics to be too "human centered" and too "productivist" since the vocation of Freire's work is to become more fully "human," to be a Subject who acts "upon" and transforms the world. But I am confident that his work would have increasingly addressed the area of climate catastrophe given his emphasis on dialogue, and he would have increasingly taken criticisms of his work into consideration and his contributions to ecopedagogy would have deepened and expanded significantly over the years, aligning itself more closely to a counterhegemonic globalization from below. I believe he would have addressed some of the considerable tensions within the eco-socialist communities and made important contributions in dialogues with eco-socialists, Red-Greens, Green anarchists and those who work within a deep ecology politics, Communalism and social ecology.

But Freire was largely concerned with developing a politics of liberation through multiple forms of literacy—he was a philosopher of praxis who was in demand mostly by teachers and teacher educators. Yet he was also interested in regional development and agrarian reform. Cultural theorist bell hooks notes that one important reason that Paulo's book, *Pedagogy in Process: The Letters to Guinea-Bissau*, "has been important for my work is that it is a crucial example of how a privileged critical thinker approaches sharing knowledge and resources with those who are in need." He traveled constantly after his exile, from a brief stay in Bolivia, a five-year stay in Chile where he became involved in the Christian Democratic Agrarian Reform Movement and worked as a UNESCO consultant with the Research and Training Institute for Agrarian Reform; a visiting appointment in 1969 to Harvard University's Center for Studies in Development and Social Change; a move to Geneva, Switzerland, in 1970 as consultant to the Office of Education of the World Council of Churches, where he developed literacy programs for Tanzania and Guinea-Bissau that focused on the re-Africanization of their countries; the development of literacy programs in postrevolutionary former Portuguese colonies such as Guinea-Bissau and Mozambique; assisting the government of Peru and Nicaragua with their literacy campaigns; the establishment of the Institute of Cultural Action in Geneva in 1971; a brief return to Chile after Salvador Allende was assassinated in 1973, provoking General Pinochet to declare Freire a subversive; and his brief visit to Brazil under a political amnesty in 1979 and his final return to Brazil in 1980 to teach at the *Pontificia Universidade Catolica de Sao Paulo* and the *Universidade de Campinas* in São Paulo. From 1980–1986, he became the supervisor of the adult literacy project for the Workers' Party in Sao Paulo. Freire worked briefly as Secretary of Education of São Paulo, from 1989 to 1992, continuing his radical agenda of literacy reform for the people of that city. Given his curiosity and his voracious capacity for addressing multiple forms of domination, I find it impossible to consider that he wouldn't engage with questions of settler colonialism, indigeneity, ecopedagogy, and many other issues involving our planetary crisis. We often expect too much from great historical figures during their lifetimes—that is only to be expected.

GY: There are times when I wonder to what extent, as a successful academic/ scholar, I have become seduced by the structures of that success. After all, we don't commit "academic suicide," where we relinquish our authority as defined within academic institutions. Our livelihood is, for the most part, satisfying. By the way, this is not to sidestep all those adjunct professors who earn significantly less money and lack the security that comes with tenure track positions. What I have in mind is where Freire argues, "One of the methods of manipulation is to inoculate individuals with the bourgeois appetite for personal success." How does one do the work that needs to be done in the name of justice and yet avoid "the bourgeois appetite for personal success"? After all, even if one doesn't have that appetite, personal success is entangled with structures that perpetuate injustice.

PM: That is an important issue, George, to be sure, and one to which I have given some serious thought. I can best speak to how I wrestled with this dilemma in my own personal journey, since for many years I was bitten by the capitalist beast of trying to achieve personal success—working in the academy, doing critical work, and enjoying the "good life." As we both are fully aware, George, universities overwhelmingly gear professors toward competition at the expense of cooperation and collaboration. There is significant—I would also say relentless—pressure on university intellectuals for receiving personal accolades for work published in the "high prestige" journals which, of course, give your work more legitimacy. I once knew a professor who gained tenure for publishing one article in the *Harvard Journal of Education*. My first contract as a professor in 1984 was not renewed because students were divided by my pedagogy and there were large marches on campus in favor of my teaching and those who felt I was being "too political" and fortunately for me, I was invited to the United States by Henry Giroux, with whom I had the great opportunity to work with for 8 years, building up a center for cultural studies. Clearly, we were not liked by the "old guard"—some of whom refused to even talk with us. With success and recognition comes risking the reproach by others who feel their work is superior, or more patriotic, or more supportive of the status quo, but have not been able to break out into the limelight. Not long ago I asked someone from a university accreditation organization to what extent they regard publications by faculty in their accreditation process. The answer was that they only count articles in the most prestigious journals. Personally, I find these journals relatively useless for doing critical, social justice research and no longer send them my work. But, of course, I can afford to do that now. I found navigating university life to be challenging.

At numerous faculty meetings I heard one Dean say that what he wanted to hire was both "mules" who would take over the burden of teaching classes—and "stars"—who were preferred, of course, over the mules. Stars were difficult to hire because this meant that many professors who were not stars needed to ratchet up their publishing game and many professors would not vote for the "star" candidates since they didn't want to work with younger scholars who had already published more than they had. At one of my first universities, there was a lot of resentment toward me because professors felt that my publishing output meant more pressure on them to publish. Once, I had a Dean who suggested to me privately upon my arrival to the university—this sounds weird, but I assure you it happened—that I was now in Los Angeles and because we had a lot of famous donors from the entertainment industry that he could recommend a plastic surgeon whenever I felt I needed some knicks and tucks to enhance my image. It wasn't a joke.

But at the outset of my work, I understood my socialist politics were far too radical to be embraced by American Universities and that I would always function as an outsider. There is such a thing as wanting to succeed as an outsider. I started traveling internationally in 1987 after Freire invited me to speak at a psychology conference in Cuba, and during that conference educational scholars/activists from Brazil and Mexico prepared gifts for me—copies of some of my works typed out in Spanish and decorated with revolutionary symbols, and souvenirs from their countries they had prepared for me in advance of the conference. I was quite stunned to think that they were familiar with my work, just as I was surprised that Freire was familiar with my work so early in my political project (I prefer the term "political project" to the term "career"). To be honest, I didn't feel my work deserved this attention but in time in might. That sentiment didn't last long. During the years 2005 and 2006, I was invited to give talks throughout Venezuela supporting the Bolivarian Revolution (always with a translator since my

Spanish was—and remains—very weak). President Hugo Chávez came to meet me in Miraflores Palace and thanked me for bringing a Freirean approach to educators in Venezuela but, in true Freirean fashion reminded me, and rightly so, that any critical pedagogy to emerge from Venezuela could not be transplanted from the outside (a Freirean insight as well) but would come from the Venezuelan people.

I was invited to appear on his television show, *Alo Presidente*, where I sat alongside another guest, the famous Nicaraguan priest and poet, Ernesto Cardinal. Subsequently I was invited to Argentina where my work was gaining attention and had conferences with the children of those who had been tortured and murdered during the dirty war. I was invited to Lapland and eventually throughout Finland where it was a similar story, and this was relatively early in my work as a professor. In Mexico, *Instituto McLaren* (which began in Tijuana but now resides in Ensenada) was begun by one of Mexico's communist parties. This early success as an outsider, can—and most often does—inflate the sense of your own worth and I remember my demeanor must have at times been insufferable to many people. There is just as much rivalry among leftist intellectuals and activists—easily as much—as on the right. An unhealthy appetite for personal success—regardless of your political affiliations—tends to encourage you to be less self-reflective about your own work, and more preoccupied with how you are viewed in the very fractious, status-driven arena of universities—places that are decidedly not driven by the cause of liberation.

Success is more predicated on acquiring grant money that filters throughout the university. To make matters worse, those of us on the left are expected to be less preoccupied with bourgeois success, and it brings about feelings of guilt. So here I was living on the Sunset Strip with movie stars as neighbors, hanging out in all the nearby clubs, rubbing shoulders with rock stars and people in the neighborhood knew me as "the Hollywood Marxist." I was even asked by a movie producer to help draft a script on Che Guevara. When I asked about the focus of the film, he replied, "Che's sex appeal." During that time, I was a professor at UCLA and a small group with Republican financial backers created a list of 30 professors which they labelled "The Dirty Thirty" and put me at the top of the list, while offering to pay students 100 dollars to secretly audiotape our lectures and fifty dollars to provide notes from our classes. This received a lot of international media attention and was denounced by newspapers and magazines in dozens of countries as the return of McCarthyism in the U.S. Such attention—even in the form of attacks—focuses you away from the original reason you joined the academy—to create ideas and analyses and innovative means of participation for the purpose of creating a better, more just world. You begin to enjoy listening to yourself speak, rather than paying attention to those seeking your assistance.

So yes, Freire was able to understand this, and speak against this form of bourgeois academic seduction. Recently one of my favorite colleagues, and a committed Freirean, now retired, received a note from a former student who is now an Assistant Professor and who has embraced an ethic of "who needs it the most" for first authorship of multiple-authored papers. Now that's especially admirable for an Assistant Professor seeking tenure, who maintained that this principle was adopted from an engagement with Freire's work that ran through all my colleague's classes. This may seem a fairly minor example, but it is profoundly Freirean and brushes against the grain of many researchers who fight their colleagues for first authorship. I found that the more I worked with and remained in solidarity with social movements outside of the academy, the more I was able to get back my original focus—although being beaten up by the Turkish military does have its price. Freire's humility and generosity of spirit were legendary. He embodied a form of what he called "armed love"—a radical love for others, even for the oppressor, a love that inspired him to risk oneself—his reputation, and even his life—for others. Now I am not making a case for martyrdom by any means. Armed love for Freire is a resistance that is both philosophical and affective—I frequently use the word enfleshed. It has a dialectical quality. Marx warned us in the famous eleventh thesis on Feuerbach: "Philosophers have hitherto only interpreted the world in various ways; the point is to change it." Philosophical problems arise out of our real-world struggles, and no one understood this better than Paulo Freire.

GY: This is my last question and seems apropos. This year marks the 100th anniversary of Freire's birth? What core truth of his would you like for us to nurture as we celebrate?

PM: Earlier you identified the fundamental importance of dialogue in Freire's work. Dialogue for Freire is not a conversation in the sense of several interlocutors exchanging ideas, despite how interesting those ideas may be, or searching for meaning through debate and discussion over hot tea but is a dialectical encounter carried out in the realm of praxis and that is what makes dialogue for Freire predominately social and political, and distinguishes his concept of dialogue from many other philosophers who use the term. The idea of dialogue in Freire's work is filled with a multitude of expansive and embracing assertions—that, for example, people who lack humility cannot enter into dialogue, dialogue requires faith in people, only dialogue can create critical thinking, dialogue requires love for people. Freire's life as a metaphysical wayfarer, scholar, political activist, public intellectual and advocate for poor and suffering peoples was guided by a search for justice that could only be realized through such an expansive and inclusive formation of dialogue. Such an authentic form of dialogue for Freire stipulates engaging both politically and pedagogically the internal contradictions that plagued society. A refusal to enter this type of dialogue has allowed the United States to be transformed, in part, into an anti-Kingdom governed by violence and oppression, and to willfully stand against people of color, against immigrants seeking a better life, against migrant workers, against refugees, against evidence-based truth and the struggle for justice. Dialogue, as Freire employs the term, lays bare the ideological and ethical potentialities for the transformation of society so necessary today as countries are increasingly embracing fascism over democracy, and the racial state. Dialogue requires treating theory as a form of practice and practice as a form of theory as we contest the psychopathology of everyday life incarnate in racism, sexism, misogyny, and capitalism's social division of labor. It is a fundamental approach to rebuilding the world on an axis of social justice.

That Freirean educators are currently under the vicious scrutiny of fast-developing repressive political forces averse to the very concept of dialogue, especially during a time when we should be celebrating 100 years since Freire's birth, should worry us all.

Part Four

CHALLENGING WHITE
FOUNDATIONS

12

THE TULSA RACE MASSACRE WENT WAY BEYOND "BLACK WALL STREET"

INTERVIEW WITH ROBIN D. G. KELLEY

There is so much grieving that Black people have yet to do. The grammar of our suffering from anti-Black racism has yet to be fully created.

As we currently deal with the pervasiveness of Black suffering, mourning and grief related to anti-Black racism, there has been a great deal of media coverage acknowledging that this year marks 100 years since the Tulsa Race Massacre, where roughly 300 people—predominantly Black people—were killed; Black churches, schools and businesses were burned to the ground, and the homes of Black people were looted. Yet, it is still not clear to me that white America is ready to acknowledge how Black people have suffered and continue to suffer under systemic white racism.

In this moment of collective remembrance of the Tulsa Race Massacre, I asked the brilliant scholar Robin D. G. Kelley to provide his reflections. Kelley offers a deep analysis that provides a counternarrative (a powerful X-ray) of the massacre that allows us to see deep issues embedded within racial capitalism that impacted poor working-class Black people and sustained Indigenous suffering.

In our discussion, we move from the importance of critical race theory as a framework for critiquing liberalism and the founding myths of the U.S., to questions of differential Black suffering, to a liberated planet. Kelley, who is the Gary B. Nash Endowed Chair of U.S. History at the University

G. Yancy (with Robin D. G. Kelley), "Robin D.G. Kelley: The Tulsa Race Massacre Went Way Beyond 'Black Wall Street.,'" in *Truthout*, June 1, 2021. [Editors: Alana Yu-lan Price and Britney Schultz]

of California Los Angeles (UCLA) and contributing editor for the *Boston Review*, provides us with complex realities that are braided and require our collective efforts without losing sight of our specific oppressions with their accompanying lived experiences. Kelley is the author of several books, including *Freedom Dreams: The Black Radical Imagination; Hammer and Hoe: Alabama Communists During the Great Depression*; and the forthcoming *Black Bodies Swinging: An American Postmortem* (Metropolitan Books).

GEORGE YANCY: According to accounts of the Tulsa Race Massacre, airplanes were used to drop firebombs on the Greenwood District in Tulsa, Oklahoma, which was known as Black Wall Street. When I think about this, the ironies abound. They say, "Black people are lazy." Yet, Black people in the Greenwood District in Tulsa were known for their affluence, economic power and self-reliant diligence. And they say, "Black people are capricious, they loot, they destroy property." Over 1,000 Black homes were burned to the ground through acts of white terrorism in Tulsa. The overlap of events at this moment is so crucial. How do you understand the current discussions of the massacre in various public spheres (including in left-wing media and mainstream media but also in conservative media) and what this says about the current political moment in relation to contestations over the existence of white supremacy, systemic racism and the struggle for racial justice?

ROBIN D. G. KELLEY: George, it is always an honor to be in conversation with you. Your questions are always incisive; they cut to the core of the issue.

Certainly, the Tulsa race massacre can possibly be one avenue for the country to "acknowledge" historic and ongoing Black suffering through some kind of truth, reconciliation and reparations process. I'm skeptical for several reasons. For one thing, we keep repeating the mantra that this story is unknown. Although it was front page news in 1921, and although a resident/survivor Mary E. Jones Parrish self-published an eyewitness account in 1923, and although Black residents filed 193 unsuccessful lawsuits against the city and various insurance companies for just compensation, we still talk as if this is all new and shocking knowledge. The Oklahoma Commission to Study the Tulsa Race Riot of 1921 (now called the 1921 Tulsa Race Riot Centennial Commission) was created 24 years ago. The indefatigable historian, Eddie Faye Gates, spent years collecting oral histories of survivors.

60 Minutes ran a devastating segment on the massacre in 1999, and I swear, every year since, journalists (print and broadcast) have announced the discovery of this terrible history and found some Black person to interview who has never heard of it. Meanwhile, literally dozens of books have appeared on the Tulsa race massacre, going back at least to the 1970s when Lee E. Williams and Lee E. Williams II published *Anatomy of Four Race Riots* (1972) and a white history professor, Rudia Halliburton Jr., published a short book aptly titled, *The Tulsa Race War of 1921* (1975). Then in 1982, Scott Ellsworth released *Death in a Promised Land: The Tulsa Race Riot of 1921*, followed by a parade of very fine books by James Hirsch, Hannibal Johnson, Tim Madigan, Alfred Brophy, and so on. . . .

The point, of course, is that for at least 40 years, there was no shortage of public information. Even before these texts appeared, it is not hard to find mention or detailed yet flawed accounts of the Tulsa massacre in the pages of leading Black scholarly journals—*Journal of Negro History, Phylon, Journal of Negro Education*, etc. (Rudia Halliburton's book began as an essay in *The Journal of Black Studies* published in 1972). Besides stacks of books—scholarly, popular, photographic, fiction and young adult—there have been plays written about it as well as several documentary films, some bearing titles, such as *Tulsa's Secret; Terror in Tulsa: History Uncovered; The Tulsa Lynching of 1921: A Hidden Story;* all before *Watchmen* and Stanley Nelson and Marco Williams's brand new and powerful film, *Tulsa Burning*.

The fact is, the Tulsa race massacre is the most thoroughly studied and discussed incident of all of the 20th-century racial pogroms, with the possible exception of the East St. Louis massacre of 1917. I've been in the business of teaching Black history for over three decades, and every colleague I know includes Tulsa in their general survey courses. So why do we continually repeat the assertion that this history is completely unknown, a secret, or so shameful no one wants to talk about it? Because the issue *has never been about not knowing*; it is about a refusal to acknowledge genocidal, state-sanctioned racist violence in the United States, a refusal to recognize the existence of fascism in this country. This is not to say the violence is simply denied by the status quo. No, rather it is disavowed by the white propertied and political classes and displaced onto "ignorant" white racist workers. This narrative obscures how the violence, fomented and promoted by the press and business interests, became a pretext to take the land—an attempted land grab that continued for decades after 1921.

But there is more. I find the whole class politics around the way we continue to frame the story of Tulsa is not only disturbing, but it actually serves to distort and erase the exploitation and oppression of the majority of Black people. And by "we," I also mean Black folks. Let me explain.

This is what we know: two days of racist violence left an estimated 300 people dead, hundreds more injured, and more than 1,200 Black-owned dwellings destroyed, along with businesses, a school, a hospital, a public library and a dozen Black churches. Before buildings were torched and planes were used to drop turpentine bombs which functioned as incendiary devices, white men and women looted Black homes and businesses, taking money, pianos, victrolas, jewelry and clothing, lamps, furniture, etc.

But in telling the story, we focus solely on "Black Wall Street," which made up just a few blocks of the 35–40 square blocks of Greenwood the mobs destroyed. All we really hear about are doctors and lawyers and entrepreneurs, Black-owned theaters and the luxurious Stradford Hotel, when, in fact, *the vast majority of Black Tulsans beaten, killed and displaced were working people.* Contrary to the myth of universal prosperity, most Black Tulsans were not getting rich. Most Black men were laborers—more than one-third employed as porters, janitors, gardeners, chauffeurs, etc.—and 93 percent of employed Black women cleaned, cooked and cared for children in white households. Not everyone rendered homeless owned their homes—many were, in fact, renters or boarders living in private homes. And many Black working-class families did manage to purchase property and construct ramshackle houses out of leftover wood from old barns or packing crates. No matter what you might have seen on *Watchmen*, in 1921, only six blocks of all of Greenwood were paved, and most Black working-class houses had outhouses, no underground sewage lines.

But in the discourse surrounding the massacre, it seems like the fate of those few blocks in and around "Black Wall Street" is all that matters. Again, Mary E. Jones Parrish set the stage by only including testimonies from Black elites and by including an illuminating appendix of a partial list of property losses that lays bare the class divide in Greenwood. First, the list only includes about 270 Black-owned homes out of a population of about 10,000. Second, only 19 people sustained losses of $15,000 or more, four of whom lost over $50,000 (J. B. Stradford, $125,000; Lula T. Williams, $85,000; O. W. Gurley, $65,000; Jim Cherry, $50,000). To be clear, $15,000 in 1921 is worth over $223,000 in 2021 dollars—though this estimate doesn't account for all the factors that determine property values, like the racial make-up of a neighborhood. Nor am I considering real wealth since equity varied and many homes were heavily mortgaged. Black-owned businesses were concentrated on North Greenwood Street as well as adjoining streets—Frankfort Ave., Cameron, East Archer, North Elgin, Cincinnati—with more expensive homes situated along Detroit, which valued between $3,000 and $7,000. But most of the homes encircling this core area, with exceptions, are valued between $1,500 and $500—in today's dollars, between $20,000 and $6,000. And some of the wealthier Black folks owned between 10 and 20 houses each, which they rented out for additional income.

We live in such a materialist, celebrity culture that we measure our "success" by class mobility, by wealth accumulation, and then we fall victim to a tired narrative that white folks destroyed "our" communities out of jealousy over of our success. While there is truth to this, and white looting is clear evidence, the "jealousy" is cultivated, nurtured in the ideology of white supremacy, usually in the guise of patriotism and nationalism, or in the capitalist replacement theory—"N*****s are coming for your jobs!" The mob was largely made up of shock troops engaged in an attempted land grab from which they themselves would not directly benefit. The first spark for the mob wasn't real estate, but another form of property rooted in patriarchy—property in women. A Black man accused of assaulting a white woman is a more effective dog whistle than Negroes with grand pianos and bank accounts. The second spark, of course, were Negroes with guns. Here we see Black solidarity and fearlessness on full display—Black World War I veterans representing all classes within Greenwood, armed and prepared to defend one of their own, their people and their property. That act of insubordination, more than anything else, convinced white folks to fuel up their planes and build an arsenal.

If we are to be honest, it was the Black working class, the Black poor who suffered the most. They didn't have insurance and very, very few had the means to file suit or make claims (though there is a lesson here about the relative poverty of Black lawyers whose clients tended to be Black working people having to deal with a racist criminal justice system!) We celebrate the resilience of the Black elite because they were able to hold Greenwood a few decades longer, but we completely ignore the Black working class, many of whom were displaced and were never able to return. This is not an oversight, it is ideological. Again, Parrish acknowledges that the Black elite are often inclined to "feel their superiority over those less fortunate, but when a supreme test, like the Tulsa disaster comes, it serves to remind us that we are all of one race. . . . Every Negro was accorded the same treatment, regardless of his education or other advantages. A Negro was a Negro on that day and was forced to march with his hands up for blocks." And yet, she chose to underscore this point with scripture from 1 Thessalonians 5:14 "Comfort the feeble minded; support the weak."

Sadly, when the blockbuster movie comes out about the 1921 massacre, Greenwood is going to look like Wakanda: wealthy elite Negroes walking around with shopping bags.

Finally, any discussion of repair and reparations, of grieving and mourning the events of 1921 and its aftermath, must grapple with the colonial violence that made Tulsa or Oklahoma and its settler regime possible.

Last year, the U.S. Supreme Court made a significant though limited ruling that half of Oklahoma is still under Indigenous jurisdiction—which includes most of Tulsa. Of course, all of the land is stolen from Indigenous people, including the coveted land upon which Greenwood sat. Some Black people got to Oklahoma by way of the forced march of the Creeks, Choctaws, Chickasaws, Cherokees, and Seminoles from the Southeastern territories in the 1830s. Some came as slaves of wealthy tribal members, others as spouses and children—part African, part Indigenous. And many died along the way. Later, Black folks joined the exodus out of the South after the Civil War by taking advantage of the Homestead Act to acquire land and create all-Black towns—Oklahoma being a prime destination. But again, on whose land? There is much rolled up in this process—Native elites owning African slaves; Africans, slave and free, being incorporated as members of the five tribes (especially the Creeks and the Seminoles). I don't think the issue of the Tulsa Race Massacre of 1921 can ever be fully resolved or "repaired" without addressing the question of both holocausts—Indigenous dispossession and African slavery. Whatever resolution will be temporary.

I know this is a long answer, but I'm simply making a plea that we think more deeply about the events of 100 years ago and their legacy—that we bear in mind that Black working-class lives matter, that we reject capitalist solutions to address the violence of racial capitalism and settler colonialism, that we never forget how this country came to be in the first place, and that we never forget what "Wall Street" signifies.

GY: As we know, there has been an attack on teaching critical race theory, which is not somehow anti-white, and has nothing to do with teaching reverse racism. Critical race theory engages theory, history and narrative as important ways of critiquing the so-called racial neutrality of law and excavates the subtle ways in which racism is embedded within social structures and the unconscious. It critically engages how these sites function to maintain racial injustice, white hegemony and power. In fact, critical race theorists would bring attention to the anti-Black dynamics of what took place during the massacre in Tulsa. Its aim is to provide for us a critical framework for understanding the racial and racist power dynamics at play during that tragic period. Yet, even as we focus our attention on the Tulsa race massacre, John Keven Stitt, the governor of Oklahoma, recently signed a bill that prohibits teaching critical race theory in schools. This is an attack on knowledge production. It is an attack on critical inquiry, and an attack on epistemological and social justice efforts to understand the systemic operations of white supremacy, and how we might critically dismantle the perpetuation of racialized injustice. In other words, Stitt's effort is one of profound bad faith, pervasive ignorance and white nation-building. His refusal (intentionally or unintentionally) to face the systemic nature of white racism helps to whitewash the U.S.'s racist and brutal history. Unfortunately, this attempt to ban critical race theory is also occurring in other Republican-controlled states. Stitt's refusal attempts to repress the necessary counter-narratives that contest the U.S.'s racist "innocence." This raises two important issues: the attack on "The 1619 Project" published by *The New York Times*, and the current explosion of discussion over Nikole Hannah-Jones's tenure fight at the University of North Carolina. We are attacked for our successes, attacked because of other's stereotypes of us, and we are attacked for holding a disagreeable mirror up to white America's face. How do you connect the dots here, Robin?

RDGK: We have always been attacked for holding up a disagreeable mirror to white America. But mirrors are not that dangerous because they reflect back what is only on the surface—the obvious, if unspoken, truth that we live in a racist country. Conservatives don't want to hear it, but liberals, especially in the era of "Equity, Diversity, and Inclusion" can get with the mirror and even embrace it. For example, you remember after Obama was elected and Republicans were holding public readings of the Constitution but skipping over the "arcane" parts sanctioning slavery as a property right and a basis for congressional representation and taxation, liberal Democrats were on their high horse, arguing that we must acknowledge the "offensive" and "politically uncomfortable" passages of the Constitution, if only to demonstrate the greatness of the document for rising above the anachronistic values of the so-called founding fathers.

The problem, of course, is that slavery was not an aberration but foundational—not only to the American economy but to the very shape of the Republic. American *liberty* was built on slavery and dispossession because liberty was fundamentally about property rights. A mirror will not show us this, but an "X-ray" will. You see, liberals hold on to the idea that in the U.S. democracy is a creed passed down to us via these great documents— this myth, if we're to be honest, has driven the liberal wing of the civil rights movement for decades and still drives it today. This is classic Gunnar Myrdal, who still lingers like an open sore in the political unconscious of the Black elite. Myrdal's main contention is that the "Negro problem" was an unresolved moral issue for white America: The conflict is between democratic, egalitarian values of the American creed and the treatment of Black people. Racist practices, therefore, are not built into the structure (of settler colonialism, racial capitalism and patriarchy) but an aberration, a constant disruption to the structure of (or promise of) American democracy.

This kind of obfuscation is visible in the mirror, but not when we use an X-ray to look at the hidden structure of our *Herrenvolk* Republic. Critical race theory (CRT) is one of those X-rays. It exposes the structure through an "intersectional" framework of race, class and gender with the intention of interrogating how power is maintained and inequality reproduced, despite a liberal legal foundation that promises inclusion and "equality." In other words, CRT doesn't just challenge right-wing myth-making, but offers a critique of liberalism and the founding myths of the United States. So why should we be surprised that the ruling class is trying to eliminate CRT? As you well know, this is not the first time CRT has been under attack (and here we must acknowledge the fissures among CRT scholars). In that respect, it shares much in common with "The 1619 Project." While "The 1619 Project" does not share CRT's more robust critique of capitalism, it succeeded in bringing to a mainstream audience the periodization that had been *de rigueur* in U.S. Black Studies for over half a century, if not longer. By arguing that "America" begins in 1619, Nikole Hannah-Jones and her fellow contributors show that our "country" was built on a colonial economy based on racial slavery, plantation production, trans-Atlantic commodity trade, and the buying, selling, mortgaging and insuring of human beings. They overturn the founding myth that America was born out of an anti-colonial war for liberty against British tyranny. Rather than portray the so-called founding fathers as the victims of colonial domination, "The 1619 Project" exposes them as part of a long line of colonizers. Consequently, the essays give the general public greater clarity as to what 1776 was about—which was hardly a rupture from the past, but rather a struggle between fractions of the same class over who would benefit from the spoils of slavery, slave-produced commerce and Indigenous dispossession.

In short, what we are facing is an ongoing discursive war that began even before the creation of a Black press. We see it unfold constantly, the last few years with the fight over Confederate monuments. Of course, these statues were products of the long discursive war, introduced mostly during the early 20th century to signal that the South actually won the Civil War. Indeed, the heyday for the erection of Confederate statues was around the First World War and after, the era of the bloody Red Summer of 1919 and the Tulsa Race Massacre. The discursive war ramped up with Trump, who announced the creation of a 1776 Commission (whose vice-chair is the notorious Black political scientist Carol Swain) to fill the curriculum with "patriotic education," in an effort to shield the nation from Howard Zinn and critical race theorists. And yet, I see all of this as a desperate regime on the defensive. Their efforts to deny Nikole Hannah-Jones a tenure-track position is a sign of desperation. That's an easy thing to reverse. So, I'm less concerned with paranoid right-wing white nationalists than I am with (neo)liberal multiculturalists who side-step the question of power, or what Gerald Horne wryly calls "left-wing white nationalists" who downplay white supremacy and mistake a settler-colonial revolt for a democratic revolution.

GY: In a profoundly courageous and clear statement before a hearing held by a House Judiciary Subcommittee, 107-year-old Viola Fletcher, a beauti-fully dignified Black woman, who is a survivor of the 1921 Tulsa race massa-cre, recalls, "*I will never forget the violence of the white mob when we left our home. I still see Black men being shot, Black bodies lying in the street. I still smell smoke and see fire. I still see Black businesses being burned. I still hear airplanes flying overhead. I hear the* screams." She adds, "*I have lived through the massacre every day. Our country may forget this history but I cannot.*" Viola Fletcher is a living witness to white terrorism. In cultural theorist bell hooks's engaging essay, "Representations of Whiteness in the Black Imagination," hooks writes, "All black people in the United States, irrespective of their class status or politics, live with the possibility that they will be terrorized by whiteness." It is this kind of terrorization of Black people that occurred 100 years ago in Tulsa. Imagine the weight of those images of Black men being shot by whites, Black bodies lying in the streets? Try to imagine numerous George Floyds lying dead in the streets. Imagine not being able to free oneself from the smell of smoke or unsee the fire. Imagine the screams that she cannot cease from hearing. What happens when she hears the sound of a plane? She speaks so powerfully to our contemporary moment when she says, "*Our country may forget this history but I cannot.*" The cowardice attack on critical race theory and "The 1619 Project" are ways in which some (many?) in this country are trying to forget this history. As Viola Fletcher says, though, ". . . *but I cannot.*" When she says "*I cannot*," I am both encouraged and yet profoundly saddened. Encouraged, because "I cannot" suggests a refusal to forget. Saddened, because "I cannot" suggests the indelible pain of anti-Black trauma. What do we say to Black people who have to live with anti-Black racist trauma on a daily basis? I ask this question because it threatens white America's tendency to forget, to downplay anti-Black racism and its systemic structure. I also ask it because, personally, I'm sick of this shit. There are times when the idea of leaving this country feels right. There are other times when living is just too hard when you know that anti-Black racism may not have an end. We carried the weight of maintaining the democratic spirit and momentum of this country, and yet we continue to be murdered by the state, and we still cannot breathe.

RDGK: These are great and difficult questions. For me, they can be distilled into three questions: How do we deal with the trauma of anti-Black racism? What do we remember and how does that shape how we move forward? Should we continue to carry the burden of "maintaining the democratic spirit of this country"?

With regard to the first question: while in principle I can agree that all Black people live with the *possibility* of being terrorized by whiteness, the possibilities are *differential* based on class, gender, age, disability, etc. I am a university professor with a good income who lives in a neighborhood where the police constantly harass homeless and underhoused people, almost all of whom are Black men and women. Or they are constantly hitting up poor Latinx men who line up in the mornings looking for temporary work. Now, in the 1970s and '80s, as a young, poor Black person, my interactions with racist state and non-state actors (e.g., racist store owners and their employees), was a daily occurrence. But in my neighborhood now, the police generally ignore me. Besides, I can also afford to limit my interactions with police and with the public, and I have documentation to prove who I am. Does any of this make me completely safe? No. But to pretend that I don't enjoy certain privileges that make me less vulnerable than other Black and Brown folks would be dishonest.

I know this is an uncomfortable topic and I've gotten attacked by folks who believe racism is undifferentiated, and every anti-Black gesture is equally traumatic. But I deal with quite a number of middle- and upper-class Black students who are traumatized by microaggressions of varying degrees. I also teach Black and Brown students who are transfers from community college, slightly older students often detoured by a year, 18 months, or two years in prison. To say that these students are traumatized differently is not to dismiss the traumas that my more privileged students endure. But as I've written elsewhere, perhaps the best way to deal with trauma besides therapy is to engage, think and struggle collectively. And this requires building a solidarity that is not based solely on seeing the world through personal experience and "affinity," but to build political communities around/against the trauma inflicted on most of the world. Here I'm thinking of war, gender violence, imprisonment, the neoliberal terrorism of privatization, austerity and dispossession, often inflicted on the world by the U.S. As Dr. Martin Luther King Jr. put it, "The greatest purveyor of violence in the world: my own government."

To the question, *What do we remember and how does it shape how we move forward?*, I want to return to Tulsa. If we only remember the loss of property and wealth and the evisceration of a Black elite, then we only imagine a potential future in which someone like J. B. Stradford could have been the Black "Hilton," where the wealthy are wealthier, and projected "reparations" payments are calculated based on accumulated property at the time of the violence. Despite recognizing that the entire community suffered, "compensation" would be differential, mirroring the very system of racial capitalism that structured enclosure (segregation), violence, deep inequality and poverty for most, and premature death. We will also forget what might be the most impactful response by the community: mutual aid, a caring culture, and the impulse toward self-defense and protecting one another. And if our memories begin and end in 1921, we are stripped of a full accounting of the process of displacement and dispossession—which begins with the inaugural theft of Indigenous lands and still hasn't ended. The story of the massacre continues for decades, with the disinvestment of Greenwood, the construction of Interstate 244, urban renewal policies, and more recently a multimillion-dollar museum commemorating Black Wall Street which many activists see as a Trojan horse to advance the ongoing movement to gentrify the Greenwood district.

In the end, we should not have to carry the weight of maintaining the democratic spirit of this country because it is not a democracy and never has been. We live in what the late Alexander Saxton and David Roediger and others described as a *Herrenvolk* Republic. We have to exit this country and its liberal humanist conceits, but that doesn't necessarily mean to physically leave. (Besides, so long as the U.S. empire exists, there is nowhere to go!). In our *Herrenvolk* Republic, liberalism was founded on a definition of liberty that places property before human freedom (and human needs), and an exclusionary definition of the human that permits various forms of unfree labor, dispossession and subordination based on "race" and "gender." And yet, we keep speaking of the Tulsa race massacre in terms of property, property rights, property destroyed. I think we need to talk about decolonization in order to advance beyond land as property toward a vision of freedom not based on ownership or possession or anthropocentrism. The land has been enslaved and needs liberation so the Earth could flourish, so people could flourish, so the historical and contemporary structures of violence might end, opening up a radically different future. It is worth remembering that Tulsa was an oil boom town, a fact we are quick to drop uncritically as further evidence of Black success! But when I speak of exiting this country, I'm thinking about our solidarity with Indigenous movements at the forefront of struggles against fracking, pipelines, fossil fuel extraction, environmental racism, pushing back the climate catastrophe.

GY: Going forward, I see no end in sight when Black people will have their humanity fully recognized, especially when it seems that anti-Blackness is fundamentally linked to white America's social DNA, its understanding of itself, its identity. James Baldwin was right where he links "the Negro problem" with the failure of white people to truly love themselves. He was also right where he notes, "All of us know, whether or not we are able to admit it, that mirrors can only lie, that death by drowning is all that awaits one there." How might we deploy history to shatter those mirrors that lie to white people and by extension free them from *needing* us as a "problem"?

RDGK: Obviously, I agree with Baldwin when he writes "mirrors can only lie." I think this whole conversation has been an effort to shatter those mirrors that lie, not only to white folks but to our people as well. That is the more uncomfortable but much needed discussion to have. In any case, as I said in the previous response, I don't think it is a matter of convincing white folks to recognize *our* humanity. The veracity of our humanity was never the issue—then or now. The problem lies with Western civilization's very construction of the human. As Sylvia Wynter, Cedric Robinson, Frantz Fanon, Aimé Césaire, and others have been saying for decades, the "Negro" was an invention, a fiction—like that of the "Indian," the "Oriental," the "Mexican," etc. Indeed, the entire structure of global white supremacy depends on such inventions, like the fictions of the Arab as non- or anti-Western and the "Immigrant" as essentially Latinx, or that Indigenous people (in North America at least) are all dead. I take it, this is what you mean when you talked about white folks needing us as a "problem."

These fabrications are enacted through violence. Once they crumble, so goes the West's liberal humanism, the massive philosophical smokescreen that enables racial capitalism to masquerade as the engine of progress, a pure expression of freedom and liberty, the only path to human emancipation. The modern world that invented the Negro, the Oriental, the Indian and the Savage as a means of inventing a biocentric understanding of the Human (European Man) was built on the theft of humans, theft of land and water, indiscriminate murder, violation of customary rights, moral economy, enclosure of the commons, destruction of the planet—outright lawlessness. And yet, as Sylvia Wynter, Alexander Weheliye, Saidiya Hartman, and Ariella Azoulay, among others, remind us, the creators and perpetrators of this violence were also the inventors of "rights" and citizenship.

Of course, some kind of reparations is an important first step to begin to come to terms with consequences of settler violence, not just in Tulsa, but Greensboro and Wilmington, North Carolina; Brownsville; Rosewood; East St. Louis; Springfield, Illinois; every part of Mississippi; Watts; Detroit; Newark; Chicago; Sand Creek; Skeleton Cave; Fort Robinson; Wounded Knee; all along the Southwest border; Attica; Soledad; San Quentin; Manzanar; the West Bank and Gaza, and beyond. . . .

Reparations carry their own contradictions, which we can save for another conversation. Certainly, how we proceed with repair depends on how we remember. But reparations are easier than decolonization, which is the answer to the question of where do we go, how to exit. In the United States, where the structure of colonial domination is completely shrouded in liberal multiculturalism, neoliberal homilies about freedom, colorblind discourse that undergirds criminalization and white supremacy, enabling 400 years of state-sanctioned serial murder to continue with impunity, power cannot be unseated merely through violence. (Of course, the very utterance of the word impunity reveals a contradiction, in that the point of law for the colonized is not protection but containment, discipline, and in some cases, genocide.) But we have no choice if we want to save the planet and free ourselves from liberal humanism. Decolonization, however, requires the abolition of all forms of oppression and violence. It means disbanding the military/police, opening borders, opening the prisons, freeing the body from the constraints of inherited and imposed normativities of gender and sexuality. It means ending war entirely, and that means the end of America as we know it.

13

THE WHITENESS OF HARVARD AND WALL STREET IS "JIM CROW, NEW STYLE"

INTERVIEW WITH CORNEL WEST

Cornel West is a preeminent public intellectual, a brilliant philosopher-gadfly and a towering thinker whose critically engaging voice and fearless speech have proven indispensable for calling out injustice wherever it exists. He is a force grounded within a prophetic tradition that refuses idols, even if that idol is democracy itself. He is a bluesman who grapples with the funk of life through a cruciform of love within a crucible of catastrophe, where despair never has the last word.

West isn't a typical professional philosopher. As a professor at Yale in the mid-1980s, he was arrested for attempting, through protest, to get the university to withdraw its investments from all companies that were doing business in Apartheid South Africa. And he relentlessly exposes the limits of disciplinary smugness and the hypocrisy of epistemological "purity."

West is arguably the most publicly visible philosopher in contemporary America, but despite his prominence and brilliance, he was recently denied the option of being considered for tenure at Harvard,[1] where he currently teaches, and where he had previously held tenure.

In a massive outcry, students at the university have mobilized in support of West,[2] describing Harvard's refusal to consider West's bid for tenure as "an urgent matter of equity and parity" and a blatant devaluation of Black scholarship that could lead to "a mass exodus of Black scholars."

G. Yancy (with Cornel West), "Cornel West: The Whiteness of Harvard and Wall Street Is 'Jim Crow, New Style,'" in *Truthout*, March 5, 2021. [Editors: Alana Yu-lan Price and Maya Schenwar]

159

At this tense decision point, as West decides whether to stay at the institution after this level of disrespect, I asked him to share his thoughts on optimism, racism, capitalism and what it means to be a philosopher of African descent within the American empire in the 21st century.

GEORGE YANCY: I was surprised and disturbed to hear about your situation at Harvard University. It is my understanding that a faculty committee was reviewing your renewal and that committee asked that you be considered for tenure. Yet, that consideration, as I understand it, was denied. I immediately thought about forms of academic institutional fear when it comes to maintaining scholars—especially Black scholars and scholars of color—who engage critically in processes of calling academic insularity into question, calling empire into question, calling forms of institutional and systemic injustice into question. Given your conceptualization of vocation as tied to a form of calling that allows suffering to speak, I immediately thought about how certain institutions might care more for their self-image and their donors as opposed to keeping scholars who cause "good trouble," as that towering figure, the late Congressman John Lewis would say. Some may very well fear the vocational work that you do so well, with so much fire, courage and love. Talk about how you understand the distinction between vocation and profession.

CORNEL WEST: Yes, that's a very important place to begin my brother, because, for me, intellectual vocation and prophetic witness sit at the very center of my work. And for me, I am just building on Max Weber in many ways, especially two great essays of his from 1917 and 1919. What it is to have a *Beruf*, a calling, is very different than having a career. When you are wedded to a vocation, when you are wedded to a calling, it is tied to the Negro National Anthem; you are lifting your voice. You are not just lifting an echo, you're not a copy, you're not an imitation. Rather, you have a distinctive, unique and singular voice to be brought to bear and that voice is found only by bouncing up against earlier voices, the voices of the dead and the voices of the quick, but it's the best voices, the most courageous voices, the most visionary voices. And it means then that you're always going to be over against establishments, over against status quos—no matter what color.

Every vocation is connected to a sense of history in which you are involved in an invocation. And every calling that you have is tied to a certain kind of recalling and interpretation of the past. And every interpretation of the past is an interpretation of the present. Or, as Michel Foucault used to say, every history of the past is a history of the present and vice versa. And, therefore, you situate yourself within a particular vocation and tradition headed toward—for me—revolution.

It's revolution in the spiritual sense, revolution in the political sense and revolution in the economic sense, which is a massive transfer of power, of respect, of wealth. It is a transfer that is not about putting others down, but it's a democratizing, it's a sharing of that respect, the sharing of that wealth, the sharing of those resources and so forth. So that radical democratic end is informed by this intense commitment to vocation, finding voice, but always situating your voice in relation to a certain tradition, or what Antonio Gramsci called a "critical historical inventory." That's Socratic, it's self-examination.

But all of us are always already in circumstances not of our own choosing, and so we have to situate ourselves in particular historical traditions, and my traditions come from the magnificent West family, Clifton and Irene West, from the Shiloh Baptist church, and from the Black radical tradition. But it also comes from the best of my teachers, Hilary Putnam, John Rawls, Tim Scanlon, Thomas Nagel, Richard Rorty, Martin Kilson, Preston Williams, one can go on and on. So, I am a fusion, I am a hybrid of the best from whence I come, and the best of my formal education, but all of them are just feeding into a particular vocation and witness, an intellectual vocation and a prophetic witness.

George, as you said in your brilliant foreword on me written for Teodros Kiros's new book, *Conversations with Cornel West* (2021), my intellectual vocation and prophetic witness are profoundly cruciform, profoundly Christian, tied to the cross, tied to service, tied to the willingness to empty oneself, to give of oneself, to donate oneself.

GY: This is how you use the term *kenosis*, which is a form of emptying. I agree with it and use it in my own work.

CW: Yes! It's *kenosis* in that very deep sense. That's why I'm always pulled by the great artists of *kenosis*. It could be Rembrandt's *The Return of the Prodigal Son*, which is *kenosis* on the canvas, the emptying of the self, of father to sons. Or it could be James Brown on the stage, the emptying of himself for four hours straight, nonstop; it could be Aretha Franklin behind the microphone, the emptying of herself. That is *kenosis* at work.

GY: And do you see a relationship between kenosis and pedagogy? Like you, I tell my students that when they come to my class that they need to be prepared for their prejudices and dogmatic assumptions to die.

CW: Beautiful!

GY: I like the idea of kenosis or emptying. As you know, Michel Foucault talks about a certain kind of death in relationship to parrhesia, or courageous speak. In fact, he sees the process of parrhesia as a risk of a kind of physical death, where one stands on the precipice of risking one's own life. What do you think about that? You talk often of having your black suit on, what you call your cemetery clothes. I want you to speak to the gravitas of this unique voice that you've crafted, a voice that is always already in relationship to your parents and your siblings. I know that you reject a Cartesian position of an insular or hermetically sealed voice. For you, your voice is always moving beyond yourself, it is rhizomatic and multi-historically grounded. My sense is that you take very seriously the idea that vocation and voice will often create deep tension in relationship to issues of empire such that one's very life is at stake.

CW: Absolutely! As you know, one of the differences between the grand Cartesian subject is that the "real problem" is epistemological skepticism. Whereas for the bluesman like myself, or the blues-woman, the real problem is catastrophe and that catastrophe is not just epistemic.

The catastrophe is bodily, it is corporeal, psychic, spiritual. It's where one wrestles with forms of death—spiritual death, psychic death, social death, civic death. All of those continually bombarding you. So, when I say that I'm a bluesman in the life of the mind, some people say, "That's kind of interesting." No! That is a particular tradition of a way of being-in-the-world.

So, if I put my cemetery clothes on every day, if I'm coffin-ready every day, it means a particular kind of catastrophe, like physical death, is always already there on a continuum with the other forms of death. And to be a Black man in a white supremacist civilization, where Black love is a crime, where Black hope is a joke, where Black freedom is a pipe dream, and Black history is a curse, then I've got to fight that no matter what. So, I'm going to love and be willing to be criminalized. I'm going to fight for freedom and be willing to be crushed. I'm going to try to provide some kind of hope and be willing to be laughed at as a joke.

So, one is radically cutting over against oneself. And then when you add the cruciform character and the tragic-comic content to it, it means that you're in but not of this empire, you're in but not of this white supremacist society, trying to be in but not of this predatory capitalist society, you're in but not of this patriarchal, homophobic society, but you know all that's inside of you, too. And that is part of the paradox, the white supremacy that is inside of me. I grew up within a patriarchal empire, so I'm going to have the patriarchy in me. So, I have to fight that every day. That's part of learning how to die. That needs to die daily in order for me to emerge as a stronger love warrior, freedom fighter, and wounded healer.

GY: What does it mean to be a philosopher of African descent within the American empire in the 21st century?

CW: You begin with the giants in your own philosophical tradition. I can talk about Lucius Outlaw; Bernard Boxill; Joyce M. Cook, the first Black woman to receive the doctorate in philosophy from Yale University in 1965 and who you knew so very well; Eugene Holmes, Alain Locke, Leonard Harris, Howard McGary, and others. These are folk, many of whom I've been blessed to know, whose voices are forever inside of me that I wrestle with. And all of us are then bouncing off of those voices of American philosophers: from William James, to John Dewey, to Alfred North Whitehead, to W. V. O. Quine, to Stanley Cavell, and then European philosophers.

There are also some who have been willing to go back to recuperate certain African philosophers. For example, Maulana Karenga has taught me a lot about Maat, which is a concept that links us to Egyptian moral philosophy. We've got Eastern philosophy from Asia. I'm very open to dialogue across the board. So, it ought to be global, but you really do need to acknowledge the degree to which certain philosophers have had more influence on your thinking. I would never want to say, as you can imagine, that there's any generic answer to what Black philosophers ought to do or say.

We've all got different voices, just like musicians.

My particular voice is one that has been deeply shaped by critiques of empire, predatory capitalism, and white supremacy in the ways in which all of these are interwoven. But what makes me a little different from some of my brothers and sisters is that I tend to look at the world through the lens of the cross, through a moral and spiritual lens. So, I'm very tied to the prophetic voices of Hebrew scripture. I view Hebrew scripture as one of the great moral revolutions in the spreading of *hesed*, which is a steadfast love and loving kindness of orphan and widow, the hungry, and the shelterless, the homeless and the oppressed.

So, when the Palestinian Jew named Jesus goes to the Temple, which is the largest edifice east of Rome, with hundreds of Roman soldiers, bankers and intellectuals, and the chattering classes, and runs them out, well, that is very much like running out elites in the White House, Pentagon, Congress,

Hollywood, Wall Street, Harvard, Yale, Princeton and Emory. And you're running them out not because you're demonizing them, but because there's too much callousness and indifference toward the poor that you see in their way of life.

You see too much commodification that makes their souls too cold and their hearts too coarse. There's too much bureaucratization that distances them from the lived experience of people who are trying to struggle. There's too much white supremacy in terms of its mistreatment of precious Black people and Brown people and so on. I'm much more explicit about the cross and the Christian tradition. Many of my precious brothers and sisters within the philosophical tradition, Black or what have you, swerve away from that particular Christian stream and strand. And that's fine with me. It's a matter of our voices bouncing up against one another yet again.

GY: Your work is not only interdisciplinary, but it is also de-disciplinary, where one may need to call into question one's own discipline as such. Your work, as a public intellectual, engages not just a specialized few, but aims to intervene within a larger conversation that has implications for the destiny of large numbers of people. I think that this vision puts you at odds with certain neoliberal assumptions within academia. This is the work that you do. Whether you're discussing the precious lives of our Palestinian or Jewish brothers and sisters, you're asking across the board for all of us to empty, to undergo *kenosis*, in relationship to all forms of corrupt power and domination. And within academic spaces, you're also calling into question forms of corruption, bureaucratization, neoliberalism and hegemonic power. I see you as an indispensable gadfly within that space. So, how do you understand what is going on at Harvard with respect to not even wanting to consider you being considered for tenure? How do you see the voice that you've developed and nurtured, the vocation that you've chosen, the gadfly that you are, in relationship to your situation at Harvard? Is there not an important relationship or tension here? Do you not see this as part of the problem?

CW: Oh absolutely. It goes back to the issue of intellectual vocation, and prophetic witness. I have always had a deep tension with the academic division of knowledge. Think about my heroes going back to Socrates and Jesus, or Ralph Waldo Emerson and William James. When Emerson gave that famous speech on July 15, 1838, the Harvard Divinity Address, they didn't invite him back for 30 years. Why? Because he spoke his mind; he said what he meant and he meant what he said and he cut radically against the grain. What was Ralph Waldo Emerson? He was a kind of poet, a kind of preacher, a kind of circuit lecturer, a kind of philosopher. But what was he? Well, he was Emerson, you know what I mean?

Think of William James on June 24, 1903, when he gave his famous speech, "The True Harvard."[3] What is the true Harvard for James? It's what he called the "undisciplinables," the people that can never be disciplined, they don't fit within the disciplines. William James had no A.B., B.A., M.A., or Ph.D. So, how does he end up being the greatest public philosopher alongside John Dewey in the 20th century? He had an M.D., that was it; but he had a calling, he had a witness. He had a form of self-confidence in his way of pursuing the life of the mind in the world of ideas to be conversant with his voice, with a whole host of other voices, but he went on his own way. He was nonconformist. He was in the academy, but not of it. He wrote his famous essay entitled, "The Ph.D. Octopus," which was published in the early 1900s. He argues that the worst thing will be intense forms of specialization, and intense forms of professionalization that will lose sight of the forest, will be shining all the nuts in the corner, with no sense of the forest, no way of connecting the parts with the whole, where the whole is always bigger than the sum of the parts.

He got one life and then, boom, he drops the mic in 1910. He dies leaving us to make sense of what he's left in his corpus. Emerson, in 1882, drops the mic and dies. And W. E. B. Du Bois was the same way. He was the student of William James. And that's just within the American context. We can go to Russia and go from Vissarion Belinsky to Anton Chekhov. And Chekhov, for me, of course, is deeper than all the Americans. He's a medical doctor, poet, playwright, short story writer, exemplary freedom fighter, prison reformer, but always looking at the world through moral and spiritual lens as a Darwinian, as a secular thinker. And what does he say about philosophers? Chekhov says that he doesn't trust philosophers because they remind him of generals, they just want to enlist people in their army. I don't want to join their army. I'll read Friedrich Nietzsche, I'll read Nicholas of Cusa, I'll read Charles Darwin. I'll read as many of them as I can, but I'm going to be Anton Chekhov, grandson of a slave. You know what I mean?

GY: I do. It is indicative of your unique voice and your ethical fortitude. This raises the question of your situation at Harvard. How does your situation speak to Black scholars, what does it communicate, especially to those who want to cultivate their voices, who refuse to be echoes, who want to engage in deep interdisciplinary and de-disciplinary work? It seems to me that there is a problematic message that is being communicated. There is a sense of communicated fear in terms of what we should or shouldn't say. I can't see any basis upon which Harvard would not even consider you for tenure. And I was so delighted to see the significant support by the Harvard graduate students, undergraduates, and others throughout the country who are pushing back against Harvard's decision. How do Black scholars and scholars of color remain strong in the face of what you're dealing with?

CW: Well, this is minimal in terms of what our brothers and sisters on the block have to come to terms with, with what Black working-class people have to deal with. The fundamental common denominator, though, is that we've got to fortify in order to fructify, we've got to be strong in order to generate fruit in the form of deeds, fruit in the form of visions, of organizations, of institutions, of structures that bring power and pressure to bear.

A little crisis of the professional managerial class of Black folk, yes, it's important, but it still pales in the face of the catastrophes of our brothers and sisters who constitute the masses of Black and poor working people. We always have to work with what we have, and we have to use what we have in order not to sell our souls for a mess of pottage. The saddest thing that happens is when those folk who adjust to injustice then parade around as a success. We're talking about greatness here.

Greatness does not adjust to injustice. It doesn't adapt to indifference and then pose and posture as if that is success. Not at all. The worst thing that could happen is that young folk think that it's just about getting into the academy to be successful, become the next wave of peacocks. That's not what it's about at all.

So, I would hope that my example, given all of my privileges and all of my blessings, will communicate the message that young people should be fortified. Don't be disrespected. We come from a great people. Black people are a world historical people whose gifts have disproportionately shaped the cultures of the world. And there's just no doubt about that, so you've got to be true to that, and you are true to that with your humility and your tenacity. And you have to be willing to speak the truth—to the powerful and the powerless.

When Harvard treats me in this way, that's a sign of its spiritual and intellectual bankruptcy. Now, it could bounce back, but you have to call it for what it is. You have to acknowledge that there's new styles of Jim Crow in the life of the mind and the country. It's just a fact.

You look at *The New York Review of Books*. Thank God there are brilliant essays by brother Brandon Terry, but other than Darryl Pinkney and Anthony Appiah, it has basically been a case of Jim Crow. How many of your books, how many of John Hope Franklin's books, how many of

Houston Baker's books, how many of Hortense Spillers' books have been reviewed? Intellectual work that's taken place in the last 40 years has been rendered invisible because of the Jim Crow quality of the ways in which they review books. And that's just one example.

We have to be honest about that and say that we can do better. And we must do better. And, in fact, if you subtract the number of Black people in the Department of African and African American Studies at Harvard and only include Black folk in other departments, Harvard looks like the National Hockey League. There's hardly any Black folks at all. That's how Wall Street looks. That's how elite formation looks. That's how Silicon Valley looks, especially at the top.

You see, that's still Jim Crow, new style. So, when people say, "Ah Brother West, you are so hard on Harvard, you're so hard on the professional managerial class," I say, "Come on." I'm not even beginning to tell the truth in terms of allowing this suffering to speak. Yes, let's pursue *veritas*. Let us take *veritas* seriously, the motto of Harvard, and see its own weak will to truth about itself. That's the best kind of witness that becomes very important. Not in a spirit of hatred or revenge. This is Coltranean all the way down. This is a love of truth, a love of beauty, a love of goodness and a love of the Holy for those of us who are religious.

GY: That sounds very Baldwinian. I'm thinking here of where James Baldwin talks about how love removes the masks that we fear we cannot live without and yet know that we cannot live within.

CW: Oh yeah. That's the genius from Harlem. Baldwin is another brother who never went to college, but at least two colleges went through him.

GY: As you know, Martin Luther King Jr. was critical of what he called the triplets of racism, materialism or capitalism, and militarism. In fact, he became very unpopular once he broadened his critique of North America beyond issues related to civil rights. As a public intellectual, as one who speaks about parrhesia, or courageous speech, talk about how you understand the intersection between racism, materialism or capitalism, and militarism. Of course, all three are linked to empire-building.

CW: Intellectual vocation and prophetic witness is tied to integrity, not popularity. It is tied to quality, not quantity. And it is tied to substance, not superficial spectacle. The very way in which you look at a problem is going to be informed by important levels of integrity, quality, political, spiritual and moral substance. So, all the talk about identity these days will not mean much at all if it is not rooted in integrity and high quality and solidarity. You see, racial identity and gender identity could just be weaponized for another middle-class project that would reproduce neoliberal politics that will unleash Wall Street greed, generate high levels of poverty, no accountability of the elites at the top, and everybody walks around with a smile, because you got some Black folk and Brown folk at the top. And it just means that the class hierarchy is more colorful, and the imperial hierarchy is more colorful, but people are still suffering. King comes from our tradition, brother. He's a wave in our ocean. You and I know about 400 years of being chronically hated and yet we keep dishing out love warriors like Martin Luther King, and Stevie Wonder, who's thinking about going to Ghana. Four-hundred years of being terrorized and yet we keep dishing out freedom fighters like Fannie Lou Hamer. Traumatized and yet we keep dishing out wounded healers like Aretha Franklin. That's a great people with a great tradition. We're human beings like everybody else, but I'm talking about the best of who we are. So, when we think of a Martin Luther King, we say, "What would the analogues in the academy look like? What would the intellectuals look like if they were fundamentally grounded in those traditions of love warriors, freedom fighters and wounded healers?" I think that is our challenge. I think that you've done a magnificent job in your corpus and you've been so true to this tradition. And I think this is true for a variety of different thinkers and philosophers, but it just means, in the end, that we love the people, we're servants of the people, that we want to use our gifts to enable others, we want to use whatever we have, to empty ourselves, to donate and give ourselves, to be of service to others, such that they can be stronger, they can be more empowered when the worms get our bodies.

GY: And it isn't easy, because we have this lingering Trumpian, neo-fascist moment.

CW: Right, but neofascism is not new to us. Not new at all.

We are bluesmen and women and we are never, ever surprised by evil, we are never ever paralyzed by despair.

14

U.S. FOUNDERS DEMONIZED INDIGENOUS PEOPLE WHILE CO-OPTING THEIR POLITICAL PRACTICES

INTERVIEW WITH BRIAN BURKHART

When spending your next $20 bill, take a good look at President Andrew Jackson's face on the cover. Remember the Indian Removal Act of 1830, which was authorized by President Andrew Jackson, and the resulting brutal Trail of Tears experienced by Indigenous peoples—and the structural and ideological terror that results from efforts to preserve white "purity," white "civilization," and white "superiority." Keep in mind that Jackson was an enslaver of Black people and engaged in genocidal practices against Indigenous peoples, which isn't to reject the genocidal implications of Black enslavement.

It is important that we never forget the deep existential, cultural, environmental and spiritual toll experienced by Indigenous peoples here in North America, and how their pain and suffering continue into the 21st century. They have had to fight against dehumanizing caricatures that depicted (and continue to depict) them as "savages," as having no real culture, or as having no real relationship to the land upon which they lived, or having shared a sense of community and spiritual belonging.

To engage past and contemporary issues facing Indigenous peoples in North America, I spoke with Brian Burkhart of the Cherokee Nation

G. Yancy (with Brian Burkhart), "US Founders Demonized Indigenous People While Coopting Their Political Practices," in *Truthout*, August 15, 2021. [Editors: Maya Schenwar and Britney Schultz]

of Oklahoma, who is interim director of the Native Nations Center at Oklahoma University and an associate professor of philosophy and affiliated faculty in Native American Studies. He is the author of several important scholarly articles and chapters that engage questions of Indigenous conceptualizations of land as kinship, questions of normativity, identity, and indigenous philosophy. He is the author of *Indigenizing Philosophy Through the Land: A Trickster Methodology for Decolonizing Environmental Ethics and Indigenous Futures* (Michigan State University Press, 2019).

In this interview, Burkhart helps us to understand what it means to be Indigenous and painfully precarious within the context of COVID-19. He explores the meaning of settler colonial ignorance, and of white settler appropriation of Indigenous ideas and land. And he helps us to appreciate the deep philosophical and spiritual implications of land as a site of particularity that grounds points of view that reject epistemological arrogance and refuse conceptions of universality that are hegemonic.

GEORGE YANCY: There are times when ignorance runs so deep that I feel as if it is not even worth responding to. I fear that responding to it gives it some measure of validity. Yet, remaining silent doesn't feel like an option. For example, in May, while speaking at an event planned by Young America's Foundation (which I'm assuming is predominantly white, though I could be wrong), politician and political commentator Rick Santorum said, "We birthed a nation from nothing. I mean, there was nothing here. I mean, yes we have Native Americans, but candidly there isn't much Native American culture in American culture." As we know, he no longer works as a political commentator at *CNN* because of his comments. When I heard about this, I immediately thought of the racist "legal" doctrine known as *terra nullius*, which is Latin for "land belonging to no one." It is part of the colonial-settler logic deployed here and in Australia. "There was nothing here"? The language denies Indigenous existence; it denies human life; and it assumes that it is whiteness that constitutes fullness and presence. "We birthed a nation from nothing?" This also has theological resonance. Theologically, only God creates *ex nihilo*. So, here we've got anti-Indigenous racism, deeply problematic and racist theological discourse, and the obfuscation of colonial-settler genocide. North America wasn't birthed from nothing. It was given "life" through a process of violent and murderous dispossession of land and Indigenous blood and tears. As a Black man, I can tell you what it's like to be called a "n*****." As a Cherokee Nation citizen and an Indigenous philosopher, speak to what it is like to hear that your presence, the lived presence of your people, was nonexistent. Talk about the racism here.

BRIAN BURKHART: George, I am grateful for the opportunity to have this conversation with you and truly appreciate your work to include Indigenous perspectives on whiteness in America. You are correct about the depth of ignorance and the struggle over responding to it. The colonial-settler ignorance is structural (as is all racist ignorance, I believe), but the function of colonial-settler ignorance is specifically targeted to the erasure or elimination of Indigenous people as people. The construction of the European as "civilized," even *human*, against the American, African and Oceanic so-called "savage" is the foundational framework of what later becomes whiteness as a way of conceptualizing and even consolidating this human-versus-animal difference as the conceptual framework of whiteness. In the colonial context, if Indigenous people are savages or mere animals, then there are no people in the lands to be colonized: no people, no culture, no laws, nothing stands in the way of taking whatever is wanted from Indigenous lands and ultimately taking the land itself in a form of settler occupation. So, the racism that is constructed around Indigenous people operates through violent processes of elimination. The function is to eliminate Indigenous people through actual ongoing genocide, but also to eliminate us conceptually. The function of the racist view of Indigenous people that Santorum is working with is, in part, to eliminate Indigenous people from history, from the history of the land, from the history of American culture. This erasure is a removal of Indigenous people to replace them on the land with European people and to replace Indigenous people in American history with white fantasies. The classic form of the so-called "first Americans," as seen in American literature and media— from *The Last of the Mohicans* to modern movies and television—is the white appropriation and deployment of the fantasy-driven Indian who must be replaced by "civilized" humans, who are necessarily white. This speaks to the struggle to simply exist as an Indigenous person in the United States. The genocide this racism incurs is not only physical but conceptual, as Santorum's comments show. We are erased from American history and culture, and from the land that we belong to.

GY: Yes. And following through on your point, part of the problem is that even when the existence of Indigenous people is acknowledged, they are deemed "savages" and "uncivilized." Many may be unaware of this, and I am thankful to sociologist Joe Feagin for pointing this out to me, but even in the Declaration of Independence, one of the U.S.'s most "sacred" documents, Thomas Jefferson wrote about "the merciless Indian savages, whose known rule of warfare, is undistinguished destruction of all ages, sexes and conditions." The contradiction here is that while it is stated in the

Declaration of Independence that "all men are created equal," Indigenous people are deemed outside of the community of those who constitute the "fully human" (read: white). Speak to some of the contemporary ways in which you understand Native American lives as *not* mattering within North America's white hegemonic polity. I'm thinking here especially in terms of Native American communities being disproportionately hit hard by COVID-19 and the resulting existential and economic crisis.

BB: This settler erasure of Indigenous people, of Indigenous humanity, from the white hegemonic polity is a structural feature of settler society. There is an existential estrangement and epistemological bad faith that goes along with this erasure on the part of mainstream white America as well. The level of maintenance and sublimation that it requires to invert the reality of American history and the reality of Indigenous humanity into the fantasy of white supremacy and the erasure of Indigenous presence, influence and humanity is beyond belief. One example in relation to the Declaration's reference to "merciless Indian savages" will help. The same Thomas Jefferson (as well as Benjamin Franklin, among many others of the so-called founders) studied extensively and had great admiration for the political structure of the Indigenous confederacies that were quite common in areas of contact they had with Indigenous people. Franklin's Albany Plan of Union in 1754 copies much of the Iroquois Confederacy's governmental structure, and much of the Haudenosaunee (Iroquois) Great Law is copied into the structure of the Articles of Confederation and the United States Constitution. The founders are quite clear-eyed in their use of Native political philosophies, structures and institutions while at the same time calling those people, from which they are formulating the most sacred of American institutions, "savages." Franklin, in his essay "Remarks Concerning the Savages of North America,"[1] describes the importance of adopting such Native views/practices.

The fantasy of erasure and dehumanization does create a significant negative impact on Native American communities, as you mentioned. COVID-19 has a glaringly negative impact, even showing up in the national media. The Navajo nation, where I have family and where I was born and raised, has been hit particularly hard, having some of the highest infection rates, serious illnesses, and even death rates higher than anywhere in the world. Part of the reason for this disproportionate impact is the chronic underfunding of health and infrastructure for tribal nations (something that the U.S. government is required to provide to Native nations by treaty), historical trauma and general health disparities as the result of centuries of displacement, forced relocation, stock reductions (in the 1930s, federal agents killed nearly 300,000 Navajo sheep, goats, and horses because they decided they had too many[2]) and other federal policies. In the Navajo nation, prevention of infection is made more difficult by the fact that 40 percent of Navajos are without electricity or running water and, of course, there is widespread food insecurity.

These historical and ongoing traumas are coming into mainstream conversations in the United States and Canada with the discovery of mass graves of Indigenous children on the grounds of Indian residential and boarding schools. Nearly 2,000 bodies have been uncovered just in Canada over the summer and in just a handful of schools that have been searched. It is clear that these so-called schools were nothing more than death camps. Even in photographic records, there is evidence of purposeful exposure to smallpox, for example. In 1907, Peter Bryce did a study of Indian residential schools in Canada and discovered a 69 percent mortality rate among the students.[3] Would you send your child to a "school" with a 69 percent mortality rate?

GY: I certainly would not, and I am sure that white people would not. As you know, *Terra nullius* and manifest destiny are concepts consistent with colonial power and the ownership, as in domination, of the Earth. If you combine these concepts with Western technological control of the Earth, which embodies a metaphysical framework that conceptualizes the Earth as infinitely exploitable, and the proliferation of ecological harms done to the Earth, I would argue that there is a sense in which human beings are perceived as "natural" oppressors of the Earth (the oppressed). And there is also a sense of estrangement vis-à-vis the Earth. It is similar to the estrangement installed between the colonizer and the colonized. This says to me that coloniality is not just a superficial ideology, but something more akin to an enduring metaphysics. The Earth is conceptualized as an "object" over which we must gain epistemological control for the sake of global capitalist greed. So, it's important, it seems to me, that we understand that this is not the only way to conceptualize the Earth, to relate to the Earth. Dominating the Earth embodies an ontology and epistemology of ecological death and disaster. As an Indigenous philosopher, speak to Indigenous ways of relating to the Earth and how the Earth is conceptualized outside of a Western worldview.

BB: Part of the estrangement that happens in the settler psyche of white supremacy and Indigenous erasure arises from a homelessness in the land. The notion of true humanness as something floating free from the land that even requires domination of the land in order to be human, as you say, is not only *not* the only way to conceptualize or relate to the Earth, but requires a fantasy of displacement from the Earth that I argue is a key structural component of the fantasy of whiteness and white supremacy. Rather than land as an object to be dominated, claimed, owned, bought or sold, Indigenous ways of relating to the Earth view land as kinship or even the relational ground of kinship. Obscuring the land discerned through a spatial point of view creates the context of homelessness in the land where humans float free from the land. The spatial point of view sees times, history and human beings as functions of relationality with the land. Obscuring the fundamental relationality of our being with land distorts how we perceive time, history and human beings apart from grounded spatiality in the land. This conceptualization of time, history and humanness are then given as a pretense of universality across all land. In contrast, Indigenous people, within the context of seeing land from the spatial point of view, hold our land with the highest possible regard and center our sense of meaning around this point. Colonial domination, in contrast, views people, time and history apart from land in order to conceive of their colonizing movements across the globe as a form of meaningful progress. The very essence of whiteness as a form of identity requires a de-spatialization and false abstraction of humanness, time and history as universals that float free from the land.

GY: Yes. Whiteness aspires to a universal and an ahistorical status. When we think about our relationship to land, most of us think about our homes. Of course, if one is experiencing homelessness, then this conception of land is inconsequential. Yet, even as I think about land and identity, I think about things that I own. And while the things that I own don't exhaust who I am, I have been seduced by conceptions of ownership—material goods that include land. And while I would like to think of Africa as beckoning a radically different relationship that I could have with land and how I think about "ownership," there is still the rift created by the transatlantic slave trade that troubles that desired relationship. You, however, are still here, though the cruel history of dispossession should never be forgotten. Talk about the importance of how land is understood in relationship to how you understand *who you are* and how place can function (or *does* function) as a site of freedom for you.

BB: Land, as the relational ground of kinship, provides a true freedom, one that cannot be found in the supposed freedom of movement and global domination that is constructed around land as object and humans that float free from the land. Seeing oneself in relation to land through the spatial point of view allows for a perspective of particularity of identity in the kinship matrix of identity that, at the same time, is inclusive of other sites of identity through other lands. Seeing oneself and others through the spatial point of view of land presents a connectivity through the land itself, which we all stand and walk upon, while maintaining the necessity of non-homogenous pockets of identity in relation to land as particular relational sites of kinship and identity.

It is exactly this structure of diversity and inclusion through the land as kinship that notions of universal truth, planetary humanness and monotheistic religion (as an evolutionary progression from primitive superstitions to universal moral laws, from a multiplicity of gods in nature to a single God existing beyond nature, time and space) are meant to obscure. This movement happens not through a progression of a revelation of ultimate reality but through an obscuring of the spatial point of view, of the connectivity and particularity of land as the kinship matrix of identity. Rather than mistaking a particular local situation for a universal truth over all land and all time, the spatial point of view grounds itself directly in the world around us. There is freedom in this point of view because one is not trapped in the abstract space (that floats free from the land) of universal truth. One can respond and adjust to the natural surroundings, and revelation is nothing more than this continuous process of adjustment within particular kinship sites of land. These kinship sites of land then become sacred because they provide a framework for moral reflection and responsibility. These sites are permanently sacred because the sacredness exists in the land itself and is not something universal that floats free from the land or merely in human or divine action which is exercised upon the land as an object.

GY: I know that Black lives don't matter in ways that white lives matter. It makes me furious. At other times, that sense of furiousness is drained to a point of what feels like dreaded hopelessness. It's hard to know that you were never meant to be human in North America. And it's exhausting to explain that feeling, that truth, to some who are white. Without conflating our individual experiences of being the objects of racism, or conflating the collective histories of our people, speak to what makes you strong, what gives you endurance in the face of so much colonial violence and continued exclusionary dehumanization. Also, how does being a Cherokee Nation citizen speak critically to the U.S. as "we" move forward through this fragile democratic experiment? And I ask this knowing that we don't owe white America a damn thing given its brutal historical and contemporary treatment of people who look like me and you.

BB: This is an important question, George, and I am grateful to you for generating the space and opportunity to speak on it. I feel the fury you reflect in even thinking about how Black and Native lives were never meant to matter in North America and the exasperation in trying to speak and explain that feeling to many white folks. Part of what makes me strong in the face of these facts and the ongoing colonial violence and dehumanization is quite literally the land itself (as I have written about in "Be as Strong as the Land that Made You: An Indigenous Philosophy of Well-Being through the Land"[4]). The groundedness that comes from seeing one's identity and responsibility coming from particular sites of land as kinship gives one a kind of strength that is capable of tethering oneself against the worst of the wind of racism, dehumanization and violence. There is a social fabric of kinship with the land itself that provides something of a protective home even in the face of land removal and genocidal forced marches, such as the Cherokee Trail of Tears and the Navajo Long Walk, and the genocidal act of the wholesale removal of Native children to boarding and residential schools. Article II of the 1948 Genocide Convention defines "forcibly transferring children of the group to another group" as an act of genocide.

Speaking of North America's fragile democratic experiment, it seems to me that it was an experiment that was meant to fail or was never really meant to be anything but obscuring the white supremacy and settler colonial power structure of the U.S. political system. As a Cherokee Nation citizen, I can critically challenge the notion of U.S. democracies through the assertion of tribal sovereignty and the rights of treaties made with the United States and with countries before the founding of the U.S. settler state. Part of the power of this challenge is that it presents the flaw in the fragile democratic experiment: both the way that the claims to democracy hide the racial hierarchy beneath the surface, as well as the way that the notion of the community of democracy arises from a notion of land as an object and people floating free from the land. This last revelation can be seen through the structure of the settler states and their claim to ownership of Indigenous nations, like the Cherokee Nation, through the Supreme Court doctrines of plenary power and Indian land title, which holds that through the Doctrine of Discovery, the federal government is the true title holder of Indian land and the legal guardian of Indigenous nations within the settler-state territory. A conversation about the political and legal structure of the U.S. settler-state opens a space for conversation about the nature of kinship beyond white supremacy and settler-state domination, both in broader political and individual terms. Rather than trying to hold on to the fragile democratic experiment within these contexts of white supremacy and settler-state domination, we can rethink the very nature of diversity and inclusion through the land, the ways that we can be connected and be distinct within a framework of relationality and moral responsibility that arises from seeing ourselves from the spatial point of view.

GY: I deeply appreciate your conceptualization of rethinking diversity and inclusion outside of white supremacy and its logics. I'm also excited by your understanding of kinship beyond settler-state domination. I also think that Black people have always had to think of freedom outside and beyond a white supremacist framework. In fact, it can be said that Black resistance and Indigenous resistance forced the U.S. to be confronted by its fundamental hypocrisy. I want to ask one last question. As much as I believe in Black solidarity and resistance, the attack on the Capitol on January 6, 2021, left me with a deep sense of political malaise. My sense is that on that day, the U.S. revealed a deep truth about itself: a sense of white authoritarian madness. Since that event, how have you been able to reinvigorate your sense of hope? Like W. E. B. DuBois, I am not hopeless, but certainly unhopeful.

BB: This is such an important question, and while I too was shocked by the attack on the Capitol on January 6, 2021, I was not particularly surprised. In particular, I think that, for Native people and Native Nations who have been constructed as wards of the U.S. settler state, the feeling that there is limited possibility in the apparatus of the U.S. settler state for the liberation of Indigenous people and nations has hardly wavered since the early days of settler colonialism on this land. However, in contrast to the clear-eye sense of the nature of the U.S. settler state as inherently oppressive and even structured around the historical and conceptual erasure of Indigenous peoples and nations as the base of its power and meaning, Indigenous people have maintained a kind of hope at the center of our resilience over the more than 500 years of our colonial occupation. This hope is not based in trust of the settler state or even its people per se but in the boundless capacity of Indigenous people and communities, whose strength comes from the land, the land out of which we come to be and from which we maintain our resiliency and strength. A sense of groundedness in the land creates a never-ending wellspring of hope for Indigenous people because the power of the settler state, of white supremacy, of patriarchy, of the domination and exploitation of the land and all its resources comes from a false sense of power that only has meaning in an ungrounded world where certain people see themselves as floating free from the land, and above it, with the capacity to own it and exploit it as an object. The power that comes from a sense of separation from and authority and ownership over the land is a manufactured and unsustainable power. Indigenous people have tried for millennia to show this to people who have attempted to dominate the earth and all the various peoples of the earth and through such have created many diverse communities of resistant to such domination. Groundedness in the earth also creates a sense of community and the possibility of ally-ship through the earth that we are a part of and all depend on as human beings. This sense of community in the earth creates natural alliances, for Indigenous people, with those who experience the white supremacist, pa-triarchal, settler violence over the earth, who just like the earth and often because of their "earthly" connection (material, physical, emotion, animal, sexual as opposed to spiritual, intellectual, civilized) are seen as exploitable and dominatable by those who conceive of themselves as floating free from the land and as above it and its people. The white authoritarian madness that comes to light in the attack on the Capitol also exposes its weakness in the constant need to remanufacture itself apart of the land that is the center of reliance and provides the contrasting continuity and foundation of hope for Indigenous people.

15

FOUNDED ON INEQUALITY, CAN THE U.S. EVER BE TRULY DEMOCRATIC AND INCLUSIVE?

INTERVIEW WITH
TRACY DENEAN SHARPLEY-WHITING

Our contemporary problem in the U.S. is not monolithic. It resides at the intersections of race, class, gender, hegemonic policing and failed leadership. The inclusive term "syndemic" is what captures more accurately our lived *zeitgeist*. It is through the framework of this synergistic aggregation of problems that I engage in a generative discussion with distinguished scholar T. Denean Sharpley-Whiting, who is the Gertrude Conaway Vanderbilt Distinguished Professor of African American and Diaspora Studies and French at Vanderbilt University, where she directs the Callie House Research Center for the Study of Global Black Cultures and Politics, and is Vice Provost for Arts and Libraries. She is author/editor of 15 scholarly books and three novels, including the *Norton Anthology of Theory and Criticism, Bricktop's Paris: African American Women Expatriates in Jazz-Age Paris* and *Pimps Up, Ho's Down: Hip Hop's Hold on Young Black Women*. In this interview, Sharpley-Whiting, articulating part of her way of understanding contemporary race relations through the lens of race realism, does not hesitate to encourage our collective need to do our part in maximizing democratic ideals.

G. Yancy (with Tracy Denean Sharpley-Whiting), "Founded on Inequality, Can the US Ever Be Truly Democratic and Inclusive?," in *Truthout*, October 31, 2020. [Editors: Maya Schenwar and Britney Schultz]

GEORGE YANCY: I mourned the death of 26-year-old Breonna Taylor, who was shot eight times as white Louisville police officers served a no-knock warrant. As Black Americans, we continue to mourn Black death. How do you envision a post-mourning for Black America? There are times when it seems as if Black life will *never* matter in white America. So, in what ways would you say we are trapped in a world where our humanity is a permanent site of precarity, where our humanity will never matter?

TRACY DENEAN SHARPLEY-WHITING: I would argue that our humanity matters very much—to us and our allies. I don't view Black life as a site of precarity but as a sometimes casualty of white inhumanity. What we've been struggling for is not necessarily for whites to value Black life, accept Black humanity or love Black people. Black people, for the most part, value Black life. . . . Self-interest is a primary lever in changing behavior—with the anomaly being poor and working-class whites continue to vote against their economic self-interest because of racism; they enjoy being white more than they abhor poverty and wage theft. With respect to policing, if you dispensed with qualified immunity—and here is where I oddly agree with Justice Clarence Thomas—law enforcement [might] act in ways that are more consonant with their public safety charge. But as long as taxpayers are on the hook, their economic self-interests don't compel them to act differently.

GY: In what way does "a sometimes casualty of white inhumanity" square with the idea that anti-Black racism is a *constant* systemic and pervasive reality throughout the body politic? Does the use of "sometimes" let the magnitude and everyday acts of racist aggressions off the hook, even as I know that you are not saying this?

TDSW: I used "sometimes" as a qualifier. As a scholar of Diaspora Studies, I think of policing in its global formations. For instance, in Brazil, a country I research with respect to sex trafficking/tourism and Black/mixed-race women and girls, policing is brutal and oftentimes lethal with no recourse. The police on the ground are largely Black.

GY: Sen. Kamala Harris is on the Democratic ticket as vice president. This is historic. Any thoughts on what this means symbolically or otherwise going forward for Black Americans, and Black women in particular?

TDSW: It is historic; and symbols, I'd argue, are extremely important as markers of how far we've come, as guideposts and roadmaps for others to follow. They are inspirational and aspirational. With Harris's ascendancy, one simply cannot overstate as well the importance of [historically Black colleges and universities] as well as Black sororities in uplift and resilience narratives.

With that said, as powerful as symbols are, racecraft embedded in the processes of statecraft will continue to act as a serious counterbalance to racial/gender progress. In real terms, Obama's presidency was important as a symbol but it did not translate into greater wealth and opportunity for Black Americans writ large as a matter of policy.

GY: In the past, Trump has tweeted that Rep. Maxine Waters is "an extraordinary low IQ person." He has characterized reporter April Ryan as "nasty" and a "loser." Most recently, he called Harris "this monster." Your work has centered on Black women, within the context of hip-hop, as progenitors of the Negritude movement, and as dehumanized through the European imaginary, as in the case of the so-called "Hottentot Venus." Given this, can you speak to the historical, gendered and racial logics of Trump's depictions?

TDSW: Though Trump is drawing upon a well of anti-Black misogyny, I don't think he fully grasps the historical waters he's wading in. He lacks that sort of intellectual breadth and is dog whistling—if, in fact, he's even aware he's doing that—at very low frequency. Indeed, I would argue that his characterizations are actually projections. He landed at the University of Pennsylvania through cheating and his father's influence and deep pockets—much like his son-in-law at Harvard. Most agree he's nasty and a loser who cheats on taxes, in business, at golf, and in his ascent with an assist from Russia to the highest office in the land. Ironically, in 2016, when I appeared with some colleagues in political science on a Vanderbilt series about the election, they were certain that he'd turned off women voters with his infamous remarks. I argued that historical data showed that white women voted Republican in higher percentages than reported—they did so when Obama ran both times. They preferred [Sarah] Palin (!) and [John McCain] to an Obama presidency. I called Trump a "monster." He's been depicted as monstrous countless times, so his name-calling signals to me his deep and abiding understanding of his flaws and failings.

GY: COVID-19 has revealed how Black people are disproportionately vulnerable to this horrific pandemic. Rather than critically understanding how health concerns are linked to poverty (think here of food deserts), there seems to be an anti-Black narrative that sees Black people as somehow responsible for their own vulnerability. What are your thoughts on the operating ideology, especially regarding Black people, of blaming the victim?

TDSW: This is how anti-Black racism at the intersection of class operates. It allows others to absolve themselves of responsibility for their fellow citizens or even understand their silence, comfort, innocence as complicity.

GY: Yes. So, how do we encourage the self-reflection needed for others to take responsibility for their fellow citizens or begin to understand the ways in which they are *not* innocent?

TDSW: Admittedly, Black folks and others have been doing the heavy lifting of trying to educate our compatriots on the question of white innocence and complicity, in particular, for a good long while. Certainly, Aimé Césaire did so with *Discourse on Colonialism,* [W.E.B.] Du Bois with *The Souls of Black Folks* and *The Philadelphia Negro*, Ida B. Wells in her anti-lynching and anti-rape crusades, Frederick Douglass with his multiple narratives of his life in bondage, Harriet Jacobs with her pleadings to white women about enslaved Black women, and James Baldwin's *The Fire Next Time* was a 20th-century clarion call. And still, with this brief, critical list, I have only nicked the surface with respect to the litany of works on the subject and activism on these questions by writers and activists of every stripe and color. The point then is we have been and *are* already doing the work—writing, protesting, participating in the political process, etc. I consider myself nonetheless a realist about racial progress in this country. I owe this line of thinking to Derrick Bell and his *Faces at the Bottom of the Well*. To that end, I don't believe American democracy, founded on gross inequalities—gendered, racial, class-clotted—will ever be fully democratic and inclusive. With that said, we should continue to move that project along, to as close to the finish line as possible. We have always had to drag our more recalcitrant white citizens along the road to progress kicking and screaming.

GY: This last question is related to the first. Broadly, what is needed for an America that is leading in COVID-19 deaths and has unabashedly shifted to a white supremacism at the highest offices in the land? Where do we go from here?

TDSW: We are in the midst of a *syndemic*—as seen with COVID-19 and anti-Black racism in the form of police brutality, mass incarceration and poverty; we are also looking at threats to a woman's right to decide what to do with her body and a health-care crisis of unparalleled proportions. We need to educate voters about participation in the political process during midterm, special and presidential elections.

Part Five

ASSAULTS ON THE BLACK BODY

16

WHITE INDIFFERENCE IS NORMALIZING SPECTACULAR ACTS OF VIOLENCE

INTERVIEW WITH ROBIN D. G. KELLEY

"I don't believe universities are inherently sites of opposition, though spaces have been created in the past and present for oppositional work," historian Robin D. G. Kelley remarked in our recent conversation about anti-Black racism and our role as Black intellectuals working within the university setting. "How do you avoid becoming a functionary, a cog in the neoliberal machine?"

Kelley—the Gary B. Nash Endowed Chair of U.S. history at the University of California Los Angeles (UCLA)—went on to reflect on how "spectacular and mundane acts of everyday racism are normalized or simply not seen" due to white indifference, and on how this indifference "is made possible by a culture that promotes individualism, values wealth as a measure of success and is fundamentally anti-democratic."

In our extensive conversation presented here, Kelley and I examine the current conservative pushback against critical discussions about race and racism, the banning of books in schools, the problem with liberal multiculturalism, and racism within the academy, efforts to create resistance against racism and class exploitation within academia, Black pain and suffering, the war in Ukraine, practices of hope, and much more.

As a philosopher, I am honored to share this space with a fellow lover of wisdom, with someone who takes seriously the life of the mind and the

G. Yancy (with Robin D. G. Kelley), "Robin Kelley: White Indifference Is Normalizing Spectacular Acts of Violence," *Truthout*, May 5, 2022. [Editors: Alana Yu-lan Price, Anton Woronczuk, and Loretta Graceffo]

lives of those who endure various sites of oppression and dehumanization. The process of loving wisdom is exemplified in our shared openness for self-examination and the combined critique of hegemonic structures. As Cornel West writes in *Democracy Matters*, "love of wisdom is a perennial pursuit into the dark corners of one's own soul, the night alleys of one's society, and the back roads of the world in order to grasp the deep truths about one's soul, society, and world."

In the conversation below, we blend philosophical analysis, historical insight and autobiography in our discussion of the social, political and existential realities of our contemporary moment.

GEORGE YANCY: I would like to discuss with you the importance of keeping a critical discourse about racism alive. And I say this precisely because of the attack by right-wing forces against educating students in schools (and by extension the demos) about the multiple dimensions of racism—historical, systemic, institutional, legal, interpersonal, and unconscious. For example, some states (Idaho, Oklahoma, Tennessee, Texas, and others) have passed legislation that is designed to prohibit critical conversations regarding the structural racism of the U.S., which includes "discussions about conscious and unconscious bias, privilege, discrimination, and oppression."[1] What do you make of such legislative moves, and what do you see activist teachers and scholars doing (or ought to do) to push back against those efforts?

ROBIN D. G. KELLEY: Thanks, George. Always great to be in conversation with you. I realize it's been almost a year since our last conversation.[2] The right-wing attacks on schools have not abated since we spoke. Of course, you know that none of this is new. I recently revisited your wonderful book of interviews, *On Race: 34 Conversations in a Time of Crisis*, and it comes up in your conversation with Larry Blum, a philosopher who writes about race in schools. In fact, the attack on so-called political correctness in the form of critiques of Afrocentrism back in the 1990s comes up in your first book of interviews, *African-American Philosophers: 17 Conversations*, specifically within the context of your interview with Lucius T. Outlaw, if memory serves.

The current attacks, like those of the 1990s, are equally about gender, sexuality, and reproductive rights. For transgender and pregnant people, the consequences in terms of denying necessary health care and the right to abortions are potentially fatal. While our conversation is primarily about race, I don't want to lose sight of this fact—not least of which, because a disproportionate number of folks affected are Black, Brown, and poor.

Some critics have compared this wave of legislation with Jim Crow laws, but for me they are akin to McCarthyism—these are outright attacks on teachers and educational institutions. Think about it. The so-called "Moms for Liberty" in New Hampshire offered a $500 reward for turning in teachers who violate the state's anti–[critical race theory (CRT)] law. In Virginia, this extremist, Laura Murphy, succeeded in getting Toni Morrison's *Beloved* banned from the school curriculum, a move which in turn helped elect Glenn Youngkin governor. The latest absurd manifestation of this attack was seeing Sen. Ted Cruz holding up Ibram X. Kendi's sweet little children's book, *Antiracist Baby*, as if it was a bomb recovered from a terrorist cell, in order to derail Judge Ketanji Brown Jackson's Supreme Court confirmation. But like I said, none of this is new. My late colleague, historian Gary B. Nash, along with Charlotte Crabtree and Ross Dunn, published an important book 25 years ago titled *History on Trial: Culture Wars and the Teaching of the Past*, which is chock full of examples. A favorite of mine dates back to 1961, when some of the good citizens of Meriden, Connecticut, backed up by the Daughters of the American Revolution, insisted on banning textbooks deemed "subversive" because they contained images of poverty, and included material on the United Nations, prejudice, mental health, and writings of "liberal, racial, socialist, or labor agitators."

The contemporary bills are equally ridiculous (and tragic since we don't have a Supreme Court willing to strike them down). The Iowa bill signed by Gov. Kim Reynolds criminalizes teaching anything considered "divisive," including subject matter that might make "any individual . . . feel discomfort, guilt, anguish, or any other form of psychological distress on account of that individual's race or sex." The individuals in question, of course, are *white* kids, and the language is based upon an assumption that white kids (and their parents) would feel shame and guilt if they had to confront the history of American racism. The feelings of Black, Brown and Indigenous children are not considered.

Now let's follow the logic here. Conservative legislators and their white parent allies believe that an *anti-racist* curriculum will make their children uncomfortable. It is not an accident that *Antiracist Baby* is held up as subversive literature, whereas there is no commensurate movement to ban books that *promote* racism: for example, Thomas Jefferson's *Notes on the State of Virginia*; the writings of John C. Calhoun; Edmund Ruffin's *The Political Economy of Slavery*; or books and articles by Samuel Cartwright, Josiah Nott, George Fitzhugh, Louis Agassiz, Herbert Spencer, William Graham Sumner, Madison Grant, Lothrop Stoddard, or Daniel G. Brinton, the eminent Harvard anthropologist whose 1890 book, *Races and Peoples*, lamented, "That philanthropy is false, that religion is rotten, which would sanction a white woman enduring the embrace of a colored man." There are too many texts to name, and these were not written by quacks but respected scholars. The only reason we know about the brutalities of slavery, dispossession and Jim Crow is because the long history of *anti-racist* struggles has exposed America as a less-than-perfect union. It should baffle all of us that any school or community would not want to teach the history of a movement that tried to make sure every person enjoyed freedom and safety, that wanted to end slavery and Jim Crow. If we live in a country that is supposedly built on the principles of freedom and democracy, wouldn't teaching about how courageous people risked their lives to ensure freedom for themselves and others be considered a good thing? Doesn't it instill those values in students? The implication of this right-wing logic is that America is great, slavery was a good idea and anti-racism sullied our noble tradition (and when the federal government attempted to ban slavery and segregation in the states, this was a case of overreach).

So let me ask you, George, what do you make of this legislative war on—let's be honest—liberal multiculturalism?

GY: Your observations, as usual, are critically insightful, and straight to the point. The draconian legislative maneuvers that you mention to repress critical discussion about the history of and current reality of U.S. racism also reminds me of McCarthyism, something out of the dystopian nightmare of *1984*. I also appreciate your honesty and clarity in calling out liberal multiculturalism in your insightful article[3] where you draw from the work of political theorist Wendy Brown. I think that liberal multiculturalism fails at being radical. I think that it is important to create academic and public spaces where deep critical discussion can take place, where parrhesia or courageous speech can take place. In this case, I'm thinking about courageous speech regarding anti-Black racism. The reality of white terrorism that Black people have had to endure must be represented, which is what *critically informed* multicultural pedagogies ought to do. We need to be creating discursive spaces that tell the truth about what it means to be Black in the U.S. It is about inclusion, representation and visibility. After all, this is what Black folk have been fighting for in terms of institutional, societal and political inclusion. But, liberal multiculturalism has a seductive edge. I say this because being "included" seems positive but it does not necessarily lead to one's liberation. This is a case where the institutional structures and norms of inclusion do the work of racial, gender, and class representation, but exclude the majority of folk who continue to suffer from racism, sexism and classism. I think that Martin Luther King Jr. had something like this in mind when he spoke of his fear that he had integrated his people into a burning house. That metaphor is so powerful. After all, who wants to be integrated into a house where a conflagration is occurring? Liberal multiculturalism says, "Yes, we see you. Now, be happy." One is seen, however, on terms that both erase one's self-representational agency and downplay or attempt to erase the brutal discursive and material conditions that prompted one (in this case Black people) to resist invisibility to begin with.

My sense is that the current legal attacks on [critical race theory (CRT)] presuppose a U.S. that has transcended all things racial and racist. Of course, this is nonsense and bad faith. I would even call it disgusting, because it stinks of lies that do violence to the lived histories of Black people in the U.S. So, not only do we suffer the physical and psychic pains of anti-Black racism, but we also suffer the pains of having that history ignored or even denied. The truth is that Black people continue to be policed and brutalized by racial capitalism, even as and after we had our first Black president. This says to me that holding political office (even the highest political office) by people who look like you and me, Robin, doesn't ipso facto do anything to radically change how anti-Black racism continues to impact Black people. If we are to radically trouble the opium of mere representation, then this will require that we critique how inclusion can function as a political cul-de-sac. Critics of CRT would rather we accept our place within the house of inclusion and pretend that we can breathe just fine from the smoke permeating the air of that house. We are required to celebrate "diversity" and "inclusion" even though our breath is being arrested, and we are being dehumanized, brutalized, and rendered abject in 21st-century U.S. Attacks on CRT are attacks on Black people's epistemological agency and our will to speak the truth.

Quite frankly, I have no need for white recognition or inclusion if this means that I relinquish my critical voice that confronts the lies of whiteness, capitalism, police brutality, poverty—all of which are inextricably linked. I agree with you that if the U.S. is allegedly predicated "on the principles of freedom and democracy," then, yes, one would think that the historical themes of courage and resistance against forms of oppression ought to be emphasized and taught. Yet, such themes are feared. It is this fear that has led to my name being put on the Professor Watchlist, which is a conversative website that places under surveillance the ideas of "leftist thinkers." This says to me that freedom and democracy continue to function, in so many ways, as nominal. There is a great irony here. Black people have attempted to make the U.S. more democratic than its monochromatically white institutions have ever willingly done. And yet our critical voices are being repressed, our engaging and courageous scholarship attacked, and our embodied psychic lives continuously under social, political and existential duress. Hence, my message is that we need to continue to push back against hegemonic structures that are unjust and designed to silence, structures that continue to exist as Black, Brown, and Indigenous people continue to be included. I assume that our inclusion is designed to communicate that we have arrived, as Sara Ahmed would argue, and that any critique at all is superfluous. For Ahmed, "diversity in this world becomes then a happy sign, a sign that racism has been overcome." So, I think that we need to resist such a happy sign and its attempt at obfuscation.

On this important and indispensable theme of resistance and push back, I would like to consider our respective disciplines. I'll begin with philosophy, which is probably the whitest field within the humanities. When I discovered philosophy at 17 years old, I had no idea that it was what the late philosopher Charles Mills called both *monochromatically* and *conceptually* white. As an undergraduate at the University of Pittsburgh, I was typically the only Black student. Every philosophical text was written by a white male thinker. It was only later, because of the influence of my mentor, Black historian and cultural theorist James G. Spady, that I came to realize that there were Black philosophers, ones with doctorates. I recall a feeling that I had been duped into thinking that I was alone, the only Black philosopher. I would also later experience a sense of alienation, of drowning in a sea of whiteness when attending philosophical conferences. Before moving to Emory University, I was the first Black professor of philosophy to be tenured in the history of the philosophy department at Duquesne University. I was also the first to teach entire graduate seminars on critical philosophy of race and critical whiteness studies. When I left, unfortunately, so did my graduate seminars. To my knowledge, there hasn't been a "replacement." Perhaps this is indicative of white institutional inertia.

Historically, the field of philosophy is dominated by white men. This reality impacts how Black people and people of color are perceived within the field. It was only later that I discovered that many prominent European philosophers (David Hume, Immanuel Kant, John Locke, et al.) were racists. Many Black philosophers did the critical work to expose the contradictions within the thought of these white philosophers, especially in terms of the ideals that they held and how those ideals were never intended to apply to Black people. David Hume thought that Black people were mere parrots. We know that he believed that Black people didn't have the capacity to generate original thoughts of their own. Black philosophers have been instrumental in critiquing the emptiness of ideal theory as an approach that belies non-ideal social, political and existential conditions (racism, sexism, classism, you name it). What we find is that the practice of white philosophy avoids issues of race and racism by ghettoizing and categorizing them as "non-philosophical." Imagine Black philosophers remaining silent on such practices. We must be honest: Mainstream academic philosophy is pregnant with all sorts of white conceptual assumptions that exclude and are hostile to Black experiences, Black life and Black knowledge production. In what ways have you dealt with the hegemonic structure of whiteness within the discipline of history and your identity as a Black historian?

RDGK: I have never met a Black faculty member my age or older, in any discipline, who hasn't experienced egregious racism in the academy. I've been through the drill many times in my 35 years in this job—stopped, questioned, frisked by campus security; mistaken by *colleagues* for a janitor or mail services employee; questioned by white students regarding my credentials, especially when teaching "U.S. history" or anything not designated "Black." Emory University, where I held my first tenure-track position in the late 1980s (and was the only Black faculty member in the history department), was a nightmare. My office was a converted broom closet, and the chair of history at the time prohibited me from teaching graduate courses, despite having my PhD in hand, a book in press and some peer-reviewed articles.

Meanwhile, junior colleagues who had either completed all the requirements for the PhD except for the dissertation or filed their dissertation after me were allowed to teach graduate students. To be fair, I had a few advocates in the department, like the distinguished Southern historian Dan T. Carter. But the biggest slight came when I learned that a faculty study group, made up mostly of younger scholars, was reading Antonio Gramsci. It never occurred to them to invite me, despite the fact that I was writing about Marxism and Marxist movements. They finally agreed to invite me when they decided to read Martin Bernal's *Black Athena* (vol. 1)—a book with which I was familiar, but far from my own field. No matter, they assumed anything "Black" was my special domain. I gracefully bowed out, but not before suggesting that they take a look at some of the Black scholars who preceded the publication of *Black Athena*, e.g., Cheikh Anta Diop, Frank M. Snowden Jr., George G.M. James, as well as my own mentor, Cedric J. Robinson.

But you posed a very specific question about my discipline, history. You have to realize that my education was totally unorthodox. I attended California State University at Long Beach, a second-tier state school, where

I earned a minor in Black studies (Maulana Karenga was one of my professors) and majored in history. I had a couple of radical Jewish professors who encouraged me to read whatever I wanted and confirmed that the historical canon was largely racist. I created my own canon: Walter Rodney, W. E. B. Du Bois, C. L. R. James, Vincent Harding, Angela Davis, Barbara Smith, William Leo Hansberry, Cheikh Anta Diop, Frantz Fanon, Marx and Engels, Lenin, Gramsci, Rosa Luxemburg, *ad infinitum*. I did most of my reading independently or in study groups organized by the All-African People's Revolutionary Party, the Communist Workers Party, and other groups. In 1983, I began graduate school in African history at UCLA, where, unsurprisingly, the canonical figures were white men: Philip Curtin, Jan Vansina, and so forth, but even some of the white scholars were fairly radical—Terence Ranger, Basil Davidson, Belinda Bozzoli, Frederick Cooper, Bill Freund. And of course, we were reading *African* scholars—B. A. Ogot, J.E. Inikori, Bernard Magubane, Samir Amin, Nina Mba, Arnold Temu, Bonaventure Swai, Issa Shivji, P. O. Esedebe, Chinweizu, etc. The debates were so different. They centered on questions of class, class struggle, the limits of nationalist historiography, underdevelopment, colonialism and decolonization. We were not losing sleep over Hegel's racist characterizations of Africa in his *Philosophy of History*, but instead read Hegel with much interest as a way to understand Fanon and, to a certain extent, Marx.

I emphasize these debates because the work my peers (comrades) and I were doing defied academic disciplines. In fact, most of my friends in grad school were not historians but filmmakers, literary scholars, budding political scientists and a small group working at the edge of philosophy. I was active in UCLA's African Activists Association, which consisted primarily of African students from the continent, many embroiled directly in national liberation struggles. For this reason, philosophy was very important to all of us.

One of the first articles I published in *Ufahamu*, the graduate student-run journal of the African Activists Association, was a long review essay on Leonard Harris's landmark anthology, *Philosophy Born of Struggle*. When it came out in 1985, I had just turned 23 and was a dedicated Marxist . . . and it shows! I'm embarrassed by most of it, but I invoke it here to illustrate the *benefits* of an inadequate education. Before reading this book, everything I knew about Western philosophy I learned in an undergraduate intro course, so to my mind Aristotle, St. Thomas Aquinas, Descartes, John Locke, Rousseau were far less relevant and important than Frederick Douglass, Alain Locke, Eugene C. Holmes, Cornel West, Angela Davis, Lucius T. Outlaw, Bernard Boxill, Johnny Washington, William R. Jones, Berkley and Essie Eddins, and of course, Leonard Harris. While I would disagree with much of the essay today, my sophomoric conclusion says a lot about why I valued philosophy: "Our oppression as a people does not afford us the luxury of relegating philosophy to the trash cans of Euro-America. . . . What Harris, et. al., has shown us is that Black thought, as distinct and diverse as it may be, does contain certain commonalities when applied to our experience. Our perspective is not that of the bearer of the shoe of racism, capitalism, and imperialism. We view our being—the phenomenology of Blackness—from underneath the foot."

So, in graduate school I studied with Cedric Robinson (author of *Black Marxism* and many other texts), Robert Hill (editor of the Marcus Garvey Papers and close friends and comrades of C. L. R. James, Walter Rodney, and others), and Mazisi Kunene (South African literary scholar and author of the epic poem *Emperor Shaka the Great*). However, when I switched my major field from African history to U.S. history because I could not get into South Africa to conduct research (after all, this was around 1985–1986), I started to bump up against the liberal version of the canonical racism W.E.B. Du Bois wrote about in his final chapter of *Black Reconstruction*, "The Propaganda of History." I remember vividly taking my written qualifying examinations in U.S. history—having only taken *one* course in the U.S. field. In those days, you were placed in an empty carrel with a typewriter and paper, and you had eight hours to answer three essay questions. The final question asked us to write a historiographical essay on a "major" U.S. historian. At first, I considered the Communist historian Herbert Aptheker but realized they would fail me immediately. Then I asked the faculty proctor, my advisor John Laslett, if W. E. B. DuBois would count, and he immediately shook his head. "He is more of a sociologist than an historian," is how he put it. I ended up writing a 10-page essay on Ulrich B. Phillips, the profession's greatest apologist for slavery. Needless to say, I passed.

I know I dwelled on my formative years in this profession, but similar problems persisted. To talk about them will seem redundant. I'll briefly mention one struggle that took up probably a decade of my career—to deghettoize U.S. labor history. For many years, there was this field called labor history that sometimes dealt with race and Black workers, but when Black scholars wrote about Black workers (here I'm thinking about '90s and early 2000s, folks like Joe W. Trotter, Earl Lewis, Tera Hunter, Venus Green, Elsa Barkley Brown, and others), we took issue with the fact that those of us working on Black workers were generally relegated to panels about Black workers or about race, when our work was throwing down the gauntlet to the entire field of labor history. I found myself in a similar situation when the U.S. history profession had announced a "transnational turn," again in the late 1990s. I was invited to a conference to talk about what this meant for "Black history" but ended up writing an essay arguing that Black struggles for freedom had been transnational and global from the beginning, and that it was the rest of the profession that was coming to these matters about a century late! My remarks were published in the *Journal of American History* as "'But a Local Phase of a World Problem': Black History's Global Vision, 1883-1950."

GY: Years ago, I knew a white philosophy graduate student who probably did lose sleep over Hegel's racism because she didn't know what he thought about Africa until she took my seminar, and this was while she was reading Hegel's *Phenomenology of Spirit* in another seminar in the same department. I'm sure that I also lost sleep after finding out about the racism of prominent white philosophers. One is led to believe that the racism, no matter how abhorrent, is incidental and unrelated to the critical period of the philosopher. Regarding your idea of creating your own canon or a counter-canon, however, is what Spady did for me. So, I was fortunate to meet him while I was still in high school. His was a clear and profound motivational impact. Spady situated my thinking squarely within Black intellectually generative spaces. This included engaging important questions and themes within the Negritude Movement, the Harlem Renaissance, the Black Arts Movement, Afro-Surrealism, Dadaism, the Civil Rights movement, Pan-Africanism, the organizational and historical importance of the Universal Negro Improvement Association (UNIA), the Nation of Islam, and engaging the lives, writings and ideas of such figures as Kwame Nkrumah, Cheikh Anta Diop, Ngũgĩ wa Thiong'o, Nnamdi Azikiew, Kamau Brathwaite, Elijah Muhammad, Malcolm X, Martin Luther King Jr., George G. M. James, Elmer Imes, Marcus Garvey, bell hooks, Geneva Smitherman, Sonia Sanchez, Paula Giddings, Katherine Dunham, W. E. B. Du Bois, Ralph Bunche, Grandmaster Caz, Eve, Kool Herc, Sister Souljah, Afrika Bambaataa, Tupac Shakur, and the entire array of racial, historical, cultural, spatial, political, musicological, sonic and aesthetic modalities within rap and Hip-Hop culture as well as so many other forms of musical expression. I have come to understand Spady's impact as both helping me to appreciate Black intellectual and cultural creativity as important in and of itself and facilitating my understanding of the insidious operations of whiteness. Concerning the latter, in "The Souls of White Folk," as you know, W. E. B. Du Bois argued that he was singularly clairvoyant regarding white folk. I think this is true of many Black philosophers and Black scholars. Du Bois writes, "I see these souls undressed and from the back and side. I see the working of their entrails. I know their thoughts and they know that I know. This knowledge makes them now embarrassed, now furious." Du Bois isn't arguing that he is possessed with some preternatural capacity. I think that he is making an appeal to what we would call a variation of standpoint theory, where social location is relevant to knowledge formation and insight into the workings of hegemonic structures (racial, gender, class). And in *The Souls of Black Folk*, Du Bois deploys the concept of the gift of second sight, which is a site of epistemological clarity and insight. Again, Charles Mills is helpful here. In "The Illumination of Blackness," he writes, "The position of Blacks is unique among all the groups racialized as nonwhite by the modern West. For no other nonwhite group has race been so enduringly constitutive of their identity, so foundational for racial capitalism, and so lastingly central to white racial consciousness and global racial consciousness in general." I agree with Mills and accept this characterization as the basis upon which Black folk (even if not all) are able to see, name and call out white racism. If we take Du Bois seriously, whiteness has created, as it were, its own disagreeable mirror. Robin, what is it that keeps many white people so wedded to whiteness? What makes them so furious when their whiteness is unveiled?

RDGK: Right. Hard questions. Before I try to answer, I want to give credit to other scholars who had come to see Du Bois's notion of double consciousness as a way of seeing "white" and "global" racial consciousness long before Charles Mills. The historian Thomas Holt had begun to make the case in his 1990 *American Quarterly* essay, "The Political Uses of Alienation: W. E. B. Du Bois on Politics, Race, and Culture, 1903-1940," and Nahum Chandler advanced perhaps the most thorough argument along these lines, first in his 1996 doctoral dissertation, "The Problem of Purity: A Study in the Early Work of W.E.B. Du Bois." One of his many original claims is that Du Bois's notion of double consciousness applied to Black subjectivity actually represents a philosophical breakthrough in the study of subjectivity as a whole, and race as a whole (not just blackness). He further develops these and other ideas in his 2013 book, *X: The Problem of the Negro as a Problem for Thought*, which is nothing short of a masterpiece. At the center of his exegesis is the idea that the so-called "Negro problem" was more than just the *raison d'etre* for modern racism but fundamentally *a problem of thought*. He makes the case that Du Bois's approach to the "Negro Question" flipped the question of Black striving into an interrogation of the modern subject under racial capitalism.

I think it is important to begin here just to remind ourselves that the point of Du Bois's "second sight" was not just to understand whiteness and the racism that produces this particular form of social pathology, but to get free. That said, I completely agree with Mills that for white people race is not only constitutive of their identity but "foundational for racial capitalism." However, enduring doesn't mean "natural" or even stable. Whiteness is a deception that people are under pressure to reproduce in order to maintain class power. Racial capitalism entails the "capture" of exploited white workers as junior partners in the settler state through the myth of white racial superiority. Cedric Robinson was spot on when he wrote in *Forgeries of Memory and Meaning*: "White patrimony deceived some of the majority of Americans, patriotism and nationalism others, *but the more fugitive reality was the theft they themselves endured and the voracious expropriation of others they facilitated.* The scrap which was their reward was the installation of Black inferiority into their shared national culture. It was a paltry dividend, but it still serves."

This dividend, I would argue, takes at least four forms:

1. Actual material benefits, which are differential according to class and gender.
2. The *expectation* of material benefits, i.e., the path to becoming a slaveholder or boss or a CEO, which should be understood as an entitlement rather than privilege, and it's one that is rarely fulfilled.
3. The everyday expression or performance of institutional power, or put simply, the racial education of what it means to *not* be white. The spectacle of racism in practice teaches white people the consequences of being Black or Brown. Hyper-policing, premature death, caging, deportation, relegation to segregated neighborhoods and dilapidated housing, houselessness, job insecurity, racially segmented occupations (consider who works in fast food, private security, janitorial services, domestic work, etc.). Sure, there are some white people who recognize injustice and propose toothless liberal bromides, such as anti-racism workshops designed to "change hearts." But there are also radicals among them who join us in fighting the beast; and others who—perhaps unconsciously insecure about their own status—actively attack and further degrade Black, Brown, Indigenous, and Asian people, often with fatal consequences and almost no accountability.
4. The majority, however, are *indifferent*—which is to say, spectacular and mundane acts of everyday racism are normalized or simply not seen. The irony is that indifference leads liberal white people to the conclusion that Black people are in the condition they're in and suffer the

way they do because of, well . . . anti-Blackness. This is just the way it is and has been. Anti-Blackness is permanent, nothing has changed, and nothing will change. Sounds familiar? It is essentially the Afropessimist lite position, and the one that most of my *white* students accept without question. I say "lite" because it doesn't require an explanation; it is a fact. My point is that, while we argue with those who claim we've achieved a post-racial nirvana, a broad segment of white America had long accepted that Black people are treated like shit because they are Black. Not by them, of course, but by all the other white folks.

Where does that leave us? As Olúfẹ́mi Táíwò points out in his new book, *Elite Capture*, indifference is made possible by a culture that promotes individualism, values wealth as a measure of success, and is fundamentally anti-democratic. Elected officials, mainly in the pockets of the "successful" class, make crucial decisions about our lives as we watch from the sidelines. Indifference means there is no sense of a public good, no moral universe to speak of. Imagine, if our political culture was oriented entirely toward caring for the whole, where no one was excluded? Institutional racism would be illegal. Our culture would not be based on the protection of private property but the principle "all of us or none of us." We'd have social housing, clean energy, publicly owned free mass transit, free medical care, food security, etc. I'm sure there would still be white people wedded to whiteness, but its value would be greatly diminished.

GY: I appreciate your reminder of the history of how Du Bois's understanding of double consciousness was taken up by other scholars and for reminding us of the liberatory implications of second sight. In fact, this last point is exactly what Mills argues in "The Illumination of Blackness." There he is playing on "illumination." In that piece, he both illuminates Blackness and demonstrates how Blackness, despite its theological and racist deployment as a site of ignorance, doom and darkness, actually illuminates the world. He argues that it is Black people, arguing from feminist standpoint theory, who are better able to see the political, institutional, affective and epistemological (though distortive) inner workings of whiteness. For Mills, white people tend to create a social world that they fail to understand. This is what he means by epistemology of ignorance, a term that he coined. He argues that whiteness, which operates politically as a racial contract, involves "a particular pattern of localized and global cognitive dysfunctions." Du Bois argues that he is able to see the "entrails" of white people. His language speaks to the transparency of whiteness vis-à-vis the Black counter-gaze.

I would also mention that Mills would certainly agree with you that "enduring doesn't mean 'natural' or even stable." I'm sure that he would argue that whiteness as both a U.S. and global phenomenon is persistent and tenacious. Structurally, whiteness embodies a form of ignorance that actively obfuscates understanding itself, an ignorance that resists and fights back. It is an ignorance that presents "itself," as Mills says, "unblushingly as knowledge." And while one might disagree with Mills's optimism regarding liberalism, one that is "free" of white supremacy, one that is no longer an illiberal liberalism, he doesn't see whiteness or white supremacy as "natural," but as socially constructed and thereby socially, institutionally and psychically changeable.

It is here that I'm more of a pessimist. In fact, while it is true that racial capitalism entails the "capture" of exploited white workers, as you put it, and situates white workers as junior partners, I would only add the fact that exploited white workers were also deemed *human* under white supremacy. There is a deep anthropological investment in whiteness, one that also has deep theologically symbolic implications. After all, to be white was to resemble Adam and Eve. It was German anthropologist Johann Friedrich Blumenbach who claimed that Adam and Eve were Caucasian. Being white (that is, not being Black) provided exploited white workers with the *racial* material affordance, as Mills might say, to reevaluate their junior partnership against the backdrop of Blackness and thereby reposition themselves as demigods. In "Killers of the Dream," Lillian Smith writes, "There, in the Land of Epidermis, every one of us was a little king."

As you know, in a major part of my philosophical work, I theorize and interrogate whiteness. I'm especially attentive to its lived dimensions, how it functions at the level of body comportment, how white people react to Black bodies within racialized spaces, how the white gaze operates, how whiteness hegemonically claims the domain of the human, how whiteness constitutes a social ontological binary, how whiteness has stereotyped the Black body as inferior, wicked, smelly, criminal, and how whiteness is invested in the degradation of Blackness. I have been under the impression that there are some whites who would rather be poor and white than to be wealthy and Black. I recall a white male student once saying to me that he would like to be Black to benefit from affirmative action. I said to him that it doesn't work like that. You must be born Black and you must continue to be Black. There was this look on his face that clearly revealed that he had to rethink his assessment of affirmative action. He wanted to be Black without living the life of a Black person within an anti-Black U.S. The more that I think about anti-Black racism, it occurs to me that there is no other wretched and abject place that is more despicable. That is, Blackness is a fundamental site of the subhuman. Many other racialized groups attempt to distance themselves from Blackness. There is this sense that one's worth and dignity is augmented the closer that one approaches whiteness. This says to me that to be recognized as "human," then I must become white. I have no desire to become white, Robin. What are your thoughts about this deeply personal sense of dread?

RDGK: I feel you. You've made a very powerful, personal and moving observation. Part of your question I think I answered above. But I will also concede that I personally have never felt that sense of dread, I suppose because I've experienced Blackness as a site of solidarity and radical critique. The invention of European Man depended on reducing us to the category of subhuman in order to justify white supremacy, slavery, and settler colonialism. Maybe I am a bad reader of Frantz Fanon, but I return to his oft-quoted line from *The Wretched of the Earth*: "It is the colonist who fabricated and continues to fabricate the colonized subject." We have consistently refused his fabrication, retained our dignity, found joy, created families, communities, movements and even proclaimed a position as the *real* humans against the inhumanity of the European/white settler. Lewis Gordon has been making this point for years, most recently in his latest masterpiece, *Fear of Black Consciousness*, where he recognizes a shift from "a suffering black consciousness to a liberatory Black consciousness in which revelation of the dirty laundry and fraud of white supremacy and black inferiority is a dreaded truth." The protectors of white supremacy should be dreading us, in other words.

Yes, I've encountered my share of white men—and they are always men—who say they wish they were Black, but to quote the title of a book edited by the late great Greg Tate, they want "everything but the burden" of being Black. Still, I encountered way more Black people, especially growing up, who said they were happy and relieved *not* to be white.

I don't want to diminish this sense of personal dread. It is real, especially when the consequences of being Black means persistent vulnerability to premature death. But I can say that personally, if proximity to whiteness has had any impact on my personal worth, it is only because it further exposes the absurdity of racism since what I mainly see are mediocre white people in high positions of power and authority. They're everywhere. It's simultaneously hilarious and terrifying!

Finally, I want to hold up the magnificent work of James Edwards Ford III, whose book *Thinking Through Crisis: Depression-Era Black Literature, The-*

ory, and Politics really gets at some of these questions. His brilliant critique of liberal trauma theory draws on Du Boisian "second sight" to recover modalities of Black radical thought and praxis, not in order to illuminate the problem of whiteness but to think *with* Black people in motion in the face of crisis. The following quote is instructive:

"*Thinking Through Crisis* critiques trauma theory for its dedication to the image of European Man. . . . Trauma theory can offer a liberal response that, at best, bears witness to suffering while offering few, if any, insights into altering the systemic factors perpetuating that suffering. Agency, in this framework, remains limited to practices already recognized and constrained by conventional liberal-democratic norms valorizing some forms of suffering and sufferers over many others. Nor can trauma theory fully account for how those living outside these norms are ignored and, when noticed, are punished for transgressing limits that were impossible to obey. *Thinking Through Crisis* stays with specific forms of life outside these norms, forms of life that consider transformation of material conditions indispensable to working through overwhelming experiences." It is precisely those forms of life and struggle outside of the norms and institutional structures of racialized class power that we need to embrace in order to stay sane and whole. This is what the Black radical tradition looks like; this is life in what Fred Moten and Stefano Harney call "the Undercommons."

GY: When you mention not feeling dread, I feel both joy and dread. There are times when I wished that I didn't feel that dread. I'm sure that there are moments when I'm overcome with "Blackness as a site of solidarity and radical critique." Yet, I wonder if such critical spaces only function as temporary reprieves, sites where we celebrate our lives as a collective with the understanding that we are an excluded people, but a people of tremendous intellectual brilliance, shared history and political praxis. Such moments take the form of marronage,[4] where, in this case, there is a separation from the established order, perhaps even law and order that are tropes of whiteness. At some point, though, we must emerge from the critical gathering, after "the Clearing" as this takes place in Toni Morrison's *Beloved*, where Black people dance, cry and love their own bodies through a more organic and dynamic sense of sociality. Within the clearing, there is a different sense of aesthetics, bodily movement, affective gravity and togetherness. The Metropole, as it were, is bracketed, but we still find ourselves faced with the terror of structural anti-Black racism in the form of civil society. In such moments, the knee of a white police officer is on the neck of George Floyd as he calls for his Momma; Eric Garner is crying out, "I can't breathe"; and Breonna

Taylor is being shot to death after her privacy is violated in the form of a no-knock warrant that increases the hegemony of state policing. To put this metaphorically and yet tragically, there are times when Black life feels like a "shooting star," a momentary streak of life across the dark sky. It's not just the temporality that I'm concerned with here, but the fact that a shooting star is *not* a star, but scattered pieces of debris or waste. Indeed, within the context of white mythmaking, Black bodies are nothing more than refuse that is disposable and yet necessary. So, even after those moments of Black solidarity, I reach for my wallet, as in the case of Amadou Diallo in 1999, and I'm shot at 41 times and hit with 19 bullets. The racial contract remains, and white law and order have been maintained. On this point, let's return to Mills and link this to another question that I have.

In doing public intellectual work, specifically in terms of writing high-profile public essays, I have been called all types of racist, vitriolic epithets by white people who have read my work on whiteness. There is this seemingly impenetrable race-evasive posture that goes into effect. I think that Charles Mills is correct that white people have created a world that they in general will not understand. There are all sorts of bad faith maneuvers. For example, some white readers of my work have argued that because I teach at a prestigious university that I shouldn't complain about racism because I have "made it." This position is problematic in so many ways. These white readers seemingly fail to understand that if I have achieved anything it is *despite* anti-Black racism. Indeed, my "success" doesn't disprove anti-Black racism. I continue to be its target. There is also the point that the consumptive dimensions of white neoliberal capitalism can find a way to benefit from what I offer in terms of intellectual labor. This is where I engage in both self-critique and the critique of other successful Black scholars who engage questions of white supremacy and racial injustice. Think about it. There are a number of us who are hired by prestigious academic institutions to teach ideas that are designed to trouble those spaces, to advance critical discourses against hegemonic ideological paradigms and practices. And while there is work to be done intramurally, how do we avoid becoming functionaries? This raises the issue of what academic radicality looks like. Perhaps I'm being a bit cynical, but neoliberalism is more than capable of absorbing what we throw at it. This is related to my earlier observations regarding liberal multiculturalism. Across domains of race and gender, a number of Black scholars and academics engage in radical pursuits that are consistent with problematic forms of capitalist accumulation: academic entrepreneurship, big salary increases and demanding large sums of money to give lectures/talks for just an hour. Not that we should take individual "vows of poverty."

However, what do you think about "radical scholarship" by scholars who nevertheless are part of a neoliberal capitalistic system and institutions that pay us and that we then, through our scholarship, help to scaffold the elite status of?

RDGK: Well, we are all a part of the neoliberal capitalistic system, but it doesn't mean we can't stand against it and produce work critical of the system. I think your life and work proves the point since the attacks you've endured are not, in my view at least, motivated solely by anti-Blackness. Rather, you do public work that threatens the status quo.

Your question is important, and fortunately for us Steven Osuna has written a thorough and powerful answer in his essay, "Class Suicide: The Black Radical Tradition, Radical Scholarship, and the Neoliberal Turn," published in *Futures of Black Radicalism*, edited by Gaye Theresa Johnson and Alex Lubin. Taking his lead from Cedric Robinson, he points to several examples of intellectuals who consciously chose to align themselves with the people, with movements resisting the status quo. Some of these organic intellectuals held university positions and some were fired for their activism. As you know, I don't believe universities are inherently sites of opposition, though spaces have been created in the past and present for oppositional work. Is this work vulnerable to commodification and neoliberal capture? Of course, but only insofar as it remains untethered to social movements. We will not always get it right, but unless we fight, we cannot hope to change our condition.

So my question to you is, how do you avoid becoming a functionary, a cog in the neoliberal machine? As a deeply committed anti-racist intellectual, dedicated to dismantling the structures we've been discussing, what do you see as your main task within the academy?

GY: I appreciate your honesty regarding the fact of our situation as academics. I think that's important as I am often confronted by my own sense of academic entitlement and how that academic position is itself a function of the neoliberal capitalistic system. For me, I confront what feels like an aporia, an internal contradiction that pulls at my conscience. I recall once giving a keynote address at Yale at the 77th Annual Meeting of The English Institute. I began my talk by bringing attention to the fact that there were so many people experiencing homelessness in New Haven, right around Yale. This was not some superficial act of virtue signaling, but an act of self-critique. Someone in the audience responded by saying something like, "Who says that *they* want to be in here with us?" For me, the response was a function of privilege—in this case both white and academic. My point was not about a perfunctory form of charity or to suggest that we were the envy of those experiencing poverty. I brought attention to the fact that we were inside, comfortable, with sufficient clothing and warm air, and that our stomachs were full. The point is that not one of us, to my knowledge, asked those on the outside if they wanted to join "us." Perhaps, for me, I'm feeling the weight of an ethical contradiction that I have not been able to shake. Hell, no matter how many books I publish or distinguished keynote addresses that I deliver, there will be people who are living in squalor in the U.S. Last I checked, there are 689 million people living in poverty[5] on a global level, of which 356 million are children.[6] When I'm teaching, it is that reality, and other social, political and existential devastating realities, that hit, and hit hard. During such times, at least for me, there is a sense of academic sophistication that is mocked by the pervasiveness of human suffering experienced by those who are deprived of basic necessities. I think that part of what helps me to contest and critique *how I am structurally situated* as a functionary or a cog in the neoliberal machine is precisely by bringing attention to the historical, institutional, habitual, aspirational, and normative forces that hail me. So, it is not clear that I am able to "avoid" being a functionary as opposed to being able to trouble that site. I bring as much critical discourse and critical affect as I can to bear upon the suffering (economically and otherwise) that takes place around us as academics. I am haunted by the real possibility that our intramural academic lives are constitutive of forms of indifference and silence regarding those persons outside the boundaries of "sacred" academic spaces. Of course, this is not to deny various forms of suffering that are explicitly and implicitly authorized within the academy itself—racism, sexism, classism, elitism, narcissism, and backstabbing. In the Yale example, I was pained and deeply concerned by the disarticulation of what we were doing within that Ivy League institutional space and what was happening on the streets outside. I was and continue to be haunted by that. I wanted to identify the elephant in the room, to have us think about what Joy James critiques as our "desire to be famous, powerful, and wealthy"[7] within the context of liberation struggle inside or outside of the academy. Sure, I got to deliver my keynote address, to engage in critical discourse about, in this case, whiteness, but I got the impression that academics within that space were problematically seduced by critical discourse itself, even as the discourse was designed to trouble the status quo. So, for these reasons, and so many more, I don't think that I will get it right, though I/we must fight, resist, protest. I also think that we must remain aware not only of how oppositional work can be compromised, but how social movements are not invulnerable to commodification and neo-liberal capture. There is nothing that logically prevents social movements from cooptation.

My task within the academy takes a specific mode of address. I call upon my students to bear witness to all forms of suffering, which means that I try to mirror as best I can my own human fallibility, my failures, but also my strengths, my courage and my capacity to risk modalities of comfort, which is, as you said, linked to the work that I do that threatens the status quo. I want my students to tarry with the weight of the global mess that we are collectively in. Tarrying, by the way, is not intended to function as a site of serenity, but crisis. More specifically, I encourage my white students to rethink and tarry with the ways in which they are complicit within structures of white domination, how their white privilege works as an af-fordance where they get to move across college and university spaces with ease without ever questioning their sense of belonging.

So, I attempt to cultivate not just a critical consciousness, but a radi-cally different way of feeling, a structure of sensitivity that occasions differ-ent ways that white students listen and are receptive to forms of suffering that call from beyond their sense of themselves as white neoliberal subjects and thereby provide a critical space where my white students are able to rethink what it means to be radically ethical in a world of global whiteness. This also involves the augmentation of their critical imaginaries. The root of what I'm doing pedagogically is to demonstrate what the Hebrew word *hesed* or loving-kindness demands of us, and how it ought to hasten what we do ethically once we leave the classroom. Pedagogically, my main task is to encourage a radical form of love that may—perhaps—generate a col-lective refusal of another day of human suffering, which would also involve nonhuman animals and the earth itself.

Given that your own work examines the global dimensions of in-ternationalist anti-racist activism, how do you understand the relationship between such activism and current antiwar work?

RDGK: Not an easy question. First, I don't recall a moment in my lifetime when there wasn't an antiwar movement or a war that wasn't fundamen-tally racist. Vietnam, Cambodia, Chile, Central America, Southern Africa, Grenada, Panama, Palestine, Bosnia, Iraq, Somalia, Libya, Afghanistan, Syria, Northern Mexico, and that's not the half of it. Wars on Communism, wars on terror, wars on drugs. Russia's brutal invasion of Ukraine is a bit different in that we're facing the threat of nuclear war, a potential escalation that might draw the U.S. and NATO directly into the fighting, and the fact of the war's "whiteness." On the one hand, a driver of massive military and humanitarian support for Ukraine is the representation of its victims as white Europeans, not like those Brown refugees from the Middle East. Of course, this erases all of the Black and Brown people inside Ukraine, African, and South Asian workers and students, the former subjected to anti-Black racism, pulled off trains, detained, denied the right to leave. On the other hand, there is the inconvenient fact that among Ukraine's combatants defending the "homeland" is the neo-Nazi Azov Regiment founded by a group of virulent white supremacists. Meanwhile, we are all expected to "Stand by Ukraine."

The work ahead is to stop this war as soon as possible, and to stop all wars. Without taking anything away from the utter devastation and suffering in Ukraine, we are obliged to keep reminding the world of the unremitting attacks on Palestinians under the Zionist state's illegal occupation and within the '48 borders, and the carnage in Yemen—both backed by the United States. Over 160,000 Yemenis are likely to experience famine over the second half of this year, and some 17 million people are currently in need of food assistance, all because of the war. And yet, the Biden administration is extending the olive branch to Saudi Arabia just to get oil, while refusing to lift the sanctions on Venezuela or make a more robust shift away from fossil fuels. Face it, war not only dooms the planet through violent destruction, but also is a primary driver of the climate catastrophe. The U.S. Department of Defense is the single largest consumer of energy in the U.S. and the world's largest consumer of petroleum. So while we might stand behind the slogan that Putin must be stopped, the U.S. and NATO must also be stopped. The urgent work of anti-racists is to end war, now and forever.

GY: There are times when I feel that anti-Black racism will continue indefinitely. Like Sisyphus, there is some movement, but that movement doesn't free us from the inexorable recursive backlash of anti-Blackness. I understand the importance of Black struggle, but what is Black struggle without end, without the end of anti-Black racism? Where is the great Exodus? After all, as Black abolitionist Henry Highland Garnet stated, "The Pharaohs are on both sides of the blood-red water." And the arc of the moral universe (assuming that it is moral) can be so long that its bending continues to feel like a straight line. I know that there is a lot here, Robin, but how is it that a people continue to face such racist brutality and terror and yet remain hopeful?

RDGK: I'd love to know your thoughts on this question. My answer is relatively brief, in part because it is the question I confront every morning

I wake up. First, if there is such a thing as the arc of the moral universe, it does not bend on its own. We bend it one way, our enemies bend it back. As the old Civil Rights song goes, "they say that freedom is a constant struggle." By acknowledging this fact, I don't feel particularly hopeful or pessimistic or optimistic, just determined.

Second, yes, of course we must end anti-Black racism, but as I argued earlier in our conversation, this doesn't mean changing hearts. It's really about bringing down Pharaoh—that is to say, dismantling power and establishing forms of accountability. It means power to the people. It means ending oppressive institutions like prisons, police, patriarchy and racial capitalism. Hopeful or not, we don't have the luxury not to fight. There is no guarantee that we will win—whatever that means—but I guarantee that if we don't fight, we lose.

GY: There are times when I think that hope is our Achilles heel. What do I mean by that? Hope is that capacity that keeps Black people yearning for more despite the setbacks, the gratuitous violence, and the fact that we continue to be treated as less than human. But what if hope is our obstacle? What if hope is the unintended assurance that further solidifies anti-Black racism? After all, hope can displace the full weight of our collective expressive rage; hope gestures toward the future, communicating that we will make it—someday. Indeed, that "we gon' be alright," as Kendrick Lamar raps. This is where I'm torn. Hope had to play a profoundly significant role in sustaining Black bodies within the slave ships, during plantation oppression, during the creation of Black codes and during Jim Crow terrorism. And it continues to sustain us today. This is not to oppose hope as resistance, because hope can function as resistance. However, what if we collectively decided, as Black people, to rid ourselves of hope, a form of hope which seems to be linked (though not totally reducible) to some form of white "acceptance," if not just white tolerance? Ridding ourselves of hope doesn't mean that we are morose; rather, it gestures toward the relinquishment of all cooperation with tomorrow's promise, one that has proven repeatedly that there is only Black death that awaits us there. My aim is not to endorse a form of nihilism, but to interrogate the ethics of hope in the face of an anti-Black world that is relentlessly hell-bent on our destruction.

17

WHITE JOURNALISTS ARE STILL USING THE N-WORD

This Is an Intolerable Assault on Black Freedom

INTERVIEW WITH ELIZABETH STORDEUR PRYOR

When I read about the two Black Capitol Police officers who were called the n-word during the storming of the Capitol on January 6, I thought about my own experiences of being called that uniquely horrible word from some white readers of my public philosophical work.

The word—which is vile, ugly, and violent—is part of an anti-Black vocabulary meant to defile Black people. The word has a long history and has been the subject of debate within academia (around who gets to say it and when) and among Black people themselves. In recent weeks, this debate has flared once more as two white journalists have ignited a heated discussion regarding their use of the n-word.

To explore these issues and more, I had the honor of interviewing Elizabeth Stordeur Pryor, who is an associate professor of history at Smith College, and the author of an award-winning article, "The Etymology of [N-Word]: Resistance, Language and the Politics of Freedom in the Antebellum North,"[1] and a 2016 monograph entitled *Colored Travelers: Mobility and the Fight for Citizenship before the Civil War.*[2]

Her new project is a historical and pedagogical study of the n-word framed by her experience as a biracial woman in the United States. Pryor

G. Yancy (with Elizabeth Stordeur Pryor), "White Journalists' Use of the N-Word Is an Intolerable Assault on Black Freedom," in *Truthout*, February 27, 2021. [Editors: Alana Yu-lan Price, Britney Schultz, and Anton Woronczuk]

is an award-winning teacher with 10 years of experience teaching about and examining the n-word; she is Smith College's faculty teaching mentor; and she conducts faculty workshops on navigating the n-word and other racist language in the classroom. Her 2020 TED talk[3] on the n-word has more than 2 million views. Pryor's work on the n-word is indispensable as the U.S. deals with its history of white supremacy and its extant unabashed re-emergence.

GEORGE YANCY: Given the history of Black anti-racism in this country, I would think that explaining to white people that the n-word is off limits would not need to be debated. However, I get the impression that some white people feel at ease using the racist slur and perhaps are unconvinced that it should not be used. This month two white journalists have reignited conversation on this topic over their use of the n-word. Donald McNeil Jr., who was a science and health journalist at *The New York Times*, used the racist slur while in Peru with high school students on a trip. He used it in conversation with a student within a larger context of discussing racist language. Mike Pesca, a podcaster at *Slate*, is said to have argued that within certain contexts it is permissible for white people to use the n-word. It seems to me that taking the position that white people should not use the n-word is uncontroversial. Perhaps I'm being overly sensitive or draconian. What are your thoughts?

ELIZABETH STORDEUR PRYOR: Stories like the ones involving McNeil and Pesca read to me like dangerous clickbait. The premise is, as Bret Stephens recently published in *The New York Times*, the thought police is coming to get you. Framed as reflections of a woke culture gone awry, these news stories remind me of the 1915 film *The Birth of a Nation* in which emancipation of 4 million enslaved people and their political elevation is drawn as a direct threat to white freedom, well-being and safety. Thus, the idea that Black people today might give voice to their displeasure at having to confront the n-word at work, at school, in a carelessly worded Slack conversation, emerges as fodder for white liberals and the conservative right to imagine themselves as victims of the overzealous hordes of Black people (and their allies) who are gunning for their freedom and their rights. It's *The Birth of a Nation*, 2.0. And in the film, the cure was the rise of the KKK. So what's the cure to this so-called unwieldy exercise of Black freedom? The media framing of these stories is pernicious.

I always think, instead, about the tremendous sacrifice it takes for the person who dares to speak up in these moments. I wonder what it took for a teenager to stand up to McNeil or report him, to put their foot down and say, "No! Why should I have to feel shame and fear and unprotected simply because you're trying to speak your mind for the sake of argument?"

Moreover, there's always more to these cases than meets the eye. The spokeswoman for *Slate* says of the Pesca suspension, *look, I'm not going to get into details, but,* "I can confirm this was not a decision based around making an isolated abstract argument in a Slack channel."

In other words, this isn't only about using the n-word once or even only about using the n-word. I see this in my own research. White people and non-Black POC every day unwittingly speak the n-word, and they don't end up losing their jobs or in the news. That's because it is not uncommon in conversations to misspeak, to stand corrected and to adjust your approach in the future . . . maybe even offer an apology. In the cases that grab the attention of the media, however, the person accused usually doubles down. They insist they have the right; they refuse to listen or even engage a conversation about the harm they cause.

This is what I'd like folks to consider: If you want to have an open debate about the n-word, why not have it while using the surrogate phrase "the n-word" instead of the actual word? The phrase is not a tool of polite society. Instead, it has radical roots. It is born out of the activism and intellectualism of African Americans in the late 1980s and early 1990s who refused to repeat the anti-Blackness hurled against them. We have the n-word phrase in our lexicon, people know what it means (or can Google it), so why say the actual word just to make a point?

GY: As a philosopher, I have made it my aim to engage philosophy within more expansive public contexts. This is important as philosophy is still perceived as abstract and socially irrelevant. Writing outside insular academic institutional contexts has its rewards, but there are downsides. For example, while some who engage in more public philosophy receive the occasional nasty message from a reader, I have received tons of hate mail. I have received email messages, voice messages left on my university answering machine, letters and postcards mailed to my office. While there are often some very choice expletives that are used, the n-word appears frequently. I cannot recall how many times I have been called the n-word. I thought that I could just brush it off, but my sense is that being called the n-word impacts one's Black body even if its full impact is not registered until later. During the white supremacist violence unleashed at the Capitol on January 6, I recall reading about two of the Black Capitol Police officers being called the n-word. In fact, one of the Black veteran officers said that he was called the n-word 15 times during that day. He cried later, which was no doubt because of the white supremacist physical violence that he experienced, but also because of the use of that ugly word. It functions like a knee to one's neck.[4] I would like for you to speak to the word's violence. I ask this because the word is not isolated from the white terror out of which it has been shaped.

ESP: At the core of the n-word is violence. It has long been a weapon of white supremacy. I think it's important, too, that you were called the n-word in reaction to your public-facing work. I have been too. I once received an email that was basically a string of anti-Black epithets (monkey, sow, the misogynistic c-word and the n-word was in there at least two or three times). I got the email because I talked to a *CNN* reporter about the pervasiveness of the terms "slave" and "master" in 21st-century public discourse. In the same way, it's important that the Black police officers, ostensibly members of the Blue Lives [Matter] camp that Trump supporters so vehemently defend, are people who wind up on the firing end of the n-word. It's precisely when Black folks speak out and assert ourselves as free people that we confront the word.

Often, my students will say that they understand the roots of the n-word, that it comes from slavery. They are right to an extent. The word appears as soon as the first 20 enslaved Africans arrive in British North America in 1619. Those captives are referred to as n-words; they are understood as Black involuntary laborers, as slaves. Over time, their labor is institutionalized within the body of Black women (a child follows the condition of the mother) and their enslavement lasts in perpetuity (me, my children and my children's children). Any person occupying that labor category in the emerging United States would be called the n-word.

But the evidence suggests the violence of that particular word (not of enslavement, of course, but of the n-word itself) manifests later. It is in the early 1800s, as African-descended people become free in the northern states—Massachusetts, Connecticut, New York—that the n-word latches on like a shackle. Suddenly, the unflattering word used to describe an actual and existing labor category is now attributed to all people with Black skin, free or otherwise, and it's meant to signify that Black servility is immutable and that Black folks are incapable of embodying freedom. So, more than anything, the n-word is an assault against Black freedom and a rallying cry of anti-Blackness for exactly that reason. When a Black cop, despite their membership among the boys of blue, defies white aggression, they are deemed nothing more than n-words, particularly because they stand up. The same is true when African Americans, such as Obama, are prosperous.

According to this thinking, any kind of Black mobility (social, political, economic) is a direct threat to white supremacy, and the person enacting that mobility [is] an n-word.

GY: Believe it or not, years ago, in one of my philosophy courses where we were talking about white privilege, one of my white male students argued that it is discriminatory to prevent white people from using the n-word. As a Black professor, it was hard to maintain my calm, but I did. I asked the class, which was predominantly white, if anyone else held that view. There was one other white male in the course who reluctantly raised his hand in agreement. There was part of me that wanted to immediately shut him down. As I recall, we had a productive discussion. He came away understanding not only why he could not use the word, but he also came away understanding the ridiculousness of the claim that he was being discriminated against. I made it clear that the logics of white privilege imply that white people have this sense that they can possess (almost as if by having a "natural right" to do so) whatever they so desire. After explaining how Black people have attempted to take some of the sting out of that word (for example, deleting the "er"), I made it clear that the word is off limits to white people—it is as simple as that. What is your pedagogy, so to speak, around using the n-word? I say this also because there are white teachers who have gotten into serious trouble using the n-word.

ESP: It doesn't surprise me at all that there are some white people, especially white men, who feel discriminated against because they are being asked not to say something. I always think of freedom of speech as a right granted to "the people" against the government, against power. It's my right as a lowly citizen to speak about the government or about certain leaders of government without facing arrest or detainment of any kind. And yet, it's interesting to me that some of the people most likely to assert the right of freedom of speech are people with access to the most power and who want to wield that power against the historically disenfranchised.

My evidence is anecdotal, but still compelling: It's at just about the time that Black students, in the early 1990s, at colleges and universities across the country begin saying the surrogate phrase "the n-word" (rather than repeating the actual word) that we hear calls against political correctness and for the rights of free speech emerging on those campuses. In other words, it's just when Black people start to set the terms of how they want to be spoken about and how language can be deployed against them (or not) that certain factions begin resisting. I'm thinking of a case called "the water buffalo incident" at the University of Pennsylvania in 1993. Five Black women, assaulted by verbal attacks and a litany of racial slurs, end up making a public statement at the end of the spring semester in which they refuse to repeat the anti-Black and misogynistic language used against them.

But as to your question: The classroom is in crisis across the United States over the misuse of the n-word. It really, really is. I talk about this in my TED talk on why it's hard to talk about the n-word. I think there are two problems operating when teachers, especially white teachers, speak the n-word out loud in class. The first is in how they use the n-word as a symbol of racism's past without giving credence to its anti-Black resonance in the present. These instructors often think speaking it out loud is important precisely because of how it shocks and that they are doing important work by letting that discomfort arise in their classroom. Perhaps this would be true if U.S. classrooms were filled only with white students who had no cultural literacy, who never met a Black person, but they're not. Black students often take the brunt of these interactions and find themselves having to either suck it up and say nothing and endure the anxiety of that, *or* to speak up and be an activist, when really, they just wanted to come to school to learn.

Under these conditions, the classroom becomes a hostile space for Black students and impedes rather than encourages learning. I also think educators would be surprised at how many white students are overwhelmed and traumatized by these exchanges. The second problem with the n-word is that teachers rarely provide historical context. We have such a profound opportunity to teach young people about race and racism through this word that's in the music they love and proliferates the culture they live in—in video games, artworks, movies. There's an assumption that everyone, if they're born in the United States, somehow has an innate understanding of the power of the n-word by virtue of their "American-ness." This isn't true, and I think by not teaching the history of the word and, of course, the history of the racism that produced it, we perpetuate its violence and create a crop of young people who end up in your class and debate you about how its discriminatory not to be able to say it.

GY: I think that all Black people have had what you call a "point of encounter" with the n-word. As I mentioned, it enters my body, and then I carry the load of its violence. Talk about your point of encounter. What does the word *do to* you?

ESP: What does the n-word do to me? Well, the anti-Black version of the word—the one that ends in "er"—ties me in knots, makes me self-conscious, brutalizes me, brings back painful memories, makes me paranoid, afraid, confused. I can't tell you how many times I've had a point of encounter and the first thing I think is "What did I do?" I blame myself. Sometimes it's taken me years to make sense of the encounter and realize it wasn't my fault at all.

I'm writing a book right now about these experiences. Plural. A whole book. I say this to emphasize that there have been many more times I've been accosted and assaulted by the n-word. The thing I'm calling a "point of encounter" is when you have a run-in with the n-word, whether in an academic setting, a debate, in popular culture or art, or if you've been the victim of a slur or witnessed someone being the victim of the slur. It was a point of encounter in my classroom that set off my research on the n-word. A well-meaning white student quoted the word in class, and I realized I had no idea what to do. I sputtered a response and tried to stop them, but they were quoting a line from a movie and repeated it.

What happened for me next, however, was really surprising. After speaking with my students about the incident and about the word, many of them started confessing. What I mean by that is they started revealing their own stories about points of encounter with the n-word—many of which happened in the classroom. I hear these stories all the time. When I give public talks, people are so generous and trusting with me and tell me stories about being called the n-word, memories that they carry all their lives.

I think of Emily Bernard's beautiful 2005 personal reflection[5] on the n-word in the classroom which she opens with Countee Cullen's poem, "Incident."[6] In it, Cullen talks about going to Baltimore as an 8-year-old child and seeing another child, white and a little bit older, on the bus. Cullen looks over at the older boy, and the boy sticks out his tongue and calls him the n-word. Cullen spent that entire summer in Baltimore, but, as the poem tells us, he remembers nothing but the word and the incident on the bus.

There's a way these moments inscribe themselves into our brains and our nerve endings. They obliterate everything else. At least they do for me. It blows my mind how many encounters I remembered once I started doing this work. And even more surprising are the ones I've forgotten. My cousin, who, like all of my first cousins is white, texted me the other day and told me she remembered when I was 15, I refused to go with her into a pizza place outside of Boston because I was convinced someone would call me the n-word. I don't remember that at all, but I've felt that feeling so many other times, I know it's true. I've passed up so many "best ice cream in the city" and "best breakfast in town" because I felt in my heart, once I saw the places, if I went inside, I might encounter that word.

GY: There will be many white people who will continue to use the n-word. And, here, I don't mean card-carrying white supremacists, but liberal and progressive whites. How might we better prepare Black students to effectively deal with the ugliness of that word, even when white people, apparently, don't intend to use it as an anti-Black racist slur? I ask this because regardless of their "good intentions," the use of that word does not lose its violent and vicious wounding.

ESP: I think the question you ask is so great because it's 100 percent true. White people will continue to use this word. They will. I recently met a law professor whose students told me that when they asked him to please stop speaking "the n-word" (they used that phrase), he said the actual word right back to them. He was that committed to using the word. And I do think white liberals are some of the biggest culprits of this.

Black people know what to do when a white person calls them the n-word as a slur, or at least, we know how to feel. We have the right to be angry and hurt and afraid and outraged. There is space for that reaction in our culture (even though, honestly, it's still been confusing to me to be called the slur). But when someone says it casually in conversation, or when teaching a lesson, or when repeating something they overheard, how am I supposed to feel then? Where is the space for me to say, *Please don't, I really don't like that*, and, in so doing, to not somehow be transgressive to so-called American ideals? Which is why I love the question. Instead of asking how we control those white speakers of the n-word (who are not going away), you ask, *How do we arm Black students against it?*

I think Black students should know it's okay to speak up about the word if they want to and it's also okay not to speak up about the word if they don't. When you're assaulted, whether that's a verbal assault or some other kind, a lot of times the feelings get bottled up and are hard to digest. Hearing the n-word, even as part of a legitimate lesson, still creates a lot of those feelings. Even when people are "just" quoting the word, what they are likely doing, especially in the classroom, is telling the story of some kind of racial violence. Why else would the n-word be in literature or a law book or a history essay? It's there to highlight an episode of racial violence. By repeating it, you're not neutral or being "just" authentic to the source material because the story you're telling is likely not neutral either. Instead, it's likely laden with the anti-Blackness of the history of the United States.

GY: There are many who would argue that any use of the n-word is prohibited. I recall that in 2007 there were many, I believe headed by the

NAACP, who assembled in Detroit, Michigan, to bury the n-word. It was a ceremonial funeral. However, I have come to terms with the complex ways in which Black people use the n-word amongst themselves. I like the agency that Black people, especially younger Black people, exhibit when they use the respelled version of the word. I see this as one way of denuding the term of its violence or metaphorically taking it out of the mouths of white people and marking it with a different meaning, a positive meaning. Perhaps a similar argument can be made for some women who use the b-word amongst themselves but who argue against men using the term. Of course, I don't wish to conflate the two words. What are your thoughts about Black people using the n-word in ways that attempt to resignify its meaning?

ESP: The n-word with the soft "-ga" is working for young Black people—artists, musicians, poets and people walking down the street. It is effective to signal Black subversion and protest. It's powerful for them. I study the early 19th century, and even then, African Americans used the n-word with each other and among each other in defiance of white definitions of the word.

In my essay on the word, I argue that the reason that this particular word emerged as a vitriolic word is because Black people were using it among each other and gave it political weight. As Black people started to become free, white minstrel performers in the antebellum North used the word as part of their attempt to authenticate their blackface Blackness on stage. They wore black cork on their faces, ragged clothes, spoke in dialect, and often used the n-word. When whites used the word, they did so to mock Black speech.

Even when Black people became free, many Black people still used the word among each other, and many working-class Black folks continued to do so among themselves. This is something that my father, Richard Pryor—the iconic Black comedian—exposed when he finally found his voice on stage in the early 1970s. It's important and groundbreaking that he called his 1974 album "That N-word's Crazy" (only with the actual word, not the phrase). His comedy demonstrates how Black people use the n-word as a form of protest.

I think the use of the n-word by Black folks is working, it's marking something, making a claim, and not until the structures are in place, like social justice and equity, will the word become meaningless. Instead of trying to control the Black use of the word, we should be more concerned with trying to dismantle the white supremacy that makes the n-word a powerful statement of Black irreverence.

GY: When I think about the n-word, I cannot separate it from white supremacy. Does the continued virulent use of the term depend upon the continued existence of white supremacy? I don't see white supremacy ending anytime soon. Hence, I don't see any end in sight regarding the violent use of the n-word. Any thoughts on this? In other words, do you see any hope for us as a nation regarding not only white supremacy, but its deployment of discursive tools that are designed to oppress?

ESP: The n-word is going no place until white supremacy comes to an end, and we have such great powerful minds at work who simply cannot even begin to imagine a world or a United States without it, or better yet, who don't want to.

Last summer, as a result of the protests over police brutality, the nation started using the phrase "systemic racism." The systemic part is important. If you imagine racism as a corrosion of your plumbing, eating away at the lead and spilling sewage into the groundwater, you wouldn't continue patching up those pipes. You'd tear them out and get brand news ones with a better and stronger material.

But somehow, even though everyone—Nike, the NFL, presidential candidates, *ABC*'s *The Bachelor*—used the term "systemic" to describe the state of white supremacy, they offered no real framework for undoing the systems. Instead, they just tried to patch it up: *Let's celebrate Juneteenth, let's take down Confederate statues.* And I'm not saying these are not important actions and symbols, because they are, but somebody needs to get in there and replace the pipes. Without new pipes, the n-word and its legacy will persist. And Black people will continue to speak their own version in protest, and likely insist that non-Black people in the United States find another way, besides the n-word, to express themselves.

18

PROTESTS UNLEASHED BY MURDER OF GEORGE FLOYD EXCEED ALL IN U.S. HISTORY

INTERVIEW WITH NOAM CHOMSKY

There has been "nothing comparable in American history" to the huge outpouring of protest unleashed by the murder of George Floyd, says world-renowned intellectual Noam Chomsky. Even at the very peak of Martin Luther King Jr.'s popularity, the mass protests that King led and inspired "didn't come anywhere close" to the massive racial justice protests that have erupted over this past year, Chomsky adds.

As the anniversary of Floyd's murder approaches, I invited Chomsky—a brilliant thinker who combines deep and unbelievable historical breadth, critical conceptual sharpness, and profound passion in his analysis of political and existential issues—to talk with me about George Floyd's death and the guilty verdict against Derek Chauvin, as well as anti-Black violence in North America and how the U.S. fomented a "gun culture."

Chomsky is an intellectual whom I have come to greatly appreciate, to admire and to think of as a friend. Through his example, I have learned how to practice disobedience and dissent in a world that is filled with indoctrination. As a rule of thumb, he has taught me that when everybody agrees on something more complicated than "two plus two equals four," we should question it.

G. Yancy (with Noam Chomsky), "Chomsky: Protests Unleashed by Murder of George Floyd Exceed All in US History," in *Truthout*, May 7, 2021. [Editors: Alana Yu-lan Price, Maya Schenwar, and Britney Schultz]

GEORGE YANCY: For some of us, witnessing the killing of George Floyd and hearing him say that he couldn't breathe brought back memories of 43-year-old Black male Eric Garner's death back in 2014, though he said, "I can't breathe" 11 times. When you think about what happened to George Floyd within the larger historical context of white racism within the U.S., how does Floyd's death speak to you? For me, it was not anomalous, but how did it speak to you?

NOAM CHOMSKY: His death dramatically symbolized 400 years of hideous crimes and atrocities, and evidently it meant that to a large part of the population. It is quite striking what happened after his assassination, as we should call it. There was a huge outpouring, nothing comparable in American history. There were huge demonstrations; there was a sense of dedicated solidarity of Black and white people marching together. They were nonviolent overwhelmingly, though the right wing would like you to believe otherwise. There was also enormous public support, with two-thirds of the population supportive of protest. There is nothing remotely like that in U.S. history.

Protests led by Martin Luther King Jr., at the very peak of his popularity, didn't come anywhere close to that. That's the result, I think, of a lot of work that's been done on the ground by Black Lives Matter and other groups which have raised the level of consciousness and awareness to the point where when this thing happened it just lit a spark, and the kindling was ready to burn. And it's had a longtime impact. I think it's changed perception and understanding considerably, and not undermined by the fact that police-perpetrated killings continue almost daily.

GY: As I was watching the guilty verdict of Derek Chauvin, I'm sure that Floyd's family had experienced some sense of relief and perhaps they could breathe again as well. Yet, it also occurred to me that in the case of finding Chauvin guilty on all three charges, there was such a low threshold to demonstrate his guilt. He had knelt on him for nine minutes and 29 seconds. I don't want to come across as pessimistic or cynical, but what do you see as "triumphant" or "progressive" regarding the guilty verdict?

NC: You know, there had been an atmosphere in the past, as you know, better than I do, in which Black lives just didn't matter. The sentiment was that if a white person was brought to trial after killing a Black person, the reasoning was that they probably had a "good reason." So, just free them. Of course, there were even worse cases where whites carried out murders and lynchings and were praised. Well, fortunately, we're past that.

But not so far in the past, Black Panther leader Fred Hampton, for example, was assassinated in a Gestapo-style murder, set-up by the FBI, who fed to the Chicago police fake stories about guns being stashed in his apartment. The police raided his apartment at about 4 o'clock in the morning and murdered him and his friend, Mark Clark. Just murdered them. The reason for killing Hampton was very simple. He was the most important of the Black Panther organizers. The FBI wanted to go after the successful organizers and Hampton was the peak of them; he had to be killed. In fact, it was the last of a long series of efforts where the FBI tried to instigate a feud between the Black Panthers and the criminal group, Blackstone Rangers, which were in Chicago.

The FBI sent fake letters to the Rangers written in fake Black dialect saying that the Panthers had a contract out on their leaders. But they were closely enough integrated, so they knew what was going on. In the case of Hampton, however, they had an FBI infiltrator, who was his bodyguard. The point is that there was a long FBI plot not just against the Panthers, but against the Black movements altogether. It took years of dedicated work by some great young lawyers, Flint Taylor and Jeffrey Haas, working on the case for years to finally get a kind of civil settlement.

This one case vastly outweighs anything that was charged against Richard Nixon. Was he charged for his use of national political police carrying out murder and assassination campaigns against Black organizers? And regarding your question, that's a big difference between then and now. Now at least circumstances are such that a jury can convict someone for the perfectly obvious murder of a Black man. But if you turn on *Fox News*, notice the reaction. Listen to Tucker Carlson, who claims that the trial of Derek Chauvin wasn't legitimate because the jury was intimidated, they were terrified that Black people were going to come and destroy their houses and kill them all. Alan Dershowitz, the so-called civil libertarian who likes to present himself as that, also claimed that the trial was illegitimate because the jury was intimidated.

We haven't freed ourselves. There's a lot of distance to go, but the killing of George Floyd did bring out something very positive in the society, namely the beginnings of understanding that there's something really hideous at the core of our history. It has come up in other ways, like the 1619 Project published by *The New York Times*. Some historians are carping about it, "You got this wrong; you've got that wrong." But it's not even relevant when, finally, we have a recognition in the main media and the country that we've had 400 years of hideous atrocities experienced by Black people. So, let's take a look at it, ask who we are and what we are. This is not something irrelevant to American history. It's the basis of U.S. economic prosperity; that's why I'm privileged.

Cotton was the oil of the 19th century. The large part of the wealth of the United States, and also Britain, and to a lesser extent the continent, was based on cheap cotton. How do you get cheap cotton? Well, by the most hideous, atrocious system of slavery that ever existed. A lot of this is just coming to light. Edward E. Baptist's book, *The Half Has Never Been Told*, provides an astonishing picture of things that maybe professional historians knew something about, but certainly the general public, even the informed public, wasn't informed about. I didn't know a lot of the things he described; they were way beyond the horrors that I knew about. A lot of this is just beginning to come out after hundreds of years. It's about time.

GY: Most certainly.

NC: And we have to look at a lot of other things. For example, why do so few Black people have access to wealth? There are many reasons. One reason is the New Deal measures, which determined that federal housing had to be segregated. And in the 1950s, for the first time, a Black man had a chance to get a decent job in an auto union job at an auto plant, to make some money and perhaps buy a house. But he couldn't buy a house, because the Federal Housing Projects (Levittown, in Long Island, New York, for example) kept Black people out.

In the U.S., wealth and housing are very closely related. A lot of people's wealth is in their house. Once Black workers finally got just a little bit of emancipation, a chance to get a job, they were told, "Sorry folks, but you can't buy a house here because we have racist laws." This ran into the later 1960s, which was finally overturned by the popular activism in the 1960s. I should say that the liberal Democratic senators who voted for this law were strongly opposed to segregation. They were not racists. They wanted nonsegregated housing, but they couldn't get anything through the Southern Democrats, who dominated the Senate. This is very similar in our own time when you can't get anything through unless you somehow get the Republican Party, which is dedicated to wealth and power, to agree. And this is a big problem in this country.

GY: In the past few months, we have heard about shooting after shooting. Could you talk about the escalating danger of gun violence? My sense is that there are profound cultural myths regarding gun ownership. Could you speak to this as well?

NC: Gun violence is increasing not just here, but one of the worst effects of the U.S. gun culture is in Mexico and Latin America. They're flooded with American guns, which are killing people at a hideous rate. Mexico is a killing field with largely American guns. In Central America, there is the same thing. You flood areas with guns where there are plenty of tensions and crises and you're going to get killings. Instead of people shouting at each other, they'll shoot each other. And it's shocking that somebody like me, for example, who doesn't know which end of the gun to hold, could go into a store in Arizona, where I live, and pick up a fancy gun and hand it over to somebody from a Mexican cartel. Basically, things like that are a curse for the world. And it just has to be cured.

The history of this is worth remembering. In the 19th century, there was no gun culture. People had guns. After all, it was an agricultural country, so farmers had old muskets to chase coyotes away and so on, but there was no gun culture. What happened apparently—and there is a good study of this by historian Pamela Haag, who has examined this in some detail—is that gun manufacturers were facing an economic crisis.

The American Civil War provided a huge market for fancy modern guns. European states were at war, they were buying up guns. But the Civil War ended, and Europe went into a temporary quiescent state. There were not a lot of wars and fighting and so the market dried up. So, they hit on the idea of trying to create a market through advertising. The first great advertising campaign began with concocting an image of the "Wild West," the kind of thing that I grew up with. There was Wyatt Earp, a sheriff who was quick on the draw, or there was the Lone Ranger who would ride to the rescue. There was nothing remotely like this in the West, but it was invented and had a big effect. I can remember it from my childhood, and we all believed it.

Of course, the bottom line of all of this was that you better buy your son a fancy rifle, or he won't be a "real man." Well, that established the basis for a kind of gun culture, and it was copied by other advertising campaigns. We all remember the Marlboro Man. You know, you want to poison yourself with cigarettes and be like a cowboy who runs to the rescue. And it turned out to be very effective. The tobacco campaign killed—though nobody knows, probably millions of people—and the gun culture is still killing people at a horrific rate, which was all escalated by the Supreme Court in 2008—the *District of Columbia v. Heller*—where Justice Antonin Scalia reversed 100 years of precedent and reinterpreted the Second Amendment to grant free access to guns by individuals. Scalia was an originalist, a textualist.

The idea here is that you don't pay attention to what the people who introduced the legislation meant by it; you're not allowed to do that. You just have to look at the text, not what it meant to the people who wrote it. That's illegitimate, not true scholarship.

So, he looked at the text and tried to show that somebody living in the 18th century would have interpreted the Second Amendment to mean disregard for militias. True or false, it's totally irrelevant. We know exactly why the founders instituted the Second Amendment. One reason was the British Army. They were the main force in the world. The U.S. barely had an army, and the British might come right back. In fact, they did a few years later, and one had to have militias to call up to protect oneself against the British.

The second reason was slavery. In places like South Carolina, enslaved Black people outnumbered white people. And there were slave rebellions going on all over the Caribbean, and they could spread here. In fact, they did. So, white people decided they needed guns for militias. But the main reason was aggression and genocide. One of the main reasons for the American Revolution was that King George III had instituted a royal proclamation which banned the colonists from going to the territory of the Indian Nations. They were not supposed to invade them. Colonists were supposed to stay east of the Appalachians, but they didn't want that. They wanted to kill and displace the American Indian people. They could then settle out there. Land speculators like George Washington wanted to move out. As soon as the British were gone, well, the white settlers needed militias, they needed guns.

Later on, the army was created, the cavalry took care of it, and through the 19th century, Indigenous nations were destroyed, attacked and expelled. They needed lots of guns for that. You see, that's why the founders needed guns, but we're not allowed to talk about that. Instead, we generally say what someone like Scalia thinks someone would've understood by the Second Amendment. And now that has become holy writ. Most people in the U.S., if you ask them what's in the Constitution, the first thing they'll say is the Second Amendment. It has just become a dominant part of the culture.

Part Six

MATTERS OF FAITH AND RELIGION

19

BLACK WOMANIST THEOLOGY OFFERS HOPE IN THE FACE OF WHITE SUPREMACY

INTERVIEW WITH KELLY BROWN DOUGLAS

The language of "American racial reckoning" has been frequently cited since the tragic murder of George Floyd and the raising of American consciousness regarding its history of systemic racism. The ongoing murders of Black people by the police, and the profound ways in which Black people must continue to struggle against forms of anti-Black inequity across various political, social and economic indices, prove that there needs to be a robust reckoning. And yet, these realities perpetuate forms of anti-Black pain and suffering that thwart and belie such reckoning.

To remind us of what is at stake, and to exhume the pain and suffering that much of the U.S. would rather not see, I spoke with The Very Reverend Dr. Kelly Brown Douglas, who reveals the anti-Black narrative that constitutes the core of this country and how that narrative is fundamentally linked to this country's collective psyche. Douglas also delineates how anti-Black theories and beliefs—even the force of white Western Christian traditional practices—have marked the Black body as "evil" and thereby eliminable. Additionally, Douglas examines how anti-Blackness impacts the lives of Black women in specific hetero-patriarchic forms and their subjugation to carceral policing. She does this while courageously maintaining a powerful form of faith that shapes how she remains focused on a future that promises the recognition of each person's sacred humanity.

G. Yancy (with Kelly Brown Douglas), "Black Womanist Theology Offers Hope in the Face of White Supremacy," in *Truthout*, June 19, 2021. [Editors: Alana Yu-lan Price and Maya Schenwar]

Douglas serves as the Dean of the Episcopal Divinity School and the Bill and Judith Moyers Chair in Theology at Union Theological Seminary. She also serves as the Canon Theologian at the Washington National Cathedral and Theologian in Residence at Trinity Church Wall Street. She is the author of many articles and books, including *Sexuality and the Black Church: A Womanist Perspective* and *Stand Your Ground: Black Bodies and the Justice of God*, and the forthcoming *Resurrection Hope: A Future Where Black Lives Matter* (Orbis Books).

GEORGE YANCY: You've talked about how you started to ask at the early age of 6 why it is that we as Black people are treated so badly. The question brings to mind the arc of our deep existential suffering from enslavement, Black codes, the collapse of Reconstruction, Jim and Jane Crowism, the criminalization and lynching of Black bodies etc. Within this historical arc, I'm also referring to Emmett Till, who was tragically and brutally murdered in 1955, and the four young Black girls (Addie Mae Collins, Cynthia Wesley, Carole Robertson and Denise McNair) who were murdered at the 16th Street Baptist Church, which was bombed by white supremacists in 1963. In our contemporary moment, I'm also thinking about the killing of George Floyd, Breonna Taylor, and 20-year-old Daunte Wright, who was recently killed by a white police officer, in Brooklyn Center, Minnesota. Also, relevant here is what happened to Afro-Latino Caron Nazario, a Second Lieutenant of the U.S. Army Medical Corps, who was held at gunpoint and pepper-sprayed by Virginia cops as he remained calm in his parked vehicle. I'm also thinking about new forms of Jim and Jane Crow, including the violence of the foster care system in relation to Black mothers, and the prison-industrial complex in terms of how Black women's incarceration specifically negatively impacts the mother-child bond, the disproportionate incarceration of Black bodies, more generally, and so on. So, what is it? Why are Black people treated so badly?

KELLY BROWN DOUGLAS: With the seemingly unrelenting attacks on Black bodies, I have become increasingly aware that the dehumanizing and deadly treatment of Black people in this country goes beyond the white supremacist foundation upon which this country was built. The almost taken-for-granted violence of white supremacy that is endemic to this nation is manifest in the systemic, structural, and cultural ways it privileges whiteness and penalizes those who are not raced white.

However, such privileges and penalties do not adequately account for the visceral assaults, sometimes fatal, upon Black bodies, as in the case of a Tony McDade, Atatiana Jefferson, or Casey Goodson Jr., and this list, horrifically, could go on and on. These consistent, malicious attacks, while grounded in whiteness, reflect more than a belief in the superiority of whiteness. Such attacks bespeak a singular, deep-seated fear, if not contempt, for Blackness itself. It is only in appreciating the pervasive and distinctive presence and dehumanizing presuppositions of an anti-Black narrative ensconced within this country's collective psyche, that we can begin to understand the intensity of white repulsion when it comes to Black bodies.

Now, it is important to recognize that anti-Black beliefs, if not theories, are deeply rooted within the Western philosophical and even Christian tradition. For instance, in his attempts to understand the diversity of human creation, Aristotle laid a philosophical foundation for an anti-Black narrative that rendered Black people as inferior and wanton beings. In so doing, he fostered the notion that Blackness signaled an immoral, if not dangerous, nature. That Blackness has been seen as a signifier for sin replete with images of the devil as Black, as exemplified throughout the Christian tradition, is one exemplar of how Christianity has provided a sacred foundation for an anti-Black narrative.

The point of the matter is: These philosophical and theological beliefs served as a precursor to what would become a well-formed anti-Black narrative.

Within the anti-Black narrative, Black people are seen as dangerously threatening. Like animals, Black people are viewed as likely to erupt into a life-threatening tirade with little provocation, and thus are considered inherently violent and to be feared. An anti-Black narrative undoubtedly arrived in America with the earliest settlers dispatched from England in 1607 to form what became known as the Jamestown Colony in Virginia.

Fast forwarding, "The Make America Great Again" vision promoted by Donald Trump brought to the surface the nation's fundamental white supremacist values as defined by an anti-Black narrative. In so doing, Trump's pledge to "Make America Great Again" (read, white again) played upon the fears about Black people as hyper-dangerous threats to white civilized America, thus provoking in white America an almost reflexive response to protect "whiteness" against the "perceived" threat of Blackness at all cost.

This could be readily seen in incidents that seemed to multiply across the country where police were called on Black people simply going about the business of being human—such quotidian activities as Black people waiting, barbecuing or birdwatching. Even worse, was when the presence of a Black body almost instinctively elicited deadly force from police, as was the case in relation to Elijah McClain, George Floyd and Breonna Taylor.

Moreover, the fact that Black people are disproportionately trapped in poverty—with its social co-morbidities of inadequate health care, substandard housing, and insufficient employment, educational and recreational opportunities—is the result of an uninterrupted anti-Black narrative. There is no getting around it: An anti-Black narrative is pervasive within America's social-cultural mindset and soil. It is for this reason that Black people are treated so badly.

GY: Thank you for saying their names, for identifying such persons by name. That act alone helps us to remember them, to recognize that they were here, that they were human beings who were subjected to what you powerfully call an anti-Black narrative. In the light of so much anti-Black racism, how do you conceptualize yourself as a Black female Christian? In other words, who are you called to be amid such anti-Blackness?

KBD: First of all, as a person of faith, I am accountable not to the unjust ways of the present, but to the just future to which God calls us. And so, in the least, I am called to speak out and stand against that which does not reflect God's just future. This is a future where all persons are treated as the sacred creations that they are. Put simply, I must speak out against any policies, systems, structures and ideologies of beliefs that negate the sacred humanity of persons because of how they are raced, gendered, sexually oriented, or because of the language they speak, country they come from, labor they perform, and any other discriminating human construct. Moreover, I must witness for that just future, which means working to create spaces and indeed a society where all persons have equitable opportunity to flourish and thrive into the fullness of their sacred humanity.

Second, as a Black female I am accountable to those Black people, especially those Black women who came before me. I think oftentimes of those Black persons who endured the realities of anti-Blackness that was chattel slavery. These were people who never breathed a free breath, never dreamed that they would breathe a freed breath, but fought for freedom anyhow. They fought for a freedom they knew they would never see, yet one they believed would one day become a reality. The freedom in which they put their faith is the very freedom that is the justice of God. It is because of their fight and belief that I as a Black female have the freedoms that I enjoy, as fraught and contested as they may sometimes be given the constructs of white supremacist hetero-patriarchal oppression. And so I am called by their struggle of faith, to continue the fight for a freedom that I may never see, but one that perhaps my children and their children will experience. This is a freedom from anti-Blackness. It is the freedom to live in a nation, indeed a world, where all Black lives matter.

GY: I hear in your response the act of giving thanks to those who have come before you, those Black people who clung to a future that wasn't certain and yet they endured. I too am thankful and indebted to them. I am often troubled, though, by the lack of national attention that is given to Black women who are subjected to police brutality, especially as compared to the national spotlight that is placed upon Black male bodies that are subjected to deeply problematic policing. Indeed, Black women and women of color (including, of course, trans women of color) undergo experiences of pain and suffering that we should not conflate with the suffering of Black men or men of color. And while this isn't about "oppression Olympics," I do think that it is important that Black women's pain and suffering under sexism, patriarchy, and racism are marked and rendered visible lest we find ourselves guilty of multiple forms of erasing Black women's lived complexity. Given the importance of your work within the area of Black womanist theology, can you describe how it helps to frame more accurately and insightfully the historical and the lived or phenomenologically complex dimensions of Black women?

KBD: Yes, you are right. Black women's pain and suffering has become virtually invisible within the wider social discourse, protest movements and collective social consciousness. As scholar Michele Bratcher Goodwin has explained, during this time of focus on racialized police brutality, the injustice perpetrated against Black women has played "off mainstage, relegated to the corner of another theater." Yet Black women are no less victimized by the ravages of systemic racism when it comes to policing and the criminal justice system. Black women are "caught within the clutches of a broken *or intentional* criminal justice system," even as they are continually "ignor[ed] as *victims*."[1]

For instance, according to the Sentencing Project,[2] "In 2019, the imprisonment rate for African American women . . . was over 1.7 times the rate of imprisonment for white women." Moreover, "African American girls are more than three times as likely as their white peers to be incarcerated." This data as well as the fact Black women's oppression has been virtually ignored evince what Pauli Murray identified as Jane Crow, which is the intersecting realities of raced and gendered oppression. More specifically, the anti-Black narrative has historically been shaped not only by color but also gender.

As is well documented, Black women became the perfect foils to white women. While white women were considered virginal, pure angels in need of protection, Black women were considered wanton, lascivious Jezebels in need of controlling. Black women were essentially entrapped within the catch-22 of a violent "intersection." For inasmuch as they did not meet the white female standard of beauty, they were not regarded as "ladies" to be respected; the more that their Black skin marked them for a way of living that defied ideal "womanhood," then more "validity" was given to the meaning of their Black body aesthetic. Their Blackness signified that they were in fact not proper women, they were not "Victorian ladies," even as it ensured that they would never enjoy the privilege of being treated as a Victorian lady, and worse yet it ensured brutal assaults against their bodies. Most particularly, it enabled white men to literally rape Black women with moral and legal impunity. In the logic of the anti-Black narrative, a Black woman could never be raped since she was an unabashed temptress and thus responsible for any such assault against her body.

Essentially, what we recognize are the realities of raced and gendered oppression that have intersected on Black women's bodies. It is because of these intersecting realities of oppression that 19th-century "Negro Club Woman" Anna Julia Cooper proclaimed, "Only the BLACK WOMAN can say 'when and where I enter, in the quiet, undisputed dignity of my womanhood, without violence and without suing or special patronage, then and there the whole Negro race enters with me.'" For it is the case, that if Black women are to live into the fullness of their humanity, then the aggregate complex of white supremacist heteropatriarchy would have to be dismantled. With this being the case, then those who are oppressed by any aspect of this oppressive complex would themselves be free. It is perhaps for this reason, that there have been no people more instrumental in keeping America's democratic vision alive than Black women.

It is indeed those persons who have been on the utter underside of justice—who have experienced the penalties of injustice—that are the best barometers for justice. Otherwise, justice is too easily confused with gaining privilege in an unjust system. This has been the case historically, as most clearly evident in the 19th-century struggle to expand the right to vote. On the one hand, white women have fought to eliminate gender requirements while on the other hand Black men fought to eliminate racial requirements and thus gain the patriarchal privilege to vote. Neither took into account that without the elimination of both racial and gendered restrictions, Black women would still be disenfranchised.

What we most clearly see here is the sovereign value attached to "whiteness" and "maleness." So, for instance, to be both white and male affords one the highest level of political, social, economic and even eccle-siastical privilege. To be white and female eliminates the claim to gender privilege, but preserves the right to race privilege (hence white women have fought for the race privilege granted white males). To be Black and male portends a "raced" male privilege, thus affording them privileges over Black, but not white, women. And so it is that historically Black men have fought to eliminate the restrictions of race. Yet to be Black and female—let alone if one is trans, gender non-conforming or queer—is to have virtually no claim to the privileges accorded in a White hetero-patriarchal society.

The bottom line is that Black women as a group are characteristically relegated to the absolute margins of political, social, economic and ecclesi-astical privilege and discourse. Yet, this marginality has not signified lack of agency as implied in Cooper's pronouncement. Clearly, Cooper recognized that Black women possess a unique perspective on the complicated, inter-secting realities of injustice in this country that has made them uniquely qualified to chart the course for not just Black freedom, but a freedom from the tyranny that is white supremacist heteropatriarchy.

So, it is no wonder that Black women have been—and continue to be—in the forefront in moving our nation to live into its better angels, including in the fights for equal rights and voting rights. And that, again, is because Black women continue to bear the full weight of the intersecting realities of white supremacist, hetero-patriarchal realities of injustice. In this regard, what Pulitzer Prize–winning journalist of the 1619 Project[3] Nikole Hannah-Jones says of Black people in general applies most especially to Black women. She says, "Our founding ideals of liberty and equality were false when they were written. Black Americans fought to make them true. Without this struggle, America would have no democracy at all."

GY: I was recently discussing Black sexuality with my undergraduates in one of my philosophy seminars and the issue of Black female sexuality was raised. We explored the horrible, caricatured, and racist cartography of the Black female as defined as "Mammy," "Jezebel," and "Sapphire." Each of these stereotypes is framed according to a distorted understanding of Black women's sexuality. Of course, Black men have also been subjected to harmful racist images. Think here of the "Black Buck." Through the lens of white supremacy, Black people have been reduced to their bodies; they are depicted as base, subhuman, hypersexual and hyper-sensual creatures without reason. How is this distorted image of the Black body related to a *white* theology and perhaps even *Western* philosophical assumptions about the body, more generally?

KBD: Yes, this indeed is the case as I have alluded to in my previous responses. But let me summarize how this has been the case when it comes to Christianity and the white theological tradition. There is no doubt that the Western Christian tradition has influenced if not provided a sacred canopy for white supremacists/anti-Black beliefs and attacks upon Black bodies, as well as justification for the social subjugation of Black people. Essentially, the Western Christian tradition opened wide the door for the possibility of utilizing sexuality as a means of devaluing and demonizing human beings. This theological perspective of the body came to prevail within the Christian tradition. Specifically, the body was seen as a cauldron of sinful passions, such as sexual lust. Simply put, this theological tradition asserts that sexuality is a cauldron of evil and is an obstacle to one's salvation if not a threat to one's very humanity.

By maintaining the evilness of sexuality, Christianity provided a theological basis for any claims that people who were deemed to be governed by sexual desires are innately evil and need to be controlled. It is in this way that Christianity has perpetuated a theological tradition that is compatible with a white supremacist, anti-Black narrative. For we are reminded that this is a narrative which regards Black people as hyper-sexual and thus dangerous. Hence, Christianity is, in the least, complicit in sustaining white attacks against the Black body. For again, inasmuch as sexuality is considered evil, so too are "hyper-sexualized" Black people. Therefore, if Black people are considered evil by nature, then to protect society from them, even if it means their death, is seen as reasonable.

To sum up here, there is a prevailing Christian theological tradition that not only sanctions Black people's dehumanization, but also suggests their demise. This theological tradition is most prominent within fundamentalist versions of Christianity that maintain a more literal approach to the Bible. It is perhaps no coincidence, therefore, that evangelical Protestantism prevails in the South where most Black lynching historically has taken place.

GY: Those are rich theological insights vis-à-vis anti-Black racism, especially in terms of the Black imago in the white imaginary. When I think about the term "redemption," I think about the process of freeing, of being extricated from captivity. So many human beings are suffering, and that suffering is unbearable. The Earth itself seems to cry out for redemption. The Black body continues to be held captive, fungible and disposable in relationship to anti-Black forces. We bear witness to our Asian brothers and sisters undergoing violence because of poisonous anti-Asian xenophobia; we grapple with those who are our neighbors that are excluded as they flee poverty and violence within their own countries; we are aware of human trafficking and labor abuses worldwide; we bear witness to femicide in Latin America and around the world. Climate change and the threat of nuclear weapons pose a heightened existential threat to life on earth. Given the wreckage that we have created, it is hard for me to believe that we will be redeemed. There are times when I wonder if we are in fact irredeemable. What is it that keeps you grounded in the face of so much dread? Does womanist theology play a role? Is there an eschatological hope that you possess? Given the gravitas that we collectively face, share your wisdom.

KBD: Actually, the answer is easy for me. That which keeps me grounded and gives me hope is the very Black faith that was handed down to me through my grandmothers, who had received that gift of faith from their grandmothers. You see, Black faith finds its meaning in the very absurdities and contradictions of Black life. For, Black faith was not born during a time when Black people were even nominally free. And perhaps that's the strength of Black faith itself—an empowering power in times of absurdity. Somehow Black people were able to affirm their faith in the justice of God, and thus in God's promise in a more just future, even in the middle of the evil that was chattel slavery. It was this faith that gave them the "courage," the determination, to fight for freedom, to fight for Black life in the midst of a society that denied Black freedom and destroyed Black lives.

As I said earlier, it is because of their faith in the freedom and promise of God that I can be here engaging in this conversation and doing the work that I do. And so, for me to give up on our society, for me to give up on our world, for me to despair, is for me to betray the faith of all of those grandmothers who kept the faith and kept fighting for justice and freedom. The way I see it is, if they could keep hoping and believing when there was certainly no reason to hope, then I have no excuse to not continue to fight for that in which they hoped—a more just future for their children and their children's children.

20

CHRISTIANITY IS EMPTY IF IT DOESN'T ADDRESS THE RACIST CARCERAL STATE

INTERVIEW WITH MARK LEWIS TAYLOR

Religion becomes an empty theological exercise if it does not address human suffering—and this includes the anguish wrought by systems of mass incarceration and policing.

I believe this deep down as a philosopher whose religious sensibilities are informed by an African American prophetic tradition that emphasizes courageous speech, deep lamentation, and outrage in relationship to those who undergo social and existential agony.

Forms of religiosity that fail or refuse to concern themselves with "the least of these" risk becoming manifestations of empty idolatry and theological abstraction that leave by the wayside those in need of compassionate community, loving grace and spiritual support.

Given the clarion call for defunding the police within the context of the killing of unarmed Black bodies, religious leaders and institutions in the U.S. must confront the evils of policing, which is undergirded by the legacy of white supremacist domination.

Policing is inextricably tied to deeply problematic normative assumptions and institutional, structural practices and policies that define as suspect, criminal and abject those who are vulnerable (racially, economically,

G. Yancy (with Mark L. Taylor), "Christianity Is Empty If It Doesn't Address the Racist Carceral State," *Truthout*, September 26, 2021. [Editors: Alana Yu-lan Price, Maya Schenwar, and Britney Schultz]

socially, psychologically). I am speaking not about "bad apple" officers, but about policing as a mode of power, control, confinement, gratuitous violence, inhuman isolation, civic death and forms of social death that must be abolished.

Increasingly, a wide range of religious communities are engaging with the struggle to abolish policing. To discuss the effort taking place within Christian communities, I spoke with Mark Lewis Taylor, who emphasizes the indispensable importance of linking the ideology and practice of carceral America with the historical Jesus, who faced a form of policing governmentality by imperial Rome that saw to Jesus's torture and execution.

As a white ordained minister and theologian, Taylor insightfully and critically engages his own whiteness, emphasizes the importance of Black resistance as agency, critiques white Christian nationalism, highlights the importance of political ontology as a crucial point of politico-religious embarkation and pulls from the wisdom of political prisoner Mumia Abu-Jamal.

Taylor is a professor in Religion and Society at Princeton Theological Seminary who earned his Master's in Divinity at Union Theological Seminary (Richmond, Virginia) and his Ph.D. from the University of Chicago. Among his most recent books are *Religion, Politics, and the Christian Right: Post-9/11 Powers and American Empire* (2005) and *The Theological and the Political: On the Weight of the World* (2011). Taylor received the Best General Interest Book Award for his 2001 book, *The Executed God: The Way of the Cross in Lockdown America* (2nd edition 2015).

In addition to years of anti-death penalty work and activism for political prisoners, including founding the group Educators for Mumia Abu-Jamal (EMAJ), Taylor remains active in solidarity work against U.S. wars and especially against U.S. dominance and exploitation in Central America. He has taught the course "Critical Race Theory as Theological Challenge" for 20 years at Princeton.

GEORGE YANCY: I'm interested in posing a question about your understanding of the historical Jesus in relation to your critically engaging work within the context of carceral logics and prisons as sites of oppression, marginalization, alienation, fragmentation and dehumanization. I am interested in the specific Christological question: "What would Jesus do vis-à-vis mass incarceration?" Cognizant, of course, of falling into a problematic presentism, speak to how you understand the telos of the historical person known as Jesus and how, were he alive today, he would respond to mass incarceration. His own crucifixion was linked to the oppressive structure of the Roman Empire, execution by the State, and those who would rather see him dead. So, there is that sense of being an outcast. I think here of Black bodies which are disproportionately imprisoned, those racially embodied persons who are seen as the abject (etymologically, "to throw away"). How could the historical Jesus not be critical of our contemporary hegemonic prison practices and ideology?

MARK LEWIS TAYLOR: I definitely agree with the answer you suggest we give: The prophetic Jew from Nazareth in Palestine would have been critical and run afoul of today's "contemporary hegemonic prison practice and ideology" in the U.S., in "lockdown America"—as he did amid the religiopolitical repression of first-century Roman Empire. Not to say and live this, while claiming some kind of faithfulness to Jesus is, as I write often, a "betrayal of the gospel," understanding "gospel" as the core meanings of Jesus's life and teachings.

Even as I make that claim, however, I want to issue two warnings. First, because of today's still problematic Christian supremacy, this claim is neither the most-needed thing to say nor the first thing that needs to be stated. The first and most important thing to voice is lament and outrage over the violating attacks today on Black people of African descent and others who labor still in the afterlife of slavery. Also, we must know the resilience and resistance by those rendered abject. Without this, any counter-carceral or counter-imperial Jesus will make little sense. I tell my students, and have stated in my Theology Department, that I am a human-in-the-world *before* I am a follower of Jesus.

This means I have to reckon with the kind of human I am—with a personal history and thus a political, racial, social, economic way of being in the world. All this is integral to—indeed, I think a precondition for—any faith claims I may want to make. This is why I have stressed (in *The Theological and the Political*) that a certain kind of political ontology of my being, of my embeddedness in societal and historical antagonisms, is preliminary to a sense of the theological. And if you permit me another reference to my own work, I emphasize in the preface to *The Executed God,* that I do not, in that book or elsewhere, propose Christian discourse as having a premium on the thinking and practice necessary for resisting and living amidst and against the carceral and imperial logics of lockdown America. "Muslims, Jews, engaged Buddhists, the Yoruba, traditions of Caribbean cultures, secular activists as well as many others abroad and in the U.S.—all must be engaged to take on Lockdown America." All this is part of resisting Christian supremacy.

My second warning is that we must exercise a strict epistemic humility in talking about "the historical Jesus." We really know very little about the historical Jesus, so little that in fact I sympathize with those who even doubt that he existed. But we need not go that far. In fact, biblical scholar Bart Ehrman—himself an avowed agnostic and humanist—has written an entire book entitled, *Did Jesus Exist?* in which he argues that a disciplined historical method will show "a Jesus of Nazareth who existed in history, who was crucified under Pontius Pilate." In her book, *Jesus of Nazareth, King of the Jews*, New Testament scholar Paula Fredriksen also emphasizes that "the single most solid fact about Jesus of Nazareth is his death: he was crucified by the prefect Pilate . . . in the manner that Rome reserved particularly for political insurrectionists, namely crucifixion." This may seem a stripped-down minimalist Jesus to many Christians today. Or they find it too fearsome a thing, since there are strong probabilities that Jesus met the fate of many if not most of the crucified: being left to the birds and beasts of prey before being tossed ignominiously into a mass lime pit. No wonder many Christians of both conservative and liberal persuasions prefer certain orthodox "grand scenarios" for interpreting Jesus's death. They look away, abstracting from this ugly history. They intone instead the grander themes: he came to forgive sins, to make expiation for human sin, to satisfy on the cross God's wrath, to pay ransom with his death on the cross to appease an angry God, to die intentionally to show self-sacrificing love, and so on—all to facilitate some exit from this world of strife.

My work, to the contrary, takes as a starting point the neglected historicity of Jesus's torture-death, his imperial execution. I ask what it means to remember *that*, and how any life can come from remembering *that*. To be crucified was a shameful, terrorizing thing. Early Jesus movements barely survived the stigmatizing that went with being associated with a crucified Jesus.

Even today, especially in the U.S., Christians prefer the grand scenario interpretations of Jesus's death to a thoroughgoing identification with Jesus as a counter-imperial, political insurrectionist who met a torturous death. I emphasize, though, that even with this more limited, "solid" historical claim about Jesus, to ask today "What would Jesus do?" and to answer "Well, he would criticize and resist today's death-dealing, torturous ways of U.S. state violence"—even that answer requires first an awareness and serious reckoning with our violent U.S. State, driven by a warrior-elite today buttressed by the ways of white supremacy, empire and a long history of European and American coloniality of power. Feeling and thinking those antagonisms, I repeat, is the condition for the possibility of a liberatory retrieval of the historical Jesus.

GY: Aware that none of us are beyond reproach, which I think helps us to maintain a certain religious and ethical humility, speak to what it is that contemporary ordained ministers and theologians have failed to do regarding the deep political, social, economic and existential problems of incarceration. I'm thinking here of the failure, assuming that this is what you would call it, of ordained ministers and theologians to embody forms of outrage that are linked to practices that are intended to liberate those who have been subjected to forms of carceral injustice. This raises the issue of praxis, a Christological mode of being-in-the-world that imitates the work of the historical Jesus. Assuming that there is a "failure" here, is it one that is linked to a certain insular, apolitical understanding of Christian theology? Is it a case of fear of enacting fomenting practices that challenge the U.S. empire and its ruling elites who support forms of carceral rule and domination? What are your thoughts?

MLT: Yes, indeed I agree. Most "ordained ministers and theologians" have "failed," and in all the ways you mention here. Having experienced as I have some versions of white evangelical Christian traditions (even if I thoroughly rejected them decades ago), and though now I work in a theological institution often seen as a flagship seminary for especially mainstream Protestantism (primarily Presbyterian mainliners, but also some evangelicals)—given all this, indeed I have to work with a profound sense of "religious and ethical humility." Better said, perhaps, I have to own a kind of complicity, an embeddedness in white institutions and ethos that conditions not only my conscious life, but also my unconscious. Thus, my whiteness will be at work in many of my reflexive gestures, opinions, modes of expression, relationships to others and at times in my selected theoretical positions, and often in spite of my best intentions. (And then, how often do we whites even have good or "the best" intentions?)

At work here is something more than "complicity," since complicity usually suggests some kind of involvement that you can become aware of and then lay aside or grow beyond. Again, my whiteness and its anti-Blackness are aspects of conditions of political being, an ontology of being white that puts Black life "under erasure," as Calvin Warren writes about it in *Ontological Terror: Blackness, Nihilism, and Emancipation*. Because this persists, due to the history and politics into which I have been thrown by sheer birth and acculturation (as well as by my individual choices and failures), there is for me great lament and outrage. Those ontological conditions include Western modernity's slavery-based racial capitalism, U.S. wars and empire-building, as these are continually reinforced by and reinforcing a heteropatriarchal gender and sexual system. I cannot just renounce all this. Nor, of course, can I go to an anti-racist training seminar to get over my "white fragility." It's a white forcefulness with which I must reckon, the very power of which is marked by my body (again, whether I intend that or not). Admitting this is the stuff of white loss of innocence. James Baldwin's essay, "The White Man's Guilt," should be read annually in all white churches. Alas, many of my white students have not read it.

Most of the church and its leaders are ensconced in a reconciliatory dreaming that starts from problems of generalized guilt and sin that "Jesus came" to do something about. This again foregrounds Christian theology's grand scenarios. This is to abstract from the problem of how one might find life, possibly, by remembering Jesus's political insurrectionary torture-death. But abstracting away from this Jesus is often a piece with Christian leaders' abstracting also from any outrage over their own thoroughgoing whiteness as a form of radical evil (again, I mean not only whatever personal manifestations of whiteness they may show, but also whiteness as racial capitalism, as gender and sexual subjugation and erasure of Black lives, etc.). This chronic abstracting is part of the heart of whiteness, as I have argued since my 1990 works, and it is a vicious thread running through various modes of subjugation. In sum, I don't think Christian leaders will be outraged about the carceral logics of our time until they/we sink into and own a lament and outrage over their/our own emplacement in a political ontology of whiteness.

GY: Speak to how you understand the relationship between coloniality and U.S. mass incarceration. When I think of the two, I think of usurpation, expansionism, exploitation, domination, control, subjugation, the attempted creation of docile bodies, marked bodies, raced bodies, dangerous bodies. I assume that part of addressing the relationship between coloniality and U.S. mass incarceration would also involve processes of decolonization, yes? If this is true, then it seems to me that we must ask (demand?) of ordained ministers and theologians to become better decolonizers. Please explore.

MLT: Again, I have to say that before ordained ministers and theologians can become "better decolonizers" or to engage in decolonizing at all, they need to counter the de-historization of Jesus's death to which they contribute by continuously narrating any number of the grand scenarios about Jesus's death on the cross. These scenarios mask the insurrectionist and mundane political meanings of his imperial torture-death. Decolonizing, or "de-linking from the coloniality of power"—as decolonial thinkers such as Samir Amin would say—requires also a "de-imperializing" commitment. Imperialism is the brutal commandeering power of colonial expansion and maintenance. If there is not a re-politicization of Jesus understood as one who not only suffered but challenged imperial practices of torture and the forced subjugation of the body, then Christian leaders and their communities will hardly find the will to be "decolonizers" at all.

If we are serious about decolonizing, the road ahead is tangled and will demand our utmost. The "colonial matrix of power" presents a foreboding set of intersecting dynamics of power. Summarizing the work of one of the most influential of decolonial thinkers, Peruvian sociologist Aníbal Quijano, I have argued elsewhere that the coloniality of power is "a matrix of four ambits of social structural and cultural practices. These include, first, *labor* (structural practices of global capital), *sex and sexuality* (structural practices of hegemonic masculinism and heteronormativity), *subjectivity* (structural practices of Eurocentric white racism), and *state authority* (structural practices of state boundary fortifications). These four ambits are not separate circles of operation. They should be seen as overlapping, with various interactions specifiable between them." In the ambit of "state authority," Christian ministers today have a special responsibility to challenge the current directions of the U.S. state. Long-existing American traditions of white supremacy are now consolidating their hold over security, military and police functions with the aid of newly energized white Christian nationalism. It has been easy for many Christian liberal ministers and theologians to distance and differentiate themselves from this Christian right wing. But they have yet to really call them out and challenge them, organize to block their fascist aspiration. During the years of George W. Bush, I attempted to sound the alarm with my book *Religion, Politics and the Christian Right: Post-9/11 Powers and American Empire.*

GY: As a white male ordained minister and theologian, how do you understand the tensions that exist between the liberation work that you do and your own whiteness? I have long argued that white religious folk have failed to give critical attention to their whiteness, especially in terms of how their whiteness is linked to structures of power, hegemony and violence. It seems to me that well-intentioned white religious folk must do the work of removing their masks of "innocence," as James Baldwin would say. Without a critique of their own whiteness, they will continue to be complicit in anti-theological structures. Then again, white racism is so deeply pervasive and encrusted, I imagine that self-critique is not enough. One can rage against the machine of whiteness and still benefit from and perpetuate racialized injustice. There must be something far more global and systemically insur-rectionist—not simply reconciliatory, but abolitionist. In short, how do you critically address your own whiteness, what insights have you learned, with respect to living the life of a white male ordained minister and theologian who is committed to social justice, especially as you also teach at an elite academic institution that has roots within slavery?

MLT: As you can imagine from the foregoing, the status as "ordained minister," which I took on over 35 years ago, is a difficult one to maintain. I grew so uneasy with the status that 15–20 years ago I went on non-active status. I am not a celebrant of its "priestly" functions and practices. I respect the many good things that some do in their roles as ordained ministers, but personally, I am no longer comfortable with such a role. It is so difficult to extract white ecclesial functioning in the U.S. from white supremacist and U.S. imperialist formations. Even "theology," at least as the guild discipline it has become, is one from which I have distanced myself (see my book, *The Theological and the Political*). There I articulate a notion of "the theological" that frees it from the doctrinal genre that usually defines it, and from the transcendentalizing discourses that usually lead theology into abstractions that slight, or neglect altogether, the concrete and historical demands of faith and practice (like remembering the death of Jesus as an imperialist torture-death, comparable to lynching, as James Cone emphasizes). But the theological of which I would now speak is one that stays close to some very ancient meanings of the term. The theological is a discourse that traces awe-inspiring spectral forces born of remembering those who suffer the deep antagonisms of history (Ignacio Ellacuría's "the crucified people"), and those who, when remembered, portend a disruption of the standing order and generate practices of struggle to birth other possible worlds.

Any of these changes though, any specter for overcoming the antago-nisms spawned by white supremacy's anti-Blackness, demand that whites lay aside our innocence. Again, I agree with you, this is crucial to emphasize. Our whiteness dogs us at every step. I might make some progress shaking off some of the more egregious marks of individual white prejudice, but my place in structural racism, my having been thrown—as I've already stated—into the political ontology of whiteness, keeps me always a racist and my reflexive thoughts and actions can always surprise me to remind me of that uncomfortable fact.

So, what then? I argue that the way forward for white folk is to find our places in a collective struggle against the structures of white supremacy. Expect yourself to make mistakes, I often say to my white students, friends and colleagues. To myself! Watch out for them. Acknowledge them when they happen, but then keep moving forward, at the cues given by the leadership of Black, Indigenous, and other leaders of color. There are times when leadership from whites against white supremacy is essential. But usually this has to happen from within a collective of movements against white supremacy. Along this route there is no gaining of purity or renewed innocence for the white individual. Such a collective route should not become another prominent adventure displaying a white person's descent into display of our valiant wrestling with whiteness and then some rising into restored, emancipatory whiteness (or worse, some claimed "no-longer white-ness"). That is to chase again the will-o'-the-wisp of purity and innocence. All too often it is only the foregrounding of yet another white hero narrative—a claimed sojourn "up from whiteness!"

GY: As a hopeful Christian theist, I am also haunted by skeptical and pessimistic sensibilities. This partly accounts for my use of the term "hopeful." It's not just the epistemological question of God's existence, but the sheer magnitude of being sick and tired of, for me, anti-Black racism. This would include questions of mass incarceration, the policing of Black bodies, the killing of unarmed Black bodies, social and civic death, the investment in Black bodies as "criminal," "disgusting," "morally incorrigible," "subhuman," "hypersexual." When I think of liberation, through what I see as a form of racial realism à la Derrick Bell, I think of truncated forms of adjustment, one after another. I think of the arc of white American history that is only prepared to bend to the extent that whiteness remains hegemonic, where hope, therefore, functions to sustain Black people from taking far more serious and perhaps dangerous revolutionary action against their dehumanization. There are times when I think that systemic forms of anti-Black racism are just too embedded within the structures and psyches of white America, and that at the end of the day, my Black humanity will still be denied. It is at these crucial times that I want to avoid the seductions of Karl Marx's dictum that "religion is the opium of the people," which implies a form of deception, where one exclusively looks beyond this life to the one (allegedly) to come. Yet, there are times when the weight of human misery is so great, and the ethical, moral and spiritual imagination (strength and capacity) of human beings seems so meager, that I think that there is nothing that will liberate us short of the eschaton, which I see not simply as a reckoning but as a day of ending all evil and suffering, something like a metaphysical intervention in human history. Do you see the tension here? Speak to this in terms of how you deal with what I'm trying to articulate.

MLT: Yes, I share in the heaviness of being "sick and tired" of my own whiteness but especially of the structural anti-Blackness with its roots in multiple streams of the past and sustained by the many ambits and levels of U.S. imperial war policy and the coloniality and neo-coloniality of power today, all of which still pulse through transnational global rule.

So, maybe I need to be very concrete here both about my own pessimism for all the reasons you note so eloquently here, but also about my own . . . well, I won't say hope, surely not optimism—but something like hope, an expectant, always proactive posture toward a meaningful and powerful "otherwise." I do find myself unable to let go of an arts-nurtured spirit of defiance toward the future, one which is in combination with many others' defiance, at work in collective practices to keep the future open.[1]

And this is where it is so important to keep our struggle broad, our focus on anti-Black white supremacy, but as understood to be sustained and animated by the multidimensional coloniality of power. And that coloniality does have a historical beginning in the constellation of modernity's colonizing powers. We are still on the way to undoing those powers. We need to delink from not only the micro- and macro-aggressions that so obviously mark white racism. We need also need to organize with people of every region who hope but also know that U.S. imperial power is animated by a transnational whiteness and accumulative systematic greed that drives down so many. This inter-regional organizing helps us know what "radical hope" looks like. I know Maya activists in Guatemala who live and fight on the underside of U.S.-backed genocide in their country and who tell me that the changes they fight and hope for will not come until their grandchildren's time. I know well one political prisoner, Mumia Abu-Jamal, who insists on finding something to laugh about every day as a way to hope. With Mumia still in prison in spite of my years of work in movements for him, the temptation to despair is real. Yes, I am convinced that movements for him got him off death row, but now he endures a "slow death row," as he puts it, with a life-without-parole sentence. While he is still in prison, I am about to retire after teaching the whole four decades that Mumia has been in prison since 1982, the same year of my first Fall as a professor in Princeton. I'm headed for retirement maybe with some comforts on the eve of death. Black activist and revolutionary Mumia is still in prison. There's the difference that whiteness makes right there! What hope can there be?

I'm not sure, but I hold onto some artistic form, some song, some poet, the love in my life and family—any of which might at the very least support in me and us a spirit of defiance toward any future that still seems overwhelmed by anti-Blackness. A lyrical but uncompromisingly political reggae song can often carry me a long way; and I confess that almost any ballad by even a white troubadour—one who is ready to sing of workers' struggles toward unity with a whole "motley crew" of international rebels against Western colonialism, white supremacy, capitalism and imperialism—can be a defiant spirit welcome to my being. It is in this spirit that I also receive the hand-painted notecards that Mumia occasionally paints and sends to me (and to others). Defiant spirit is especially operative in such sites of organized liberatory action as the Campaign to Bring Mumia Home. Indeed, as you say, this future means holding open the possibilities for "dangerous revolutionary action," but these will have to come when the most victimized by colonizing white supremacy call for it and dare to seize, and make, the right time for it. Churches whose dreams, prayers, communal rituals, and practices fail to dare that revolutionary action, or even to welcome it, are usually inhaling the kind of religion as opium about which Marx rightly warned.

We need prayers, practices and actions that align us with a spirit of defiance for another future. And I do look for this on *this* side of what Christian theologians call "the eschaton," and on *this* side of what Afropessimists term "the end of the world," fixing as they do on that one phrase plucked from midway in a poem by Aimé Césaire and from amidst the complex work toward a new future that Frantz Fanon pointed to. We cannot wait for some "end of the world." I'm not proposing we just get busy with many activities of liberal reformism instead. That's deadly too. Instead, with the arts nurturing a spirit of defiance, we need to break liberals' "freedom-speak" open to a more radical thinking and acting toward freedom. We need to create new spaces and discourses that defy any future that looks only like more of the same. The arts nurturing defiance, if well-crafted and at work in social movements, help me (us?) "taste" that future and to live defiantly toward it. In the meantime, I recall Mumia's words that I have cited often, about the urgency and possibility of resisting the U.S. and its imperial force: ". . . what history really shows is that today's empire is tomorrow's ashes, that nothing lasts forever, that to not resist is to acquiesce in your own oppression."

I know these words do not assuage the angst amid the repression of now, but they do display an intelligent spirit of defiance toward the future—not as desperate individual heroics, but within collective movement practices. I myself don't prioritize "metaphysical intervention." When contemplating threatening futures, this language often assumes some power that will break into our historical, socio-political and natural and planetary living from some outside sphere, plane or realm. With philosopher Jean-Luc Nancy, I always want to ask, "What outside?" I have further followed

Nancy in looking not so much toward an "outside" but more to an "other," to an emergent "otherwise" to the colonizing brutalities of our time. This is neither a drive for other-worldly transcendence nor the championing of a secularist immanence. It is to watch and work for what Nancy termed a "transimmanental" world. Here there is a real crossing over ("trans-"), into an "other" world, but a crossing that remains within emergent and conflictual historical, socio-political transformations of our natural and planetary being ("-immanental"). I know this is complex language, but so is "metaphysical intervention." But I see that phrase as too readily accommodating the apolitical and ahistorical "divine-scenario" thinking and practice, which I mentioned above and which often allows Christian leaders to evade addressing this world's ontologies of repression. To be sure, I know of and value those communities that *do* speak of such interventions, but these are usually uniquely crafted types of apocalyptic political radicalisms, and therefore rare.

GY: The state of being sick and tired is so recursive. Not only in terms of clearly anti-Black racist realities, but also in terms of those realities that can mean the extinction of life as we know it. As a child I recall being so afraid (obsessively) of what would happen if there was a nuclear holocaust. The thought of the global existential devastation was just too much to imagine as a child. Yet, here I am as an adult reliving many of those experiences, especially having read recently that the Doomsday Clock has been set at 100 seconds to midnight. This would have horrible implications for the earth as such. How do you think about such catastrophes theologically?

MLT: Yes, I hope it appears that I hear you on this. Being "sick and tired" is indeed recursive. It is also, I sense, an always persisting dimension deep within the being of activists and thinkers most needed to sustain defiant hope. This is especially so if we as scholars dare struggle to be what Joy James terms "radical subjects," those who seek to maintain connections with collectivities inside, but especially outside of academe, who are in struggle against the white supremacy that laces poison into the corporate warrior state that embodies the dynamics of the coloniality of power today. For those of us in neoliberal academe, if we are there as "radical subjects," we endure a kind of incoherence with our profession, rather than settling for being the "activist scholars" that James, and others like Rob Nixon have problematized. The "activist scholar" all too often works with a sense of professional coherence with neoliberal academe.

And along the way of my own being sick and tired, I too am haunted by the extinction of life by nuclear war. I recall the drills of my elementary school years in New Mexico and Kansas, practicing then how to cover our heads while crouching under our desks in case of nuclear attack by the USSR! More importantly, I now know that in a sense the U.S. is already among "the most nuclear bombed countries in the world," as anthropologist Joe Masco puts it in his stellar book, *Nuclear Borderlands*. That claim was the fruit of his analysis of the trajectories of nuclear fallout across the lower 48 states, from the years of nuclear bomb testing in the U.S. Southwest. Mass amounts of that fallout were deposited in the very Northeast part of Kansas where I grew up. This nuclearist threat against life is not only the portent of a spectacular violence, but also a "slow violence," as described by Rob Nixon, who notes the poisoning of generations that resulted also from U.S. bombings of Iraq that deposited onerous levels of depleted uranium there, thus sickening and deforming the bodies of Iraq's people and land.

All this is, as you say, "catastrophe" (from Latin, an "overturning" of things, a "turning over"). This comprehensive antagonism against life should call forth theological reflection and critique. Various groups remember and name their catastrophes in different ways. There are the Aymara of Peru remembering their "conquest" at the hands of Spain (*Pachakuti*, "total disruption of space/time"), also Jews' language of "holocaust" (as *Shoa*), Palestinians' remembrance of massive loss of land, loved ones, ongoing mass incarceration and illegal occupation by the Israeli state (*Nakba*), the trans-atlantic middle passage and slavery endured by Africans and Blacks (*Maafa*) or twentieth century Maya peoples in Guatemala remembering their late twentieth century massacres as simply "*la violencia.*"

From the theological viewpoint I set out earlier in this interview, such catastrophic modes of history's structural suffering show populations becoming what Spanish philosopher and theologian in El Salvador, Ignacio Ellacuría, termed "crucified peoples." He himself in 1989 was subject to massacre by a U.S.-backed battalion along with his housekeeper and daughter and five other liberation scholar/priests. Crucified peoples are those subjected to collective murder, mass human destruction, loss of land and the ruination of their nature-systems. It is an imperial tool of rule, using publicly displayed death by torture (like lynching in the U.S.) to instill fear and control the dominated. It targets whole subordinate peoples as well as individuals. We must think deeply about the dialectics at work in these crucifixion scenes, these sites of white supremacy and settler colonial violation and destruction.

In the days of future nuclear war and mass extinction of life, I ask: will we all, like so many of the already crucified become victims of our own crucifying imperial rule? Viewed from a long range perspective, I think that "anti-Black racist realities" and the "realities of extinction of life as we know it" by nuclear war—these need to be thought in conjunction (not "analogically" or certainly not as "the same"). They *are* distinctive sites of ontological terror. Also, different kinds of arguments for each can be made about their ontological primacy or comparative importance vis-à-vis the other. But they also both share in a dialectic of colonizing catastrophe, wherein two dynamics of abstraction are in continual intertwining. The first is *abstraction as distancing*, the pulling away of human rhetoric, social practice, ideologies and religious viewpoints from concrete worlds of nature and bodies. Perhaps, dramatically exemplary of this is the "paper entrepreneurialism" of finance capital, emblematically visible in corporate power's paperwork and digital transactions processed in urban skyscrapers or elite enclaves of the rich. They are routinely isolated from face-to-face exchanges with the very rural poor or those of urban barrios and ghettos who suffer the brunt of transnational capital's concentration of wealth. Second, intertwined with the abstraction's distancing is *abstraction as destruction*, the creation of an endless supply of material things and ever-shifting values, such that the poor's worlds are left destroyed by deprivation of material goods most needed for life and dignity. Both types of abstraction are at work in almost every case of war. Sanitizing mythologies, as Chris Hedges emphasizes in *The Greatest Evil is War*,[2] present war as "virtue" and so distance many of us from its concrete horror, even while war's destructive ways hide in the crevices of this distancing abstraction. War comes with its brutal chaos, dismembering and leaving ruined our most real and cherished worlds.

Anti-Blackness' racist reality involves distancing from, the abandonment of the Black body, leaving it in ruin, but also often constructing it as the mark, the symbol of what ruin looks like. Here the historically and socially subjected and reduced body, made nothing, is "blackened" (Zakiya Imani Jackson); it becomes, and I agree here with this part of Afro-pessimism, constructed as a kind of ontological marker of ruin, dehumanized, a kind of "no-thing," positioned as antithetical to the human. Nuclear extinction—again however distinct—also shows the abstraction as distancing from sentient human flesh and earth ("we'll deter one another through "mutually-assured destruction"/we'll use "only" strategic and limited nuclear weapons/we'll "contain" this/ we'll "survive" this). But this abstractive distancing only feeds abstraction's impending destruction, the charring (another "blackening"), the melting, the rubble of built-up structures, the ooze of bodies, then the years of winter and slow poisoning. Read Dr. Michihiko Hachiya's *Hiroshima Diary* of Japan's 1945 ordeal of nuclear war to encounter the terrifying reality of what may, in fact, be an understatement of what future extinguishing terror would be. Talk about "chickens coming home to roost": here white supremacy's blackening of African bodies across centuries of its imperial coloniality—this reduction, this extinguishing of Black being to "no-thing"—redounding upon "civilization and all humanity, making all to be "crucified peoples" of racial imperial rule, reducing to nothing all humanity and most of earth's creatures.

Theology that traces the antagonisms of life—and this is what I take theology at its best to do—will lay bare and neither hide from nor mask the actuality and potentiality of this terrorizing end. Unmasking that potentially barren future is a prerequisite for any dreaming and for any real defiance of terrorizing futures. After that unmasking, we might then bring peoples' together, if only as huddled masses yearning for some otherwise. Then—as peoples have done when living through or in anticipation of the terrorizing loss of flesh and earth (as *Pachakuti*, the *Maafa*, *Shoa*, *Nakba*, or more)—we might all desperately undertake a collective "theological" task, experimenting with the myths and symbols, the stories, the visions large and small, as well as our deliberative analyses, which can open us as earth's peoples to new ways of meeting the future, to defy (not deny) the terror.

I cannot say what precisely we humans will do or become. I do sense, though, that this means laying aside any Christianity that claims to alone be adequate—and also any "Abrahamic faith" or any of the great so-called "religions." It seems feeble but necessary to seek instead the often maligned wisdom of earth's indigenous peoples, living and sometimes flourishing after and at the edges of threatened extinction. *"!No nos aniquilaron!/They have not annihilated us!"* as Indigenous peoples marched and chanted in 1992 at the fifth quincentennial of Europeans' enslaving conquests in the Americas. So, I turn for some defiant wisdom and hope to Laguna Pueblo writer Leslie Marmon Silko's words from one of her characters, Yoeme, in Silko's novel *Almanac of the Dead*—difficult as these words are, dismissible as they can seem:

> Old Yoeme had always said the earth would go on, the earth would outlast anything man did to it, including the atomic bomb. . . . Once the earth had been blasted open and brutally exploited, it was only logical the earth's offspring, all the earth's beings, would similarly be destroyed. The earth would have its ups and downs; but humans had been raping and killing their own nestlings at such a rate. Yoeme said humans might not survive. The humans would not be a great loss to the earth.

Maybe we need to analyze *this*. Give it nuance, depth, content. Challenge it, if you will. But what would it mean to *live* this?

21

WHITE SUPREMACIST CHRISTIANITY DRIVES TRUMP'S LOYAL MOB

We Must Scream It Down

INTERVIEW WITH SUSANNAH HESCHEL

Two months have now passed since mobs of mostly white people descended on the Capitol in an attempt to overthrow the results of November's election, but I am still haunted by images of the mob's racist violence such as the noose that they put on display and the shirt of a white man in the crowd that read, "Camp Auschwitz."

These details were more than symbolic—they point to historically materialized forms of horrific anti-Black and antisemitic racism that continue to be stoked by white supremacist strains of Christianity.

As we struggle against this violence, we can draw from the deep wellsprings of African American and Jewish prophetic traditions that speak truth to power and counter oppression.

In moments like these I often turn to the work of Rabbi Abraham Joshua Heschel, who was one of the leading Jewish theologians and prophetic figures of the 20th century. He was also a close friend of Dr. Martin Luther King Jr. and joined King to march from Selma to Montgomery in March 1965.

Rabbi Heschel's writings produce a profound love for those who suffer and a profound sense of outrage against those who perpetuate that suffering.

G. Yancy (with Susannah Heschel), "White Supremacist Christianity Drives Trump's Loyal Mob. We Must Scream It Down," in *Truthout*, March 12, 2021. [Editors: Alana Yu-lan Price, Britney Schultz, and Anton Woronczuk]

At this moment in U.S. history, as we witness the rise of unabashed white supremacy and the proliferation of lies and mistrust, we desperately need to channel the prophetic urgency and clarity of voices like his.

Where are the courageous voices who will call out all forms of religious idolatry that are entwined with profane understandings of Christianity? Is racism anti-theological? In what ways might we continue to hope while in the claws of despair? And where are we headed—into chaos or into community, given such pervasive violence and indifference in the world?

In this engaging interview, Rabbi Heschel's daughter, Susannah Heschel, speaks in her own powerful voice, and weaves her father's prophetic courage and wisdom into our conversation. Susannah Heschel is the Eli M. Black Distinguished Professor and chair of the Jewish Studies Program at Dartmouth College. She is the author of *Abraham Geiger and the Jewish Jesus*, *The Aryan Jesus: Christian Theologians and the Bible in Nazi Germany*, and *Jüdischer Islam: Islam und jüdisch-deutsche Selbstbestimmung*. A Guggenheim Fellow, she is currently writing a book with Sarah Imhoff, entitled, *Jewish Studies and the Woman Question*.

GEORGE YANCY: One of my favorite quotes from Rabbi Abraham Joshua Heschel is "The prophet's word is a scream in the night." For me, it points to his own deep sense of pain felt when others suffer, and the sense of outrage that he felt when it came to our inhumanity toward each other. I wanted to scream as I watched with sorrow and outrage the events unfold at the Capitol. How would you characterize the meaning and importance of your father's use of "scream" within the context of what we witnessed collectively at the Capitol? There is something sonically visceral expressed in his use of that term.

SUSANNAH HESCHEL: What does it mean to be a prophet? We conventionally think of prophets as people who foretell the future, but my father's understanding of the Hebrew prophets of the Bible is entirely different. "What manner of man is the prophet?" he asks. A person of agony, whose "life and soul are at stake in what he says." Who hears our despair? As you note, my father writes that the prophet's word is "a scream in the night," a scream to shatter our indifference. The prophet screams out the horror of human suffering, giving voice to the "silent sigh of human anguish."

When we watched the horrific video of police murdering George Floyd, we saw his desperation and agony, and we watched a murderer kill him. We saw police bystanders who stood there, utterly indifferent, doing nothing to save this man's life. We wanted to scream.

White Americans shoulder grave responsibility for that moment. My father writes, "Some are guilty, but all are responsible." We are not guilty of murder, but we have to assess our responsibility: Are we not bystanders, responsible for the racism that led to the murder of so many Black men, women and children? George Floyd was murdered by the racism that has gone unchecked for centuries, the systemic racism that organizes this country according to principles of white supremacy.

The soil of this country is soaked with the blood of Native Americans we slaughtered and Black Africans we brought to this country to enslave. Enslavement left us with a heritage of its sadism in our culture and with the screams of enslaved people still ringing in our ears. Remember, my father said that, "the blood of the innocent cries forever. Should that blood stop to cry, humanity will cease to exist." Have we all become indifferent bystanders, unable to hear the scream in the night? Do we not hear the cries of the tortured and murdered? If we are to preserve our own humanity, we must become prophetic witnesses.

As you have shared when you were at Dartmouth College as our Montgomery Fellow, some white Christians in this country left Sunday church services to hunt a Black man, woman or child to torture and then hang in full view of a throng of white onlookers, taking photographs before going home for their Sunday dinner. During World War II, Nazi death camp guards tortured and murdered Jews and then went to church services. How is that even possible? What should we do once we conclude our prayers? Do we leave our houses of worship only to engage in brutality? What kind of worship is it, then?

Our worship services require revision to make clear to congregants why they gather to pray, and that God demands, first and foremost, justice before we even gain the right to stand before God and pray. A life of cruelty cannot be combined with a life of pretended piety: "I hate, I despise your feasts," God tells us through the prophet Amos, "let justice roll down like water and righteousness like a mighty stream."

Dr. King and my father used similar language and spoke of God not as the "unmoved mover" of Aristotle, but as the "most moved mover" of the Bible, a God of pathos who responds to us. Central to my father's theology is his assertion that God has passion and is involved in human history, affected by human deeds. This means that God suffers when human beings are hurt, so that when I hurt another person, I injure God. How can a self-proclaimed "religious" person pray on Sunday morning and then torture and murder on Sunday afternoon? This is not prayer; this is not living as a witness to God.

What does it mean to be a witness? My father writes that while the Ten Commandments prohibit images of God, God created human beings in the divine image. We are the only permitted images of God, but what does it mean to be an image of God? To be an image, my father writes, is to be a witness: "God is raging in the prophet's words." The prophets are witnesses to God's passion for justice. Indeed, citing an old Jewish tradition, my father writes, "I am God and you are my witnesses; if you are not my witnesses, then I am not God."

GY: Your father also wrote that, "The history of interracial relations is a nightmare." He understood how racism defiles the human soul and disgraces our common humanity. The ugly, dreadful and deadly reality of racism in this country haunts U.S. history and lurks within the fragile struts that maintain our democratic experiment. At the Capitol, I recall seeing a sign or flag that read, "JESUS SAVES." Deploying that message within the context of the racist and violent attack at the Capitol recalls other moments of vile contradiction within white Christianity, such as times when many white Christians gathered to watch Black bodies being castrated, brutalized and burned. And while this form of racism is *not* intrinsic to Christianity, many white Europeans committed gruesome crimes in the name of Christianity. Your father's words characterize racial and religious bigotry in terms of evil, the sheer absence of reverence. How would your father characterize our contemporary nightmare, and what advice would he have for religious leaders as we live through this 21st-century nightmare?

SH: Those self-proclaimed religious leaders who grant sanction to racists, spread lies and intolerance, claim they speak in the name of God, faith and morals; I say my Bible has been taken captive by a fascistic movement masquerading as apocalyptic Christianity. All around this country, we see truth and justice covered with chains, enslaved by selfishness and the lust for power and empire. These are indeed a people who hear and do not understand, see and do not perceive.

To these people, I quote Jeremiah:

> They know no bounds in deeds of wickedness; they judge not with justice the cause of the fatherless, the rights of the needy. Shall I not punish them for these things, says the Lord, and shall I not avenge myself on a nation such as this? An appalling and horrible thing has happened in the land: the prophets prophesy falsely and the priests rule at their direction; my people love to have it so, but what will you do when the end comes? (Jeremiah 5:28-31)

How do we find hope in a time of despair? How do we keep the optimism of Isaiah at a time when the words of Jeremiah express our mood of desolation? But we must also ask: How can we abandon poor God to those who reject truth and trample on justice?

Let us remember that in the Bible, the words of God come to us from the prophets, not the priests, and not the kings. We are desperate for prophets in our time, those who will speak clearly to remind us, as my father did, that racism is "unmitigated evil." My father stated clearly and sharply that "we forfeit the right to worship God" if we continue to uphold a racist society. He called upon all houses of worship to repent and recognize their sins, including their sins of perverting the fundamental teaching of all religious traditions: that *God is either the creator of all life or of no life.*

Prayer is the home for the soul, my father wrote, but worship must not be reassuring. My father's friend, Rev. William Sloane Coffin, used to say that prayer must comfort the afflicted and afflict the comfortable. My father wrote that prayer must be subversive, disturb our self-righteousness and complacency. The experience of prayer should be like the experience of hearing the prophets: a rousing call to conscience. The prophets have been mocked for their passionate outrage about injustice, and my father asks, if we mock the prophets as "hysterics," then "what name should be given to the abysmal indifference to evil which the prophet bewails?" Who are we, the complacent, the bystanders?

GY: I am also deeply intrigued by your father's integration of God-talk vis-à-vis the ways in which we mistreat, oppress and marginalize others. Your father's eyes were always focused on human beings, on our past and present mistreatment of other human beings. I see this as his horizontal vision, one that is unafraid to name and call out the social evils that we as human beings create and perpetuate. Yet, what I would call his vertical vision is always operative as well. God is always there, especially manifested in our fellow human beings. Your father writes, "To act in the spirit of religion is to unite what lies apart, to remember that humanity as a whole is God's beloved child." What is important to note here is that the term "religion" comes from the Latin *religare*, which suggests a community *bond* between human beings and God. Speak to the need for a form of God-talk in our moment, especially given so much religious hypocrisy, where religiosity appears to be tethered to forms of political idolization, where Donald Trump, apparently, can commit no wrong, no harm, no acts of injustice, where he has, for some, become "infallible."

SH: Perhaps what we need is not talk about God, but greater awareness of the presence of God. The problem my father poses in his books is how we can cultivate in ourselves the ability to sense God's presence, whether in nature, Torah, other people—and in justice itself. First, we have to realize what we are capable of—a sense of awe and amazement, heightened sensitivity to others, awareness of our own vulnerability.

A Hasidic thinker of the 19th century made a distinction between having a sense of the absence of God's presence—moments when we lose our ability to recognize that the whole earth is filled with God's glory—and a sense of the presence of God's absence, meaning moments when we fall into a pit of despair and sense that there is, perhaps, a place in our world that is vacant, without God.

In these days, some of us feel we are in an abyss of despair, terribly worried about the overwhelming problems we face as a society and a country, unsure of how we can emerge.

We also see people who were driven by a lying president, inciting them to riot, to rage against all norms of proper behavior and thereby fall into an abyss as well, though not of despair but of rebellion, the vacant abyss in which God is absent.

Together we need to raise ourselves from despair and rebellion. In Hasidic tradition, we need help to lift ourselves out of the abyss, to leave behind fear and resentment, and accompany our return to conscience and commandments.

What we must remember, my father always emphasized, is that evil is never the climax of history. Justice will rise up and prevail. Out of despair, let us find hope and inspiration in Dr. King and my father, in their teachings and in their relationship.

For my father, the prophets always held out a vision and a hope: "There is bound to come a renewal of our sense of wonder and radical amazement, a revival of reverence, an emergence of a sense of ultimate embarrassment, and ultimate indebtedness."

GY: Your father and Dr. Martin Luther King Jr. were friends, but also close in terms of theological vision and sociopolitical praxis. Both rejected the evils of racism and economic injustice. Both were concerned about the poor, the orphaned, the despised, the "disposable." Many want to know where we go from here. So, will it be chaos or community? And how might the voices of these two figures, who stand within the tradition of a theology of social justice, help us in this moment of deep divisiveness, help us to find a way out of so many anti-democratic forces?

SH: Yes, will it be chaos or community? Apocalypse or prophecy?

The political religion of the Nazis was not about religion but fascism masquerading as Christianity. My great concern is that fascistic movements have until now never been halted by political arguments—not by Democrats, Communists, Socialists or Christians. The challenge before us is great, and the temptation to despair is enormous.

Throughout the course of history, political movements have used religion to gain power and have sought to undermine the prophetic tradition. They are movements characterized by terror and a desire for social control and constriction, warning of death and destruction rather than offering hope and redemption. Today we have a Christian Right that swaggers with a promise of salvation for the elect and ignores the here and now of our lives, our desperate need for justice and a beloved community. Rather than care for the Earth and its bounty, they care for money even at the price of utter destruction of the land, poison of our bodies, contempt for our fellow animal creatures.

Such movements are bolstered by a death-glorifying theology. What we see is a white supremacist movement reviving an insidious politics of race. In the Nazi period, some Germans used Christianity to promote racism and antisemitism. When I wrote a book about them, *The Aryan Jesus*, I learned how frighteningly easy it can be to pervert religion and destroy its moral credibility. Some German bishops and pastors were so enthusiastic about Hitler that they called him a "savior." Shockingly, I have heard American Christians say the same about Trump. In Germany, Hitler's Christian supporters threw the Old Testament out of the Bible and proclaimed Jesus an Aryan, not a Jew.

Trump has had a similar effect in this country, with rallies that arouse emotional excitement. Some religious leaders—Catholic, Protestant and Jewish—have viewed him as a "savior" figure. In both contexts, Germany and America, the desecration of basic moral decency did not dissuade religious leaders, but brought a thrill of naughty violation of the fundamental propriety and doctrinal discipline of religion and society.

Why are some Jews in America and in Israel Christianizing Zionism and their own moral values with white supremacy? Is Trump more appealing than Judaism? Let me warn them: Smearing themselves with white supremacy will result in the suicidal destruction of Judaism.

Have my fellow Jews forgotten that the central teaching of Judaism is compassion and justice? The ultimate expression of God for the prophets is not wisdom, magnificence, land, glory, nor even love, but rather justice. Zion, Isaiah declares, shall be redeemed by justice, and those who repent, by righteousness. Justice is the tool of God, the manifestation of God, the means of our redemption and the redemption of God from human mendacity.

What has happened to our conscience, to our judgment, to our duty as citizens to say "no" to the subversiveness of our government, which is ruining the values we cherish by carrying out deadly policies? Is America, is democracy, the great rock of ages, to become a temporary moment in history?

How do we emerge from the abyss of despair and lift fellow human beings out of their abyss of rage? How do we become God's beloved disciple when we feel like God's suffering servant?

I wish to share a few poignant verses from the Bible:

Who will speak for me, asks God, who will remember the covenant of peace and compassion? Can we abandon despair and find the inner resources to respond like Isaiah, who said, Here I am, send me. (Isaiah 6:8)

And yet in anger, Habakkuk reminds us, we must remember mercy. (3:2)

To live a life of moral grandeur and spiritual audacity is a profound challenge; we must all begin by practicing small acts of courage and truth. David, on his deathbed, tells Solomon: Be strong and of good courage; Fear not, be not dismayed; for the Lord God is with you. God will not fail you nor forsake you until all the work for the service of the Lord is finished. (1 Chronicles 28:20)

Part Seven

THE POLITICS OF CATASTROPHE

22

MOURNING IS A POLITICAL ACT AMID THE PANDEMIC AND ITS DISPARITIES

INTERVIEW WITH JUDITH BUTLER

As corpses pile up and makeshift morgues struggle under the burden of the COVID-19 pandemic, questions of vulnerability and mourning have become ever more acute. How do we mourn mass death amid a pandemic, and how is our mourning political?

Theorist Judith Butler—whose recent work has focused on philosophies of both vulnerability and mourning—argues here that "learning to mourn mass death means marking the loss of someone whose name you do not know, whose language you may not speak, who lives at an unbridgeable distance from where you live." And the public mourning that is required in this moment also requires asking difficult political questions about the conditions that have structured the magnitude and disparities of the epidemic.

In the exclusive *Truthout* interview that follows, Butler shares their analysis of how to think about vulnerability to COVID-19 in political terms, what it means to mobilize and learn from private grief and mass mourning, and the role of academia and intellectuals in the current crisis. Butler is known for their decades of work in philosophy, feminism and social activism worldwide. A professor in the Department of Comparative Literature and the Program of Critical Theory at the University of California, Berkeley, they are the author of numerous influential books, including *Gender Trouble, Precarious Life, Notes Toward a Performative Theory of Assembly,*

G. Yancy (with Judith Butler), "Judith Butler: Mourning Is a Political Act Amid the Pandemic and Its Disparities," in *Truthout*, April 30, 2020. [Editors: Alana Yu-lan Price, Britney Schultz, and Anton Woronczuk]

The Force of Nonviolence and most recently, *What World is This? A Pandemic Phenomenology.*

GEORGE YANCY: Trying to articulate what it feels like to live through this shared pandemic is difficult. I move through feelings of profound grief, intolerable isolation and even fantasies of apocalyptic dread. At other times, there is a sense of hope and clarity. One among many things that is very clear to me, though by no means new, is just how interconnected we are, just how misleadingly and dangerously we have behaved and treated others under neoliberal assumptions and practices. We are, after all, as you have argued, "Given over from the start to the world of others." Your point couldn't be more germane as we find ourselves within the midst of an unprecedented global vulnerability. Speak to how you're thinking about vulnerability at this moment, especially in terms of how that vulnerability isn't equally distributed.

JUDITH BUTLER: On the one hand, the pandemic exposes a global vulnerability. Everyone is vulnerable to the virus because everyone is vulnerable to viral infection from other human beings without first establishing immunity. Vulnerability is not just the condition of being potentially harmed by another. It names the porous and interdependent character of our bodily and social lives. We are given over from the start to a world of others we never chose in order to become more or less singular beings. That dependency does not precisely end with adulthood. To survive, we take something in; we eat, we breathe. We are impressed upon by the environment, social worlds and intimate contact. That impressionability and porosity define our embodied social lives. What another breathes out, I can breathe in, and something of my breath can find its way into yet another person. The human trace that someone leaves on an object may well be what I touch, pass along on another surface or absorb into my own body. Humans share the air with one another and with animals; they share the surfaces of the world. They touch what others have touched and they touch one another. These reciprocal and material modes of sharing describe a crucial dimension of our vulnerability, intertwinements and interdependence of our embodied social life.

On the other hand, one part of the public response to the pandemic has been to identify "vulnerable groups"—those who are especially likely to suffer the virus as a ravaging and life-threatening disease and to contrast them with those who are less at risk of losing their lives from the pathogen. The vulnerable include Black and Brown communities deprived of adequate health care throughout their lifetimes and the history of this nation. The vulnerable also include poor people, migrants, incarcerated people, people with disabilities, trans and queer people who struggle to achieve rights to health care, and all those with prior illnesses and enduring medical conditions. The pandemic exposes the heightened vulnerability to the illness of all those for whom health care is neither accessible nor affordable. Perhaps there are at least two lessons about vulnerability that follow: it describes a shared condition of social life, of interdependency, exposure and porosity; it names the greater likelihood of dying, understood as the fatal consequence of a pervasive social inequality.

GY: Coupled with your reflections on vulnerability are such themes as mourning and grief. I take very seriously the fact that, at this moment, there are so many who are unemployed. Yet, COVID-19 has made unambiguously clear the deep forms of economic instability that have always been there, that are intrinsic to our ways of living, our ways of being complacent with huge economic differentials, of massive income and wealth gaps. In short, people are mourning and grieving because they are simply not economically secure. How do we mobilize such mourning and grief and tarry with it, so that it has something to teach us now and going forward?

JB: For those who are homeless or unemployed, the economic forecast in 2020 could not look bleaker. Without a working and equitable health care system, the affirmation of health care as a public good and a mandate of government, the unemployed are left to scramble for alternatives to avoid falling ill and dying for lack of care. This is the stunning cruelty of the U.S. that shocks large portions of the world. Many workers are not just temporarily out of work, but are registering the collapse of their work worlds, the prospect of no paycheck, homelessness, a pervasive sense of being abandoned by the society to which they should rightly belong.

Before the pandemic, the future horizon was already closing or had closed for many people forced to move between jobs, who saw no real increase in wages, and found that rents, debts and medical costs belonged to the expanding category of "the unpayable." Their entire sense of future is structured by that unpayable debt: it becomes a form of bondage, infinite and without end.

The radical increase in poverty now means that anxiety and fear become for many the norm: *How will they eat? Will they eat less often and less well? Will they find shelter? How will they survive and those who depend upon them?* Many are anxious because they do not yet know who or what they have yet to lose, what parts of the world will be irrecoverably lost or reanimated in new and truncated form. Those grieving now may well be bracing for more grief, not knowing from which direction it will arrive. The grief over the sudden loss of someone's life is bound up with a sense of shock that this is now a world in which such losses can and do and will happen.

GY: Many of my students, both undergraduate and graduate, have been grieving in a different way. Some have said to me that academia feels useless and going to classes during this time just doesn't make sense. In fact, those students in philosophy have been particularly vocal. They are finding it hard to read abstract texts that seem oblivious to our current existential predicament. Any advice?

JB: Some young people, including students of mine, worry that they are being asked to grieve the loss of hope itself. But theirs is not a mindless desperation. They do not accept the lies and false promises of the profiteers or the politicians that call for reopening of the workplace without any regard for the lives that could not survive the infection.

My graduate students don't make decent wages as it is, often living in overcrowded rental apartments, forced to pay high rents in the Bay Area, and sometimes suffering from food insecurity. Now they are asking what path in academic life is still open for them. They live with a profound uncertainty during this time even as they seek to ground themselves in an informed understanding of the pandemic. They are in urgent need of debt forgiveness and a livable wage and are drawn to strike actions to make their clearly just demands heard.

As a teacher and adviser, I ponder how to hold steady for the young when one's own foundation is rocked and rocking? In higher education, we are confronted with hiring freezes, furloughs, the freezing and cancellation of academic and postdoctoral positions. The arts and the humanities were already struggling for decent funding in a higher education market that tends to reward the STEM fields without seeing how interconnected our kinds of knowledge are.

The basic questions—how to live, how to face mortality and how best to make sense of the world—are ones that drive the humanities still and again. The crisis of values we are facing is enormous as cost-benefit schemes of values are imposed upon the management of life, too often designating the precarious as dispensable lives. It is no wonder that people are turning to poetry and song, writing and visual art, history and theory on new digital platforms to make sense of their pandemic world, to reflect upon the question: *When the world as we know it falls apart, what then?*

GY: I am often speechless when I see the piling up of corpses and makeshift morgues as so many of us perish as a result of this pandemic. Often after a mass shooting, even if it is forgotten soon thereafter, we, in the U.S., engage in public forms of grieving. For many families, burial rituals cannot be performed given the spread of the virus. What deep impact do you think this will have on families and how might we rethink public forms of grieving?

JB: A difficult question: How to mourn mass death? Under conditions of pandemic, losses are for the most part borne in private. We are returned to the household (if there is one) as the site for mourning, deprived of the public gathering in which such losses are marked and registered and shared. The internet has more fully claimed its place as the new public sphere, but it can never fully substitute for the gatherings, both private and public, that allow losses to be fathomed and lived through with others.

A purely private form of mourning is possible but cannot assuage the cry that wants the world to bear witness to a singular loss. And with public losses of this magnitude and quick succession, there are political questions that are linked with the demand for public mourning: *Why were health facilities so badly underfunded and unprepared? Why did the president disband the committee tasked with preparations of pandemics of this kind? Why are there not enough beds or ventilators? Why are Black people, incarcerated people and migrants more at risk of dying than those who have been afforded decent health care for years?* All these lost lives are grievable, which means that they are lives worthy of acknowledgment and support, equal in value to every other life, a value that cannot be calculated.

The images of bodies piled high in Ecuador or stacked in closets in New Jersey or Northern Italy convey that the infrastructure of hospitals is overwhelmed and underfunded and those conditions were not in place to respect the dead. The images shock; they tell a story about public health infrastructure, demands on health-care workers, the emotional cost of social distancing when loved ones cannot receive the body and the dead body becomes a logistical problem: stacked, counted, transferred, stored. The images flit by as sensational clips.

Sequestering enforces both a sense of ambient death and a shared practice of deflection: "Let's not focus on the negative!" Learning to mourn mass death means marking the loss of someone whose name you do not know, whose language you may not speak, who lives at an unbridgeable distance from where you live. One does not have to know the person lost to affirm that this was a life. What one grieves is the life cut short, the life that should have had a chance to live longer and more, the value that person has carried now in the lives of others, the wound that permanently transforms those who live on. What someone else suffers is not one's own suffering, but the loss that the stranger endures traverses the personal loss one feels, potentially connecting strangers in grief.

GY: You know, it seems to me that we are not even allowing ourselves to grieve as a nation. Perhaps this is because so many are dying every day. Then again, for those whom the economy is the bottom line—especially for those who have expressed the desire to give their lives so that the economy is thriving again, which is really just getting back to a state of normal economic instability and precarity—it's not clear to me that they understand the importance of expressing a nonmarket-related grief. Their only grief seems to be related to the fact that the capitalist machine is taking a hit. It's as if many are not undone or un-sutured by the death of other human beings; rather, they are panicked by the fact that capitalism is being upended. What does this say about the moral logics (or lack thereof) regarding some in our country?

JB: Yes, we see the discourse on "the health of the nation" slide into another on "the health of the economy." But Social Darwinism has taken hold in some circles, especially in the discussions of "herd immunity." Some argue that the economy must be reinvigorated even if the virus is left more free to circulate, threatening the lives of the most vulnerable people. That those who are most likely to survive the virus (imagined as young, equipped with health care from the onset of life, able-bodied, white and without preexisting conditions) would go back to work and the university while the rest of us stay sheltering in place rests on a particular kind of lie.

Although some claim that the vulnerable—a new class—would remain "protected" by staying out of the workplace, that simply means the intensification of unemployment for many. And it is no "protection" because those healthy "immunes" will doubtless transfer the virus and affect their communities, including their parents and grandparents, and all those who cannot afford to stay home. Because "the vulnerable" are not deemed productive in the new quasi-Aryan community, they are not valued lives, and if they die, that is apparently acceptable, since they are not imagined as productive workers, but "drains" on the economy. Although the herd immunity argument may not make this claim explicitly, it is there.

To restart the economy without universal health care is to sacrifice the lives of those whose health or health care has never been adequate. It is to intensify those forms of social and economic inequality that disproportionately affect Black people and all those who qualify as "vulnerable" in the pandemic. It is not enough to point out that the productive worker back in the workplace and the public sphere will probably survive the viral infection, establish immunity, and go on working; that worker is a potential spreader when infected. This is a price that some are willing to pay, but we should look carefully at the ethics and politics of such a decision. For the "health" of the economy, the virus spreads and damages the health of the population, especially those who are precarious and most at risk of dying.

GY: For me, this level of market worshipping and market domination at the expense of collective human life was nauseatingly clear, despicably immoral, especially when I read that Trump allegedly offered German scientists, who were working on a possible coronavirus vaccine, money to acquire exclusive rights to the possible vaccine for the U.S.[1] This sort of move, if true, speaks to the necro-political intersection between cruel and unabashed nationalism, capitalistic greed, and the perverse desire to control who dies and who lives. The thought of this is monstrous. What does this say about differential vulnerability, and those who have already been marked as "grievable" and "un-grievable"?

JB: I see that there are writers and academics who are taking both utopian and dystopian positions. The utopians tend to celebrate the global time-out as an opportunity to remake the world and to realize the socialist ideals embodied in the communities of care that have recently emerged. I can understand that.

The dystopians tend to project into the future the intensification of state control and surveillance, the loss of civil liberties and the unshackling of market forces, including the crude kinds of market rationality that intensify social and economic inequalities. I can understand that, too.

We are confronting an intensified struggle and the results cannot be predicted. Political anxiety accelerated because conventional forms of mobilization are not available during lockdown. However, some very impressive international exchange is taking place among research institutes seeking to develop a vaccine at the same time that some pharmaceuticals are clearly positioning themselves for obscene profits.

The German company, CureVac, from whom Trump tried to secure exclusive U.S. rights to any future vaccine, proceeded seemingly to push out the CEO who tried to make that deal.[2] They proceeded then to affirm their commitment to international norms of health care distribution that mandate that those most in need will be first to receive any developed treatment. The development of strong and binding international standards will go part of the way to make sure that whatever effective treatments emerge do not become the expensive and exclusive property of those who can pay. The unequal access to health care could intensify or it could be effectively addressed. That is the key point of struggle.

GY: There is no rule book that specifies what "public intellectuals" are to do during unprecedented crises like this one. Do you have any suggestions for those of us who might have access to larger public spaces? Then again, perhaps this question is itself symptomatic of a deeper problem that creates a false distinction between "public intellectuals" and those who "are not." Perhaps the question moves us away from what COVID-19 requires—the full critical and loving energy of the demos.

JB: My sense is that we have moved from the period of "public intellectuals" to a broader demand for the "public humanities." Many students and recent Ph.Ds. are asking how they can bring their humanities backgrounds into public service, how they can overcome the divide between academic and public cultures, and to show how important the humanities are for understanding the world in which we live and making a new path toward a more just and reflective society.

Although some do wait for the anointed public intellectual to speak, most are, in my experience, eager to create conditions for conversation, creative and critical work that expand our ideas about why language, literature, visual arts, history, are important for understanding our world. That world cannot be reduced to "the economy" or "the nation" and neither is it fully defined by the pandemic. A sense of the world can wax and wane, as Ludwig Wittgenstein once said. Whose task is world-making in the face of radical disorientation and loss? The rush to Netflix in the midst of ambient death could be understood as a self-anaesthetizing practice, deflecting from reality. But maybe we are drawn to the question of who draws and redraws the world?

Some of the most important insights into devastating historical experiences emerge from stories and images refracted through another time and space. Alexandria Ocasio-Cortez remarked recently that in one of the districts in Queens she represents, the people speak 200 languages. Translation is a wondrous and critical aspect of the everyday life of that multilingual community. Our public institutions would do well to help us think through different media about persistence and loss, what connects and divides humans across communities, languages and regions, and what role the critical imagination has during times in which crisis and futurity are clearly the issues.

GY: We first did this interview in 2020, and it is now late 2022. So, I would like to end with a question regarding your newest book, *What World Is This? Pandemic Phenomenology*. The question regarding the world (and its plurality of responses) presupposes a place, a standpoint, within the world from which to pose that question. I think here of such problematic terms, along with their normative assumptions, as the "First World" and the "Third World" and all the social, political, and economic vulnerabilities that are differentially experienced/lived. This includes differential ways of being exposed to ecological catastrophes. Since I was a young boy, I have been terrified by the idea of a nuclear conflagration. Such an event wouldn't just entail the obliteration of a specific group of people from the earth, but it could lead to the obliteration of all life on earth as we know it. That fear is especially palpable as the Doomsday Clock has been set at 100 seconds to midnight. As we think about ecological disasters and pandemics, the idea of a nuclear apocalypse would entail the potential obliteration of any human subject who would pose the question, "What world is this?" For you, what is necessary to prevent the elimination of the very conditions in terms of which questions are even askable? What must we do so that our capacity to breathe, to touch, to engage in world-making, isn't made impossible because of our having exercised global genocidal extinction for which there is no justification?

JB: So much philosophical reflection assumes that the world was there, as background, and that philosophy distinguishes the human both from other animals and from the living earth on which we depend and which it is our responsibility to safeguard from destruction. So many people live now with a sense of existential anxiety, feeling that destruction is happening and that there is no way to find or pull the emergency break. That fear of a destruction that is already upon us is surely about the ecological catastrophe that humans have brought into reality, but it is also, as we speak, about the nuclear warfare that Putin threatens to use, the rise of authoritarian rule and its specific forms of violence, and the rising numbers of people killed from anti-Black violence and femicide. My sense is that we have to overcome the traditional distinction between earth and world, and listen to those who argue that the planetary is the more proper framework. We will not assume the humility and the responsibility required to check destruction until we come to understand ourselves as part of a dynamic and fragile set of inter-related living processes and relations. In other words, there is a radical humility that takes the human out of the center of the world-picture at the same time a new sense of obligation that emerges from our radical and irreversible interdependency. We can only ask, what world is this?, if we are already in that world, implicated in the very processes that provoke fear and terror, aspiration and solidarity. Hannah Arendt objected to those who decided moral issues on the basis of individual conscience. She felt that they tended to lose sight of the world or to contribute to its effacement. She thought no ethics was worthwhile that did not ask what future we want for the world. It is understandable why so many now despair and say that we can no longer ask the question because the future is uncertain, but that form of pessimism has to be countered by a radical imaginary, one that is not based in reality, as it were, but in the potentials we can still find among ourselves—potentials for renewal and regeneration delinked from human narcissism.

23

TRUMP'S LYING ABOUT COVID AMOUNTS TO TREASON

INTERVIEW WITH EDUARDO MENDIETA

Our very democracy has been on the edge of catastrophe, not only because of a president who lies as a way of life, but because of many who have come to accept his lies as "truth," or who have lost any concern with truth in the name of apotheosis and hubristic party line politics. How does the language of treason function within this context, especially in terms of derelict "leadership," disrespect for the Constitution, and the failure to be concerned for hundreds of thousands of Americans who have died from COVID-19? In this interview, Eduardo Mendieta, who is professor of philosophy at Penn State University, and editor, co-editor, and author of many books, including *The Adventures of Transcendental Philosophy* and *The Philosophical Animal: On Zoopoetics and Interspecies Cosmopolitanism*, boldly and insightfully delineates what is at stake when morality, hope and truth are seriously under attack.

GEORGE YANCY: I would argue that truth-telling, transparency, and critical intelligence are central to any thriving democracy. Speak to how our fragile democratic experiment is being tested—perhaps even crushed—under Trump's dangerous penchant for lying.

EDUARDO MENDIETA: Let me begin by underscoring what you say about the relationship between truth and democracy by way of reflecting on

G. Yancy (with Eduardo Mendieta), "Trump's Lying About COVID Amounts to Treason," in *Truthout*, November 1, 2020. [Editors: Maya Schenwar and Britney Schultz]

our 1776 "Declaration of Independence." Paragraph two begins: "We hold these truths to be self-evident, that all men are created equal, that they are endowed by their Creator with certain unalienable Rights, that among these are Life, Liberty and the pursuit of Happiness . . ." In the introduction to her recent and powerful history of the United State, *These Truths*, Jill Lepore informs us that Thomas Jefferson had originally written, "We hold these truths to be sacred and undeniable" and that Benjamin Franklin crossed those words, and suggested instead "self-evident." Lepore then notes that, "Truths that are self-evident are laws of nature, empirical and observable, the stuff of science." I take it that our "Declaration of Independence" was also a declaration *for* a government based on truth and denunciation of the rule of untruth, lying and mendacity. Democracy is the governance of the people, for the people, by the people, as Abraham Lincoln put it, that lives "in truth." Democracy, in other words, has an epistemic dimension. This means that there is not only a politics of truth in democracy, but also the truth of democratic politics. My colleague Nicolas de Warren and I have named this entanglement of truth and democracy "democratic honesty." Honesty has two pillars: truthfulness and integrity. Democratic honesty is not only an epistemic virtue of democratic citizens, it is just as importantly also an epistemic virtue of "democratic" societies.

Now, turning to Trump's assault on truth, I would have to say that it is not so much his relentless lying, mendacity, dishonesty, deception, and hypocrisy that is worrying, but that Trump is a national phenomenon. And that no matter how rapidly he is "fact checked"—and his lies are unmasked and called out as lies—that nonetheless there is a sizable group of citizens who believe him, who have remained loyal to him, notwithstanding the piles and piles of lies, his brutality, his crassness, his belligerence, and vulgarity. What is just as worrying is that our government is in the grip of Republicans who not only tolerate all of this, but who enable it and weaponize it. His lying is one thing. More important, in my view, is how he has frontally and in plain view of everyone attacked all those institutions that hold up the integrity of our democratic commitment to truth. He attacks science, the law, the media and the ballot. He attacks experts, lawyers, judges and journalists, everyone and anyone who is labeled a "never Trumper." In his very grotesque and Machiavellian way, he has undermined the integrity of all those institutions that hold up our democracy, make it honest, just, fair, accountable, transparent and trustworthy.

GY: Trump initially downplayed (and continues to misrepresent) the dire seriousness of COVID-19. We now know, thanks to the interviews conducted by journalist Bob Woodward, that Trump has been lying. As of this interview, over 215,000 Americans have died of COVID-19. This catastrophe is beyond words. Existential bad faith is one thing, but Trump's behavior seems homicidal. What do you make of this manner of "leader"? And must we not hold him accountable for the blood that is on his hands?

EM: The language I would use would be "dereliction of duty" and "treason." The president of the U.S. swears to uphold the Constitution and protect the American people. And he swears on a Bible. Trump has depleted our democratic lexicon of terms to use about his malfeasance and utter contempt for the rule of law, and our American commitments to rights and equality before the law. He has also eroded down the meaning of the word "unprecedented." That he knew already so early in the pandemic about COVID-19's mortality and lethality and that he "decided" not to act accordingly is simply criminal, and should be to all of us, simply astonishing and unprecedented. I would say that lying and downplaying the virus, when he knew its dangers, is a form of treason, because he decided that his reelection was more important than the well-being of our fellow citizens. He is not only criminal, but also treasonous.

On the other hand, let me also underscore that every life lost to the virus that could have been brought under control is a wasted life. We must also note, and this a huge point to note, that the deathly effects of the virus have been more adversely and severely suffered and shouldered by African Americans and Latinos. The APM Research Lab reports that African Americans are 3.4 percent more likely to die of COVID-19 than a white American.[1] Viruses don't discriminate, but our institutions do, and above all our health care system does, and of course, our labor market system does, and so a virus is not simply a thing of nature, but a political fact. I read about the contrast between how many U.S. citizens died during Vietnam, or World War I, and so on, and how many have died because of COVID-19. I am not sure that is the right way to think about it. A pandemic is a sociopolitical fact, not death as "it is what it is." Many of these deaths could have been prevented, but our "protector"-in-chief decided not to. In this pandemic, who died, who will die, who will remain vulnerable and infectable is a political decision.

GY: As we know, Trump is the symptom of a larger systemic problem of white racism. Indeed, he is a product of a larger historical sedimented history of xenophobia, sexism, and homophobia, a larger history inextricably linked to white male patriarchy. Given this, I guess that the real issue has to do with the end of white supremacy. I have no optimism. What about you?

EM: You and I have been committed for most of our lives to this long-term struggle for the soul of our country, to rescue it from its long history of racism, sexism and its amnesia of the genocide of our Native American brothers and sisters. A pandemic is not genocide, but a virus can be used as what the French called a "*dispositif*"—an apparatus or device—for racial killing. You know that I am an optimist and I have argued for skepticism of the mind and optimism of the heart. These days, however, I am not feeling optimistic, of either the mind or the heart. I feel that far too many Americans have decided that America is "theirs," and not "our" America. The America we all built over the last centuries, one that is most inclusive, just, egalitarian, more available to all kinds of people—that in the recent past has cowered in the shadows of racial hate—*that* America is being rejected. Some want the old America back. Yet, I don't know what to make of the sociological data coming out about how the post-George Floyd killing protests are the most racially integrated demonstrations we have seen in the U.S.—by far, more inclusive than those of the civil rights era. It seems like "racial justice" is not simply a "Black" thing, but an "Us" thing, an "American" thing. However, the resurgence of white supremacy, and that some white supremacist groups have been working on "igniting" a civil war—a racial war—and that the president won't condemn their acts of hate and violence, and in fact condones and encourages them, should make many of us be pessimistic.

GY: Philosophy is concerned with truth, even as there are some philosophers who deny we can ever have access to "things as they really are" or access to some grand metaphysical reality. Trump is not a philosopher who worries about the status of truth. Rather, he is someone who doesn't give a damn about truth. Yet, philosophers *should* give a damn. How do you understand the role of us philosophers under this Trumpian "post-truth" nightmare?

EM: Indeed, the question of truth is at the heart of philosophy. Kant told us that there are three fundamental questions: What can I know? What ought I to do? What can I hope for? Then, he said that these three questions boil down to one: What does it mean to be human? I always found Kant's questions generative, especially that they are one question: What it means to be human. What I take from Kant's three questions is that morality, hope and truth are entangled, interdependent and mutually supportive. I can't know what I ought to do if I don't know what the facts of the matter are, and I can't know that if I don't have access to truth (or ways of verifying), and I can't hope, if what I think I ought to do based on the facts will not have any relevance or efficacy, that what I will do will change things. Holocaust deniers, for instance, make all this so evident. And all those, too, who have challenged the efforts to think about enduring effects of centuries of slavery in the U.S. . . . Those who deny facts, history, what happened, are refusing the basis on which we can act and hope. There is no democratic hope without democratic honesty, truthfulness, and integrity.

Trump is, in his own way, ceaselessly shouting at us: *We can't know anything* (unless it confirms his worldview), *we can't know what the right thing to do is* (unless it is for his glory), *and you can't hope that what you do that is right will have any efficacy* (for that is up to him to decide). That is giving him too much credit, perhaps. We philosophers know that to be human is to be a creature of responsibility, truth, and hope. We are human by the speech that holds us together. Lying and untruth are an assault on what makes us the social beings of language that we are.

"Post-truth" is the fake news of Trumpites. Truth is out there: It is a virus, it is climate change, it is gravitational waves, it is the truth that journalists discover—the documents, the emails, the tweets, the trail of deception and malfeasance, and obstruction of justice—there is the truth by which and on which we decide collectively to forge a collective future. There is no democratic future without democratic truth.

GY: Some look to the vigorous protests here and globally, following the tragic killing of George Floyd, as a sign of hope for something better. What do you see as the necessary steps that will move not just the U.S. forward, but also the broader world—a world where white nationalism has become a global danger, a different kind of global pandemic?

EM: That the post-Floyd demonstrations went global is extremely significant. First, because as manifestations across the world, they were global manifestations of solidarity with our struggles against police violence and for social justice. Second, they are also significant because they are also an expression that state violence, racial violence and social injustice are intolerable anywhere and everywhere. I think they are manifestations of a growing global racial justice consciousness and movement. This can't be neglected. These protests are also taking place in the midst of a global health crisis and pandemic that have made it all too evident that we live in "one world." There are no vaccines for the virus that can be developed by one country; there is no way that we can inoculate just one country and expect the virus will be contained. The economic effects have devastated communities across the world—although shock waves have impacted more the United States and poorer countries than Europe and Asian countries, where there is less systemic and enduring poverty. Viruses that are zoonotic—born in animals that then infect humans—are going to become more frequent because of climate change.

Over the last century, since the end of World War II, we have become aware at a global level of how profoundly interdependent we are. Trump's nationalism, chauvinism, isolationism, his anti-internationalism, all his know-nothing-ism and adulation of white supremacy belong to a time that is long past. We are past the time when the United States was the sole world power. It is time that we rejoin the global community.

GY: And yet, the world community is so balkanized, with many countries taking a turn toward a political strongman. I'm not even sure of how we might achieve the beloved community here in the U.S., let alone within the context of a "global community." I say this as the Doomsday Clock has been set at 100 seconds to midnight. In the light of that shrinking timeline, we may not have enough time left to rejoin the global community. What are your thoughts?

EM: Let me circle back to my argument that Trump engaged in treason of the United States when he politicized the response to the Pandemic. After we began this conversation in 2020, the *New York Times* published an amazing story based on careful journalism. The article was written by Matt Apuzzo, Noah Weiland, and Selam Gebrekidan.[2] It is entitled, "Trump Gave W.H.O. a List of Demands. Hours Later, He Walked Away." The article details how Trump had sent Andrew Bremberg, the U.S. ambassador in Geneva, to present to Tedros Adhanom Ghebreyesus, the Director General of the World Health Organization, seven demands. These demands were in fact extortions that aimed to turn the W.H.O. into a political arm of Trumpism. But even before Bremberg could follow his meeting with Ghebreyesus, Trump announced on April 27, 2020, on the White House lawn, that he was pulling the U.S. out of the W.H.O. and would stop sending our contributions to it. The demands made and the speech Trump gave on that day are vulgar, egregious, and constituted criminal acts of betrayal regarding people in the U.S. and within the context of the world community. Yet, they reveal something additionally important, namely that health is a global challenge and a global responsibility. The W.H.O. has been at the forefront of making sure that developing nations also have access to COVID-19 vaccines. Today, we can see how this pandemic, with its shock waves to the global economy and society in general, reveal in my estimation three fundamental truths that are all too evident for us to neglect. First, that we are part of a global community that is relationally vulnerable, i.e., we are vulnerably co-dependent. Second, that the growing and abysmal inequalities within and across countries exacerbate our relational vulnerability. The more some of us are vulnerable, the more the whole fabric is fragile and ready to be torn, and thus the more we are all affected. This is very clearly illustrated by the effects of the pandemic on our economy and the "frontline workers," which has sent ripples affecting supply lines, which in turn have catalyzed into a global inflation. This in turn is affecting production and supply lines. And to boot, we are now dealing with the Russian war of aggression against Ukraine, a war that has already added to the energy and food supply lines, which in turn affect all regardless. Third, and notwithstanding the presence of so-called populist strong men, like Trump and Bolsenaro, and so on, there is a global sense of a collective will to collaborate on global solutions to problems that are irrevocably and irrefutably global: climate change, pandemics, food supply lines, migration, and national and global poverty. I like to think we can learn collectively, and the Pandemic, its inflation, and now the War in Ukraine, are hard lessons from which we must learn.

24

BIG PHARMA CARES MORE ABOUT PROFITING FROM COVID THAN HUMAN SURVIVAL

INTERVIEW WITH NOAM CHOMSKY

The election of Joe Biden has not demolished the Republican Party, or that party's ongoing attempts to block policies that might give humanity a chance at survival. Moreover, the advent of the Biden administration has not negated some of the most persistent threats we face. In this interview, renowned intellectual Noam Chomsky discusses the importance of critical thinking, the deep existential threat of the climate crisis, the possibility of nuclear annihilation, and the tragic continuity of U.S. foreign policy between presidential administrations. Chomsky also emphasizes the urgency of ending the tyranny of pharmaceutical companies and making COVID-19 vaccine technology available to all.

GEORGE YANCY: For you, in its current instantiation, the Republican Party is willfully attempting to undermine the conditions for the survival of human society itself. When I think about this, it is clear to me that political parties place profound emphasis on gaining power. Without necessarily psychologizing this, is it that the Republican Party embodies a death wish or some kind of profound nihilism?

G. Yancy (with Noam Chomsky), "Chomsky: Big Pharma Cares More About Profiting From COVID Than Human Survival," in *Truthout*, May 10, 2021. [Editors: Alana Yu-lan Price, Anton Woronczuk, and Maya Schenwar]

NOAM CHOMSKY: There's a lot of factors, but some of them are on the surface, before we get into psychology. First of all, Trump had an enormous effect. There were plenty of problems in the party, but he just poisoned it and by now he owns it. He was a genius at tapping into all of the poisonous currents that lie right beneath the surface in America, which includes white supremacy, and "Great Replacement" conspiracy theories. He knew very well how to bring up such poisons, mobilize them, and turn them into a raging force of terrified people who think the world is coming to an end. That's the kind of genius that Adolf Hitler had, and others who are not very pretty people. And Trump still has these people; they have taken over the party. David Brooks, who is a longtime dedicated Republican, argues that the GOP is far worse than we think.[1]

Let's take climate change. When you examine the climate policy, there are things that happened that tell us a lot about American politics. If you go back, just before Trump, which is the last time when Republican leaders could actually talk without the Trump shadow, it's very interesting to look at the Republican primaries. I'm referring to a time when there is the cream of the crop of the Republican leadership. There's no Trump yet. Every single one either denied that climate change is happening or said if it's happening then they don't care. There was one Republican, former Ohio Gov. John Kasich, who was described as the "sane" one, as the adult in the room. He was considered so decent that he was invited to speak at the 2020 Democratic Convention. He was considered a "good Republican." I think that he was the worst of the lot. If you look back at what he said, he was the one person who said, "Yes, global warming is happening, humans are responsible for it, and the science is right." But as governor of Ohio, he said that we in Ohio are going to use coal and not apologize for it.[2] He was aware that they were destroying the world, destroying the prospects for human life, but he said that he would do it and not apologize for it. Now, that's the "sane" person in the room that you invite to Biden's Democratic National Convention speech. That tells you something about the mentality—and not just the Republicans.

But why did the Republican Party become such dedicated denialists? This wasn't always true. It wasn't true in 2008 when John McCain ran for president. He did have a climate plank in his platform, not very much, but something. Other Republicans in the Senate were beginning to consider. They were considering moderate measures to do something about global warming. Well, the Koch brothers, who own a huge energy conglomerate, heard about this effort. They had been working for years to try to ensure that the Republican Party didn't make a move toward trying to do anything that would harm their profits. Perhaps some of the Republicans may have been true believers, maybe they really were, but who cares? Maybe Hitler really believed that the Jews were poisoning civilization, and that he and others believed that they had to save themselves, but it doesn't matter if they believe it or not. So, if David Koch talked himself into it, I don't care. The Koch brothers were devoting themselves to controlling the party, making sure it didn't have any hint of concern for climate change. When they heard about this deviation, they went into overtime to try to cut it off at the pass. As a huge juggernaut, they engaged in massive lobbying, threats, buying off senators and astroturfing. Everything you could think of. Then the Republican Party shifted: "There is no more a serious climate problem." And since this, they have been a party of denialists. And the leadership is dedicated to this. They have a media echo chamber at *Fox News*. They had Rush Limbaugh, when he was around, and others. When it comes to the voting base, well, that's their world; they turn to *Fox News* for their source of information. They are being bombarded with this stuff and the results are clear.

There was a recent Pew Research Institute poll that had very interesting results.[3] It gave people a choice of 15 options for what they thought was a major problem. And they divided it into Republicans and Democrats. Democrats were not all that great I should say, but among the Republicans, it's shocking. One of the least important issues for them was climate change. It's only the most important question that's ever arisen in human history. Is our species going to survive in any recognizable form? This question has to be answered right now—this generation. However, climate change, along with sexism, was ranked the least important issue. What's at the top of the list? Well, "illegal" immigrants and the budget deficit. And notice the budget deficit became an issue this January. Before that it was not a problem. It was great to have a budget deficit, because the Republicans were creating it to enrich their constituency of great wealth. So, it was fine to have a budget deficit. However, as soon as the Democrats come in, the budget deficit is the most urgent problem we face, along with an assumption that there will be a "hoard of illegal immigrants" who are going to carry out the "Great Replacement," and carry out genocide against the white race. You know the litany.

Well, if people are living in that world, you can kind of understand why about 40 percent of Republicans say that it's right to use political violence to protect the country from what's "happening." But you can't even call it surreal. It's often from outer space, but it's working. Take a look at Marjorie Taylor Greene. For her, it's literally from outer space. After all of the ridiculousness got exposed, her funding shot into the stratosphere. She is now getting more support than anyone else.[4] And you can see it from people who believe this. Incidentally, these are not poor people. The Robert Pape studies and other studies, for example, Anthony DiMaggio's work, show that the main Republican Trump base is moderately affluent. It's people who are above the median. Not very rich, but people who own stores, run construction businesses, insurance salesmen. What used to be called the petty bourgeoisie, those above the median but not great. These are people who see their traditional lives being taken away from them. They have been harmed by neoliberal policies where their communities may be collapsing. You go to a rural town in the United States and their businesses are closed down, the bank is shuttered, and young people are leaving their traditional "happy" white Christian, white supremacist environments. . . . Well, that is all disappearing. You can build this up to the "Great Replacement," where the idea is that they're all trying to take it away from us and kill us all. All of these things feed together, but right on top of it, you have a highly corrupt, cynical leadership which is willing to be bought off to become deniers of what's happening, which happens to be on the verge of destroying human life on Earth.

And incidentally, it's not the first time that this has happened. Just go back 50 years to Richard Nixon and the Southern strategy. It's not very different. Nixon recognized that you have to have limited civil rights, very limited, for African Americans. By doing so you're going to alienate the Southern white population. In this way, he's going to set up a racist party, which will pick up white Southern votes. It was perfectly open; it wasn't concealed. A few years later, in the mid-1970s, the Republican strategist Paul Weyrich had a flash of light and realized that if the Republican Party pretended to be opposed to abortion, they could pick up the huge Evangelical vote and make inroads into the Northern Catholic vote, a lot of whom were Democrats. I stress *pretended* as the leading figures in the Republican Party were what we now call pro-choice. Ronald Reagan, when he was governor of California, in the 1960s, passed one of the strongest legislations giving women the right to choose. The same with George H. W. Bush, and the same with the rest of them, but they turned on a dime. They all became passionately anti- abortion. The whole anti-abortion policy, within this context, is a fraud. . . . You can't even call it cynicism. I don't know what's the right word. It's evil incarnate, and it's running across the board.

And you can't blame just [Republicans]. Take the current situation with vaccines. Unless vaccines go to the Global South, to the poorer countries, to Africa, to Asia, unless they get vaccines quickly, the virus is going to mutate. It's already happening, you get more lethal strains. You may get something like Ebola, which is so lethal you can't do anything about it. Pretty soon it's going to spread back to Europe. You guys are all going to die. What are they doing? Holding on to the vaccines, refusing to give them to Africa and Asia. It's not just beyond immoral, especially considering what Europe did to these areas over the centuries, it's suicidal. It is the importance of greed and ensuring that I have what I need which overwhelms everything. A large part of it is protecting the so-called intellectual property rights of the big pharmaceutical corporations. We've got to make sure that they make exorbitant profits, even if we kill ourselves. . . . This is a malady that is deep-seated. An important step was taken by President Joe Biden when he announced that the U.S. would support a temporary waiver of patent rights at the World Health Organization. That will initiate a long negotiating process with many pitfalls, and will not relieve the horrendous crisis in India or the immediate problems of lack of vaccines for the poorer areas. Much more must be done, without delay.

GY: I think that this raises the issue of the crucial importance of education. You've argued that education is often a site of indoctrination, which you link with the essential point that critical questions are not being asked, where there are not enough people who are being disobedient. Do you still hold this position? I suspect that you still hold this to be true because I don't think that many of us are asking those necessary questions. And we don't seem to be disobedient, especially in ways that challenge how we are not being good stewards of the Earth, not only in terms of climate change, the use of fossil fuels, but in terms of how we are finding ourselves on the precipice of a nuclear war.

NC: Along with global warming, another enormous threat to survival, which is not even discussed is the threat of nuclear war. Anyone who's looked at the record will know that it is virtually a miracle that we've escaped total destruction over the last 75 years. There's case after case, sometimes often just by accident, where we came perilously close to the missiles going off, which means basically the end for us all. Human intervention, at the last minute, blocked such a devastation. There are cases of very reckless actions by leaders, including those who many people—not me—respect. Think here of John F. Kennedy. His very reckless actions brought us very close to the brink of terminal war. You look over the record, and it's just shocking, but it's getting worse. . . . Trump's worst crimes are his environmental policies and his nuclear policies. There was an arms control regime which had laboriously been put together since Dwight Eisenhower, bits and pieces, but it was something at least. When in office, the main thing that Trump understood was, "Let's wreck things! I want to be on the front page, and I have no clue what to do so I'll wreck things." That was basically the policy. And one of the things that he wrecked was the arms control regime, step by step, every piece he could destroy. He didn't just wreck it, but wrecked it with a declaration: "I want you to come in and join me." Immediately after dismantling the [Intermediate-Range Nuclear Forces Treaty] in August 2019, which was the Reagan-Gorbachev treaty, which had been very valuable in reducing the threat of war in Europe, Trump sent off missiles, which had obviously been prepared, which violated the treaty. He's telling the Russians, "Hey, boys. Join us in this fun game of destroying everything." Trump destroyed the Open Skies Treaty, which goes back to Eisenhower. Trump was within hours of destroying the last of the treaties. In fact, it was Biden who came in literally hours before the New START Treaty—which Trump had been avoiding Russian efforts to extend—was about to expire. And meanwhile [Trump] was building new, more destructive weapons, and moving into weaponizing space, which others will follow. This is asking for suicide. People in the arms control community are well aware of it, and warning about it, but it barely gets mentioned.

Biden, unfortunately, is picking up the military program. It's already well beyond anything that we need. Going back to your question about being disobedient, I would put it a little differently. I would stress just questioning. There is a rule of thumb that everyone should have in mind. It should be built-in from childhood. If everybody agrees on something that's more complicated than two plus two equals four, a light should go off in your head. Nobody can agree totally on anything moderately complicated. So, if everyone agrees, then it's probably deep indoctrination, and there's some scam going on behind it. You should believe that in the sciences, in ordinary life and certainly in political life.

So, what are the things that every right-thinking person believes? We've got to face the threat of China and the threat of Iran. Everyone believes it, and so it's obviously a question of some complexity. So, ask yourself: What's the threat of China and what's the threat of Iran? Well, you start asking that question, then the whole ideological system collapses. You start pushing it, and you know a lot of things are wrong, but they are not threats. So, Iran has a rotten government, not as bad as the ones we support like Saudi Arabia but pretty rotten. But is that a threat to us? Suppose Iran was developing nuclear weapons, which we have no reason to believe. Would that be a threat to us? If Iran had a nuclear weapon, could they use it, could they arm a missile with it? If they did, the country would be vaporized. The ruling clerics, which are not my favorite people, or yours, have no particular instinct for immediate suicide and losing everything that they have. American intelligence says the same thing. In the past they said if [Iran had] a nuclear program, then it would be part of their deterrence strategy. Why does a country have a deterrence strategy? Well, because somebody is ready to attack them. Who's ready to attack them? The countries that are at war with them already, which is the United States and Israel. When the United States boasts of carrying out cyber war that destroys Iranian facilities, that's an act of war. When Israel assassinates nuclear scientists and blows up facilities, that's an act of war. We are openly and proudly at war with Iran. So, should they develop a deterrent capacity? Is that a threat to us if they do? In a way, yes. If a country wants to rampage freely in the region, and they don't want to have deterrence around, yes, that's kind of a threat.

Pursue this further, you see more. There are a lot of things China shouldn't be doing. The internal repression in China is serious. Not as bad as a lot of things we do but serious. Yes, they should not be doing that, though it isn't a threat to us. And, unfortunately, we can't do much about it. We can do a lot about the repression we're carrying out, but we don't want to talk about that. And in the South China Sea, which has enormous commercial and security significance to China, they are violating international law and carrying out acts that they shouldn't be carrying out. The answer to that is not to send a Naval armada into the South China Sea, which could lead to possible provocations, which could explode. And if anything does explode, we're all finished. There can't be a nuclear war with China or with Russia. We're all dead if that happens. That's not the way to do it. The way to do it is with diplomacy and negotiations. There are opportunities, which may not come out perfectly, but to take one of Trump's rare true statements: "You think our country's so innocent?" The one true statement that he was able to make in a flood of lies. You know, the same is true with provocations on the Russian border. Notice, the Russian border, not the Mexican border. That's not the place to have provocative military exercises, it's not the place to put up anti-ballistic missile installations, which is what Barack Obama did, which have dual use and can be used not only for surveillance but even guidance. You just don't do that if you want to live in a world that survives.

The basic and significant point, going back to dissent, and it should be repeated, is that if there's too much agreement on some complicated question, you should be suspicious. Complicated questions should be debated.

Part Eight

REALIZING (OR IMAGINING) THE POSSIBLE

25

BLACK TRANS FEMINIST THOUGHT CAN SET US FREE

INTERVIEW WITH CHE GOSSETT

How can we move beyond a mindset dictated by the logic of prison, policing and anti-Blackness? What is "abolition feminism"? And how do the politics of gender, including the criminalization of trans and nonbinary people, dovetail with our understandings of race? How can deconstructing racialized gender binaries help us move toward justice and liberation?

To confront these questions, I spoke with Che Gossett, a Black nonbinary femme writer and critical theorist specializing in queer/trans studies, aesthetic theory, abolitionist thought, and black study. Gossett is currently the Racial Justice Postdoctoral Fellow at the Center for Contemporary Critical Thought at Columbia University, and a Visiting Fellow at Harvard Law School's Animal Law & Policy Program.

GEORGE YANCY: Within a context where Black people, Indigenous people and people of color (or BIPOC) continue to be victims of a form of racist and capitalist carceral punishment, can you speak to the importance of what is being called "abolition feminism"? Please define the meaning of this important term and speak to its relevance at this critical moment in U.S. history and global history.

G. Yancy (with Che Gossett), "Black Trans Feminist Thought Can Set Us Free," in *Truthout*, December 9, 2020. [Editors: Alana Yu-lan Price, Maya Schenwar, and Britney Schultz]

CHE GOSSETT: My knowledge of the term abolition feminism derives from Angela Davis and Gina Dent's critical labor.[1] I think of it as an open invitation to the unfinished liberatory struggle for abolition that is also a Black feminist struggle against anti-Blackness and heteropatriarchy and forms of carceral and white feminism that continue to perpetuate these forms of what Hortense Spillers calls "grammars of capture." Abolition feminism would not only entail the abolition of the normative version of "feminism," as opposed to its reform, and is not just a project of negative freedom but one that is immanent to and animate within already existing ensembles of struggle. Spillers's definition of Black feminism as a "critical disposition" is that it is "a repertoire of concepts, practices, and alignments," that "is progressive in outlook and dedicated to the view that sustainable life systems must be available to everyone; it also stands up for the survival of this planet."[2] This concept really resonates with me and I see this as critical to a formulation of "abolition feminism."

Black trans women and femmes have historically and contemporaneously battled criminalization and policing, the precarious violence of lumpen proletarianization within the capitalist political economy—underground economies of drag and sex were and are criminalized—and also the violence of the anti-Black and anti-trans libidinal economy. My thinking here is informed by Lindon Barrett in terms of how race is conceived as a set of libidinal and corporeal protocols, that is, where "Race is conceived of as a set of libidinal prohibitions"—an economy wherein Black trans people face anti-Black and anti-trans patriarchal violence that is both legal and extralegal. In this moment, I am also thinking about Layleen Polanco, who died at Rikers, in the women's facility, where the carceral liberals and carceral feminists would have imagined her to be *safe.* As CeCe McDonald reminds us, prisons are safe for no one.

The premature death of Black trans women continues now in the middle of the COVID-19 epidemic. I went to a powerful protest here in New York City over the summer for Black trans life,[3] which was modeled after the 1917 Silent Parade. The march this summer was a powerful surge of rage and mourning where an estimated 15,000 people attended.[4] This felt like a seismic shift. Black trans demands continue and there's dedicated mutual aid and organizing happening that made that moment possible. The Brooklyn Liberation, The Okra Project, Marsha P. Johnson Institute, For the Gworls, GLITS, and Black Trans Femmes in the Arts have all been doing incredible work at this historical juncture. GLITS just opened the first by and for trans housing complex, and all of these organizations and formations center formerly incarcerated trans people and sex workers.

Black trans women and femmes have not only been at the epicenter of the struggle against racial patriarchy—even while being exiled from and unthought of by feminism—but also there's an analysis, a study of racial patriarchy that is made available to us through the 1970s political formations: an archive of zines and political grammar (fag, non-men, street queen, etc.) that continues and that is essential to and indispensable for the struggle against racial patriarchy and carceral violence in the present tense.

GY: How do we creatively cultivate spaces that exist outside of carceral logics and anti-Black logics?

CG: I'm not sure that we can ever fully in this "world" create spaces that exist entirely outside of anti-Blackness and its carceral technologies, since we are always under duress. I think one of the incredible lessons of the abolitionist movement, which is a form of critique and praxis, is that abolition is both an interior and external practice. I think of Jared Sexton's brilliant synopsis: "Slavery is the threshold of the political world, abolition the interminable radicalization of every radical movement." The radicalization is perennial. And rather than falling for the ruse of political immunity to carceral logics and anti-Blackness, perhaps knowing that this protracted struggle is one that preceded us, and will continue after, can sustain us.

There's a powerful line in Frantz Fanon's *The Wretched of the Earth* that speaks to contamination and the illusion of purity and the need for an entangled effort: "Everyone must be involved in the struggle for the sake of the common salvation. There are no clean hands, no innocent bystanders. We are all in the process of dirtying our hands in the quagmire of our soil and the terrifying void of our minds."

Black thought has always been "thought of the outside" (to repurpose Maurice Blanchot). Part of this thinking of the outside is the project of moving against and beyond the coordinates of what Sylvia Wynter termed "our narratively condemned status" in her incredible essay "No Human Involved," which she wrote following the brutal assault and viral circulation (the digital afterlife of slavery) on Rodney King.

Wynter's "Towards the Sociogenic Principle" holds out a theoretical and political horizon for life beyond/against the racial and colonial figure of the Human, which she so brilliantly terms a genre. In this pathbreaking essay, Wynter parts ways with functionalism—the theory that the mind is what it does—and argues for sociogenesis: "If the mind is what the brain does, what the brain does, is itself culturally determined through the mediation of the socialized sense of self, as well as of the 'social' situation in which this self is placed." For Wynter, not only is Man a genre but so too is (the theory of) Mind. Within a context where the mind-body problem is maintained, with its positing of an *a priori* universalized consciousness, the phylogenetic/ontogenetic dyad is a symptom of whiteness in that it ignores sociogeny and it can take that position of epistemic pseudo- or quasi-ignorance as a result of not experiencing racialization. In this sense, mind is seen as universal and given, as opposed to constructed.

To modify and repurpose theories of mind that posit underlying laws that determine the necessity for consciousness in the face of the question as to why living creatures, humans in particular, require conscious experience at all, Wynter extends Fanon's theorization of sociogeny. She brilliantly shows how thinking with Fanon opens up "insights into the laws which govern the realm of lived subjective experience, human and nonhuman, which govern therefore, the interrelated phenomena of identity, mind and/or consciousness."[5]

Wynter makes a lateral move and offers, via her theorization of the Human as a genre, a de-hierarchization of life/subjectivities. This to me, especially in this moment of what anti-Black capitalist planetary destruction might look like, speaks to other formations and orchestrations of life that work toward new iterations of livability and inhabitability of this planet.

GY: I have written about how cisgender Black men have suffered under the gaze of whiteness, how they have been rendered both invisible and hypervisible. Within the context of the U.S.'s anti-Black imaginary, Black men are deemed criminals, thugs and brutal animals. My work here presupposes a gender binary that I leave untroubled. Could you speak to how violence operates precisely at the site of the gender binary?

CG: The violent figuration of Black people as criminals, thugs and brutal animals—"beasts," since they are imagined creatures, not actual animals—is also sexualized and gendered against Black trans, queer and gender nonconforming people. This can be seen with the anti-Black and anti-trans viral lithograph of Black trans sex worker Mary Jones in 1836. She was demonized as "monstrous" as she testified that she had "always dressed this way amongst people of my own colour." Or, think about the news media referring to the Black, gender-nonconforming queer young people known as the NJ4[6]—whose struggle was the center of the documentary *Out in the Night*—who defended themselves against patriarchal and homophobic attacks and were prosecuted as a result, and referred to as a "wolf pack." It is this aestheticization of anti-Blackness that we face in trying either to force us to be "normal" or in figuring us as disposable. Again, this is the discursive violence of what Wynter calls "our narratively condemned status."

Blackness is gender trouble. The etymology of cisgender itself presumes a correspondence between assigned sex and gender, which fails to account for Blackness. Thinking here of Black feminist and Black trans studies' deconstruction of sex and gender, of Spillers's "ungendering" and also the work of Riley Snorton[7] and also Zakiyyah Imani Jackson[8] on the anti-Black logic of binary sexuation. As Snorton argues, "captive flesh figures a critical genealogy for modern transness, as chattel persons gave rise to an understanding of gender as mutable and as an amenable form of being"—this happens through fungibility. The slave is the ground for "modern" gender and sexuality.

In her writing on fungibility in *Scenes of Subjection,* Saidiya Hartman expands the conceptualization of the commodity form by showing how the figure of the slave as commodity is situated not only in the political but also within a libidinal economy of what Frank Wilderson calls "gratuitous violence." Hartman and Fred Moten[9] think of the commodity that speaks (which Marx only imagines) and, moreover, the commodity that screams. Black thought begins with the un-apprehension of being. Marx beyond Marx (to sabotage Antonio Negri). Hartman writes about the relationship between libidinal economy and political economy that is consecrated in the commodity form and its fungibility and trans-positionality. In a paragraph worth quoting at length, she argues:

> The relation between pleasure and the possession of slave property, in both the figurative and literal senses, can be explained in part by the fungibility of the slave—that is, the joy made possible by virtue of the replaceability and interchangeability endemic to the commodity—and by the extensive capacities of property—that is, the augmentation of the master subject through his embodiment in external objects and persons. Put differently, the fungibility of the commodity makes the captive body an abstract and empty vessel vulnerable to the projection of others' feelings, ideas, desires, and values.[10]

Black queer and trans and feminist thought provide an arsenal of critique and praxis that allows us to think rigorously both about violence, and to think again alongside Frank Wilderson's brilliant grammar, the demand for "gratuitous freedom." The violence that you are describing is part of a broader matrix of the gender binary that constantly seeks to imperil and outlaw Blackness, despite the failed optimism of appeals to what Jared Sexton calls "borrowed institutionality."

GY: How might the discourse and praxis of Trans Studies help us to move forward, to a world where justice and radical love prevails?

CG: Blackness is gender trouble.

One of the problems of the heralded moment of "trans visibility" is the assumption that trans is perceptible and knowable, that you can visually isolate trans or that there are more authentic versions of trans than others, which implies a kind of hierarchical and vertical visual economy. Trans visibility so often means surveillance, especially by non-trans people and also by the security state—from TSA at airports to the welfare line. This is rigorously studied and dismantled by Toby Beauchamp in *Going Stealth: Transgender Politics and U.S. Surveillance Practices*[11] and in Eric Stanley's brilliant essay on visibility as an anti-trans optic (and operation).[12] I'm interested in how trans artists through their visual theorizing are subverting that order through iterations of trans "opacity" and troubling aesthetics as a racial and patriarchal regime. For example, Ser Serpas,[13] who in a show in 2017 at the gallery Current Projects exhibited as "self-portrait," undercuts the autobiographical notion of the self and its portrait, titled *penultimate warrior.* The "self-portrait" was an incinerated armchair that she had lit on fire after throwing estradiol on it. The armchair isn't an armchair anymore; rather than perfected, it is undone. Trans as gender in ruins.

Thinking about another intervention and troubling of trans linearity and visibility within the frame of trans studies is Eva Hayward's "More Lessons from a Starfish: Prefixial Flesh and Transspeciated Selves."[14] Hayward presents an alternative to the medical linear narrative of trans women and femme embodiment as ontological insufficiency and corporeal lack—the idea that to transition requires a supplement to an originary lack that is then solved by reassignment surgery that would make one into a "real" woman. Instead, Hayward shows how every cut is a fold, how there's no lack but instead a transition of body from itself to itself.

Finally, in thinking about Black trans art and the afterlife of slavery, it's important to bring attention to the incredible aesthetic, cinematic and archival labor of the filmmaker and artist Tourmaline.[15] Hartman argues that the afterlife of slavery is an aesthetic problem and I see the work of Tourmaline as both an inhabitation of that problem, through speculative cinematography and what Hartman terms "critical fabulation." Tourmaline's film *Salacia*,[16] which is now in the permanent collection of both the Museum of Modern Art and the Tate in London, as well as her films *Happy Birthday Marsha*[17] and *Atlantic is a Sea of Bones*[18] helps us imagine the Black trans aesthetics of abolition, as well as think of the historical temporality of

Blackness and transness beyond the limits to and effacements of the archive of slavery.

GY: Che, since our last conversation (2020), so much continues to change or perhaps I should say, deteriorate. I admire your realism where you note that "knowing that this protracted struggle is one that preceded us, and will continue after, can sustain us." Yet, there are times that I fear that there will be no us. And by "us" I'm thinking about "humanity," specifically in the form of our climate crisis. Talk to me about what needs to happen *right now* before we have ended life on this planet as we know it.

CG: I think that the climate crisis is one of the most pressing and imperative issues threatening the survival of all forms of life on the planetary axis, and then vertically, or transversally, we see this unfolding along the colonial and racial "color line" that W. E. B. Du Bois so cogently and presciently theorized. Addressing racial capitalist exploitation and slow and fast death— one nexus would be the agribusiness and the necropolitical factory farm—is one site where this massive scale problem of environmental harm can be directly confronted.

26

REACHING BEYOND
"BLACK FACES IN HIGH PLACES"

INTERVIEW WITH JOY JAMES

With the advent of the Biden administration, it's a crucial time to examine the role anti-Blackness plays not only when it comes to overt white supremacist actions, but also the actions of the government—and other forces of power—more broadly.

What does Black suffering look like historically? What is the complex relationship between "progressive" racial politics and the subtle operations of capitalism? How is Black suffering monetized, especially within the context of celebrity activism? How do we ensure that our efforts to resist anti-Black racism are congruent with fighting on behalf of Indigenous peoples?

To come to terms with these pressing questions, I spoke with Joy James, who is Ebenezer Fitch Professor of Humanities and professor in political science at Williams College. She is the author of *Resisting State Violence; Transcending the Talented Tenth; Shadowboxing: Representations of Black Feminist Politics*; and *Seeking the Beloved Community: A Feminist Race Reader*. James has edited volumes on politics and incarceration, including *Imprisoned Intellectuals* and *The New Abolitionists*.

GEORGE YANCY: Black suffering is pervasive; its arc long. As a scholar-activist who takes seriously such themes as radical politics and abolitionism, when will Black suffering "bend"? Or is it the case that Blackness is always

G. Yancy (with Joy James), "Reaching Beyond 'Black Faces in High Places': An Interview with Joy James," in *Truthout*, February 1, 2021. [Editors: Alana Yu-lan Price, Anton Woronczuk, and Maya Schenwar]

already a site of "permanent" suffering or oppression? To put this meta-phorically, are we still in the holds of slave ships? When I ask this question, COVID-19, and Black vulnerability to it, feels almost normative vis-à-vis the death of Black people.

JOY JAMES: It is always good to be in dialogue with you, George. Your first question relates to an existential theme that we discussed years ago about "misery" following the publicly displayed police executions of Eric Garner in Staten Island and Michael Brown in Ferguson.[1]

I do not think that Blackness as a permanent site of suffering/oppression is the defining marker of who we are. I would say that white supremacy and its violent iterations are clearly historically documented. Think here of enslavement, the convict prison lease system, black codes, Jim Crow, voter disenfranchisement, redlining, and the spectacular war and violence as reflected in Tulsa, Oklahoma's, Black Wall Street 1921 bombing, and burning and mass murders of Black residents, in which white police looted and lynched, re-enacted decades later by Philadelphia police in the 1985 bombing of the MOVE house and city employees deciding to burn down an entire Black neighborhood. White supremacist culture is a permanent site of predatory consumption, extraction and violation. Its aggressions seek to distract from the dystopia depicted in T. S. Eliot's *The Waste Land* (also marked by Eliot's reported affinity to antisemitism).

Oppression and devastation preceded and engineered the creation of the "Black"; we are just in a long dirge in which resistance and rebellion follows repression and adds shouts, prayers, and expletives. How do we resist? We do so in innumerable ways through arts and activism, betrayal and code switching as "shape shifting" (as noted by a brilliant webinar, "Octavia Butler: Slow Read-A-Long"[2] led by young Black feminist intellectuals/artists).

We are in the "hold": slave ships, dungeons, prisons, jails, Immigration and Customs Enforcement (ICE) family centers (in Texas, Haitian families form 40 percent of the population[3]) and "womb collector" hysterectomies that seem to "favor" Black women/mothers. Yet the rebellion of whistle blowing was done by a sister, Dawn Wooten,[4] who reported both medical violations and medical neglect concerning COVID-19. From the hold of a slave ship to solitary confinement in prison or psych wards, our people fight for life in the presence of death by caring for ourselves and others.

GY: When I think about the theme of Black leadership and hope, I think that there were many who may have conceptualized Barack Obama's presidency as the panacea for anti-Black racism, that he might help the arc of the moral universe to bend. I think that such an expectation was unreasonable for many reasons, one being that he was commander-in-chief, head of the American empire. My question has to do with radical political change and its possible realization from within the space of state power. I'm thinking here of Kamala Harris but trying to do so beyond her symbolic significance as the first Black and South Asian American woman to hold such political power. What can she do that might be identified as politically radical? After all, as you have argued elsewhere, hegemonic structures exist alongside a diversity of Black faces. As with Obama, her allegiance is to the American empire first. What would it take for "insiders" to bring about radical change, counter-hegemonic change or is the instigation for genuine radical change only possible as "outsiders"?

JJ: We both work for private corporations defined as nonprofit educational institutions. We have no romantic illusions about the nature of our jobs. We were hired to affirm and stabilize the elite university/college. We can demand accountability for white supremacist/(hetero)sexist eruptions and ask for security (which can be denied or curtailed), but we do not pretend that these institutions exist to bring justice to the world or function in the interests of the oppressed (particularly if such institutions are gentrifying neighborhoods and taking donor money from right-wing oil/gas mogul Charles Koch). If you don't have illusions about your day job and its functions to stabilize (while admonishing excessive violence from) racial capitalism, why would you have illusions about the government/state investment in racial capital?

No one forced Barack Obama to be the first Black *imperial* president for a nation whose democracy was built on racial conquest and rape. He wanted the gig. Black people, working class or laboring poor or dispossessed of paid labor, did not draw up petitions to draft Obama to primary Hillary Clinton (whose policies were more neoliberal progressive than Obama's in the 2007/2008 primary). White wealthy donors seemed to be his early backers along with a slice of the Black elite that had not yet peeled off from the Clintons. Anti-Black racism was furthered by Clinton policies and never seriously challenged by Obama policies.

If the big ask now is to "see Black faces in high places," then enjoy the Biden-Harris administration. It is definitely better to not be taxed to pay for violent white nationalists and the salaries and pardons of white-collar and war criminals. However, no longer being taxed to pay for predatory rogues, rot, and incompetence is not the definition of transformative justice. Empires thrive on violence and racial capitalism.

Harris campaigned on "Joe." Not just for the president-elect's policies (which are not based in transformative justice) but for his persona as the caring white leader who can bargain with those who empowered white nationalism and the devastation of the health and well-being of the laboring poor and working class. Biden's revolving door of the Obama administration attempts to re-center D.C. into a romanticized past. There should be more money for jobs and social welfare programs—as much money as corporations and bureaucrats deem "prudent" from those exploited and abandoned by the corporate state and its racial/sexual/religious anima. With the (neo)liberals back, expect less autonomy for independent thinking as everybody will be charged to "get on board" with the elite-driven programs that never adequately addressed white supremacy, poverty, and violence against women, children, LGBTQ and are not designed by those most negatively impacted by racial/colonial capitalism.

Black masses are consistently told by the Black elite pundits, academics, nonprofit leaders, or movement specialists to stay in line and follow. But follow whom? What is the possibility that Obama and Harris have been sold to Black people by corporate/state elites as responsive to the needs of the Black mass and the impoverished and denigrated? Biden's only strong competitor was Bernie Sanders who campaigned on Medicare for All[5]—until Black civil rights icons merged in the political machine with the Obama/Clinton DNC to warn folks not to go "too left" and to stop asking for "free stuff." How much misery from 20 million COVID-19 cases and over 400,000 deaths in the U.S. could have been mitigated or prevented if universal health care existed? Where Black politicians and advocacy Democrats share the same donor base and think tanks, and propaganda networks with the Democratic National Committee (DNC), it is illogical to expect transformative justice. There are possibilities with the incoming representatives such as Cori Bush and Jamaal Bowman, and the sort of rogue Democratic Socialists of America (DSA), if their roles as productive disruptors and creators for the (Black) masses are not cannibalized by the party machine.

GY: Given the previous question, how do we engage in "free discourse," that is, a discourse that challenges how liberals have defined freedom and liberty? What does a political vision of freedom look like outside of logics that maintain the status quo, that imprison not just our discourse but our political imaginative capacities?

JJ: Free discourse is the ability to be radical in service to the disenfranchised and imprisoned without being attacked. Obama instituted the most repressive laws against whistleblowers/investigative journalists. To stop the white (Black?)-washing of the Obama legacy and acquiescence to heirs apparent, radicals would have to negotiate the terms of struggle, and sacrifice and insults for attempting to illuminate contradictions, hegemonic betrayals, and ideology masking performative politics within celebrity activism/education and accumulation from the monetization of Black suffering. There is razor-like irony at play in performative politics inching towards the Achilles' heels of radicals. Black radicals are lectured to stop being so "lefty" by Joe and Barack (and others who castigate as "purity politics" analyses which decades ago would have been described as principled rather than opportunistic). Despite the millions protesting against the police murders of George Floyd, Breonna Taylor, police and white supremacist killings and dishonoring of our people (Anjanette Young in Chicago[6]) or deaths due to medical neglect such as MD Susan Moore for whose death no one will be accountable; her last testimony to us warned: "Being Black up in here, this is what happens."[7]

Historically, anti-Black violence was used to enslave and accumulate wealth for non-Blacks, including Indigenous tribes granted "civilized nations" status if they trafficked/enslaved Black people. Some doubt New Mexico Congresswoman Debra Haaland, named the first Indigenous secretary of the interior by Biden, will positively respond to the Choctaw-Chickasaw Freedmen/Black Indian petition[8] to seek tribal recognition and monetary/land support. Anti-Black violence was also embedded in Biden's choice for new Secretary of Agriculture Tom Vilsack; the former Ag guy in the Obama administration who expedited Black farmers' loss of their lands and livelihoods due to denial of civil rights protections. Violence from 18th century slave ships to 21st-century Obama administrators enabled accumulation through Black loss. One can monetize Black suffering and raise revenue through private prisons, repressive charter schools, Wells Fargo fraud[9] targeting Black homeowners. Those opposed to anti-Black violence and dispossession can also monetize Black suffering by refashioning the narratives, stories, and trauma into marketable writing and lecturing, visuals in fashion wear, public relations, voter registration/mobilization, nonprofit sector jobs, punditry on news shows/podcasts. Black misery is profitable for racists and anti-racists.

Making money is a precondition of surviving under capitalism (rent, food, competent health care, clothing, education, etc.). Yet Black street activists or imprisoned activists—whose heads are cracked open by violent cops/guards and white supremacists—take the greatest risks for transformative justice and reap the smallest percentage of monetary gains from advocacy democracy.[10] Explaining Black people or anti-Black terror to non-Blacks, reassuring Blacks that there is a way to evolve out of predatory anti-Blackness without revolutionary struggle is lucrative. Those funds garnered from the narratives whose radical love leads to radical risk rarely go back into Black institutions, community centers, houses of worship, food banks, freedom schools and most importantly, *transformative political education*, what Fred Hampton defined as the only real weapon against oppression.

GY: The Black Lives Matter movement is crucial as a dynamic process of bringing attention to various forms of anti-Blackness. Meanwhile, Indigenous struggles are often erased even in the middle of racial justice movements. Speak to the theme of solidarity here. I'm thinking of Martin Luther King Jr., where he says that "Injustice anywhere is a threat to justice everywhere." It seems to me that marginalized people can't claim liberation until Native Americans are also liberated. In fact, Native American suffering, or so I would argue, is often elided.

JJ: There were debates before an abolitionist platform changed its motto statement[11] from a quote by a Black academic to a declaration for sovereign rights by an Indigenous Dakota leader seeking to secure the roads into the reservation despite a Trump-leaning governor. The attempts of a collective of radical Black women abolitionists to highlight Article 16 of the Ft. Laramie Treaty as "abolitionism" was permitted as a *momentary* intervention. Radical Black women and allies could only temporarily refocus the abolitionist motto. We later circulated a statement asserting that Indigenous nations/elders—not Black, white, or people of color (POC) academics—determine the status of those who claim to belong to Indigenous communities (and build careers as representatives of said communities). Still later, we brought attention to the Choctaw-Chickasaw Freedmen's petition challenging anti-Black racism[12] to New Mexico Congresswoman Deb Haaland, the first Indigenous nominee for secretary of the interior.

In the U.S., we grapple with white supremacy, "POC" ethnic chauvinism toward Indigenous people, and anti-Black racism among Indigenous people. We lack consensus on how progressive multiracial "coalitions" should respect the desires of Black working/laboring class people and Indigenous reservation communities to define their needs and assert autonomy. Revolutionary acts respect global Indigenous autonomy and culture, including Indigenous peoples in Africa, Australia, the Americas and beyond.

Derrick Bell analyzed "interest convergence" in which the strongest party steers the coalition and so betrays the needs of the less empowered by the racial state and capital. Alliances with hegemonic wealthy white liberals tilt the balance of the scales. If Indigenous elites are white wealth–identified, they will not align with Black people unless they are also white wealth-identified. Either way, Black masses are marginalized.

I am curious about why Afropessimism is so vilified for its contributions not just its limitations. Its contributions are to cut through the smoke and mirrors of banal coalitions that castigate Black people for being "too Black," that is, for addressing the need to be free from anti-Blackness/white supremacy through a political project that forecloses compromise (the "virtue" of coalitions that are not dominated by radical Black masses). Perhaps we could focus on what we have in common as Indigenous, Black Indigenous and Blacks: rebellion, hence the need to free our political prisoners such as: Leonard Peltier, Mutulu Shakur, Mumia Abu-Jamal, Joy Powell, Russell Maroon Shoatz, Sundiata Acoli, Veronza Bowers, Ruchell Cinque Magee, and others who rebelled against conquest and genocide.

Let's see if we can form an alliance around the recognition of the rights of Black Indigenous people alongside the recognition of non-Black Indigenous rights to land and autonomy. Also, let's see if we can discuss reparations with specificity, not generalizations; that this is imperial democracy built on stolen Indigenous land and with stolen Black labor. Let's see if we can collectively mourn the mass rapes of Black women baked in the three-fifths clause of the U.S. Constitution so that former slavery-bond states (southern "red states") deployed terror for reproduction to accumulate political power and pro-plantation presidencies. Let's see if we can fight the murders and disappearances of Black women/girls/trans interlocking with the battles to stop the murders and disappearance of Indigenous women/girls/two-spirit people.[13] We need each other as allies in struggle, but as Black people our struggles remain distinct; it is not a hierarchy in oppression, it is a *specificity* in combating it that we as radicals demand.

GY: Joy, you have written about spirituality and Black feminist thought. As an approach to healing so much human suffering, speak to the importance of a specifically *spiritual* awakening that is necessary for this country. Also, in what ways does your understanding of spirituality overlap with Black feminist thought in terms of rethinking relationality, community, and humanity?

JJ: Spirituality and trauma forced me to recognize the limited capacity of bourgeois Black feminist thought and reflect on how the ideological markers of Black feminism were blended into hegemonic discourse and "progressive" marketing.

Two thousand and twenty-one is the 50th anniversary of the Attica rebellion. Think about how those in Attica maintained the structures of their captivity under pain of torture or death, until they chose to risk life to defeat a living death. Trustees and imprisoned nurtured and nursed each other and performed the labor under penal slavery (the 13th Amendment to the U.S. Constitution codifies enslavement to incarceration) that allowed the massive prison to exist. Rejecting the first or early stage of contradiction and caretaking and collaboration, the captives decided to organize a prison strike for human rights and dignity. They allowed spirit to lead them into mass movement and rebellion (some were inspired by the assassination of George Jackson[14]).

After taking over the massive prison, they had to rebuild community as a maroon camp within a prison, setting up a food delivery system, waste removal, political education, a medic site, security, spokespersons to address the press and public about their Liberation Manifesto.[15] Spirit formed community out of chaos, amid precarity and extreme vulnerability they were able to forge unity and purpose for transformative justice.

From that third stage, captives were moved to the fourth and final stage, that of war resister when the racial state born with a lust for slavery treated the rebellion for human and civil rights as an act of war and responded with Vietnam military surplus (imperial wars amplify domestic supremacist violence); the National Guard called in by president and governor killed Black and Brown resisters, maroons, community builders and defenders; later guards would torture and murder rebels once the prison was retaken.

Four spirit-filled stages—conflicted caretaker, movement activist, maroon, war resister—in which one risks life to achieve life outside of the fetid hold of the slave ship, and in the process, one's "losses" transform into victory in which the birth of rebellion becomes a story of origins and birth making. To rebel, to have any moment of freedom meant that the world was in the moment born anew, the air—fresher, songs—sweeter, fear and dread, exhilarating with hope mixed with despair.

GY: Joy, since we last spoke in 2021, your expression, "being in the hold," has stayed with me. The expression speaks to the gratuity of Black trauma, where Black spirituality in terms of its resistance is constantly challenged. Indeed, the expression functions as a radically descriptive and haunting account of the reality of Black life, which seems to be always haunted by death. I want to create a space here for you to discuss the state of Missouri's plan to execute Kevin Johnson on Nov. 29, 2022. When I think about his situation, I am haunted by what it means to be in the hold. Whether he is executed or receives life in prison, speak about both what is at stake here for Kevin and what you see as the larger dreadful carceral implications that his situation raises.

JJ: As you know, the state of Missouri killed thirty-seven years old Kevin Johnson by lethal injection on November 29, 2022, for killing a white police officer whom Kevin, at age nineteen, thought was partly responsible for the death of his twelve-year-old brother Joseph (Bam-Bam). Working with Missourians for Alternatives to the Death Penalty (MADPMO) and Kalonji Changa (see *Truthout*), I had the opportunity to share a phone conversation with Kevin in November as people mobilized to stop state murder. The state denied his nineteen-year old daughter (now orphaned with a five-month-old son) the right to witness her father's execution. Before the state killed him, I heard special prosecutors argue that the death sentence meted out to Kevin and the racially-biased jury selection were determined by a white supremacist prosecutor. I listened for and hoped for forgiveness (Kevin and MADPMO asked for life imprisonment), so that a teen who had lost her mother when she was four by a civilian murderer would not lose her father by state murderers. You and others have "humanized" Kevin by sharing the ordeals he survived as a child dealing with poverty and abuse. These conditions are not aberrational in the U.S. or around the globe. My communities—known and unknown (to me)—will seek provisions and care for his daughter and grandson. On November 29, 2022 in the late morning, my kin—known and unknown—appeared on RSTV/Black Power Media. The day of the execution of Kevin hundreds, thousands of observers and practitioners gathered in varied sites. Gifts were shared. On the BPM platform Sunni Patterson, a beautiful poet and healer, offered libation and prayers. Kalonji Changa, organizing with working class/poor/imprisoned people and political prisoners, structured the digital platform and informed communities. Dylan Rodriguez, activist academic and radical abolitionist, named the wars waged by white supremacy, capitalism, and imperialism as systemic, brutal, extractive, and anti-life. On the same day that state violence terminated Kevin's life, legalized murder brought the four of us, mostly as strangers, together. We held space in the hold for rage, grief, radicalization. You felt this death as well, George; it altered you. We are permanently scarred in the hold; we are also sanctified there in our encounters not only with death but with each other as we care for agape. We connect, mutate, and grow capacity for consciousness. Thus, we cultivate courage to resist the hold as a zone of death and dishonor funded by taxation.

Part Nine

WHITE MOB MENTALITY

27

THE CAPITOL SIEGE WAS WHITE SUPREMACY IN ACTION

Trial Evidence Confirms That

INTERVIEW WITH PENIEL E. JOSEPH

New footage aired at the impeachment trial of Donald Trump has flooded the U.S. once again with images of the violent mob that stormed the Capitol last month, reigniting our horror and attempt as a nation to make sense of the event.

What we witnessed was white supremacy on full display. There were Confederate flags, nooses, symbols of antisemitism. There were members of "alt-right" groups such as the Proud Boys. Combine these facts with the reality that the white mob was there to overturn legitimate votes, especially votes cast by majority-Black voters who played a significant role in electing now-President Joe Biden, this was a case of white power and white rage unhinged. And we must not forget about the two Black Capitol police officers who were called the n-word multiple times. Given Trump's white nationalist fervor and white racism, the majority white mob reflected his image, his anti–Black, Indigenous, and people of color (BIPOC) sensibilities. All of this confirms that the Capitol Siege represented the brazen reemergence of white supremacy in our country.

Two east Texans described the mob violence as an attempt at a "second revolution,"[1] while GOP Sen. Roy Blunt has sought to describe it as a right-wing equivalent to the Black Lives Matter upswell of protest against police brutality.[2] Both of these formulations are hard to stomach.

G. Yancy (with Peniel E. Joseph), "The Capitol Siege Was White Supremacy in Action. Trial Evidence Confirms That," in *Truthout*, February 13, 2021. [Editors: Alana Yu-lan Price and Britney Schultz]

"Revolution," connotes the attempted overthrow of an existing power structure that is oppressive and unjust, but the "oppression" articulated by the majority-white mob who stormed the Capitol was actually a fabricated stew of conspiracy theories about election theft and the existence of threats to white supremacy.

Meanwhile, to conflate what took place at the Capitol with what took place on the streets of the U.S. (and around the world) last year regarding resistance to police brutality is to denude the latter of righteous indignation against current and historical systems of racial injustice.

The emergence of unabashed white supremacy was certainly on display at the Capitol on January 6, which is not to say that every white person there was a card-carrying member of a white supremacist group. The unprecedented storming of the Capitol and the brazen reemergence of white supremacy in our country, forced a set of questions regarding the meaning of revolution.

As I considered these things, I wondered what Malcolm X and Martin Luther King Jr. might think. To tackle these questions, I spoke with Peniel E. Joseph, who is the Barbara Jordan Chair in Political Values and Ethics and Founding Director of the Center for the Study of Race and Democracy at the LBJ School of Public Affairs and Professor of History at the University of Texas at Austin. Joseph's most recent book is *The Sword and the Shield: The Revolutionary Lives of Malcolm X and Martin Luther King Jr.*, which was named by *Time Magazine* as one of the 100 Must-Read Books of 2020.

GEORGE YANCY: During the storming of the U.S. Capitol on January 6, the term "revolution" was bandied about. When I think about Black revolutionary discourse and Black revolutionary consciousness in the U.S., I think about Black people who have had enough of white racism, its violence against and dehumanization of people who look like me. My point is that the discourse of Black revolution is grounded not just in self-determination or even armed struggle, but steeped in bringing an end to anti-Black racism, the brutalization of Black bodies and the reality of systemic racial discrimination and oppression. And even if one opposes armed Black struggle, as Martin Luther King Jr. did, one certainly understands that Black people are sick of being treated as sub-persons. So, what do you make of the discourse of "revolution" or "insurrection" vis-à-vis the largely white-led attack on the Capitol? The attack wasn't motivated because of the weight of "historical anti-whiteness." The U.S. was *not* founded upon anti-whiteness. What then was at its core, especially when one considers the demonstrable racist oppressive plight that Black people lived under and continue to live under? What I'm suggesting is that the term "revolution" that was used by some within the white mob was not only a misnomer but was denuded of a single thread of political integrity and righteous indignation.

PENIEL E. JOSEPH: I absolutely agree. The white riot at the U.S. Capitol echoes the racial terror and violence that we witnessed during America's first two periods of Reconstruction. In that sense, it might be considered a morally reprehensible and politically indefensible counter-revolution, the kind that brought Black America to its "nadir" during the Reconstruction's afterlife, the period of the White Redeemer South. "Redemption" sought to deny Black citizenship and dignity by use of racial violence and systemic massacres and pogroms (later 19th century, peaking with the Wilmington, North Carolina, white riot of 1898 that displaced duly elected Black and white officials with unapologetic white supremacists).

GY: What I witnessed at the Capitol was an expression of white nationalism. When I think about the founding of North America, I think about white nationalism. So, historically, white nationalism is inseparable from colonialism, xenophobia, brutality, land confiscation, and anti-BIPOC racism. White nationalism is also predicated upon social ontological logics that are hierarchical, where white people are deemed human while non-whites are judged to be ersatz, inferior, evil, insects, vermin. In short, white nationalism is an expression of white power. When I witnessed Black people in the streets in the summer of 2020 in the U.S. and around the world protesting the killings of unarmed Black people, I saw Black power being expressed, but I didn't see people displaying anti-white racism per se, especially as many white people were also in the streets speaking truth to power and affirming that Black lives matter. Some, I imagine, will want to conflate the protests by majority youth-led BLM protests with the violent attack on the Capitol. Black people want racial justice, they protest because they are not regarded as fully human. Help us to understand the differences in these separate events so that we avoid false equivalences and forms of obscurantism that are designed to "justify" white violence.

PEJ: There is no moral equivalency between slavery and abolition. I say this from the outset, because the problem with comparing Black Lives Matter protests for racial justice with white supremacist insurrections to live in an authoritarian neofascist state that circumscribes Black lives is rooted in this remarkable resilient fallacy.

Even Barack Obama used this trope to save his presidential candidacy during his March 18, 2008, "Race Speech" in Philadelphia. He compared

Jeremiah Wright's Black Liberationist Theological critique of American imperialism to white resentment against affirmative action. This was lauded as the best speech on race matters since Lincoln. So, we face an uphill climb on this matter.

The best thing to say is that BLM activists are, in the tradition of Dr. King's "beloved community"[3] and Malcolm X's human rights movement, trying to create a world that is free of racial injustice, economic inequality, violence, war and exploitation. Their pursuit of intersectional justice and centering of Black radical and queer feminism to their policy agenda stands in stark contrast to white rioters who are not only racist but don't believe in democracy.

GY: Given your wealth of knowledge regarding the different philosophical positions of Malcolm X (who later became known as El-Hajj Malik El-Shabazz) and Martin Luther King Jr., speak to how both might conceptualize this moment in U.S. history. I am thinking not only about the storming of the Capitol, but the unabashed reemergence of white supremacy. This isn't to deny that it has always been there. After all, white supremacy is like the Hydra of Lerna; it can grow many heads. There are many who see Malcolm and Martin as holding diametrically opposed views, but within our current moment, what would they agree upon philosophically and tactically as we live through this emergence of white terrorism?

PEJ: My new book, *The Sword and the Shield: The Revolutionary Lives of Malcolm X and Martin Luther King Jr.*, speaks to how Malcolm and Martin started as adversaries, turned into rivals, and ultimately became each other's alter egos. They understood that true liberation required King's radical Black citizenship and Malcolm's concept of radical Black dignity.

King focused on not just ending racial oppression but reimagining citizenship as including a universal basic income, the end of poverty, violence and racism, decent housing fit for human beings and food justice. Malcolm imagined Black dignity as eradicating what he called White World Supremacy. He wanted freedom not just in Harlem, but in Haiti, from New Orleans to Nigeria, from Brooklyn to Benin to Bandung, Indonesia.

They would both agree that what we have seen is not surprising, considering their deep knowledge of history and interest in racial slavery to the present. King's understanding of the searing racial wilderness that Malcolm often described came later, but when it arrived, King stalked this planet like a pillar of fire, a prophet whose scathing critique of white supremacy, war, violence and racism made him a pariah in a land that had only recently feted him as America's Apostle of Nonviolence, Prince of Peace, and the youngest Nobel Peace Prize recipient in history.

GY: In his famous "I Have a Dream" speech on August 28, 1963, which he delivered on the steps of the Lincoln Memorial, King said, "I have a dream that one day this nation will rise up and live out the true meaning of its creed: We hold these truths to be self-evident, that all men are created equal." In New York City, on May 1, 1962, Malcolm X said, "What is looked upon as an American dream for white people has long been an American nightmare for black people." Peniel, what do you see moving forward? Do you see a dream or a nightmare?

PEJ: I believe that the struggle for Black dignity and citizenship is the key to building a "beloved community" premised on recognizing Black people as human beings and devoted to guaranteeing intersectional justice for all people. The COVID-19 pandemic impacted all of us, differently, based on race, class, able-bodied-ness, gender, sexuality, geography, etc. What folks try to smear as "identity politics" is the actual realization that universality cannot be primarily seen through the lens of white male privilege. To defeat white supremacy, eradicate anti-Black racism, and achieve a different, more racially just and equitable country is the movement for our time. The future of American democracy rests on centering racial justice as the beating heart of the entire body politic.

I remain hopeful because of the depth and breadth of not just protest, but also organizing that has been witnessed this past year. BLM has proven to be a game-changing social movement that both rests on the shoulders of past icons such as Malcolm and Martin and expands the boundaries of the Radical Black Liberation Tradition in so many fruitful and important ways.

By centering the most vulnerable within the Black community— women, LGBTQIA, children, the cash poor, mentally ill, HIV positive, incarcerated, homeless—we are able to imagine a more liberated future for all of us. I truly believe Malcolm X and MLK would have marched arm in arm with BLM activists in the continuing search for that future based on their fervent belief that another, better and more just, world is possible.

GY: Peniel, I want to return to the theme of nightmares. Since our discussion (2021), I'm angered and deeply frightened by the fact that we are now down to 100 seconds to midnight. I'm thinking here of a world-shattering nuclear conflagration. I know that Dr. King wasn't just critical of racism and capitalism/materialism, but he was also deeply critical of militarism. Under this horrible scenario, perhaps none of us will survive. Speak to this issue of standing, as it were, on the nuclear precipice, and are there any voices within the Black tradition of radical thought that might help us *now*?

PEJ: I do think that there are numerous voices in the Black Radical Tradition that can help us at this pivotal "midnight" moment in the history of American democracy. I think the work of Angela Davis is especially crucial here. Davis offers a generative, inspiring, and complex notion of freedom rooted in an expansive vision of what W. E. B. Du Bois characterized as "abolition-democracy." This concept, articulated by Du Bois in *Black Reconstruction*, which I would argue is his most important work of history, relates not simply to the elimination of racial slavery, but to the structures of punishment, dehumanization, and violence that upheld this system during antebellum slavery and its afterlives from Reconstruction to the present.

Abolition-Democracy in the Reconstruction era could be found in the writings and activism of Frederick Douglass, Ida B. Wells, and many other proponents of Radical Reconstruction. Davis' writings on slavery, shifting meanings of freedom, prison and police abolition knit together three generations of Reconstructionists. What's imperative at this moment is to mine the Black Radical Tradition and Radical Black Feminist Traditions to reimagine the meaning of freedom beyond myths of American Exceptionalism. We need to recognize the power of narratives and the way in which redemptionists narratives of the Lost Cause have damaged and disfigured our collective democratic possibilities and potential. The writings of Toni Morrison, Manning Marable, Barbara Smith, Malcolm X, Martin Luther King Jr., Toni Cade Bambara, Eddie Glaude, Fran Beal, Gloria Hull, Beverly Guy-Sheftall, Imani Perry, Keisha Blaine, Ashley Farmer, Daina Ramey Berry, Audre Lorde, Cornel West, Cathy Cohen, Beth Richie, Robin D. G. Kelley, Laurence Ralph, Kimberle Crenshaw, bell hooks, Yohuru Williams, and so many more help to amplify this abolitionist-democracy tradition. We need to re-engage with the narrative power of the Black Radical Tradition, something the 1619 Project, the Black Lives Matter Movement's policy agenda, the writings of activists, scholars, prisoners, and the Black quotidian engage in. The story we need to tell is an urgent one, powered by a Reconstructionist vision of a multiracial democracy courageous enough to defeat the high tide of white backlash, racial reaction, and state sanctioned violence once and for all.

28

CAPITOL MOB REVEALS ONGOING REFUSAL TO ACCEPT BLACK VOTES AS LEGITIMATE

INTERVIEW WITH ERIC FONER

What will history make of the horror and disbelief experienced by the world on January 6, when the United States Capitol was violently broken into and vandalized by Trump supporters who attempted to stop the counting of the Electoral College votes legitimately won by President-elect Joe Biden?

The painful and unforgettable events that transpired that day, leaving five people dead, not only speak to the fragility of American democracy but also reveal deeply embedded realities about white supremacy and its current and historical efforts to undermine democratic institutions and ideals.

In this interview, Eric Foner, one of the U.S.'s most prominent historians, provides an important historical framework for understanding these recent tragic events. Foner argues that the Capitol mob reflects other moments in our racially fraught history, revealing a common thread: the "inability or unwillingness to accept African Americans as legitimate members of American society, and to accept African American votes as legitimate."

Foner is the DeWitt Clinton Professor Emeritus of History at Columbia University and the author of numerous books, including *The Fiery Trial: Abraham Lincoln and American Slavery*, which in 2011 won a Pulitzer Prize for History, and most recently, *The Second Founding: How the Civil War and Reconstruction Remade the Constitution*.

G. Yancy (with Eric Foner), "Capitol Mob Reveals Ongoing Refusal to Accept Black Votes as Legitimate," in *Truthout*, January 12, 2021. [Editors: Alana Yu-lan Price and Maya Schenwar]

GEORGE YANCY: Your range of work as an American historian is extraordinary. And after recent events regarding the insurrectionist efforts of the mob of white rioters who attacked the nation's Capitol, I think we need your voice. So, what was your initial response as you watched or heard about what took place on January 6 as so many white people engaged in violence against democracy to stop the process of confirming that President-elect Joe Biden had won the election?

ERIC FONER: The day before the attack on the capitol, I was on the phone with a former student of mine who works in Washington, D.C. I mentioned that it would be best to stay indoors tomorrow because all these people are coming in. . . . I literally said that I wouldn't be surprised if they just try to storm the Capitol to try to stop the counting of the electoral votes. Now, I'm not a security expert. But I wouldn't be surprised if eventually it comes out that some of the DC or the Capitol Hill police were in cahoots, or at least were sympathetic and didn't really feel like doing anything to stop them. But be that as it may, I was appalled and shocked. This is the logical end of Trump's presidency. He has been inciting hatred and violence for years and now it has come home to roost for all of us. As an historian, I was particularly shocked by seeing the Confederate flag displayed in the Capitol. I can't think of another time in history where the Confederate flag was prominently on display. Maybe there was such a moment. I don't know. But again, that's Trump. He has, among many other things, closely identified himself with the Confederacy, with the Confederate flag, Confederate monuments, and all that. It is pretty clear what people who carry the Confederate flag around think it says. This is not just heritage, so to speak. It's not just respect of history. This is a symbol of white supremacy. Everybody knows that. You don't have to have a Ph.D. in history to know that.

GY: For sure. And seeing the Confederate flag in the capitol was the materialization of white supremacy within this building that theoretically symbolizes freedom.

EF: Yes. Absolutely. I was in a good mood until this happened because that very morning the two victories of a Black man, Raphael Warnock, and a Jewish man, Jon Ossoff, elected to the Senate in Georgia, had been announced by the networks. But change can happen. That was a remarkable thing in and of itself. If one knows about the history of Georgia, one knows how remarkable it is. This is a state that was critical to the Confederacy. It is where there were many lynchings of Black people over the years, where a Jewish man, Leo Frank, was lynched in the early 20th century. Where the Atlanta Massacre took place in 1906. Where you had Herman Talmadge as governor on a strict white supremacist platform. But in terms of Warnock and Ossoff, change can happen. In other words, I don't want to take the events in the Capitol as conclusive—that's it. No, there are signs of hope, as well as signs of real outrage here. So, it was a mixed day in many ways; a very positive thing happened for Georgia and a horrific thing happened in Washington.

GY: That's a nice segue to what I see as a strange tension, the juxtaposition between the storming of the capitol and the election of Warnock, as Georgia's first Black senator, and Ossoff, as Georgia's first Jewish senator. And while you've spoken to this, I would like you to say more. How are those progressive victories to be squared with the attack on the capitol and by extension, an attack on democracy?

EF: Those two victories are very important for those of us who would like to see a more progressive program here in the United States. They were the result of very hard work by a lot of people. You know, the Democratic Party, over the years, has, I think, fallen into the trap of demographic determinism. How many times have you heard people say, "Oh, in 2045 there's going to be a nonwhite majority in the country?" Maybe that's true, but that's not political destiny, by any means. In fact, the most recent election in 2016 showed what happens if the Democrats just take for granted the votes of African Americans and Hispanic Americans. A lot of them voted for Trump. So, it's not guaranteed that a nonwhite majority necessarily means that you'll end up with progressive politics. You have to go out and work hard in Georgia, like Stacey Abrams and others over the last several years have worked very hard to register people, to make sure they get out and vote, to tell them to get their friends and relatives out to vote. And it paid off in Georgia. It's a lesson to everybody that change is possible, but it's not easy and it's not inevitable and it's not just a kind of natural flow of events. You've got to get out there into the trenches. And they did that in Georgia and I commend them absolutely for turning that state around.

GY: I agree. And I agree with your point about the myth of inevitable victory. People must make things happen in progressive ways. But, you know, there is a sense in which America is seen by many Americans as buttressed by a kind of theological destiny, where American "exceptionalism" speaks to a kind of unique mission and superiority that the U.S. has been bestowed.

How do you think about the concept of "American exceptionalism" in relationship to the events on January 6?

EF: You know, to my mind, as a historian, American exceptionalism is the great obstacle to understanding America. It's built into our culture. It's very hard for us, even for those who realize how ridiculous it is, to get away from it. But it is ingrained in our culture. And it has all sorts of deleterious effects. You can start at a very simple level and say, well, "American exceptionalism" means that American history is different from other histories of other countries. Well, but that's obvious. Chinese history is not the same as French history which is not the same as Brazilian history. So to say that different countries have different histories isn't saying very much. But, of course, if we move up the ladder a little, American exceptionalism says more than that. It says that we have nothing to learn from the rest of the world. There's no point in knowing about the rest of the world because we are so exceptional that what applies to them doesn't apply to us.

This struck me years ago when Obamacare was being debated in the Congress. We're aware that every other country has some kind of health care system, but nobody said why don't we see what these other countries are doing. What's going on in Germany or France or England or in Canada? They're not all the same. They all have distinctive systems, but maybe we can learn something from their experiences. Nobody thinks we can learn anything from other people. And that's very different from the Progressive Era a century or so ago. Americans really wanted to learn from other places about the processes of urbanization, industrialization, class conflict, which were happening all throughout the industrialized world. And American reformers and social scientists went over to Europe to see what policies were being adopted there.

A very good historian, Daniel T. Rodgers, wrote a book entitled *Atlantic Crossings*, which has to do with the idea of going back and forth. Now they don't go back and forth. America tells other people what to do. Sometimes we tell them verbally. Sometimes we tell them by force of arms. Think of Iraq, for example. If you don't want to be like us, then we're going to force you to be, whether you want it or not.

Interestingly, Abraham Lincoln, was an American exceptionalist. The Gettysburg Address says, look, we are the only democracy in the world and the Civil War is about whether democracy will survive in the world. But Lincoln did not believe that the United States should run around the world, telling everyone what to do. He opposed the Mexican War. He held that it was by example that we were going to have influence, not by force of arms.

Unfortunately, the example we set on January 6 is not likely to persuade other countries that we are a model they want to emulate.

GY: That's right. We're already being severely questioned by the international community. As you explained American exceptionalism, the hubris and procrustean sensibilities of America are so damagingly clear. Do you see white racism as tangential to this exceptionalism, or integral to it?

EF: White nationalism, as they call it, is built into our history in numerous ways. It's not the only thing, but the American nation, created by the revolution, was premised on westward expansion. Read James Madison at the Constitutional Convention where westward expansion is seen as the destiny of the American Republic. But that, of course, assumes just displacing all the Native Americans who were said not to count. And the economy that is going to fuel westward expansion is a slave economy. It's the labor of African American slaves that's going to produce the wealth that will enable this. So, it's right there from the beginning. The first Naturalization Act, in 1790—that's at the very beginning—said that only white people can immigrate to the United States and become citizens. Blacks couldn't; no Asians. This is a white country. That was their basic premise. Now, of course, the Declaration of Independence also says all men are created equal. And there's your tension. Which part of the Declaration do you actually want to adhere to? That's the contradiction we saw between the Georgia election and the riots in Washington.

GY: I think here of Frederick Douglass who said, "The fourth of July is yours, not mine. You may rejoice, I must mourn."

EF: Yes. Frederick Douglass embraced the promise of the Declaration, even while he condemned the United States as a land of hypocrisy, because people talk about freedom, but in fact they deprive millions of their freedom. So this tension existed. Unfortunately, the white nationalist element here has been reinforced greatly by President Trump during his four years in office. He's not the only one, by any means, but he's certainly very vocal about it. And we have to be very careful, because American exceptionalism assumes that by nature we possess a democratic culture, but this isn't true as we witnessed on January 6. There are many other strands within our experience which are not democratic and are not exceptional. Trump doesn't really think that we're exceptional. He thinks that he is just another authoritarian ruler like his pals Tayyip Erdoğan, Vladimir Putin, Xi Jinping, or others around the world. That's not very exceptional. That's a certain mode of governance that a lot of people in the United States seem to find attractive.

GY: Although you have spoken about this before, it is so incredibly important that I think that it bears mentioning here. Compare January 6 to the event in 1873, in Colfax, Louisiana, where members of a Black militia were murdered by white people who were armed and who seized control of the local government from elected Black officials. And also the 1898 coup by armed white people in Wilmington, N.C. In this case, they rejected or ousted the elected biracial local government. What do you see as the common ideological thread running through these three horrific events?

EF: I think the common thread is an inability or unwillingness to accept African Americans as legitimate members of American society, and to accept African American votes as legitimate. Remember that President Trump came into politics by way of the Birther Movement. President Obama just wasn't an American, Trump said. For Trump, Obama simply had no right to be president. To those with a historical sensibility, this reminds us of the Dred Scott decision of 1857, which said no Black person could be a citizen. I'm sure Trump is not that familiar with the Dred Scott decision, but the idea that this is a white country is there; anyone else is an interloper, an alien. That's what unites all these things, and the belief that white people have the authority to overturn the results of African American voting. It happened in Colfax, Louisiana, it happened in Wilmington, N.C., and it happened many times in Reconstruction with Black people trying to go to the polls. Black people gained enormous power in the Reconstruction period after the Civil War. They gained the right to vote. Something like 2,000 Black people held public office from the U.S. Senate down to Justice of the Peace, and so on. This galvanized a tremendous violent white backlash of terrorism, which we saw a little bit of on January 6. The violence back then, of course, was much worse. The Klan killed hundreds of people. You had white leagues, Knights of the White Camelia, you had these white nationalist violent terrorist groups operating in many parts of the South aiming at overturning biracial Reconstruction. That sense that there's something illegitimate about Black political power is deeply rooted in many sectors of our society.

GY: It's dialectical, isn't it? Philosopher Simone de Beauvoir, in *The Second Sex*, argues that "no group ever sets itself up as the One without at once setting up the Other over against itself."

EF: Yes. Around 1900, just as the South was fully imposing the Jim Crow system taking away the right to vote from African Americans, Rudyard Kipling wrote his famous poem about the white man's burden. It was a message to the United States from England. Basically, the British Empire, even though it was at its height, was waning. He felt that the United States had to take up the burden. What was the burden? It was ruling over nonwhite people. That was the white man's burden. It's a hard thing to do. Nonwhite people may not want to be ruled over. But the white man, as the belief holds, has got to do it for civilization, for humanity. Kipling didn't ask France. He didn't ask Germany. He asked the United States, even though we didn't really have a big empire. We had Puerto Rico, we had Hawaii, but we didn't have a giant empire like the European countries. You know, the greatest example of the white man's burden was in the South where white people had reestablished, after the Civil War Reconstruction, their ability to rule over nonwhites. At that time, there was a big sense that the United States was the rising power. And the old empires were waning or would wane. Remember that's around the moment when Australia was putting into effect what they called the White Australia policy. This is happening around the world and that's the moment when the United States becomes an imperial power along with the rest of them. It's part of our history, but it isn't the only part. I think that if we look at people like Frederick Douglass and W. E. B. DuBois, you'll find a different strand, obviously, which survives to this day. There's the conflict there, a different vision of what America ought to be in juxtaposition to imperial rule.

GY: When Trump refers to making America great again, given this imperial history, one wonders what he can possibly mean.

EF: Yes. When was America great? Trump never actually says when America was great. A lot of people say it was in the 1950s when there were good jobs available, good pay, manufacturing, stable communities. It didn't include Black people. Black people still couldn't vote in the South, segregation was still widely enforced. It's a politics of resentment, which is Trump's politics: When people, mostly white men, but not all, cannot come to terms with the changes in our society over the past 50 years, whether it's the Civil Rights Revolution, the changing status of women, the impact of globalization, which has been very deleterious in a lot of communities, changing demographics with immigration, etc. People who don't like all that think there was a time when America was great, when none of that happened, when people from India and China and all these places were not pouring into the country, when Black people "knew their place," women "knew their place," white men could get good solid jobs. Exactly when that was is hard to say, but, nonetheless, that's what we're going to restore according to Trump.

GY: As you know, Dr. Martin Luther King Jr. paraphrased abolitionist minister Theodore Parker. King says that the arc of the moral universe is long, but it bends. Taking a long view as a historian, would you say that American history demonstrates or contradicts that assumption?

EF: King admired Parker a lot. This is ultimately a religious concept. I'm not much of a religious fellow so it's not the way I think. It would be nice to believe it. Unfortunately, as I said at the end of my most recent book about the Reconstruction constitutional amendments and what happened to them later on, there is no guaranteed line of progress. Rights can be gained and rights can be taken away. King was obviously not quiescent. He wasn't saying let's just wait around until things get better. You've got to bend the arc yourself.

29

TRUMP HAS ADOPTED A "VIVA DEATH!" APPROACH TO THE PRESIDENCY

INTERVIEW WITH NOAM CHOMSKY

As protests against racist police violence rock the country, fascism ascends in the Trump White House and the COVID-19 pandemic persists, this country is at a pivotal moment. I spoke about this flash point in history with Noam Chomsky, known as the father of modern linguistics, who is one of the world's most prominent public intellectuals and the author of over 100 books, including *Hegemony or Survival, Failed States, Optimism Over Despair, Hopes and Prospects, Masters of Mankind* and *Who Rules the World?*

In the following interview, Chomsky provides insight on how we can best grapple with the current moment—and prepare for the sobering future.

GEORGE YANCY: Before I ask you about COVID-19, I'd like to start by asking your thoughts on the horrible murder of George Floyd and how you understand the protests that have occurred throughout the U.S. and the world. I am especially interested in your response to Trump's rhetoric to deploy the military to suppress a so-called insurrection.

NOAM CHOMSKY: "Horrible murder" is right. But let us be clear about the murders of Black Americans going on right now. The brutality of a few racist policemen in Minneapolis constitutes a small part of the crime.

G. Yancy (with Noam Chomsky), "Noam Chomsky: Trump Has Adopted a 'Viva Death!' Approach to the Presidency," in *Truthout*, June 5, 2020. [Editors: Alana Yu-lan Price and Maya Schenwar]

It has been widely noted that death rates from the pandemic are far higher among Black people. A current study found that "Americans living in counties with above-average Black populations are three times as likely to die of the coronavirus as those in above-average white counties. This slaughter of Black people is partly a result of how resources were devoted to dealing with the crisis, mostly "in areas that happened to be whiter and more affluent." But it is rooted more deeply in a hideous record of 400 years of malevolent racism. The plague has been taking different forms since the establishment of the most vicious system of slavery in human history—a prime foundation of the country's industry, finance, commerce and general prosperity—but has at most been mitigated, never brought close to a cure.

American slavery was unique not only in terms of its viciousness, but also in that it was linked to skin color. Within this system, every Black face was marked with the emblem, "Your nature is to be a slave."

Other sectors have been harshly treated. Jews and Italians were so feared and despised a century ago that the 1924 racist immigration law was designed to bar them from the country, sending many Jews to crematoria. In support, racists of the day could plead that we had to protect ourselves from the Jews and Italians running the major criminal syndicates, from creatures like Meyer Lansky and Al Capone and Bugsy Siegel. But they were finally assimilated. The same happened with the Irish.

With Black people, however, it is different. They are deemed permanently unassimilable in a society cursed by racism and white supremacy. For the victims, the effects are compounded by the lasting socioeconomic gaps engendered by the curse, intensified by the neoliberal assault of the past 40 years, a great boon to extreme wealth, a disaster for the more vulnerable.

The slaughter of Black Americans proceeds under the radar. The president, whose malice knows no bound, has been exploiting the focus on the pandemic to pursue his service to his prime constituency, great wealth and corporate power. One method is eliminating regulations that protect the public but harm profits. In the midst of an unprecedented respiratory pandemic, Trump has moved to increase air pollution, which makes COVID-19 far more deadly,[1] so much so that tens of thousands of Americans may die as a result, the business press reports. As usual, deaths are not randomly distributed: "Hardest hit are low-income communities and people of color," who are forced to live in the most dangerous areas.

It is all too easy to continue. The protesters know all of this very well. They need no studies. For many it is their lived experience. The protests are not just calling for an end to police brutality in Black communities, but for much more fundamental restructuring of social and economic institutions.

And they are receiving remarkable support, as we see not only from actions all over the country but also from polls. An early June poll "found 64 percent of American adults were 'sympathetic to people who are out protesting right now,' while 27 percent said they were not and 9 percent were unsure."[2]

We may compare this reaction to another occasion when similar protests occurred: 1992, after the acquittal of the Los Angeles police officers who beat Rodney King almost to death. A week of riots followed, with over 60 deaths, finally quelled by the National Guard backed by federal troops sent by President Bush. The protests were mostly limited to Los Angeles, nothing like what we are seeing today.

Trump has one overriding concern, his own welfare: *How can I use this tragedy to enhance my electoral prospects by firing up the most racist and violent components of my voting base?* His natural instincts call for violence: "the most vicious dogs, and most ominous weapons, I have ever seen." And send in the military to teach the "scum" a lesson they'll never forget.

Trump's plan to "dominate" the errant population by violence elicited widespread anger, including bitter condemnation by former chairmen of the Joint Chiefs of Staff along with expressions of sympathy for the protestors. Former Joint Chiefs of Staff chairman Admiral Mike Mullen wrote: "As a white man, I cannot claim perfect understanding of the fear and anger that African Americans feel today. . . . But as someone who has been around for a while, I know enough—and I've seen enough—to understand that those feelings are real and that they are all too painfully founded."[3]

The changes in the past two decades are perhaps a sign that large parts of the population are coming to recognize long-concealed truths about our society, a ray of light in dark times.

GY: We are often told that the United States is the most powerful country in the world. We are fed on a diet of "American exceptionalism." Yet, globally, we have the highest number of deaths due to COVID-19. We were systemically unprepared. How do you explain this incongruity, and what role does Trump play in all of this?

NC: The lack of preparedness has three basic causes: capitalist logic, neoliberal doctrine, and the character of the political leadership. Let's run through them briefly in turn.

After the 2003 SARS epidemic was contained, scientists were well aware that a pandemic was likely and that it might be caused by another coronavirus. They also knew how to take measures to prepare. But knowledge is not enough. Someone must use it. The obvious candidate is the drug companies, which have all the resources needed and huge profits, thanks in no small measure to the exorbitant patents granted them in the mislabeled "free trade" agreements. But they were blocked by capitalist logic. There's no profit in preparing for a possible catastrophe down the road—and as economist Milton Friedman intoned at the dawn of the neoliberal age 40 years ago, the sole responsibility of the corporation is to maximize shareholder value (and management wealth). As recently as 2017, the major drug companies rejected a European Union proposal to fast-track research on pathogens,[4] including coronavirus.

The other candidate is the government, which also has the necessary resources and has played a significant role in developing most vaccines and drugs. But that path is blocked by the neoliberal doctrine that has prevailed since Reagan, who informed us that government is the problem—meaning that decisions must be removed from the government, which is to some extent influenced by citizens, to the unaccountable private tyrannies that were the primary agents (and beneficiaries) of the neoliberal triumph. So, government is barred as well.

The third factor is individual governments. Keeping to the U.S., President George H.W. Bush had established a [President's] Council of Advisors on Science and Technology (PCAST) to keep the president abreast of important scientific issues. One of President Obama's first acts on taking office in 2009 was to commission a PCAST study on how to deal with a pandemic. It was provided to the White House a few weeks later. The science-oriented Obama administration proceeded to put in place a pandemic infrastructure which planned early response to infectious disease threats. That was in place until Jan. 20, 2017, when President Trump took office, and within days began to dismantle the entire executive branch science infrastructure, including the preparations for pandemic,[5] and indeed moved on to reject science generally from a role in informing policy, reversing the bipartisan initiatives since World War II that have been critical for developing the modern high-tech economy.

To drive further nails into the coffin, Trump disbanded programs in which scientists worked with Chinese colleagues to investigate coronaviruses. Each year, he defunded the Centers for Disease Control and Prevention (CDC). That continued with his budget proposal of February 2020 while the pandemic was raging, calling for further CDC cuts (while raising subsidies to fossil fuel industries). Scientists were systematically replaced by industry officials who would ensure that private profit is maximized whatever the impact on the irrelevant public.

Trump's decisions accord with the judgment of his favorite pundit, Rush Limbaugh, to whom he awarded the Presidential Medal of Freedom. He instructs us that science is one of the "four corners of deceit," along with academia, media and government, all of which "exist by virtue of deceit." The guiding maxim of the administration was articulated more eloquently by Franco's leading general in 1936: "Down with intelligence! Viva death!"

As a result, the U.S. was "systematically unprepared" when the pandemic hit.

GY: In February, Trump said that COVID-19 would just disappear, that "one day, it's like a miracle, it will disappear." He was profoundly mistaken and then blamed China, even "racializing" the disease. Some would claim that Trump has blood on his hands because of his gross mishandling of COVID-19. What are your thoughts about this?

NC: Tens of thousands of Americans died as a result of Trump's dedicated service to his primary constituency: extreme wealth and corporate power. His malevolence persisted after the disease struck. A few weeks after discovery of the first symptoms last December, Chinese scientists identified the virus, sequenced the genome, and provided the information to the WHO and the world. Countries in Asia and Oceania reacted at once and have the situation largely under control. Others varied. Trump brought up the rear. For two crucial months, U.S. intelligence and health officials tried to capture the attention of the White House, in vain. Finally, Trump noticed—possibly when the stock market crashed, it has been reported. Since then it has been chaos.

Not surprisingly, Trump and his minions have been thrashing around desperately to find some scapegoat to blame for his crimes against Americans, oblivious to how many more people he slaughters. Defunding and then pulling out of the WHO [World Health Organization] is a sadistic blow against Africans, Yemenis, and many other poor and desperate people who had been protected from rampant diseases by WHO medical aid even before the coronavirus struck, and are now facing new catastrophes in addition. They are dispensable if it will improve his electoral prospects.

Trump's charge against the WHO, which is too ludicrous to discuss, is that it was being controlled by China. By pulling out, he increases Chinese influence. But it is unfair to criticize him for foolishness. The outcome only underscores the fact that he never cared about this in the first place.

GY: Speaking of responsibility and blood on one's hands, a certain interpretation of individual rights seems to override a collective social responsibility for many in the U.S. who are not observing the recommendations of the WHO and the CDC, including a blatant rejection of wearing masks. What would you say is fueling this anger and lack of responsibility toward the health and safety of others?

NC: Republicans overwhelmingly have faith in the president, no matter how much his actions harm them. His god-like image is amplified by those who surround him, thanks to his successful campaign to get rid of everyone but fawning sycophants, like the second-in-command, Secretary of State Mike Pompeo, who muses that God may have sent Trump to earth to save Israel from Iran. Pompeo's fellow evangelicals, the largest base of Trump supporters, likely agree. And they hear much the same generally from the Republican Party, which has virtually abandoned any shred of integrity and abjectly worship him whatever he does. Much the same is true of his media echo chamber. Studies have shown that the primary source of information for Republicans is *Fox News*, Limbaugh, and *Breitbart*. In fact, an interesting dyad has developed: Trump issues some random pronouncement, it is hailed by Sean Hannity as a path-breaking discovery, and the next morning Trump turns to *Fox News* to find out what to think.

Surveys of public opinion reveal the consequences. A Pew poll in April, when Trump's responsibility for the growing disaster was beyond serious debate, found that 83 percent of Republicans and Republican leaners rated Trump's response to the outbreak as either excellent or good[6] (as compared with 18 percent of Democrats and Democratic leaners). They are listening to a president who had been comparing the virus to "regular flu," and who in mid-April tweeted instructions to his supporters to "LIBERATE VIR-GINIA, and save your great 2nd Amendment. It is under siege!" The 2nd Amendment has not the slightest relevance, but Trump knows what buttons to push. He was, transparently, urging his troops to take up arms, part of his more general attempts to encourage armed protestors to violate orders in states with Democratic governors[7] (like Virginia), at a time when there were almost 50,000 recorded deaths.

Let's kill more Americans, not just Yemenis and Africans, if it will improve my electoral prospects. "Down with intelligence! Viva death!"

When we exclude the Astroturf operations and the fervent loyalty of the voting base, it's not clear that much is left of an appeal to "individual rights" in any meaningful sense.

Nor is it clear that the protestors are overriding social responsibility. They evidently don't see it that way. They would be appalled at the idea that what they are doing is similar to people with assault rifles running around the streets shooting randomly, though the comparison is apt. They do not think they are endangering anyone. Rather, they are following their revered leader in protesting an effort by the radical left, maybe on instructions from China, to destroy their elementary rights and even to take away their guns.

All further signs that the country is in deep trouble—and in the light of U.S. power, the world with it.

GY: Apart from Trump's incompetence, what needs to be done globally so that we might both prevent another pandemic and what must we do to be better prepared in the future?

NC: I don't feel that "incompetence" is quite the right word. He's quite competent in pursuing his primary goals: enriching the very wealthy, enhancing corporate power and profit, keeping his base in line while he stabs them in the back, and concentrating power in his hands by dismantling the executive branch, and so intimidating congressional Republicans that they timidly accept almost anything. I didn't hear a peep from them when Trump fired the scientist in charge of vaccine development for daring to question one of the quack cures he is promoting. There is dead silence from these ranks as he carries out his purge of inspector generals, who impose some controls on the swamp he has created in Washington, also insulting one of the most respected Republican senators, 86-year-old Chuck Grassley, who devoted his long career to establishing this system.

It is an impressive achievement.

What has to be done globally is to follow the advice that scientists are providing. A new pandemic is likely, probably worse than this one because of global warming, which may become climate roasting with another four years of the Trump plague. Steps have to be taken to prepare for it, the kind that were recommended in 2003 and were in small part pursued until Trump wielded his wrecking ball. There should be international cooperation in seeking coronaviruses and other potential hazards, developing the scientific understanding needed for rapid development of vaccines and drugs to alleviate symptoms, and implementing contingency plans to be put in place if a pandemic strikes again.

For the U.S. in particular, that means extricating the society from neoliberal dogma, which has had bitter consequences in the domain of health (and many others). The business model for hospitals, with no waste or spare capacity, is an invitation to disaster. More generally, the highly inefficient privatized health-care system is a terrible burden on the society, with double the costs of other developed countries and some of the poorest outcomes. A recent *Lancet* study estimates its annual cost at almost $500 billion and 68,000 extra deaths. It is outrageous that the U.S. cannot rise to the level of other societies and instead relies on the most cruel and costly system of universal health care: emergency rooms. If you can drag yourself to one you can get care—followed perhaps by a healthy bill.

The same neoliberal dogma prevents the National Institutes of Health from proceeding beyond essential research and development for drugs to testing and distribution, bypassing the private companies and implementing the provisions of U.S. law, constantly ignored, which require that drugs produced with government assistance (virtually all) be available to the public at reasonable cost. The most careful studies of these matters that I know of are by Dean Baker, who estimates enormous savings with no loss of innovation if such measures are introduced (see his book *Rigged*, available free[8]).

This is only a bare beginning. There are deep social, cultural and institutional problems that should be addressed.

GY: Assuming that the November election is close, do you see Trump deploying the ruse of voting fraud to remain in power? If that happens, what do you foresee in terms of this playing out politically?

NC: Trump and associates are already pushing that scam energetically, not for the first time. They know that they head a minority party and must resort to deceit and fraud to maintain political power. And for them, a lot is at stake. Another four years would enable them to guarantee that their far-right policies will prevail for a generation no matter what the population wants. That's been the goal of the McConnell strategy of placing the judiciary, top to bottom, in the hands of young far-right jurists who can block programs that are in the public interest. Loss of the current opportunity might doom their project. For Trump personally, the prospects of loss may be severe, even if he is psychologically capable of accepting it like a normal human being. He may be vulnerable to serious legal charges if his immunity is lost. And with the Republican Party having surrendered to his authority, North Korean–style, he faces few impediments. We can leave the rest to the imagination.

GY: I realize that this sounds dystopian, but who is to say that Trump, out of sheer lust for power, will not galvanize a militia to back his desire to stay in power? Any thoughts?

NC: Can't be ruled out. As widely recognized, the country is facing a longer-term constitutional crisis. The Senate is a radically undemocratic institution, to a lesser extent the electoral college. For demographic and structural reasons, a small minority of white, Christian, rural, traditional, often–white supremacist voters can maintain control to an extent even beyond what racist Southern Democrats exercised before Nixon's "southern strategy" brought them into the Republican fold. And this is virtually unchangeable by constitutional amendment. It's not out of the question that in Trump's hands, the impending crisis may come about very soon.

GY: Noam, I know that you prefer not to talk much about yourself, but at 91 how are you personally dealing with our surreal historical moment living under COVID-19?

NC: In narrow personal terms, it's not a severe difficulty for my wife and me. For many others, it's a radically different story. The moment is indeed surreal. The future will be shaped by how we emerge from the crisis. The forces that are responsible for it, and for the neoliberal assault on the population that has, demonstrably, intensified it sharply, are not sitting back quietly. They are working relentlessly to ensure that what emerges is a harsher and more authoritarian version of what they had created in their own interest. There are popular forces seeking to grasp the current opportunities to reverse the disasters of the recent past and to move forward to a far more humane and decent world. And, crucially, to confront the far more severe crises that are looming.

We will recover from the pandemic, at a terrible cost. We will not recover from the ongoing melting of the polar ice sheets and the other consequences of the roasting of the earth that will make many of the areas of human habitation unlivable before too long if we continue on our current course. Another four years of the Trump malignancy will sharply increase the difficulties of dealing with this impending catastrophe—even if we escape the threat of terminal nuclear war that Trump is escalating by dismantling the arms control regime that offered some protection and racing to develop new and more dangerous means of destruction that undermine our diminishing security.

NOTES

INTRODUCTION

1. Frantz Fanon, *Black Skin, White Masks*, trans. Charles Lam Markmann (New York: Grove Press, 1967), 138.

2. Ruth Wilson Gilmore, *Golden Gulag: Prisons, Surplus, Crisis, and Opposition in Globalizing* (Oakland: University of California Press, 2007), 28.

3. James Baldwin, *The Fire Next Time* (New York: Modern Library, 1962/1995), 7.

4. Cornel West, *Democracy Matters: Winning the Flight Against Imperialism* (New York: Penguin Books, 2005), 211.

5. Baldwin, *The Fire Next Time*, 94.

6. Peter L. Berger, *Invitation to Sociology: A Humanistic Perspective* (Garden City, New York: Anchor Books, 1963), 79.

7. West, *Democracy Matters*, 208.

8. West, *Democracy Matters*, 208.

9. Baldwin, *The Fire Next Time*, 94.

10. Paulo Freire, *Pedagogy of the Oppressed*, New Revised 20th Anniversary Edition (New York: Continuum International Publishing Company, 1997), 70.

11. Freire, *Pedagogy of the Oppressed*, 71.

12. See the important work of Fred Evens regarding the dynamic interplay of voices and their fecundity. See *The Multivoiced Body: Society and Communication in the Age of Diversity* (New York: Columbia University Press, 2008) and *Public Art and the Fragility of Democracy: An Essay in Political Aesthetics* (New York: Columbia University Press, 2019).

13. Luce Irigaray, *An Ethics of Sexual Difference*, trans. Carolyn Burke and Gillian C. Gill (Ithaca, New York: Cornell University Press, 1993), 75.

14. Judith Butler, *Precarious Life: The Powers of Mourning and Violence* (New York: Verso, 2004), 29.

15. Regarding my own experience of vile, anti-Black white racist hatred that followed my attempt to speak courageously and publicly about whiteness, see my book: *Backlash: What Happens When We Talk Honestly about Racism in America* (Lanham, MD: Rowman & Littlefield, 2018).

16. Judith Butler, *Giving an Account of Oneself* (New York: Fordham University Press, 2005), 64.

17. Luce Irigaray, *An Ethics of Sexual Difference*, trans. Carolyn Burke and Gillian C. Gill (Ithaca, New York: Cornell University Press, 1993), 74

18. Irigaray, *An Ethics of Sexual Difference*, 75

19. Irigaray, *An Ethics of Sexual Difference*, 75.

20. Irigaray, *An Ethics of Sexual Difference*, 74.

21. Baldwin, *The Fire Next Time*, 8.

22. Audre Lorde, *Sister Outsider: Essays and Speeches*, new foreword by Cheryl Clarke (Berkeley, CA: Crossing Press, 1984), 41.

23. Rosalyn Diprose, *Corporeal Generosity: On Giving with Nietzsche, Merleau-Ponty, and Levinas* (Albany: State University of New York Press, 2002), 13.

24. Freire, *Pedagogy of the Oppressed*, 71.

25. See Jill Stauffer's important book, *Ethical Loneliness: The Injustice of Not Being Heard* (New York: Columbia University Press, 2015).

26. Butler, *Precarious Life*, 27.

27. Butler, *Precarious Life*, 27.

28. Abraham Joshua Heschel, *Abraham Joshua Heschel: Essential Writings*, ed. Susannah Heschel (Ossining, NY: Orbis Books, 2011), 178.

29. Heschel, *Abraham Joshua Heschel*, 74.

CHAPTER 1

1. George Yancy, "Dear White America." *New York Times*, December 24, 2015. https://archive.nytimes.com/opinionator.blogs.nytimes.com/2015/12/24/dear-white-america/.

2. Christopher Newfield and Michael Meranze, "When Are Access and Inclusion Also Racist?" Remaking the University. Accessed December 28, 2022. http://utotherescue.blogspot.com/2020/06/when-are-access-and-inclusion-also.html.

3. Marjorie Cohn, "Calling Chauvin a 'Bad Apple' Denies Systemic Nature of Racist Police Violence." *Truthout*, April 19, 2021. https://truthout.org/articles/calling-chauvin-a-bad-apple-denies-systemic-nature-of-racist-police-violence/.

4. A. Sivanandan, *A Different Hunger: Writings on Black Resistance*. London: Pluto Press, 1987.

CHAPTER 2

1. See comments section after the article, George Yancy, "Dear White America," *New York Times*, December 24, 2015, https://archive.nytimes.com/opinionator.blogs.nytimes.com/2015/12/24/dear-white-america/.

2. George Yancy, "Dear White America," *New York Times*, December 24, 2015, https://archive.nytimes.com/opinionator.blogs.nytimes.com/2015/12/24/dear-white-america/.

3. James Baldwin, "A Letter to My Nephew," Progressive.org, December 1, 1962, https://progressive.org/magazine/letter-nephew/.

4. "Middle Passage," *Encyclopædia Britannica*. Accessed December 28, 2022, https://www.britannica.com/topic/Middle-Passage-slave-trade.

CHAPTER 3

1. William C. Anderson, "On Juneteenth, Let's Commit to Learning How to Abolish Oppressive Institutions," *Truthout*, July 10, 2020, https://truthout.org/articles/on-juneteenth-lets-commit-to-learning-how-to-abolish-oppressive-institutions/.

2. Joe R. Feagin, *How Blacks Built America: Labor, Culture, Freedom, and Democracy* (New York: Routledge, 2016).

3. Joe R. Feagin and Harlan Hahn, *Ghetto Revolts: The Politics of Violence in American Cities* (New York: Macmillan, 1973).

4. Joe R. Feagin, *Racist America: Roots, Current Realities, and Future Reparations: Remaking America with Anti-Racist Strategies* (New York: Routledge, 2000); Joe R. Feagin and Kimberley Ducey, *Racist America: Roots, Current Realities, and Future Reparations* (New York: Routledge, 2019).

5. See "On Views of Race and Inequality, Blacks and Whites Are Worlds Apart," Pew Research Center's Social & Demographic Trends Project. Pew Research Center, August 27, 2020, https://www.pewresearch.org/social-trends/2016/06/27/on-views-of-race-and-inequality-blacks-and-whites-are-worlds-apart/.

6. See AntiRacism Study Dialogue Circles, https://www.asdicircle.org/.

7. W. E. B. Du Bois, *The Souls of Black Folk* (New York: Bantam Classic Books, 1989 [1903]), 186–87.

8. W. E. B. Du Bois, *The Gift of Black Folk: The Negroes in the Making of America* (Garden City Park: Square One Publishers, 2009 [1924]), 57.

9. Ralph Ellison, "What America Would Be Like without Blacks," *Time*, April 6, 1970, 109.

10. Angela Y. Davis, *The Meaning of Freedom: And Other Difficult Dialogues* (San Francisco, CA: City Lights Open Media, 2012), Kindle loc. 2321–24, 2394–95.

CHAPTER 4

1. Adrienne Maree Brown, "After Attempted Coup, We Must Fight White Supremacy and Sow Revolutionary Love," *Truthout*, January 10, 2021, https://truthout.org/articles/after-attempted-coup-we-must-fight-white-supremacy-and-sow-revolutionary-love/.

CHAPTER 6

1. "'I Can't Breathe': Footage Shows David Dungay's Death in Custody—Video." *The Guardian*, July 16, 2018, https://www.theguardian.com/australia-news/video/2018/jul/16/i-cant-breathe-footage-shows-david-dungays-death-in-custody-video.

2. "Mob" is a colloquial term identifying a group of Aboriginal people associated with a particular place or country. It is used to connect and identify who an Aboriginal person is and where they are from. Mob can represent your family group, clan group or wider Aboriginal community group. https://deadlystory.com/page/tools/aboriginal-cultural-support-planning/cultural-planning---frequently-asked-questions/what-is-the-difference-between-mob-clan-tribe-language-group#:~:text='Mob'%20is%20a%20colloquial%20term,or%20wider%20Aboriginal%20community%20group.

3. EWN online, "This Joke about Aboriginal Women Has Trevor Noah under Fire." YouTube, July 24, 2018. https://www.youtube.com/watch?v=dAh1RYzG4hg.

4. "'Wild Black Women' Take on Trying to Educate Trevor Noah." NITV. Accessed December 29, 2022, https://www.sbs.com.au/nitv/article/wild-black-women-take-on-trying-to-educate-trevor-noah/x7nibbeof.

5. "Aboriginal Women Are Black Women Too." NITV. Accessed December 29, 2022, https://www.sbs.com.au/nitv/article/aboriginal-women-are-black-women-too/rk06gdo2t.

6. Lane Sainty, "Here's the Video of an Aboriginal Man Yelling 'I Can't Breathe' as Officers Hold Him Down." BuzzFeed, July 16, 2018, https://www.buzzfeed.com/lanesainty/aboriginal-man-david-dungay-death-in-custody.

7. "'System Is Broken': All Children in NT Detention Are Aboriginal, Officials Say." *The Guardian*, May 30, 2019, https://www.theguardian.com/australia-news/2019/may/31/system-is-broken-all-children-in-nt-detention-are-aboriginal-officials-say.

8. Tim Soutphommasane, "The Whitlam Government and the Racial Discrimination Act." The Australian Human Rights Commission, November 6, 1970, https://humanrights.gov.au/about/news/speeches/whitlam-government-and-racial-discrimination-act.

9. Chelsea Bond, "Talkin' down to the Black Woman." *Australian Feminist Law Journal* 45, no. 2 (2019): 185–89. https://doi.org/10.1080/13200968.2020.1837536.

10. George Yancy, "bell hooks: Buddhism, the Beats and Loving Blackness," *New York Times*, December 10, 2015, https://archive.nytimes.com/opinionator.blogs.nytimes.com/2015/12/10/bell-hooks-buddhism-the-beats-and-loving-blackness/.

11. Chelsea Bond, "The Audacity of Anger," *The Guardian*, January 31, 2018. https://www.theguardian.com/commentisfree/2018/jan/31/the-audacity-of-anger.

CHAPTER 7

1. Olivia Konotey-Ahulu, "London Housing Prices 2021: Property Boom Left Black Britons with Nothing," Bloomberg, May 18, 2021, https://www.bloomberg .com/news/features/2021-05-18/uk-property-wealth-data-2021-show-big-gap -between-black-and-white-homeowners.

2. Claire Alexander and Jason Arday, "Aiming higher: race, inequality and diversity in the Academy," Runnymedetrust.org, 2015. https://assets.website-files.com/61 488f992b58e687f1108c7c/617bcf1cd124685da56a014c_Aiming%20Higher.pdf.

3. From the time of this interview in mid-2021 to the end of 2022, this number has increased to about forty. For more information, see Nicola Rollock, "Staying power: The career experiences and strategies of UK Black female professors," (2019),. https://www.ucu.org.uk/media/10075/Staying-Power/pdf/UCU_Rol lock_February_2019.pdf.

4. See https://www.universitiesuk.ac.uk/sites/default/files/field/downloads /2021-07/bame-student-attainment.pdf.

CHAPTER 8

1. Naima Mohamud, "Afro Hair: How Black Finns Are Taking on Racism," BBC News, September 1, 2019, https://www.bbc.com/news/world-africa-49543502.

2. Mildred Armah, "Rotorua Girl, 12, Bullied over Her Skin Colour Urges Schools to Address Racism and Anti-Black Bullying," *1 News*, accessed December 29, 2022, https://www.1news.co.nz/2021/03/31/rotorua-girl-12-bullied-over -her-skin-colour-urges-schools-to-address-racism-and-anti-black-bullying/.

3. Matthew Haag, "Mississippi Senator's 'Public Hanging' Remark Draws Backlash before Runoff," *New York Times*, November 12, 2018,. https://www.nytimes .com/2018/11/12/us/politics/public-hanging-cindy-hyde-smith.html.

4. Matthew J. Mancini, "Pig Law," *Mississippi Encyclopedia.* Center for Study of Southern Culture, April 14, 2018, https://mississippiencyclopedia.org/entries /pig-law/.

5. See https://www.freewestpapua.org/.

6. "China: Covid-19 Discrimination against Africans," Human Rights Watch, October 28, 2020, https://www.hrw.org/news/2020/05/05/china-covid-19-dis crimination-against-africans.

7. Stephanie Busari, Nimi Princewill, Shama Nasinde, and Mohammed Tawfeeq, "Foreign Students Fleeing Ukraine Say They Face Segregation, Racism at Border," CNN, March 4, 2022, https://www.cnn.com/2022/02/28/europe/students-allege -racism-ukraine-cmd-intl/index.html.

8. RNZ (June 30, 2022), New Zealand designates American Proud Boys and The Base terrorist organisations, RNZ, https://www.rnz.co.nz/news/politi cal/470065/new-zealand-designates-american-proud-boys-and-the-base-terrorist -organisations.

9. C. H. Elers and P. Jayan, "This is us": Free speech embedded in whiteness, racism and coloniality in Aotearoa, New Zealand. *First Amendment Studies* 54, 2 (2020): 236–49.

10. R. Menakem (2017), *My Grandmother's Hands: Racialized Trauma and the Pathway to Mending Our Hearts and Bodies* (Las Vegas, NV: Central Recovery Press, 2017).

11. D. Awatere, *Māori sovereignty* (Broadsheet, 1984).

CHAPTER 13

1. Anemona Hartocollis, "Cornel West Is in a Fight with Harvard, Again." *The New York Times*, March 3, 2021. https://www.nytimes.com/2021/03/02/us/cornel -west-harvard-tenure.html.

2. The Harvard Crimson, "UC Endorses Petitions in Support of Cornel West and against Statements by J. Mark Ramseyer: News: The Harvard Crimson." News | The Harvard Crimson. Accessed December 29, 2022. https://www.thecrimson.com /article/2021/3/1/uc-passes-west-support-statement/.

3. Fullreads, "The True Harvard at FullReads." Accessed December 29, 2022. https://fullreads.com/essay/the-true-harvard/.

CHAPTER 14

1. National Archives and Records Administration, "Founders Online: Remarks Concerning the Savages of North America." Accessed December 29, 2022. https:// founders.archives.gov/documents/Franklin/01-41-02-0280.

2. Southwest Indian Relief Council—SWIRC—helps Native Americans throughout the southwest United States—Southwest Indian Relief Council. Accessed December 29, 2022. http://www.nativepartnership.org/site/Page Server?pagename=swirc_hist_dustbowl.

3. Travis Hay, Cindy Blackstock, and Michael Kirlew, "Dr. Peter Bryce (1853–1932): Whistleblower on Residential Schools." CMAJ, March 2, 2020. https://www .cmaj.ca/content/192/9/E223.

4. Brian Yazzie Burkhart, "Be as Strong as the Land that Made You: An Indigenous Philosophy of Well-Being through the Land." *Science, Religion and Culture*, vol. 6. Accessed December 29, 2022. http://researcherslinks.com/current-issues /Be-as-Strong-as-the-Land-that-Made/9/26/2127/html.

CHAPTER 16

1. Rashawn Ray and Alexandra Gibbons, "Why Are States Banning Critical Race Theory?" Brookings, March 9, 2022. https://www.brookings.edu/blog /fixgov/2021/07/02/why-are-states-banning-critical-race-theory/.

2. George Yancy, "Robin D.G. Kelley: The Tulsa Race Massacre Went Way Beyond 'Black Wall Street.'" *Truthout*, June 1, 2021. https://truthout.org/articles /robin-kelley-business-interests-fomented-tulsa-massacre-as-pretext-to-take-land/.

3. Robin D. G. Kelley, "Black Study, Black Struggle." *Boston Review*, November 23, 2021. https://www.bostonreview.net/forum/robin-kelley-black-struggle -campus-protest/.

4. H. Kris Hirst, "Maroons and Marronage: Escaping Enslavement." ThoughtCo, February 3, 2019. https://www.thoughtco.com/maroons-and-marronage-4155346.

5. United Nations, "End Poverty in all its Forms Everywhere." Department of Economic and Social Affairs, Statistics Division. Accessed December 29, 2022. https://unstats.un.org/sdgs/report/2021/goal-01/.

6. UNICEF, "Child Poverty." October 16, 2022. https://www.unicef.org/social -policy/child-poverty.

7. YouTube, "How the University De-Radicalizes Students, Professors, and Social Movements": A Conversation With Joy James and Rebecca Wilcox The Political Theology Network Mentoring Initiative hosted this event on January 28, 2022, February 18, 2022. https://www.youtube.com/watch?v=IjeWk4VGNGk&t=3976s.

CHAPTER 17

1. Elizabeth Stordeur Pryor, "The Etymology of [N-word]: Resistance, Language, and the Politics of Freedom in the Antebellum North." *Journal of the Early Republic* 36, no. 2 (2016): 203–45. https://doi.org/10.1353/jer.2016.0028.

2. Elizabeth Stordeur Pryor, *Colored Travelers: Mobility and the Fight for Citizenship before the Civil War*. Chapel Hill: The University of North Carolina Press, 2020.

3. Elizabeth Stordeur Pryor, Why it's so hard to talk about the N-word | TED Talk. Accessed December 29, 2022. https://www.ted.com/talks/elizabeth_stordeur _pryor_why_it_s_so_hard_to_talk_about_the_n_word/transcript?language=en.

4. Woojin Lim, "George Yancy: To Be Black in the US Is to Have a Knee against Your Neck Each Day." *Truthout*, July 17, 2020. https://truthout.org/articles/george -yancy-to-be-black-in-the-us-is-to-have-a-knee-against-your-neck-each-day/.

5. Emily Bernard, "Teaching the N-Word." *The American Scholar*, September 1, 2005, http://theamericanscholar.org/teaching-the-n-word/.

6. Countee Cullen, Incident. Accessed December 29, 2022. http://holyjoe.org /poetry/cullen.htm.

CHAPTER 19

1. Michelle Goodwin, "The New Jane Crow: Women's Mass Incarceration." *Just Security*, March 15, 2021. https://www.justsecurity.org/71509/the-new-jane-crow -womens-mass-incarceration/.

2. "Incarcerated Women and Girls," The Sentencing Project, November 23, 2022. https://www.sentencingproject.org/fact-sheet/incarcerated-women-and-girls/.

3. Nicole Hannah-Jone, "Our democracy's founding ideals were false when they were written. Black Americans have fought to make them true." *New York Times Magazine*, 2019, 14.

CHAPTER 20

1. This is spelled out in more detail in Mark Lewis Taylor, "Political Theology: Reflecting on the Arts of a Liberating Politics." In *Theological Perspectives on Life, Liberty and the Pursuit of Happiness*. Editors, Ada-María Isazi-Díaz, Rosemary Carbine, and Mary McClintock Fulkerson. New York: Palgrave Macmillan, 2013, 83–98.

2. Chris Hedges, *The Greatest Evil Is War*. New York: Seven Stories Press, 2022, 119–120.

CHAPTER 22

1. Jake Johnson, "Trump Administration Seeks Exclusive Rights to Potential Coronavirus Vaccine." *Truthout*, March 16, 2020, https://truthout.org/articles/trump-administration-seeks-exclusive-rights-to-potential-coronavirus-vaccine/.

2. "The Race for a Vaccine," *New York Times*, April 1, 2020, https://www.nytimes.com/2020/04/01/podcasts/the-daily/coronavirus-vaccine.html.

CHAPTER 23

1. "Color of Coronavirus: Covid-19 Deaths Analyzed by Race and Ethnicity." *APM Research Lab*. Accessed December 30, 2022, https://www.apmresearchlab.org/covid/deaths-by-race.

2. Matt Apuzzo, Noah Weiland, and Selam Gebrekidan, "Trump Gave W.H.O. a List of Demands. Hours Later, He Walked Away." *New York Times*, November 27, 2020, https://www.nytimes.com/2020/11/27/world/europe/trump-who-tedros-china-virus.html.

CHAPTER 24

1. David Brooks, "The G.O.P. Is Getting Even Worse." *New York Times*, April 23, 2021, https://www.nytimes.com/2021/04/22/opinion/trump-gop.html.

2. Ben Geman, "Ohio Gov. Kasich Concerned by Climate Change, but Won't 'Apologize' for Coal." The Hill, February 3, 2016, https://thehill.com/policy /energy-environment/113214-ohio-gov-kasich-concerned-by-climate-change-but -wont-apologize-for-coal/.

3. Reem Nadeem, "3. Americans' Views of the Problems Facing the Nation." Pew Research Center—U.S. Politics & Policy, July 25, 2022, https://www.pew research.org/politics/2021/04/15/americans-views-of-the-problems-facing-the -nation/.

4. "Small-Dollar Donors Get behind Headline-Grabbing Lawmakers," Open Secrets News, April 21, 2021, https://www.opensecrets.org/news/2021/04/small -dollar-donors-q121-headline-congress/.

CHAPTER 25

1. SFUPublicSquare, "Angela Davis and Gina Dent | Abolition Feminism: Dreaming a New Reality." YouTube, September 22, 2022, https://www.youtube .com/watch?v=urjluhp0MVM.

2. "The Scholarly Journey of Hortense Spillers," *BrandeisNOW*. Accessed December 30, 2022, https://www.brandeis.edu/now/2019/february/hortense -spillers-qa.html.

3. Anushka Patil, "How a March for Black Trans Lives Became a Huge Event." *New York Times*, June 16, 2020, https://www.nytimes.com/2020/06/15/nyregion /brooklyn-black-trans-parade.html.

4. Anushka Patil, "How a March for Black Trans Lives Became a Huge Event." *New York Times*, June 16, 2020, https://www.nytimes.com/2020/06/15/nyregion /brooklyn-black-trans-parade.html.

5. Wynter, Sylvia, "Towards the sociogenic principle: Fanon, identity, the puzzle of conscious experience, and what it is like to be 'Black.'" *National identities and sociopolitical changes in Latin America* (2001): 30-66.

6. "Out in the Night—the Award-Winning Documentary." *Out in the Night*, The Award Winning Documentary. Accessed December 30, 2022, https://www .outinthenight.com/meet-the-nj4/.

7. C. Riley Snorton, *Black on Both Sides: A Racial History of Trans Identity* (Minneapolis: University of Minnesota Press, 2017).

8. Zakiyyah Iman Jackson, *Becoming Human: Matter and Meaning in an Antiblack World* (New York: New York University Press, 2020).

9. Fred Moten, *In the Break: The Aesthetics of the Black Radical Tradition* (Minneapolis: University of Minnesota Press, 2003).

10. Saidiya V. Hartman, *Scenes of Subjection: Terror, Slavery, and Self-Making in Nineteenth-Century America* (New York: W. W. Norton, 2022).

11. Toby Beauchamp, *Going Stealth: Transgender Politics and U.S. Surveillance Practices* (Durham, NC: Duke University Press, 2019).

12. Eric A. Stanley, "Anti-Trans Optics: Recognition, Opacity, and the Image of Force." *South Atlantic Quarterly* 116, no. 3 (2017): 612–20. https://doi.org/10.1215/00382876-3961732.

13. Margaux Bang, "Artists to Watch: Meet the Emerging Talent from Our Latest Issue of L'Officiel Art." *L'Officiel*, January 18, 2021. https://www.lofficielusa.com/art/artists-to-watch-spring-2020-round-up.

14. Eva Hayward, "More Lessons from a Starfish: Prefixial Flesh and Transspeciated Selves." *WSQ: Women's Studies Quarterly* 36, no. 3–4 (2008): 64–85. https://doi.org/10.1353/wsq.0.0099.

15. Tourmaline, "Filmmaker and Activist Tourmaline on How to Freedom Dream." *Vogue*, July 2, 2020. https://www.vogue.com/article/filmmaker-and-activist-tourmaline-on-how-to-freedom-dream.

16. "Anything We Want to Be: Tourmaline's Salacia: Magazine: Moma." The Museum of Modern Art. Accessed December 30, 2022, https://www.moma.org/magazine/articles/360.

17. "Happy Birthday, Marsha!" *Happy Birthday, Marsha!* Accessed December 30, 2022. http://www.happybirthdaymarsha.com/.

18. "Alternate Endings, Radical Beginnings Video & Artist . . ." Visual AIDS. Accessed December 30, 2022. https://visualaids.org/blog/aerb-tourmaline-statement.

CHAPTER 26

1. George Yancy with Joy James, "Black Lives: Between Grief and Action." *New York Times*, December 23, 2014. https://archive.nytimes.com/opinionator.blogs.nytimes.com/2014/12/23/black-lives-between-grief-and-action/?_r=0.

2. "Octavia E. Butler Slow Read: A Participatory Live Show Discussing the Book!" Eventbrite. Accessed December 30, 2022. https://www.eventbrite.ca/e/octavia-e-butler-slow-read-a-participatory-live-show-discussing-the-book-tickets-110569179392.

3. "Black Immigrant Lives Are under Attack." RAICES. Accessed December 30, 2022. https://www.raicestexas.org/2020/07/22/black-immigrant-lives-are-under-attack/.

4. José Olivares and John Washington, "'A Silent Pandemic': Nurse at Ice Facility Blows the Whistle on Coronavirus Dangers." The Intercept, September 14, 2020. https://theintercept.com/2020/09/14/ice-detention-center-nurse-whistleblower/.

5. Jonathan Michels, "The Fight for Medicare for All Made Some Important Progress in 2020." Jacobin. Accessed December 30, 2022. https://jacobin.com/2020/12/medicare-for-all-2020-coronavirus-progress.

6. Gregory Pratt, "Mayor Lori Lightfoot Was Told by Staff in November 2019 That Anjanette Young Raid Was 'Pretty Bad'." *Chicago Tribune*. Accessed December 30, 2022. https://www.chicagotribune.com/politics/ct-lightfoot-anjanette-young-raid-emails-20201230-dhnc67ikorawdhm5a2xw7s4x7u-story.html.

7. "'This Is How Black People Get Killed': Dr. Susan Moore Dies of Covid after Decrying Racist Care." Democracynow.YouTube, December 30, 2020. https://www.youtube.com/watch?v=7v1Oyp_bBGk.

8. "Sign the Petition." Change.org. Accessed December 30, 2022. https://www.change.org/p/debra-haaland-deb-haaland-stand-against-modern-day-jim-crow-in-indian-country.

9. Derek Seidman and Gin Armstrong, "Scandal-Ridden Wells Fargo Rips off Customers While Funding the Gun Industry and Carceral State." *Truthout*, March 30, 2018. https://truthout.org/articles/scandal-ridden-wells-fargo-rips-off-customers-while-funding-the-gun-industry-and-carceral-state/.

10. Marina Sokolova, "Advocacy Democracy Modes: Benefits and Limitations." Accessed December 30, 2022. https://www.e-belarus.org/article/advocacydemocracy.html.

11. "Chairman Harold Frazier (Cheyenne River Sioux Tribe)." COVID-19 in Indian Country, May 8, 2020. https://www.indianz.com/covid19/2020/05/08/chairman-harold-frazier-cheyenne-river-sioux-tribe-2/.

12. "Sign the Petition." Change.org. Accessed December 30, 2022. https://www.change.org/p/debra-haaland-deb-haaland-stand-against-modern-day-jim-crow-in-indian-country.

13. Carolyn Smith-Morris, "Addressing the Epidemic of Missing & Murdered Indigenous Women and Girls." Cultural Survival, March 6, 2020. https://www.culturalsurvival.org/news/addressing-epidemic-missing-murdered-indigenous-women-and-girls.

14. Joy James, "George Jackson: Dragon Philosopher and Revolutionary Abolitionist." AAIHS, August 27, 2018. https://www.aaihs.org/george-jackson-dragon-philosopher-and-revolutionary-abolitionist/.

15. The Working Class. "Attica Prison Liberation Faction, Manifesto of Demands 1971." libcom.org, January 6, 2012. https://libcom.org/article/attica-prison-liberation-faction-manifesto-demands-1971.

CHAPTER 27

1. Patrick Cunningham, "Two East Texans Arrested for Capitol Hill Riot Called for 'Second Revolution,' Charged with Several Federal Crimes." KTALnews.com. KTALnews.com, March 7, 2021. https://www.ktalnews.com/news/state-news/texas/two-east-texans-arrested-for-capitol-hill-riot-called-for-second-revolution-charged-with-several-federal-crimes/.

2. Melissa Macaya, Meg Wagner, Veronica Rocha, Melissa Mahtani, and Mike Hayes, "Gop Senator Compares Capitol Riot to Summer Protests in Seattle and Portland." Cable News Network, February 11, 2021. https://www.cnn.com/politics/live-news/trump-impeachment-trial-02-10-2021/h_49bdbff95a1a6f96b80429059136d977.

3. See the "We are the Beloved Community Quotes" page. Accessed December 30, 2022. https://www.wearethebelovedcommunity.org/bcquotes.html.

CHAPTER 29

1. Sharon Zhang, "Trump's EPA Is Unleashing the Pollution That Makes Us Vulnerable to Covid-19." *Truthout*, April 14, 2020. https://truthout.org/articles /trumps-epa-is-unleashing-the-pollution-that-makes-us-vulnerable-to-covid-19/.

2. Grant Smith, Joseph Ax, and Chris Kahn, "Exclusive: Most Americans Sympathize with Protests, Disapprove of Trump's Response —Reuters/Ipsos." Reuters, June 2, 2020. https://www.reuters.com/article/us-minneapolis-police-poll-ex clusive/exclusive-most-americans-sympathize-with-protests-disapprove-of-trumps -response-reuters-ipsos-idUSKBN239347.

3. Mike Mullen, "I Cannot Remain Silent." *The Atlantic*, June 2, 2020. https://www.theatlantic.com/ideas/archive/2020/06/american-cities-are-not-bat tlespaces/612553/.

4. Daniel Boffey, "Exclusive: Big Pharma Rejected EU Plan to Fast-Track Vaccines in 2017." *The Guardian*, May 25, 2020. https://www.theguardian.com /world/2020/may/25/exclusive-big-pharma-rejected-eu-plan-to-fast-track-vac cines-in-2017.

5. Jason Karlawish, "A Pandemic Plan Was in Place. Trump Abandoned It - and Science - in the Face of Covid-19." STAT, June 9, 2020. https://www.statnews .com/2020/05/17/the-art-of-the-pandemic-how-donald-trump-walked-the-u-s -into-the-covid-19-era/.

6. Ted Van Green and Alec Tyson, "5 Facts about Partisan Reactions to Covid-19 in the U.S." Pew Research Center, July 27, 2020. https://www.pewresearch.org /fact-tank/2020/04/02/5-facts-about-partisan-reactions-to-covid-19-in-the-u-s/.

7. Scott Martelle, "Opinion: Wait, Trump Wants to 'Liberate' Michigan but Not Georgia?," *Los Angeles Times*, April 23, 2020. https://www.latimes.com/opinion /story/2020-04-23/trump-liberate-michigan-but-not-georgia.

8. Dean Baker, *Rigged: How Globalization and the Rules of the Modern Economy Were Structured to Make the Rich Richer*. Washington, D.C.: Center for Economic and Policy Research, 2016.

ABOUT THE CONTRIBUTORS

Brian Burkhart is a Cherokee Nation of Oklahoma citizen and director of the Native Nations Center at the University of Oklahoma, an associate professor of philosophy and affiliated faculty in Native American Studies. His work centers around Indigenous concepts of knowing, being, valuing, and justice in relationship to land as well as the connections of race and coloniality to ideas of land and the exploitability and domination of land as an object. He is the author of *Indigenizing Philosophy through the Land: A Trickster Methodology for Decolonizing Environmental Ethics and Indigenous Futures* and *As Strong as the Land that Made You: Indigenizing Governance and Well-being through the Land* .

Judith Butler is Distinguished Professor in the Graduate School at the University of California, Berkeley. They are the author of several books including *Gender Trouble*; *Bodies that Matter*; *Precarious Life*; *Frames of War*; *The Force of Nonviolence*; and *What World is This? A Pandemic Phenomenology*. Their books have been translated into more than twenty-seven languages. From 2015–2020, they served as a principal investigator of a Mellon Foundation Grant that supports the International Consortium of Critical Theory Programs on whose board they now serve as cochair. They are active in several human rights organizations, having served on the board of the Center for Constitutional Rights in New York City and presently serves on the advisory board of Jewish Voice for Peace. They were the recipient of the Andrew Mellon Award for Distinguished Academic Achievement in the Humanities (2009–2013), were elected as a Corresponding Fellow of the British Academy in 2018, and to the American Academy of Arts and Sciences in 2019. In 2020, they served as President of the Modern Language Association. They are the recipient of fourteen honorary degrees and several international awards.

Noam Chomsky is Laureate Professor at the University of Arizona and Institute Professor emeritus at MIT, where he taught for fifty years. He is the author of many books on linguistics, philosophy, cognitive science, international affairs, and social and economic issues. He is recipient of many scientific awards and honorary degrees in the United States and abroad, and a member of many scientific societies.

Kelly Brown Douglas is the dean of Episcopal Divinity School at Union Theological Seminary in New York City and the Bill and Judith Moyers Distinguished Professor of Theology. Douglas is the author of many books in the field of womanist theology, racial reconciliation, and sexuality in the Black church, including *The Black Christ, Stand Your Ground: Black Bodies and the Justice of God* and her latest book, *Resurrection Hope: A Future Where Black Lives Matter.*

Akwugo Emejulu is professor of sociology at the University of Warwick. Her research interests include the political sociology of race, class, and gender and women of color's grassroots activism in Europe and the United States. She is the author of several books including *Precarious Solidarity*, *Fugitive Feminism*, and *Minority Women and Austerity: Survival and Resistance in France and Britain.* She is coeditor of *To Exist is to Resist: Black Feminism in Europe.*

Joe Feagin is the Distinguished Professor in Sociology at Texas A&M University. He has done internationally recognized research on racism, sexism, and political economy—published eighty scholarly books and more than two hundred articles. His books include *Systemic Racism; How Blacks Built America; Elite White Men Ruling; Racist America* ; and *The White Racial Frame.* He is recipient of the American Association for Affirmative Action's Lifetime Achievement award and the American Sociological Association's W. E. B. Du Bois Career of Distinguished Scholarship award.

Eric Foner, the DeWitt Clinton Professor Emeritus of History at Columbia University, is one of the country's leading historians. He is the author of many books on the Civil War and Reconstruction, including *Reconstruction: America's Unfinished Revolution; The Fiery Trial: Abraham Lincoln and American Slavery*; and *Gateway to Freedom: The Hidden History of the Underground Railroad.* He has curated several museum exhibitions on American history and is one of only two persons to serve as president of the three major professional organizations: the American Historical Association, Organization of American Historians, and Society of American Historians.

Che Gossett is a Black nonbinary femme writer and critical theorist specializing in queer/trans studies, aesthetic theory, abolitionist thought, and black study. Gossett is currently the Racial Justice Postdoctoral Fellow at the Center for Contemporary Critical Thought at Columbia University, and a Visiting Fellow at Harvard Law School's Animal Law & Policy Program.

Susannah Heschel is the Eli M. Black Distinguished Professor and chair of the Jewish Studies Program at Dartmouth College. The author of *Abraham Geiger and the Jewish Jesus*; *The Aryan Jesus: Christian Theologians and the Bible in Nazi Germany*; and *Jüdischer Islam: Islam und jüdisch-deutsche Selbstbestimmung*, she and Umar Ryad have coedited, *The Muslim Reception of European Orientalism*. She has also edited *Moral Grandeur and Spiritual Audacity: Essays of Abraham Joshua Heschel*. Her forthcoming book, written with Sarah Imhoff, is *Jewish Studies and the Woman Question*. The recipient of five honorary doctorates, she has held research grants from the Carnegie Foundation, the Ford Foundation, the National Humanities Center, the Guggenheim Foundation, and the Wissenschaftskolleg zu Berlin.

Joy James is Ebenezer Fitch Professor of the Humanities at Williams College. James's edited anthologies include *Imprisoned Intellectuals*; *The New Abolitionists*; *Warfare in the American Homeland*; and *The Angela Y. Davis Reader*. James's most recent books are *In Pursuit of Revolutionary Love* and *New Bones Abolition: A Tribute to Erica Garner and Captive Maternal Agency*. "The Womb of Western Theory: Time, Theft, and the Captive Maternal" reflects James''s organizing with radical communities resisting state violence.

Peniel E. Joseph is the Barbara Jordan Chair in Ethics and Political Values; founding director of the Center for the Study of Race and Democracy; associate dean for justice, equity, diversity, and inclusion at the LBJ School of Public Affairs; and distinguished service professor and professor of history at the University of Texas at Austin. An internationally recognized scholar-activist and author and editor of seven award-winning books, most recently *The Third Reconstruction: America's Struggle for Racial Justice in the Twenty-First Century*. He is a frequent national commentator on issues of race, civil rights, and democracy. A fellow of the Society of American Historians and a contributing writer for CNN.com, he lives in Austin, Texas.

Robin D. G. Kelley is the Gary B. Nash Endowed Chair in U.S. History at UCLA. His books include *Thelonious Monk: The Life and Times of an American Original*; *Hammer and Hoe: Alabama Communists During the Great Depression*;

Race Rebels: Culture Politics and the Black Working Class; *Yo' Mama's DisFunktional!: Fighting the Culture Wars in Urban America*; and *Freedom Dreams: The Black Radical Imagination*. His essays have appeared in several publications, including *The Nation*, *Monthly Review*, *The New York Times*, *American Historical Review*, *American Quarterly*, and *The Boston Review*, for which he also serves as Contributing Editor.

David Kyuman Kim is the executive director of the Center for Comparative Studies in Race & Ethnicity at Stanford University. Prior to coming to Stanford, Kim was professor of religious studies and American studies at Connecticut College. His work focuses on agency and moral culture, race and religion, and critical approaches to the study of love. Kim is author of *Melancholic Freedom: Agency and the Spirit of Politics*, coeditor of *The Post-Secular in Question*, and *Race, Religion, and Late Democracy*. His current book projects are *The Public LIfe of Love* and *The Hope Index*.

Woojin Lim is a philosophy student at Harvard University. He is editor-in-chief of the 2021 volume of *The Harvard Review of Philosophy* on political resistance. As a Fellow at the Edmond & Lily Safra Center for Ethics, he works on the ethics and governance of emerging technologies.

Mari Matsuda is an artist and critical race theorist. Her art can be viewed at marimatsudapeaceorchestra.com. Her books include *Where is Your Body, Essays on Race, Gender and the Law*, *Words That Wound, Critical Race Theory, Assaultive Speech and the First Amendment*, and *We Won't Go Back, Making The Case for Affirmative Action*.

Peter McLaren is Distinguished Professor in Critical Studies, College of Educational Studies, Chapman University. He is codirector and international ambassador for global ethics and social justice of the Paulo Freire Democratic Project, College of Educational Studies, Chapman University. He has served as chair professor, Northeast Normal University in Changchun, China, where he is honorary director of the Center for Critical Studies in Education. Professor McLaren is the author and editor of approximately fifty books and hundreds of professional publications on education and social justice. His writings have been translated into over twenty-five languages. He received his PhD in education from the Ontario Institute for Studies in Education, University of Toronto, Canada. He is the cofounder of Instituto McLaren in Ensenada, Mexico.

Eduardo Mendieta is professor of philosophy, Latina/o studies, affiliated faculty at the School of International Affairs, and the Bioethics Program at Penn State University. He is the author of *The Adventures of Transcendental Philosophy* (Rowman & Littlefield, 2002) and *Global Fragments: Globalizations, Latinamericanisms, and Critical Theory*. He is also coeditor with Amy Allen of *Decolonizing Ethics: Enrique Dussel's Critical Theory* , and with Ben Jones, *The Ethics of Policing*. He is working on a monograph on *Latinx Philosophy: A Manifesto*. He is the 2017 recipient of the Frantz Fanon Outstanding Achievements Award.

Pedro Noguera is one of the nation's leading scholars on issues related to race, inequality, and education. Prior to coming to USC to serve as the Emery Stoops and Joyce King Stoops dean of the Rossier School of Education, he was a Distinguished Professor of Education and holder of endowed chairs at UCLA, NYU, Harvard University, and the University of California, Berkeley. He is the author of fifteen books. His most recent book, *A Search for Common Ground: Conversations About the Tough Questions and Complex Issues Confronting K-12 Education in the United States Today* with Rick Hess was the winner of the American Association of Publishers Prose Award in 2021. Noguera is the son of Caribbean immigrants, and proud of his roots in Brooklyn, New York. He is the father of five, grandfather of five, and a lover of books, sports, gardening, travel, and cooking.

Adele N. Norris is senior lecturer in sociology and social policy in the Faculty of Arts and Social Sciences, University of Waikato, Hamilton, New Zealand. Adele's scholarship engages black feminist methodologies to explore state-sanctioned violence against Black and Indigenous people. She is a coeditor of the 2020 volume *Neo-Colonial Injustice and the Mass Imprisonment of Indigenous Women*. She writes on topics of anti-Blackness within the New Zealand context, black hair discrimination, white cultural imperialism, and imprisoned Black intellectual thought.

Elizabeth Stordeur Pryor, associate professor of history at Smith College, is the award-winning author of "The Etymology of [N-Word]: Resistance, Language, and the Politics of Freedom in the Antebellum North" and a 2016 monograph entitled *Colored Travelers: Mobility and the Fight for Citizenship before the Civil War.* Her TED talk on the n-word inspired her forthcoming book: a meditation on the n-word, biracial identity, and her relationship with her father, iconic Black comedian Richard Pryor. She is a Distinguished Lecturer for the Organization of American Historians and on the Advisory Council for the Society of Historians of the Early American Republic.

David R. Roediger teaches American studies and history at the University of Kansas. He was educated in Illinois public schools, completing undergraduate work at Northern Illinois University. He holds a PhD from Northwestern, where he studied under Sterling Stuckey. He edited the Frederick Douglass Papers at Yale University. His books include *Seizing Freedom*; *The Wages of Whiteness*; *The Sinking Middle Class*; *How Race Survived U.S. History*; *Class, Race, and Marxism*, and (with Elizabeth Esch) *The Production of Difference*. Roediger has been president of the American Studies Association and the Working Class Studies Association and active in labor support, antiapartheid, and antifascist movements, as well as the Chicago Surrealist Group.

T. Denean Sharpley-Whiting is the Gertrude Conaway Vanderbilt Distinguished Professor of African American and Diaspora Studies and French at Vanderbilt University where she is also vice provost for arts and libraries and directs the Callie House Research Center for the Study of Global Black Cultures and Politics. She is author/editor of fifteen books and three novels, the latest of which includes the L'Harmattan edition, *La Vénus hottentote: écrits, 1810 à 1814, suivi des textes inédits* and *Bricktop's Paris: African American Women Expatriates in Jazz-Age Paris and The Autobiography of Ada Bricktop Smith, or Miss Baker Regrets*.

Mark Lewis Taylor, PhD is Maxwell M. Upson Professor of Theology and Culture at Princeton Theological Seminary. Among his most recent books are *Religion, Politics and the Christian Right: Post 9-11 Powers and American Empire* (2005) and *The Theological and the Political: On the Weight of the World.* (2011). Taylor received the Best General Interest Book Award for his 2001 book, *The Executed God: The Way of the Cross in Lockdown America* (2nd edition 2015). Over years he has been committed to ending antideath penalty, to solidarity work in Mexico and Central America, and works support work political prisoners (he is founder of EMAJ-Educators for Mumia Abu-Jamal). Further publications and resources are available at www.marklewistaylor.

Chelsea Watego is a Munanjahli and South Sea Islander woman, professor of Indigenous health at Queensland University of Technology and director of the Institute of Collaborative Race Research. A public intellectual, her scholarship has drawn attention to the role of race in the production of health inequalities. She has led the formation of Indigenist health humanities as a new field of research, which is committed to the survival of Indigenous peoples via a foregrounding of Indigenous intellectual sovereignty. Her debut book *Another Day in the Colony* released in 2021 has been met with critical acclaim.

Cornel West is the Dietrich Bonhoeffer Professor of Philosophy and Christian Practice at the Union Theological Seminary in New York City.

Frank B. Wilderson III is Chancellor's Professor of African American Studies at UC Irvine. During the apartheid era he spent five and a half years in South Africa where he was one of two Americans to hold elected office in the African National Congress and was a cadre in the underground. His books include *Incognegro: A Memoir of Exile and Apartheid*, winner of the American Book Award, The Zora Neale Hurston/Richard Wright Legacy Award, and an NEA Fellowship; *Red, White, & Black: Cinema and the Structure of U.S. Antagonisms*; and *Afropessimism*, which was long listed for the National Book Award.

George Yancy is the Samuel Candler Dobbs Professor of Philosophy at Emory University and a Montgomery Fellow at Dartmouth College, one of the college's highest honors, and was the University of Pennsylvania's inaugural fellow in the Provost's Distinguished Faculty Fellowship Program (2019–2020). At "Academic Influence," Yancy is cited as one of the top ten influential philosophers in the last ten years, 2010–2020, based upon the number of citations and web presence. He has published over two hundred combined scholarly articles, chapters, and interviews appearing in professional journals, books, and at various news sites. He has authored, edited and coedited over twenty books. He is well-known for his influential essays and interviews at *The New York Times* philosophy column "The Stone," and at the prominent nonprofit news organization, *Truthout*. Lastly, Yancy is "Philosophy of Race" book series editor at Lexington Books.

INDEX

Milton Keynes UK
Ingram Content Group UK Ltd.
UKHW011534220823
427290UK00004B/18